Arapaho Stories, Songs, and Prayers

Arapaho Stories, Songs, and Prayers

A Bilingual Anthology

ANDREW COWELL
ALONZO MOSS, SR.
WILLIAM J. C'HAIR

University of Oklahoma Press : Norman

Also by Andrew Cowell

(edited and translated with Alonzo Moss, Sr.) *Hinono'einoo3itoono/Arapaho Historical Traditions.* Told by Paul Moss (Winnipeg, Manitoba, 2005)

(with Alonzo Moss, Sr.) *The Arapaho Language* (Boulder, Colo., 2008)

(edited with Patricia Limerick and Sharon Collinge) *Remedies for a New West: Healing Landscapes, Histories, and Cultures* (Tucson, Ariz., 2009)

Library of Congress Cataloging-in-Publication Data

Cowell, Andrew, 1963–
    Arapaho stories, songs, and prayers : a bilingual anthology / Andrew Cowell, Alonzo Moss, Sr., and William J. C'Hair.
        pages cm
    Includes bibliographical references and index.
    ISBN 978-0-8061-4486-3 (cloth)   ISBN 978-0-8061-5966-9 (paper)
    1. Arapaho Indians—Folklore.   2. Arapaho language—Texts.   3. Arapaho mythology.   4. Arapaho Indians—Songs and music—Texts.   5. Arapaho Indians—Prayers and devotions.   I. Moss, Alonzo.   II. C'Hair, William J. III. Title.
    E99.A7C68 2014
    398.2089'97354—dc23
                                                                        2014004400

The paper in this book meets the guidelines for permanence and durability of the Committee on Production Guidelines for Book Longevity of the Council on Library Resources, Inc. ∞

Contents

Legends/Myths

Animal Stories

Anecdotal Stories of Wondrous Events

Anecdotal Stories

Prayers and Ceremonial Speeches

Song Texts

Arapaho Orthography
and Pronunciation

Consonants

b	pronounced like English *b* in most cases; more like *p* word-finally, preconsonantally, and preceding *h*
c	pronounced like English *g* as in "giant" most of the time; more like *ch* in "child" word-finally, preconsonantally, and preceding *h*
h	pronounced as in English but simply as an outbreath preconsonantally and word-finally
k	pronounced like English *g* in "good" most of the time; more like *k* word-finally, preconsonantally, and preceding *h*
n	pronounced as in English
s	pronounced like English *s* in "sit"
š	pronounced like English *sh* in "ship." Formerly used by at least some Oklahoma speakers but noted only by Albert Gatschet in transcription. Equivalent to *s* for all other speakers.
t	pronounced like English *d* in "did" most of the time; more like *t* word-finally, preconsonantally, and preceding *h*
3	pronounced like English *th* in "three"
w	pronounced as in English
x	pronounced like *ch* in German "Lach" or like Greek *X* (chi)
y	pronounced as in English
'	a glottal stop, as in English "uh oh" between the "uh" and "oh"

Vowels

e	pronounced like English *e* in "set"
i	pronounced like English *i* in "sit"
o	pronounced like English *o* in "hot"
u	pronounced like English *u* in "put"
ee	pronounced longer than *e*
ii	pronounced longer than *i* and sounding more like English *ee* in "feet"

oo	pronounced longer than *o*
uu	pronounced longer than *u* and sounding a little more like English *oo* in "shoot"
ei	pronounced like English *ay* in "say"
oe	pronounced roughly like English *ie* in "pie"
ou	pronounced like English *ow* in "blow"
eii	longer than *ei,* sometimes sounding like *ei'i* or even *ei'ei*
oee	longer than *oe,* sometimes sounding like *oe'e* or even *oe'oe*
ouu	longer than *ou,* sometimes sounding like *ou'u* or even *ou'ou*

Sequences of three like vowels constitute two separate syllables, pronounced either as VV-V (*bóo-ó* 'road') or V-VV (*ní-iinon* 'tipi'). In modern Arapaho these are often shortened to *bó'ó* and *ní'inon,* but in this anthology we have kept the older pronunciation.

Pitch Accent

English words have a stronger emphasis (accent) on one or more syllables. Arapaho has the same feature but raises the pitch of the syllable instead of giving it a stronger emphasis, thus producing a "pitch accent." This is shown with a pitch accent mark over the vowel in question, as follows: *hinén* 'man'; *bééte'* 'bow'; *bóoó* 'road'. Changing the location of the accent can change the meaning of the word, so it is important to mark the pitch accent.

Samples of Arapaho words and pronunciation, with sound files, can be found online at http://www.colorado.edu/csilw/alp/pronunciation_c.html (consonants) and http://www.colorado.edu/csilw/alp/pronunciation_v.html (vowels)

Introduction

Traditional American Indian oral narratives constitute one of the great heritages of the individual tribes. Moreover, many would argue that they are an important part of the American and world heritage in general, provided that specific tribal origins, authors/tellers, and intellectual property rights are duly respected. Many of the great collections of these narratives were made in the late nineteenth and early twentieth centuries. Unfortunately, a significant number (though certainly not all) of the narratives collected during this time were obtained only in English translation. Thus neither tribal individuals nor general readers and scholars have access to the original texts. This is a crucial loss. No one would have appreciated the oral origins of Homer's *Iliad* and *Odyssey* if we did not have access to them in the original Greek, and oral-formulaic theory would not have developed as it did to explain their structure (Lord 1965; Parry 1971).

A related situation occurs when narratives were in fact collected in the original language but were published only in English translation. This is the case with many of the texts in George Dorsey and Alfred Kroeber's great early collection, *Traditions of the Arapaho* ([1903] 1997), though the majority of those texts were originally gathered in English. Another common situation involves texts that were collected in the original language in the past but have never been published at all. This is the case with work by the linguist Truman Michelson, who recorded many Arapaho texts in the original language that have remained neglected in the National Anthropological Archives (NAA) since the early 1900s. These last two situations would appear less problematic than the first one, because we do at least have the original Arapaho-language narratives in manuscript form.

This sense of comfort is greatly misplaced, however. The manuscript recordings of Arapaho were made by linguists with imperfect knowledge of the language, using orthographies that fail to represent all the sounds in the language accurately. Thus, despite the existence of translations, it may be hard even for a linguistic expert to determine exactly what was being

1

said in Arapaho. The solution to this problem is to turn to native speakers, who can clarify virtually all the obscurities in the manuscripts when working in combination with linguists. But Arapaho, like most American Indian languages, is now endangered, spoken only by those over the age of sixty. In a few years no fluent speakers of Arapaho might be left, if language revitalization efforts do not succeed. In such a situation, much of the value of the Arapaho-language manuscripts would be lost, along with the full beauty, richness, humor, subtlety, and complexity of the Arapaho oral narratives.

This volume is intended as a resuscitation of those Arapaho-language manuscripts and, more generally, as a celebration of Arapaho oral narrative traditions in all the richness of the original language. Alonzo Moss, Sr., and William C'Hair (native speakers of Arapaho) and Andrew Cowell (a linguistic anthropologist) provide retranscriptions of century-old Arapaho manuscripts into the modern Arapaho orthographic system. We also provide retranslation of the material, with linguistic, stylistic, thematic, and general cultural commentary offering a context for each of the texts. This volume includes all documented Arapaho narrative and ceremonial texts collected before 1930 but not ethnographic texts or missionary translations.

The volume is also a resuscitation of many of the narratives themselves and the language in them. Some of the narratives included here are still commonly told today, but a number were unknown to modern Arapaho consultants. Many vocabulary items in them have become archaic or obsolete in modern Arapaho. We hope that users of this book will appreciate the ability to have renewed direct contact with Arapaho narrative traditions dating from the 1880s to the 1920s, in their original form, and we also hope that the volume will inspire other resuscitations of the rich body of American Indian manuscripts.

The Arapaho Indians

The Arapahos historically occupied the High Plains; their range centered on what is now Colorado and Wyoming as well as surrounding areas and included extensive forays into the Rocky Mountains both east and west of the Continental Divide (see Fowler 1982, 2002; Trenholm 1986 for full histories). Since at least the eighteenth century and the arrival of the horse, they were classic nomadic bison hunters, living in tipis and practicing a ceremonial life centered on the Sun Dance, sweat lodge ceremonies, and vision quests (see Hilger 1952 and Anderson 2001 for anthropological surveys). The stories here contain many references to the Sun Dance (*hósei-hóowu'* 'offerings lodge'). This is a three-day ceremony held during the summer in which at least in theory the entire tribe participates. Young men who have decided to participate dance, fast, and pray for the three days, accompanied by singers and drummers. They seek healing and strength for themselves, their relations, and the entire tribe. The rest of the tribe encamps around the ceremonial lodge where the event is held (see Dorsey 1903). The Northern Arapahos possess two special sacred items: the Flat Pipe and the Wheel, which have been handed down by the Creator. These items are often referred to in the stories. Each is in the possession of a ceremonial Keeper and must never be left unattended. The objects play an important role in ceremonies and are considered living sources of power. Also central to many ceremonies and narratives is the Thunderbird, a supernatural eagle. The blinking of its eyes produces lightning, and its calls produce thunder. The Thunderbird is an intermediary between the Creator and the Arapahos, providing visions and power to those participating in the Sun Dance or vision quests. The Arapahos also had a series of highly developed (but now defunct) age-grade societies, which corresponded to allied roles in the tribe. All the men in the tribe progressed through these societies as they matured (see Kroeber [1902–1907] 1983; Dorsey 1903; Fowler 2010). Allied roles as well as separate organizations also existed for women (see Fowler 2010). These societies all incorporated their own ceremonies, songs, and sacred and secular duties. They appear in a number of places in the stories.

The Arapaho language (see Cowell and Moss 2008) is a member of the Algonquian family, along with other western languages such as Blackfeet, Cheyenne, and Gros Ventre as well as northern, midwestern, and eastern languages such as Cree, Ojibwe, Micmac, Penobscot, Abenaki, Massachussett, and Powhatan. The Arapahos separated from their Algonquian kin at some indeterminate time in the past. Since then the language has become quite different from other Algonquian languages, especially in its sound system. It is completely unintelligible even to the neighboring Cheyennes, though it is still closely related to Gros Ventre. Arapaho is what linguists call a polysynthetic, agglutinating language, meaning that a number of different ideas are often combined together to form a single "stem" (*woteekóóhu-* 'drive to town'; *benohóóxebei-* 'water horses'). Many prefixes and suffixes are attached to the stems to form long, complex words, which often approximate full English sentences (*niibéétwoteekóóhunoo* 'I want to drive to town'; *héétwoncésisbenohóóxebeinoo* 'I will go start watering the horses'). Note that these are common expressions, not at all exceptional words. The creation of even longer, more complex and unusual verbal expressions is a highly admired aspect of eloquent speech in Arapaho. The punch lines of many stories involve such forms, which are unfortunately impossible to translate well into English.

The Arapaho people gradually split into a northern and a southern branch, probably in the nineteenth century due to the founding of the fur-trading posts of Fort Laramie on the North Platte River in Wyoming and Bent's Fort on the Arkansas River in Colorado. This split was never absolute, and the two groups have maintained close contact with each other through time. The differences in their speech are less than those between speakers of English from Mississippi and Pennsylvania.

The Fort Laramie Treaty of 1851 awarded the Arapahos the area from the North Platte River to the Arkansas River, from the Continental Divide eastward into present-day western Kansas and Nebraska. The discovery of gold in the Denver area in 1858, however, exacerbated the division between the two branches of the Arapaho people, led to the Sand Creek Massacre in 1864, and eventually forced the Arapahos out of Colorado. The Southern Arapahos settled on a reservation in western Oklahoma in 1867, while the Northern Arapahos eventually settled on the Wind River Reservation in Wyoming in 1878.

The Arapahos shared a traditional culture with other northern plains tribes such as the Lakhotas, Cheyennes, Crows, Blackfeet, and Gros Ventres. Their traditional myths and legends, as well as their cultural values, have much in common with those of these other groups and the Plains Indians more generally—a feature likely enhanced by the shared Plains Sign Language. Alfred Kroeber (Dorsey and Kroeber [1903] 1997) notes many of these connections, which are also clear in his collection of Gros Ventre narratives (1907).

The Origins of This Volume

Many of the manuscripts included here were initially located by Lisa Conathan at the National Anthropological Archives and brought to the attention of Andrew Cowell, who then located more material himself. Initial transcription of some of the material was funded by the Endangered Language Fund at Yale University. A sabbatical (funded in part by the American Council of Learned Societies, with research funding from the Hans Rausing Endangered Language Documentation Programme at the University of London) allowed Cowell to work with Alonzo Moss, Sr., and William J. C'Hair on the manuscripts and also led to a full appreciation of their great literary value. Special thanks also go to Otto Borsik for help in initial retranscription of the prayers and speeches.

The Northern Arapahos in Wyoming have recently been quite active in language documentation and revitalization efforts (see Wiles 2011: 103–105, 154–57 for recent accounts and photos). The Southern Arapahos in

Oklahoma have been much less active until very recently. For a variety of historical and sociological reasons, the Arapaho language began to be lost much earlier in Oklahoma than in Wyoming. Today it is likely that no fully fluent speakers of the language are left in Oklahoma. Yet prior to the 1950s the Southern Arapahos were the source of most Arapaho language documentation. As a result, almost all of the texts in this volume come from Oklahoma. This collection thus constitutes the missing "southern voice" of the Arapahos, which has been largely absent from the revitalization and documentation efforts of recent years.

Ironically this gift from the Southern Arapahos has been made possible in a crucial way by two Northern Arapaho individuals, Alonzo Moss, Sr., and William J. C'Hair, the co-chairs of the Northern Arapaho Language and Culture Commission. Both have spent many hours reviewing these texts with Cowell, offering not only answers to problems of transcription and translation but also invaluable insights into the style and meaning of the texts. Modern documentation of Arapaho began with Zdeněk Salzmann's work on Northern Arapaho. He completed a dissertation on the language in 1963 and published a number of articles during the 1950s and 1960s. His field research was done between 1949 and 1961. In the late 1970s the Northern Arapaho tribe initiated language maintenance and revitalization efforts and contacted Salzmann for help developing a writing system, a dictionary, and curricular materials. Moss and C'Hair both became involved with language efforts at this time.

Alonzo Moss, Sr., was born on June 30, 1938, on the Wind River Reservation, in Fort Washakie. He spoke Arapaho as his home language and did not learn English until elementary school. His father, Paul Moss, was a noted storyteller and ceremonial elder. Alonzo attended St. Stephens Catholic Mission School and later obtained his General Educational Development (GED) certificate. He worked as a top-notch lumberjack for many years before applying for a job as an English assistant at Wyoming Indian High School in 1979. At that time Ralph Hopper, an older relative who had worked with Zdeněk Salzmann in the past, provided copies of Salzmann's papers. Alonzo was able to figure out Salzmann's Arapaho transcription system from those documents. When the tribe began working with Salzmann soon afterward to develop its modern popular writing system, Alonzo's uncle Pius was one of Salzmann's consultants for his dictionary (published in 1983). Alonzo sat in on several of Salzmann's sessions with the old people, which helped inspire him to begin recording and transcribing the stories of his father, Paul (see Moss 2005). Alonzo's knowledge of the writing system, along with his fluency in the language, led to a position as Arapaho language curriculum developer at Wyoming Indian High School and then as a classroom language teacher as well. He was one of the early members of the Northern Arapaho Language and Culture Commission, acting as assistant and transcriber for the older speakers (who never learned to write). He has produced a great deal of work in conjunction with Andrew Cowell over the years, including an Arapaho grammar. He has also done a great deal of curriculum development and data collection on his own. Alonzo was the Indian of the Year at the Anadarko, Oklahoma, American Indian Exposition in 2010; a keynote speaker at the Algonquian Conference in Vancouver, British Columbia, in 2006; and the marshal of the Lander, Wyoming, Fourth of July Parade in 2012.

William C'Hair was born in 1943 on the Wind River Reservation, in the St. Stephens area. He was raised by his grandparents, who spoke only Arapaho, and spent much of his childhood years listening to stories told by the older people in the evenings. He graduated from Riverton, Wyoming, High School in 1961, as one of the few Arapaho students who both attended and graduated from high school off the reservation at the time. William was sent to a bilingual curriculum workshop in Anchorage, Alaska, by the tribe when it first began exploring language documentation and first met Zdeněk Salzmann there. He worked a great deal with Salzmann in the early 1980s, serving as a key intermediary with the older speakers. As Salzmann and the tribe discussed how to adopt Salzmann's original linguistic orthography to local needs, C'Hair came up with the idea of using *3* to replace English *th* in the Arapaho orthography, so that each sound would have a single letter and also could easily be typed. Along with four other speakers he initiated the Northern Arapaho Language and Culture Commission, which Alonzo Moss, Sr., joined later. Due to his knowledge of the writing system, William was a key member of the commission from the St. Stephens/Arapahoe, Wyoming, side of the reservation and has since become co-chairman. He and his family are noted traditional singers. He is also an official tribal announcer, a ceremonial position that entails announcing at formal events ranging from funerals to honoring ceremonies to the Sun Dance. William has contributed extensive data to Andrew Cowell over the years.

The Original Consultant/Narrators

The original collectors (discussed below) worked with a number of Arapaho individuals. All the consultants included here were men, though George Dorsey and Alfred Kroeber did work with at least a few women. This is due to two primary factors. First, all of the linguists preferred to work with bilingual Arapahos when possible, and fewer women in the very earliest reservation days obtained a degree of education that allowed them to be bilingual.

Second, the linguists themselves were all men: from an Arapaho cultural perspective, it was problematic, though certainly not impossible, for individual women to work with white male researchers. Women tell stories just as much as men do among the Arapahos. Except for sacred stories that are restricted to high-level ceremonial leaders (such as the creation story, which is told fully only in the Rabbit Lodge), all men and women have equal rights to tell all kinds of stories.

Albert Gatschet was the first linguist to arrive in Oklahoma to work with the Arapahos, in 1882. He worked almost entirely with younger men who had gone to the Carlisle School in Pennsylvania and learned English there. Some of these were sons of prominent families, sent to Carlisle by parents who wanted to show their allegiance to new forms of cultural possibility. Other children were from families too poor to feed them, including orphans who lacked any other support (Fowler 2010: 127–32). Many of them do not seem to have worked with later linguists.

Later linguists worked with a somewhat different set of informants, combining much older, mostly prestigious elders with younger interpreters. This was the pattern for much of the work of Alfred Kroeber and Truman Michelson. For example, it appears that Michelson's Northern Arapaho consultant storytellers were all leaders within the tribe, often chiefs, councilmen, or both. The young interpreters seem to have diminished in number as time went on, but to have increased in specialization, often working with multiple outsiders. Their prestige and standing increased thanks to this work. The two most important Southern Arapaho interpreters, Cleaver Warden and Jesse Rowlodge, were both important political figures in later times, after their work with the linguists, as was the Northern Arapaho John Goggles. This pattern culminated in the work of James Mooney and later Truman Michelson: the Arapaho translator/consultants were effectively doing the anthropological work themselves to a large extent and sometimes left extensive manuscript collections. Thus every text in this volume, especially those collected by Kroeber and Michelson, must be seen in part as a performance and a marker of both sociocultural and political prominence and/or ambition. A fairly controlled set of decisions likely determined which stories were told and who told them.

This was dictated by both the needs and limitations of the linguists and the influence and ambitions of the consultants, not to mention subtle internal controls exercised by the tribes themselves on who would be allowed access to the linguists and be socially recognized as a representative of "the culture." As such, this volume is one more testament to the system of cultural mediation that was central to Arapaho society and political influence throughout the second half of the nineteenth century and all of the twentieth century (see Fowler 1982). In this system, access to education and good control of English has been a central aspect determining both internal tribal hierarchy and the structure of relationships between the Arapahos and the Euro-American world.

At the same time the Arapahos have maintained a strong respect for traditional knowledge and practice. In some cases traditional and ceremonial roles have been partially segregated from business and political roles, especially in the period of modern tribal government beginning in the 1930s with the Indian Reorganization Act (see Fowler 1982: 172–76 for the Northern Arapahos); historically, multiple avenues of social advancement have existed in the tribe.[1] The consultants here represent a fruitful combination of traditionalism and innovation rather than a segregation of these elements. Generally, some of the most influential Arapaho leaders in both north and south have been "innovating traditionalists" who have combined strong knowledge of traditional language, practice, and ceremony with a willingness to support new innovations in lifestyle, governance, and ceremony. Yellow Calf is a prime example in the north (see Fowler 1982; Wiles 2011), while Cleaver Warden and Jesse Rowlodge are examples in Oklahoma.

Alexander Yellowman (one text and songs) is mentioned several times (often simply as "Aleck") in Gatschet's manuscript notes. He appears to have been both a translator and a cultural informant for material provided by others as well as a provider of texts and songs himself. Yellowman, born about 1867, is listed in the U.S. Indian Census Schedules, 1903 Census of the Arapahoe Tribe in the Oklahoma Territory. He is also listed as having been a student at Carlisle Indian School.[2] In 1888 his sister married Cleaver Warden, a key consultant for many anthropologists and linguists working in Oklahoma ("Carlisle"), so it seems reasonable to believe that he was from a fairly prominent and well-connected family. In his notes (MS 213, p. 307) Gatschet says that Yellowman's name is *hine[n] nihooneih* 'Yellow Man' or what appears to be *3ooxteh'eit* 'Cut Belly'. On the same page he notes that Yellowman had a brother named *yeiy* 'Otter'. The Yellowman family name remains prominent in Oklahoma today among the Southern Arapahos.

Henry North (also listed as Henry Shave Head: one text and songs) was born about 1870 and was listed as attending the Carlisle School at the age of ten in the 1881 U.S. Census of the Oklahoma Arapahoe. He graduated from Carlisle and returned to Oklahoma sometime in the late 1880s or early 1890s (he is mentioned as resigning a post at the Agent's Office in August 1893). Thus he was available as both consultant and interpreter during Gatschet's later fieldwork in 1892–93. He also worked with Kroeber. He raised a family and was a successful farmer at the Seger Colony and around Geary, Oklahoma (Berthrong 1976: 252). He was never able to work in the trades for which he had been trained at Carlisle and was disappointed and frustrated later in life (Fowler 2010: 128, 132, 218). His Arapaho names were *heninooo* 'Kettle' and *bicinen* 'Little Man', or more properly 'Funny Little Man'. He passed away in March 1936, listed as sixty-eight years old ("Carlisle").

The "Dan of Carlisle" (songs) that Gatschet mentioned in his notes dated 1882 was almost certainly Dan Tucker. He thus has the honor of being the first named Arapaho linguistic consultant in Oklahoma. Tucker is the only Arapaho with the first name "Dan" listed as attending the Carlisle School, and is listed (misspelled "Dan Ticker") in the 1903 census of enrolled Arapahos as having been born about 1861. He was an orphan (Fowler 2010: 118) and graduated from Carlisle in 1882, which would have allowed him to be home by the summer of that year, when Gatschet says in his notebook that he was working with "Dan of Carlisle." Tucker later married a white schoolteacher from Darlington and in 1893 was a successful farmer and rancher with a substantial bank account ("Carlisle"). By 1910, however, his occupation was listed as "none." In later life he remained marginal to Arapaho traditional lifestyles but also unable to benefit from his Carlisle education (Fowler 2010: 265, 270). His Arapaho name is given by Gatschet as *wox seseih*, glossed as 'Noisy Bear' but more properly 'Angry/Fierce Bear'.

Paul Boynton (one text, songs), whose Arapaho name was *be'eekuuni'* 'Red Feather', was another Arapaho attendee at the Carlisle School. Boynton spoke both Cheyenne and Arapaho. His father was an Arapaho chief who was supportive of the transition to schooling and farming (Berthrong 1976: 166, 213), whose name was *nisice nookook* 'White-Eyed Antelope' (Gatschet, NAA, MS 231, p. 242). White-Eyed Antelope himself was the son of the sister of Left Hand, so Boynton was (in the American English sense) the grandnephew of that famous Arapaho chief. (Fowler 2002: 15). His mother's name was *bici'ei* 'Funny Face'.[3] As of 1893 he was filling "some county office" ("Carlisle") and was thus available to work with Gatschet toward the end of his time in Oklahoma. After working with Gatschet, Boynton worked especially closely with James Mooney around the turn of the century due to his involvement in the Ghost Dance movement (Mooney [1896] 1973: 655, 923, 971) and held an allotment near El Reno (Berthrong 1976: 199–200, 313).

Oscar Wilde (songs) is listed in the 1903 Census of the Arapahoe Tribe in the Oklahoma Territory as having been born about 1872. He would thus have been twenty-one in 1893, which is exactly the age listed by Gatschet in his notes. His Arapaho name was *wo'tee*[*n*] 'Black'. Albert Gatschet's field notes (NAA, MS 231, p. 241) list his father as *honouu3i'* 'Hanging'; his mother as *ceeteehteeyou'u*(?) 'Blue Beads'; and his brothers as *howohookuu* 'Feathers Standing on His Head' (literally 'Many Feathers') and *neecee beesei3* 'Big Chief'. His nickname was *hoxo3itoo* '[Does Things by] Short-cut'. He is not listed in the 1903 census.

Little Shield (Northern Arapaho) (one text) was the son of a prominent chief who fought in the wars of 1864–67 and died about 1878. His full name was Calvin Little Shield. The 1900 Northern Arapaho census indicates that he was born about 1860 (and gives his actual Arapaho name as Crooked Wrist). He was married to Sings in the Pine (English name Edna), also born about 1860. He is listed as an Arapaho chief in the 1880s (who sent a child to the Carlisle School), as a prominent leader in the 1890s, as a head councilman prior to 1920, and as the second most influential council leader in the period leading up to 1920. He was thus a key Arapaho leader, heavily involved in the process of "productive accommodation" with white society (Fowler 1982: 89, 115, 140–41, 152). Little Shield was almost certainly monolingual in Arapaho, and John Goggles translated his story.

John Goggles (Northern Arapaho, 1883–1952; six texts) is the only narrator who bridges the period between the early manuscript documentation and the time when modern documentation began with electronic recording and a phonemic writing system. He worked with Truman Michelson as a young man in 1910, both providing narratives himself and translating into English for monolingual speakers, and was a key consultant for Zdeněk Salzmann when he began working in Wyoming in 1949. The 1900 Northern Arapaho census lists him as born about 1883, with the Arapaho name Red Shirt, the son of Goggles (Lloyd Goggles) and Lump on Shoulder (Levina Goggles). He was an important leader in the Native American Church or Peyote Ceremony and was a councilman during the 1930s, though, interestingly, he was not considered an "educated" Indian at the time. This is likely because he remained a traditionalist oriented toward the language, oral narratives, and Peyote Ceremony, although he spoke English. In contrast, at least one councilwoman of the 1930s was assimilated enough to be unable to speak Arapaho (Fowler 1982: 125, 159, 182, 193). The Goggles family remains prominent at Wind River to this day. Goggles is remembered by Alonzo Moss, Sr., as having a very deep and nasal voice, which matches Salzmann's recordings of him done from 1949 to 1951. Goggles was a great-uncle to William C'Hair and thus bridges the time to the present.

Wolf Bear (Northern Arapaho, English name Ward Plummer; one text) is listed in the 1900 Northern Arapaho census as being born about 1852. He was married to Hollering Woman (Gail Plummer), who was born about

1865. He had two sons living with him at the time, Joseph and Leo, as well as a niece, Matilda Bitner. He was almost certainly monolingual in Arapaho, and John Goggles translated his story. One of Alonzo Moss's grandmothers was also from the Bitner family.

White Breast (Northern Arapaho, English name White Bird Jenkins; one text) is noted as being eighty-one years old by Michelson in 1910 and is thus the earliest-born of all the known narrators in this collection. The 1900 Northern Arapaho census lists him as born about 1831. He was married to Old Woman (English name Mockingbird), who was born about 1832. Sherman Sage reports that White Breast was wounded in a battle with the Utes near Steamboat Springs, Colorado, in the nineteenth century (Toll 1962: 24). He was a scout for the U.S. Army in 1877—a position available only to respected Arapaho warriors. White Breast later was listed as a subchief who sent a child to the Carlisle School and eventually took up farming, as an example to his fellow tribespeople. Nevertheless, he was also initiated into the Dog Lodge Age-Grade Society in 1904. Thus he, like Little Shield, could be seen as a key leader in the process of "productive accommodation" with white society, but he clearly remained deeply committed to Arapaho traditions as well (Fowler 1982: 59, 74, 89, 121). White Breast was almost certainly monolingual in Arapaho, and John Goggles translated his story.

Charles Crispin (Northern Arapaho; translator) was the son of Tom Crispin, a tribal interpreter who was involved in many activities on and off the reservation (including a trip to Colorado to document Arapaho history, culture, and place-names related to Rocky Mountain National Park) as well as a tribal councilman, who passed away in 1935 (Fowler 1982: 103, 132, 153–54, 164, 170, 175). Tom's wife was Sarah, born about 1874. Charles Crispin is listed in the 1900 Northern Arapaho census as born about 1898. He worked with Truman Michelson in the 1920s as an interpreter.

Cleaver Warden (twenty-three texts, songs) dominates the material collected by both Alfred Kroeber and George Dorsey in Oklahoma. Warden provided many of the texts himself. Because he was fluent in English thanks to his time at Carlisle, he provided the English translations of many texts provided by others in Arapaho as well as translations for his own texts. He also wrote extensively in English on Arapaho traditions from an ethnographic point of view. In addition to his work with Kroeber, he was hired by the Field Museum in Chicago to work for George Dorsey. Much of the work published under Dorsey's name was really gathered and written up by Warden. As Jeffrey Anderson (2001: v) argues in his discussion of the working methods of Kroeber and Dorsey in Oklahoma and their collaboration with Warden, Cleaver Warden could really be considered a co-author of the material that they produced. Anderson (2001: xiv–xvi) provides additional biographic information on Warden, as does Fowler (2010). Warden is almost certainly the single individual of the Arapaho tribe who has contributed the most to documenting and preserving the earlier tribal traditions. He continues to be recognized as such today in both Oklahoma and Wyoming, and his image still occurs widely even in Wyoming on posters, calendars, clothing, and artwork produced by the Northern Arapahos. His Arapaho names were *hooko'oox* 'Saddle' and *hitouunen* 'Gros Ventre' (Kroeber MS 2560a, Notebook 6, p. 63). Alonzo Moss learned a great deal from Cleaver's son Jim Warden, who was of the same generation as Alonzo's father, Paul. Jim visited Wind River every summer for the Sun Dance, and the Doris Duke Oral History Collection at the University of Oklahoma contains much information from him. Alonzo is the great-grandson (Arapaho way) of Cleaver Warden.

Jesse Rowlodge (one text) was the principal assistant to Truman Michelson in Oklahoma. He was born in 1884 and was interviewed extensively in 1968, providing details about both his life and Arapaho culture.[4] In addition to providing translations for many of the texts that Michelson collected, Rowlodge also transcribed and translated texts himself—most notably autobiographies of Medicine Grass and Mrs. White Bear, who were born in the 1850s and 1860s. Those texts, extremely rich in vocabulary related to traditional lifeways, have been retranscribed and retranslated by Cowell and Moss but will be published elsewhere. Rowlodge also translated directly into English to help produce Michelson's publication "Narrative of an Arapaho Woman" (1933), a text that Moss recently translated back into Arapaho. In addition to working with Michelson, Rowlodge worked with many other anthropologists and linguists. He was also very active in Arapaho politics for many years. Donald Berthrong (1994) has written an article examining Rowlodge's role as a political intermediary for the Arapahos. Loretta Fowler (2002, 2010) also provides extensive documentation on Rowlodge's life. His Arapaho name was Mystical Magpie (Fowler 2010: 114).

Philip Rabbit (also known as Philip Rapid; eight texts) is listed in the 1903 Census of the Arapahoe Tribe as having been born about 1882. He attended the Carlisle School, listed as Philip R. Rabbitt. Kroeber writes the name as C. Philip Rabbit/Rapid. It is unclear whether this is a different person (perhaps the father of the Carlisle attendee?) or not. So far as can be determined, all the other individuals from whom Kroeber gathered Arapaho-language texts were Carlisle attendees, so it seems likely that the Philip Rabbit that he worked with was the one born in 1882. His occupation in 1910 was reported as "none" ("Carlisle"). His Arapaho name was *niihobei* 'Goes Along' or 'Accompanies' (Kroeber, MS 2560a, Notebook 6, p. 63).

Caspar Edson (two texts) attended the Carlisle School and by 1893 was listed as a farmer attached to the Darlington Agency ("Carlisle"). He was employed at the Darlington Agency for a number of years and was also a successful farmer who accumulated significant savings (Berthrong 1976: 284). Edson was involved in the Ghost Dance and served as a consultant to James Mooney in his work on that topic (Mooney [1896] 1973: 780). He is listed in the 1903 Census of the Arapahoe Tribe as having been born about 1869. His Arapaho name was *niitowutou'* 'Strikes First' (Kroeber, MS 2560a, Notebook 6, p. 63).

Benejah (Ben) Miles (two texts) is listed in the 1903 Oklahoma Arapaho census (as Beajah Miles). He was born about 1868 and was married to Cora Miles. They had three children: Robert, Viola, and Rosalie, born in 1898, 1901, and 1903, respectively.

Eleven of the texts in the collection are anonymous. The preceding discussion covers consultants who provided material but does not cover authors/creators of songs (such as Ghost Dance Songs). Information on these figures, notably Sage and Sitting Bull, can be found in Mooney [1896] 1973 and Fowler 2002, 2010.

The Original Collectors

This volume represents the work of a number of non-Arapaho individuals who collected texts over many decades between roughly 1880 and 1930.

Albert S. Gatschet (1832–1907) was born in Switzerland. After receiving training in linguistics in Europe, he immigrated to the United States in 1868 and joined the Bureau of American Ethnology in 1879, though his work with American Indian languages had already begun earlier. Gatschet was among the first systematic field collectors of American Indian language data and did early documentation on quite a number of languages, especially in the Southeast and in Texas. A good deal of his material remains in manuscript form, including the Arapaho documentation, and apparently has never before been used by linguists who have worked on the language. The Arapaho material is in MS 231 at the National Anthropological Archives, consisting of two notebooks totaling over 300 pages, containing vocabulary, texts, and song texts, with a smaller amount of material in MS 61 (including much information on plant names and ethnobotany).[5] The vocabulary includes numerous words not otherwise documented for Arapaho, especially in relation to the natural world, place-names, and tribal names. The material is dated 1880–93, making these the earliest examples of texts recorded in Arapaho. This is the first publication of these texts in any language.

James S. Mooney (1861–1921) was born in Ohio of immigrant parents from Ireland. He was a largely self-trained anthropologist, who began working for the Bureau of American Ethnology in 1885. He is most noted for his documentation of the Cherokees and of the Ghost Dance religion on the Great Plains. He published the Arapaho Ghost Dance Songs included in this collection, along with extensive notes and commentary on the songs. Mooney also recorded some of the Arapaho songs. Unfortunately, rather than recording the Arapahos themselves, he recorded himself singing the songs.[6]

Alfred L. Kroeber (1876–1960) was born in New Jersey to immigrant parents from Germany. He was one of the great anthropologists of the twentieth century. Kroeber is best known for his work on the languages and cultures of California, as he was based at the University of California at Berkeley for many years. Kroeber's first substantial linguistic work was on the Arapaho and Gros Ventre languages as part of the Morris K. Jessup expedition in 1899 to 1901, under the auspices of the American Museum of Natural History in New York City. As part of that expedition, Kroeber collected numerous items of Arapaho material culture, along with accompanying documentation. He also collected extensive language notes and texts in both Arapaho and English. While the material items from this work were deposited at the American Museum of Natural History, the linguistic material (twenty-nine notebooks) was deposited at the Bureau of American Ethnology and is now part of the National Anthropological Archives collection. Kroeber recorded the texts here in Arapaho. He also recorded additional texts (published in Dorsey and Kroeber [1903] 1997), apparently in English only, as no manuscript evidence of Arapaho versions has been found in the National Anthropological Archives. These texts were almost certainly given in Arapaho but simultaneously translated into English by his collaborator (Cleaver Warden) and written down only in English. All the texts with Arapaho versions come from Oklahoma consultants.

Kroeber published a three-volume ethnography of the Arapahos, focused heavily on material culture, and a one-volume collection of narratives in conjunction with George Dorsey, which contains many of the texts in this translation (in English only). Additional texts collected by Kroeber were not published in the 1903 volume (Dorsey and Kroeber [1903] 1997) and appear here for the first time in any language. Kroeber also returned to his data and published "Arapaho Dialects" in 1916, which includes three brief texts in Arapaho along with a grammatical sketch (fairly accurate in its description of inflectional morphology and list of lexical items but quite inaccurate in its description of derivational morphology, lexical prefixes, and attempts at morphemic analysis). Anderson (2001) contains a careful discussion of Kroeber's work with the Arapahos in 1899 in Oklahoma and 1900 in Wyoming (with more details in Anderson 2013).

Kroeber's texts are all from NAA, MS 2560a. This manuscript has twenty-nine notebooks (though some are missing), but all the texts come from notebook 3 (July 15, 1899, and after), notebook 5 (July 19 and after), notebook 6 (August 7 [or earlier] and after), notebook 9 (August 14 and after), notebook 10 (August 22 [or earlier] and after), notebook 12 (August 23 and after), and notebook 13 (no dates, but obviously after August 23). All of the notebooks date from his 1899 visit to the Southern Arapahos.

George O. Dorsey (1868–1931), although he did extensive research on Arapaho culture and ceremony and collected many narratives (much of this work actually done by Cleaver Warden), seems to have worked entirely with English translations. None of his texts were apparently recorded in Arapaho. Those texts are published in Dorsey and Kroeber [1903] 1997 and in Dorsey 1903. Anderson (2001, 2013) discusses his work with the Southern Arapahos in 1901–1902.

Natalie Curtis Burlin (1875–1921) was born in New York City. She studied Western music in both the U.S. and Europe before becoming interested in American Indian music in the early 1900s, working first with the Hopi tribe. Curtis was a pioneering female ethnomusicologist and published *The Indians' Book* in 1907. It contains linguistic transcriptions and musical notations of songs from a number of different tribes, including several from the Arapahos. All the material attributed to Curtis here comes from that book. She pushed for greater Indian rights with Teddy Roosevelt and later went on to study African American music. Additional details on her work can be found in Curtis [1907] 1968: v–viii.

Frances A. Densmore (1867–1957) recorded a number of Arapaho song texts with musical notation but seems to have worked entirely in English, as she provides no original Arapaho versions of the songs. Her recordings still exist at the Southwest Museum in Los Angeles, so the Arapaho texts could still be resuscitated. Densmore worked in Oklahoma. Her work with the Arapahos was a relatively small part of her career.

Truman Michelson (1879–1938) did his early training in Indo-European languages before shifting his interest to American Indian languages. He was employed by the Bureau of American Ethnology beginning in 1910. Michelson collected data from a number of different American Indian languages, with a special focus on the Algonquian languages, most particularly Fox (Mesquakie). He made at least one visit to the Carlisle Indian

School in Pennsylvania to work with Arapaho speakers there, but the majority of his collecting was done in Oklahoma and Wyoming from 1910 to 1929. The texts that he collected are found in several different manuscripts now at the NAA. None of Michelson's Arapaho material has been previously published in either English or Arapaho.

Edward S. Curtis (1868–1952) is primarily known as a photographer of the supposedly "vanishing Indian" in the early twentieth century. As part of his work, however, he collected fairly extensive amounts of vocabulary and also some short texts (normally songs), along with much other ethnographic information. His twenty-volume set on *The North American Indian* was financed by J. P. Morgan and covered dozens of different tribes, including the Arapahos.

The Contents of This Volume

This collection includes creation stories, etiological narratives that explain origins of various aspects of Arapaho culture and society, trickster stories, comic and/or moralistic animal stories, legendary stories of key culture heroes and mythological figures, and anecdotal stories. Arapaho makes a general distinction between traditional myths and modern stories. This distinction exists for many Plains Indian groups (Dorsey [1904] 1995: 22, on Wichitas, and [1906] 1997: xx, on Pawnees), as well as among the Algonquian peoples generally (Buszard-Welcher 2005, on Potawatomis; S. Preston 2005 and R. Preston 2005, on East Crees; DePasquale 2005, on Swampy Crees; Brittain and MacKenzie 2005, on Naskapis). The terms used for the two types of stories in Arapaho are *heetéetoo* 'old myth' and *hoo3ítoo* 'modern story'. It should be noted, however, that in modern Northern Arapaho the meaning of the terms has changed for many speakers: *heetéetoo* has come to mean a mythical story in a more or less Euro-American sense, in that the stories are described as being "fairy tales" (by Moss but certainly not by C'Hair), while *hoo3ítoo* has come to mean a true story (from an Arapaho perspective), which is taken more seriously (by Moss at least). In former times *heetéetoo* included creation stories, some etiological narratives (related to ceremonies in particular), and legendary stories or myths plus trickster stories, whereas *hoo3ítoo* included moralistic or comic animal stories as well as other etiological narratives (related to processes of transformation within the natural world but not to ceremonies) plus modern historical narratives.

Beyond the broad two-part division, Arapaho narratives are categorized primarily based on contents and main characters. Creation stories recount the origins of the world. Certain etiological stories recount the origins of the Sun Dance ceremony, the various age-grade societies and their associated ceremonies, and the sweat lodge ceremony and the sweat lodge itself. Myths or legends generally revolve around various key mythological characters. Some of these characters are culture heroes, who brought benefits to the Arapahos in the past and/or were thought to watch over the Arapahos in the present. These included Star Child, Sun Child, Lime Crazy, and Found-in-the-Grass. Some were nonhuman sources of power and protection (notably the Thunderbird), while others were largely seen as dangerous and threatening (the Water Monster, Tangled Hair/Open Brain, the Little People, the Beheaded Ones).

A special character is Nih'oo3oo (Trickster, usually pronounced *nihóó3oo* today but spelled in this collection as recorded in the older sources), who is not associated with any particular human or animal form and is a being unto himself. Many of his adventures are integrated into the broader mythology of the Sun Dance, but others are independent narratives. The many Nih'oo3oo narratives could be said to form an overall cycle, as noted for the Winnebagos (Radin 1972) and other tribes. Many are included here (details are discussed in the introductions to the individual texts).

Animal stories are typically humorous, while also teaching moral lessons, and are considered especially appropriate for children. Common characters in these stories include Rabbit, Skunk, Fox, Wood Tick, and Bear, though others appear as well. Many animal stories have an etiological component, focus on processes of transformation, and symbolically link various moral or cultural lessons to objects or phenomena in the natural world.

Anecdotal stories generally are presented as true accounts and sometimes provide localization in terms of time, place, or personal names. We have divided these stories between purely "realistic" accounts and those that involve some kind of "wondrous" power or transformation.

It might also be useful for readers to think about what is *not* in this volume, in particular in comparison to the other current major anthology of Arapaho narratives, by Paul Moss (2005). The Moss narratives are considered historical narratives (*hoo3ítoono*) and thus true. Those narratives focus heavily on humans—Arapahos in particular—who accomplish "wondrous" things by going through proper ceremonial procedures and obtaining greater-than-human powers. The accomplishments involve hostile encounters and warfare with both other tribes and U.S. soldiers, hunting, horse theft, recovering stolen horses, and dealing with evil spirits that visit the tribe. In all cases the central focus of the stories is actually on the ritual way in which Arapaho individuals attain special powers that they can then use to aid the tribe as well as themselves. The ceremonial process tends to receive as much attention as the final exploit (or more). Quite often animal or spirit helpers are involved in the stories, which typically end with "heroic" success.

In contrast, a number of stories here involve only animals. Others involve animal-human interactions; but in these stories such encounters tend to be highly problematic ("The White Dog and the Woman," "The Woman and the Horse," "The Woman and the Porcupine"). Rarely if ever does the animal serve as an intermediary providing access to greater-than-human power or as a direct helper of humans, as in Paul Moss's stories. Intertribal warfare, horse theft, and great hunting exploits are rare or completely absent in these stories, as well as recognizably Arapaho ceremonialism.

This is just another way of saying that these stories are myths (*heetée-toono*), which recount origins and creations as well as the working out of proper relationships among animals, humans, and the other powerful creatures of the world as well as with the natural environment. In these stories we see things *becoming* what they later will be in the human world—for example, the crow becomes black, the buffalo come to inhabit the world, the horse becomes the one who will bear burdens but will not be hunted, and the practice of leaving offerings at springs on war expeditions is first established. The stories of Paul Moss assume that this process has already occurred (with the exception of his story "The Eagles"). Only when this process has been completed can Arapahos carry out ceremonial activities with confidence, knowing that relative positions within the world have become largely fixed, and only then can animals and humans enter into stable and helpful relationships. The world is still a place of potential "wondrous" events. But greater-than-human power has become predictably available—through ritual—for aiding in hunting, taking horses, protecting the tribe in battle, and similar activities. Paul Moss's stories show a confidence in the way the world works and the ways in which skillful and privileged Arapahos can manipulate it through ritual and power. In contrast, these stories focus much more on mystery, surprise, unexpected encounters, and confusion. In particular, the narrators place much more emphasis linguistically on characters' shifting perspectives, ironic reversals of expectations, and doubt ("modality" in linguistic terms). This is especially true in the Nih'oo3oo (Trickster) stories but also in other narratives. Paul Moss's stories (along with the songs, speeches, and prayers in this volume) generally could be seen as performative rituals, which not only tell about but actually enact the ritual processes needed to obtain greater-than-human power. The narrative texts in this collection, in contrast, recount the coming-into-being of the world of relationships upon which the very possibility of that ritual rests.

Arapaho Narrative/Poetic Style

We should note first that *heetéetoo* were told only at night and only in the wintertime. Jesse Rowlodge said, "You know after a rain when the little bugs start swimming around in the water—fly—then stories are over for the year . . . And besides they got only to be told at night."[7] Listeners occasionally had to say *hííí* 'snow' to show that they were still awake—otherwise the telling came to a halt.

Markers of Traditional Narrative Language/Style

Several key elements mark traditional narratives as separate from other forms of speech in Arapaho. (See appendix B for grammatical abbreviations used in this book and more complete information on Arapaho grammar in general. Cowell and Moss 2008 is a complete grammar of the language.) Most importantly, a special narrative past tense, marked by the prefix *hé'ih-*, requires verbs to take nonaffirmative inflections (Cowell and Moss 2008: 81–84). Thus rather than affirmative inflections (Cowell and Moss 2008: 75–80), as in *nih-cebísee-t* 's/he walked', one finds *hé'ih-cebisee*. A variant of this is the dubitative proclitic *he'(i)=* used with conjunct order subjunctive inflections (Cowell and Moss 2008: 87–89): *he'=cebisee-hék*. Unlike *hé'ih-*, the dubitative construction is virtually unused in modern Arapaho but is fairly common in the narratives from Oklahoma. A second important prefix is *he'ne'(i)-* 'then, so then, next', which is used when the action indicated is consequential to preceding action. This prefix contrasts with everyday *ne'(i)-* of the same meaning. Note that these forms are used for narrated, reported events; in direct discourse characters within narratives use the everyday prefixes of spoken Arapaho. Somewhat confusingly, everyday spoken Arapaho uses a separate element *ne'(i)=*, which is a proclitic (roughly speaking, a more loosely attached prefix, which precedes all person and tense/aspect prefixes) rather than a prefix and which is used for back reference, meaning 'that [is/was how many/how much/where/when, etc.]' (Cowell and Moss 2008: 423–25). In traditional narratives, this also becomes *he'ne'(i)=* (*he'ne'=nih-'iisí-nihii-t* 'that is what s/he said'). *Ne'=* is used with past and future tense and different aspectual markers (ongoing versus completed, for example), whereas *ne'-* is inherently past and punctual. In the present tense in spoken Arapaho, *ne'=* becomes *nee'=*; thus in traditional narrative it thus becomes *he'(i)nee'=*.

One inflectional feature specific to traditional narratives is the use of final *-n* to mark obviative/fourth person (explained further below), as in *hé'ih-cebísee-n* 's/he (obv.) walked'. In everyday speech this sentence (in the negative present tense) would be *hoow-cebísee*, with no distinction between proximate/third and obviative/fourth person. Similarly, some of the older texts show a distinction between third and fourth person singular with subjunctive inflections: *-ohk/-hok* versus *-ohkon/-hokon* (and similarly with the variant *-ehk*). This distinction is not retained even in traditional narratives today.

Finally, the special citational verb *heeh(i)-* (intransitive), *hee3-* (transitive) means 'said' and 'said to', respectively. In traditional narratives conjunct order subjunctive inflections are always used (*heeh-éhk* 's/he said'; *hee3-oohók* 's/he said to him/her/them'; *hee3-éihók* 's/he/they [obv.] said to him/her'; etc.), whereas in everyday speech these forms have affirmative order inflections, though they have a formal tenor even there. Note also that one sometimes sees the less formal citational forms *hé'ih-'íi-* 's/he said' and *hé'ih-'íi3-* (transitive) in traditional narratives, though more in modern Arapaho than in the texts here. Note finally that all of these special narrative features are only used with third (or fourth/obviative) person, never with first or second person—which only occur in dialogues, and where everyday grammar is used. Table 1 illustrates the forms discussed (affirmative inflections are used except where indicated).

Note that *nih-* is also used in past tense relative clause constructions ('the one who . . .) and that in this case traditional narrative and everyday speech both use *nih-*. Thus a traditional narrative could have a sentence such as *hé'ih-noohób-ee híni' nih-cebísee-t* 's/he saw the one who was walking'.

Table 1

	Traditional Narrative	*Everyday Speech*
Past Tense	hé'ih- (+ NONAFF) he'(i)= (+ SUBJ)	nih-
Consequential Past	he'ne(i)-	ne'(i)-
Back Reference	he'ne'=	ne'=
Back Reference, present	he'nee'=	nee'=
Citation (intransitive) less formal	heeh(i)- (+ SUBJ) hé'ih-'íi- (+ NONAFF)	héíhi- nih-'íi-
Citation (transitive) less formal	hee3- (+ SUBJ) hé'ih-'íi3- (+ NONAFF)	hee3- nih-'íi3-
Obviative, NONAFF	- n (sing.)	- (sing.)
Obviative, SUBJ	-ohkon (sing.)	-ohk (sing.)

Common Additional Features
of Traditional Narratives

The preceding linguistic features are the only elements that unequivocally identify traditional narratives. But a number of other features are quite characteristic of narrative. One of these is the formulaic conclusion *néé'ei'íse'* 'that is how far the story goes' or more loosely 'that is how the story ends'. Virtually the same concluding line occurs widely within Algonquian traditional narratives (Costa 2005; Leman 2005). Nih'oo3oo/Trickster stories have their own common formulaic opening: *Nih'óó3oo hé'ih-'oowúniihísee* 'Nih'oo3oo was walking downstream'. A fairly common stylistic feature of formal narratives is redundant usage of citational forms, such as "He said, 'Let's go over there,' he said." Some narrators make extensive use of the particles *noh* 'and' and *'oh* 'but' at the beginnings of lines almost as a line marker, especially prior to reported speech. Many narratives have a summational line at their conclusion, especially etiological and trickster narratives, such as "and that's why people don't marry in that way" or "and that's why white people cut their hair," using the proclitic *(he')ne'=*. Of course individual style and elements vary from narrator to narrator. See Moss 2005 for an extensive discussion of the stylistic features of a single Northern Arapaho narrator, Paul Moss, active in the 1980s and 1990s. He used a number of characteristic structures and lexical formulas not documented here as well as many that are common in the texts here. See also Cowell 2002 for a comparison of that narrator's style with another Northern Arapaho storyteller, John Goggles, recorded around 1950 by Zdeněk Salzmann (and also represented in this collection).

Note should also be made of a common feature of Algonquian languages: the distinction between proximate and obviative third persons. One third person in a narrative is considered central and most important (proximate), while other characters are considered less important and thus obviative. Nouns and verbs referencing these characters have special obviative or "fourth person" marking. Note that proximate status can change across the course of a narrative, and manipulation of this status is a key component of storytelling. The following is an example, from the beginning of the narrative "Big Belly's Adventure":

> Bih'ih he'ih-'iinoo'ei.
> Deer [a personal name] went hunting.
>
> Hitox-oohók wot=hih-tousi-ni'eihi-n hisei-n.
> He came upon an extremely good-looking woman.

The normal singular (i.e., proximate) form of 'woman' is *hisei*. Here, however, the narrator chooses to select the individual named "Deer" as the most prominent, and thus proximate, third person. 'Woman' is marked for obviative status (*hisei-n*). Similarly, the verb *tousini'eihi-* 'extremely good-looking' receives a final *-n*, indicating that it is referring to the obviative woman, not the proximate Deer. Finally, the verb *hitox-* 'meet, come upon' has the ending *-oohok*, indicating that the proximate Deer has come upon the obviative woman. Had it been the obviative woman who came upon proximate Deer, then the verb would have had the ending *-eihok*. The narrator could also have chosen to have Deer be less prominent and thus obviative, in which case the word would have had obviative marking (*bih'ih-ii*) and the verb 'hunting' would have had a final *-n*. All of the specific grammatical details of this procedure are complex (see Cowell and Moss 2008: 349–54), but it is central to Algonquian narration.

Also note that Arapaho has free word order. In addition, due to the availability of extensive inflectional prefixes and suffixes, nouns are normally not stated after their first mention, as long as the reference remains clear. Thus the choice to use a noun at all is often an important stylistic feature. When nouns are used, placement before the verb is the more salient position compared to placement after the verb, so this is also a key stylistic device. This is nearly impossible to capture well in English, with its fixed word order. In general, new and highly salient information goes in the sentence-initial position in Arapaho (see Cowell and Moss 2008: 7–12, 370–71, 399–416), so this position is key for stylistic manipulation.

Lexical and Grammatical/Structural Archaisms in Traditional Narratives

Narratives also tend to contain archaic words or phrases, although it is tricky to judge exactly what this label means here because all the narratives date from nearly a century ago: what is archaic now might not have seemed so then. Nevertheless, examples, at least from a modern perspective (such as Moss and C'Hair's), include fixed constructions, such as:

1. Dubitative *wot* = + *wh*-question prefix, nonaffirmative inflection, producing a sense of both narrative pastness and also a dubitative sense of 'you wouldn't believe . . . :
   Wot = *hih-tousi-ni'eihi-n!*
   DUBIT = PAST-how/what-pretty(AI)-4S
   'how unbelievably pretty she was!' ("Big Belly's Adventure")

2. Interrogative *koo* = (proclitic) + dubitative *wot* = (proclitic), nonaffirmative inflection, producing a sense of complete contrariness to
   desire or expectation:
   Koowót = hinenítee   *he' = e'inón-e' tih-'esówobéíh-t.*
   INTERR.DUBIT = person DUBIT = know(TA)-4/3S that/
   when-sick(AI)-3S
   'no one would have even guessed that she was sick' ("The White
   Dog and the Woman")

3. Emphatic/exemplary *(hii)yóhou* =, nonaffirmative inflection, producing a sense that someone is "as . . . as can be!"
   [hii]yóhou = hoxóotéíhih!
   How.EMPH = cute(AI.DIM)
   'it's as cute as can be!' ("The White Crow")

Another common form of archaism is the use of individual words, particularly highly colorful and specific expressive particles. Many of these begin
with the element *wo'úu-*, which generally indicates social disapproval:

Wo'uu-ceecii3owu', *he'ih-koo-koxkoh-u' hiix!*
But would you believe it, she stabbed her husband instead! ("The Faithless
Woman and the Kiowa")

Wo'uu-noononoho', *howoh tih-beeseenebeti-noo.*
What in the world will people say, especially since I thought so much of
myself. ("The White Dog and the Woman")

A number of other *wo'uu-* forms appear in the texts, and including such
a form seems to be a highlight (especially for C'Hair) if not a requirement
of many of the texts. Many more details on archaic words and constructions
occur in the notes to the stories.

Large-scale Organizational Features

Many scholars have noted large-scale organizational features in traditional
narratives (Hymes 1981, 2003; Tedlock 1983; Sherzer and Woodbury 1987).
We have intervened to label large sections in some cases, particularly in
longer narratives ("The Beheaded Ones," "Open Brain or Tangled Hair").
As explained in Cowell 2002, however, we are wary of making too strong a
claim about the organization of narratives recorded for non-Arapaho audiences for documentation purposes only, especially when they had to be
transcribed by hand. Narratives of Paul Moss told to Arapaho audiences in

the 1980s commonly run to thirty minutes or more, while few of the narratives recorded here by Michelson in particular would approach even a fifth of that length. Some of this difference is related to genre, but it is also related both to the audience in question (a linguist versus appreciative native Arapaho speakers) and to the recording techniques (line-by-line written transcription versus audio or video). While the shorter narratives do have structure, that structure may be quite different than in longer narratives and deceptively over-regularized in some cases.

Alonzo Moss notes that repetition and elaboration are key features of Arapaho storytelling and that avoiding them would be "un-Arapaho." "They can make them real short," he says, but "that's not Arapaho." He is especially attuned to this stylistic feature and finds both stories recorded by Zdeněk Salzmann (1956a, 1956b) and the shorter narratives in this collection to be lacking in this regard. Nevertheless, where important structural features seem clear, we point this out in the introductions to specific texts. We do divide some texts into sections (marked by subheads). Moss and especially C'Hair were quite attentive to divisions at the level of "parts" of long narratives such as "The Beheaded Ones," and "Open Brain/Tangled Hair," which are based on clear divisions or parallelisms in content. They were less focused on smaller-scale divisions of a few lines each, based on grammatical or lexical structures and parallelisms, as in "Nih'oo3oo Pursued by the Rolling Skull" and "Nih'oo3oo Sharpens His Leg and Dives on the Ice." This is not to say that Moss and C'Hair did not recognize these features: indeed, when he talks of the "repetition" found in good stories Alonzo Moss stresses the subtle lexical or grammatical parallels, which highlight key thematic connections and moral lessons. He notes that the texts "mean nothing in English," due to the loss of these features in translation. C'Hair and Moss see this kind of organization as less clearly "structural" in nature, however. Thus divisions of this sort presented in the texts (using just indentations rather than subheads) are more subjective. Cowell based them on comments by Moss and C'Hair plus his own appreciation of the narratives. These divisions are not necessarily recognized as such by the native speakers.

All texts are presented in a line-by-line format, with each line corresponding to a sentence or a complete clause. This is done so that the text and translation can be aligned as clearly as possible, not as a claim that the texts are specifically "poetic" in the Euro-American sense of that term. This format should not be taken as "the" denotation of poetic lines in the Arapaho texts, especially as we lack any access to data about delivery style, speed, pauses, and so forth. Readers should note that we tend to agree with the argument of Robert Bringhurst (1999: 168) that "patterns of vision [and] patterns of thought are more potent than patterns of sound" in the organization of what he calls "Classical" American Indian myths, though the sound patterns should certainly not be neglected. The traditional "sacred number" in Arapaho culture is four, with seven being a secondary sacred number. This is a key element in the larger structure of several texts as well as in the plots: the trickster, for example, is not supposed to do things more than four times but always fails to stop at that point.

Individual "Style" in Traditional Narratives

These narratives contain a good deal of stylistic variation, as one might expect. Some is no doubt due to differences of genre and may also be due to the relative effort invested in the stories as the narrator worked with the transcriber. But individual stylistic variation is also certainly present, and we try to point this out in the introduction to each story.

One fairly pervasive style might be called "flat." It typically does not involve extensive use of uncommon or highly descriptive words and phrases on a regular basis. Instead fairly common lexical items are used, without extensive adjectival or adverbial modification and specification. Such a style is not notably "colorful." In place of a large variety of words or detailed description, the style relies on repetition or near repetition with small variations and on parallel grammatical structures to create larger units of organization and larger thematic connections across a text. Within such a carefully constructed repetitive framework, small variations can be highly salient for the listener/reader. In addition, when a particularly striking or colorful word or phrase is used, it stands out all the more strongly in relation to the flatter surroundings. Some stories seem to exist almost entirely as setups for such lines (see Bauman 1986: 54–77; and Bringhurst 1999: 212; see "The Arapaho Migration across the Missouri River to the . . ." and "Nih'oo3oo Sharpens His Leg and Dives on the Ice" for examples of this style).

This style often relies on the evocation of extremely rich and complex systems of belief, practice, and ceremony through only brief mentions and allusions, which resonate powerfully with a knowledgeable Arapaho audience even as they leave outsiders unmoved. Extremely complex juxtapositions of images or beliefs may be created for the listener, without ever providing much in the way of explicit detail or description. This type of style is possible in a relatively small, face-to-face community with a great deal of shared knowledge, practice, and belief, relatively speaking, as well as a widely shared narrative tradition, which creates a close-knit textual community. Such a style can be highly efficient and is certainly not "flat" in its effects on knowledgeable listeners. It does however feature not just an absence of verbal fireworks but an apparently willed preference for verbal simplicity and parallelism in order to enhance structural balance and intricacy as well as to highlight the rare moments of extreme verbal creativity and render them more salient.

In contrast, we could also talk about a "dynamic" style, which works hard to use less common and more precise descriptive elements, taking pleasure in verbal creativity and ingenuity. Long, complex, and highly unusual polysynthetic words and phrases are a key component of this style, as is the use of a number of expressive particles, many of which have quite detailed meanings, such as those beginning with *wo'úu-* mentioned above. Such a style might be said to do more of the work for the listener and to rely less on the listener to pick up allusions and evocations or subtle parallelisms across many lines of text, in comparison to the flat style. A good example of this style is "The Faithless Woman and the Kiowa."

These are of course just two extremes on a continuum, and variation of style from moment to moment within a story is itself an important technique. In this collection Cleaver Warden stands out for his use of both the dynamic style and the flat style, choosing one or the other as the primary style for different stories. Philip Rapid/Rabbit shows similar variation (as suggested by the contrasting stylistic examples just mentioned, "The Faithless Woman and the Kiowa" and "Nih'oo3oo Sharpens His Leg and Dives on the Ice"). John Goggles, in contrast, sticks almost entirely with the flat style.

Another distinction, related to the dynamic style in part, is the density of use of modal prefixes and proclitics that serve to express either the author's or a character's relationship to or view of events, rather than being just a description of the events themselves. Arapaho is rich in prefixes such as *hiixowúh-* 'it sure looks like it to me [though I can't say for certain]'; *yóhou=* 'what an exemplary instance of . . . !'; *híínoonónox* 'to his/her great astonishment'; *wót=hih-tóus-* 'you've never seen a more . . . one'; or *yó'oh-* 'people say or think it's so, but I sure don't think so' as well as many different particles beginning with the admonitive form *wo'úu-* (see the examples given above). Some of the narratives, including many by Cleaver Warden, show rich use of these forms to manipulate point of view and make subtle character judgments. Warden uses them to especially good effect in trickster narratives to highlight the ironic differences between the trickster's beliefs and expectations and the reality of situations. All of the shorter narratives by John Goggles are virtually lacking in these forms, even at climactic moments. His two longer narratives do show examples of them, but certainly not with the density of some of Cleaver Warden's texts.

Whether this makes Warden's texts "better" is of course not an answerable question, as it depends partly on speaker judgments. But certainly William C'Hair always seemed to show a special appreciation for Cleaver Warden's texts as we worked together, while some of John Goggles's texts struck Cowell as being somewhat perfunctory in nature. Alonzo Moss agreed, noting that there are "too many *hé'ih*'s in there" in relation to the Goggles texts here as well as those collected by Salzmann (1956a, 1956b). In other words, for him the texts lacked enough dialogue and elaboration of detail through subordinate clauses and other structures and were reduced to too many lines of simply 'this happened' then 'that happened' then 'the next thing happened'. Moss says that a well-told story "makes it real clear" what the teller is trying to convey and that this involves more than just telling the events. Either explanations or speaker perspectives on the events are needed. C'Hair likewise noted the importance of clarity and respect for "traditional order" in good stories, by which he meant both the order of events told and also a correspondence to social order.

At the same time, Moss noted that he really appreciated "words I've never heard before," by which he means creative polysynthetic combinations, like a clause or sentence never heard before in English. This is a key criterion for all older native speakers to whom Cowell has talked. It is especially important for comic moments. In a somewhat different sense, another native speaker, Robert (Bobby Joe) Goggles, made the following remarks in a discussion with C'Hair recorded in 2006:

Yeah, yeah wonoo3ee' nuhu'; kookon nihii, kokoh'eeneetowoo nuhu' heteenetiitoon,
Yeah, yeah, there is a lot of this [Arapaho language] that is gone; well, I just think about our language,

toh'uni woo3ee' hoowooh'uni, nih'iisinihiini'.
because there is a lot that is no longer around, of what we used to say.

Hoo3oo'o' tih'iineeseenentoohokoni'.
Some of the people were left behind/split off as we moved around.

'oh wootii nooxeihi' nee'eeneetou'.
And I guess maybe that is where [the missing elements of the language] are at.

Wohei nihii, howoo nuhu' heeteetoono, wohei nuhu' nehe' hoonoo3itoonetiitooni', wootii nee'eeneetou'.
Well, and also these old myths, well, the way they told each other stories, I guess that's where it's at.

This statement could be understood specifically in relation to the present and ongoing language loss, in which case these stories could be considered a treasure house of missing vocabulary and expressions. But traditional narratives tend to contain archaic elements even when language loss is not occurring, so the statement can also be understood to mean that the narratives contain especially rich and unusual vocabulary, without which we cannot have a full appreciation of the Arapaho language and its creative potential. Cowell's own personal judgment of the narratives is that Warden and Philip Rabbit are the most interesting narrators in this collection and that Warden is unsurpassed in the Arapaho canon in his subtle handling of shifting points of view and psychological states. Neither Warden nor Rabbit, however, matches the structural complexity and elaboration achieved by Paul Moss in his narratives of the 1980s (Moss 2005).

"Meaning"

Our first concern in this project has been accurate documentation of what Arapaho speakers were saying as they performed these texts and also to make the more or less literal meanings of their statements clear, recognizing of course that nothing is ever simply "literal." The language has been the grounding point of everything else in the volume. When we move beyond what the stories "say" to what they "mean" interpretively, or what social functions they accomplished in Arapaho society, we have tried to ground all such remarks in the introductions and notes in very minute attention to the linguistic content and structure of the texts. Indeed, we usually have not sought to say what texts "mean" for "Arapaho culture" in general at all, for a number of reasons. Most comments about potential meanings relate to specific words or textual details.

Studies of oral performance and oral narratives consistently show that much of the meaning and social effect produced by a story is a result of the context surrounding that performance (see Basso 1990: 99–173 for just one among many possible examples). Thus telling a Nih'oo3oo story in a particular setting can serve as an indirect criticism of a member of the audience who is suggested to have acted like Nih'oo3oo. In such cases the details of the text will change to fit that context. As C'Hair says, "Depending on the audience is the way you tell them. They're very susceptible to the audience." Moss adds: if people "laugh like heck," then a teller will add more to the story to make it even funnier.

For a traditional narrative, then, the potential meanings and social tasks accomplished are as infinite as the contexts and are never fully contained in the story itself. All stories are potentialities waiting for a performance in context to realize (some of) that potential. To suggest what "the" meaning(s) of a story are would be to ignore this truth and vastly underrepresent the potential of the story. For the same reason, a story potentially has infinite individually performed versions, with no one variant being authoritative. This collection contains multiple versions of several stories. Unfortunately, other than knowing that they were performed for an outside collector of narratives, we have little other information about the specific context of performance. Hence we have limited ability to explain the variations, which are often the secondhand record of those varying contexts.

At the same time, this perspective can go too far, in that there are clearly messages and perspectives embedded in the stories themselves. Some of these may be very broad, linkable to Arapaho culture in general. They could be derived just from the texts themselves and a more general knowledge of Arapaho culture (or anthropological theory). They could in principle be accessible even through translations, without the original language. Claude Lévi-Strauss (1978) has done such interpretations using Arapaho stories. Jeffrey Anderson (2013: 95–114) does the same with the specific theme of quillwork. With a few exceptions, this book includes very little of that kind of discussion. C'Hair and Moss were almost completely uninterested and/or unresponsive when Cowell made suggestions of this sort on a few occasions. Moss added that he was always told with regard to books on the Arapahos: "Don't listen to the whites. They're going to write what the other whites want to hear." Nevertheless, some of the introductions contain phrases like "Cowell suggests" or similar remarks, to distinguish his thoughts and proposed readings of this kind from the rest of the introductory material. Even in these cases the remarks are grounded specifically in the language, coming from someone who is a near-fluent understander and good speaker of the language and has spent many years visiting Wind River. But the vast majority of the introductions reflect a true dialogue of Cowell, Moss, and C'Hair, though filtered mostly through Cowell's words. Neither Moss nor C'Hair was interested in writing independently or recording long statements for verbatim inclusion in this book.

Probably more interesting than Cowell's occasional suggestions are the Arapaho-specific interpretive traditions that accompany the stories. The same types of traditions accompany any literature: this is why Euro-Americans take literature classes. They seek not just to read novels and poetry but to find out what critics and scholars have said about what it all "means." A rich tradition of such interpretations is associated not just with stories in Arapaho but with material culture items such as beadwork, painting, quillwork, and other arts (see Kroeber [1902–1907] 1983; Anderson 2013), ceremonial imagery and practice (Dorsey 1903), and place-names

(Cowell and Moss 2003). The interpretations are typically not truly "contained" in the story in the sense that they could be derived merely from its literal contents and/or a general knowledge of Arapaho culture. Rather, a consultant is needed to explain such interpretations, which are passed down orally along with the stories and of course constantly reworked and rethought along with the stories. Moreover, these interpretations typically are tied to individuals, families, or clans and can vary considerably across the tribe, even for events as salient as the Sun Dance. Variation apparently is less broad for that event, however, or for sacred practices such as quillwork, than it is for stories. Unfortunately, while Kroeber did a good job obtaining such information for material culture items, he (and other story collectors) did a poor job of this with stories, though he recorded intriguing bits (see "The Skunk and the Rabbit," "The White Dog and the Woman," and "The White Crow" for three examples of comments from his notes).

In part, this lack can be mitigated by comments from Moss and especially from C'Hair. When Moss was growing up, he heard mostly historical, true narratives at home (such as in Moss 2005) and war stories as well as reservation-era and modern stories. He rarely heard or discussed the myths and legends such as those in this book, with the partial exception of Nih'oo3oo stories. As a result, Moss has been more interested in the linguistic side of the narratives as we worked on this volume than in the interpretive side and was especially sensitive to wordplay, sexual allusions, and similar elements. He says that "the stories are the best teachers of the language" (recalling Robert Goggles's remarks cited above). He also notes that there is "a little bit of humor in a lot of them," by which he means that they often contain hidden humor, jokes, and double meanings that the reader has to be on the lookout for.

C'Hair (who was raised by his grandparents), in contrast, did grow up listening to many of these stories, which to this day remain a key part of his interpretive framework for understanding life, family, and ceremony. For example, when we discussed "The Little People," he noted that one had been seen in the area the previous week. As a result he was relatively more interested in the interpretive side of the stories and provided many comments that appear in the introductions and notes. His family tradition is only one among others, of course, and no doubt has changed over time. But one of the narrators here (John Goggles) was one of his great-grandfathers, from whom he heard stories himself as a child. Thus he has retained significant parts of at least one interpretive tradition that must have existed around these stories when they were collected. See the introductions to "Found-in-the-Grass" and "The Turtle Fetches Up the Earth from the Bottom of the Waters," which include two nearly verbatim examples of his explanations for parts of those narratives. Moss, Cowell, and C'Hair have worked together over many years. Moss and C'Hair preferred to provide commentary to Cowell, which he would then organize and present formally. Hence Cowell in particular felt that it was virtually impossible to attribute each remark in introductions and notes to one source (though sometimes this is done). For the most part we present a single descriptive voice, with Cowell as the writer. But the reader should recognize that differences in perspective on these stories exist among all three editors.

Both Moss and C'Hair were quite reluctant to provide speculative interpretations of the stories or details within them, even from an Arapahocentric framework (as opposed to a theory/anthropology-centric one), when they did not have access to sure cultural knowledge or a received interpretive tradition. They both take a similar attitude toward explaining what obscure personal names mean when they are asked about this by non-Arapaho speakers, and for the same reason: "Every year it changes like that, even our language changes," Moss says. "I don't want to just make things up." Thus they both share a cultural conservatism toward speculation, also reported by Anderson (2013) in relation to quillwork. Cowell has commonly found the same attitude in discussing narratives with contemporary storytellers.

We should not make too much of this conservatism, however, because it is balanced by a great deal of innovation. Not included in the introductions are a number of remarks from William C'Hair and his younger brother Wayne about modern reinterpretations of some of these stories within their extended family. For example, in "Blue Bird, Elk Woman, and Buffalo Woman," the Blue Bird is revived based on the discovery of a single one of his feathers. The C'Hairs note that this shows that the Arapahos knew about DNA and the possibility of cloning. When *Sputnik* was launched in 1957, their older relatives told them that this had been predicted in the story "Nih'oo3oo Loses His Eyes," when the eyes were thrown up into the sky. The C'Hairs knew a different version of the story "The Beheaded Ones," in which a series of houses are encountered: stone, wood, metal (as in this version), and finally glass, with the glass house being the one where the evil creatures are beheaded. They note that this story was a prediction and vision of the future and of modern architecture. William C'Hair also commented that one lesson of "Nih'oo3oo and Whirlwind Woman" is to avoid marrying "fast" women, in the sexual sense. Finally, the C'Hairs note that the version of "When Nih'ooo3oo Witnessed the Sundance" (of the mice) that they know emphasizes that Nih'oo3oo hears the sound of the Sun Dance but cannot figure out where it is coming from, seeing only a seemingly innocuous elk skull. He finally discovers the source of the drumming. This was a prediction or beforehand knowledge of radio, they say.

These are all examples of interpretive traditions (and new versions of the stories themselves) that evolved after the material in this book was collected from 1880 to 1930. They illustrate the way in which some of the stories continue to live on and be adapted as meaningful cultural vehicles. Of course we hope that this book will help this process to continue into the future. These examples also show that many Arapaho-specific meanings and interpretive traditions are not literally contained within the stories themselves and cannot be easily predicted or anticipated based on either the story's content or general cultural knowledge. Moreover, they illustrate a tendency to find meaning at the level of specific independent detail as much as at the level of overall coherent wholes. Most of the reinterpretations cited above as well as many of the interpretive traditions noted in the introductions to individual narratives illustrate this point. They seize on key details, without necessarily seeking a global coherence with all the other details in the story. Indeed, such interpretations often ignore other elements in a narrative that might contradict the proposed interpretation. This is not seen as problematic. Contemporary Arapaho society offers a great deal of freedom for individuals to take what they can find from narratives and use them (or just small parts of them) however they can. Arapaho elders will often evaluate whether specific details were left out of a story that should have been included, but Cowell has rarely if ever heard these individuals argue that someone's *interpretation* of a story or its parts is "wrong," though they will often propose their own alternatives. This type of approach to narratives provides an additional understanding (Cowell believes) of why Moss and C'Hair were often resistant to speculative, global interpretations of texts.

These modern reinterpretations generally illustrate how some Arapaho people look for patterns and images in their traditional literature that allow them to make sense of the changing world. In so doing, they fit their perception of that new world into a traditional set of motifs, structures, and vocabulary, which is perhaps an inherently conservative gesture. Yet the very same process simultaneously brings new or renewed meaning to the narratives in ways that can be highly innovative, as just illustrated. This is the way in which any living literature functions. The C'Hairs, as well as other contemporary Arapaho storytellers (including one from Moss's family), feel that knowledge of the future and the technologies and events that it will bring is embedded in the structure and content of the narratives, waiting to be discovered. The task of the listener—and even the teller—is not necessarily to understand everything in the narrative but simply to absorb and convey the structure and contents, knowing that its value and meaning will perhaps be recognized and become useful at some future point. As Robert Goggles said when talking to William C'Hair: "Wootii nuhu' cee'inonoo3oo' hiiwoonhehe' . . . 'oh hinee hosei3iihi', wootii hoote'einei'i-nou'u, toonheet, heetniisoo' huune'etiit, huut no'uuhu'" (It seems like this [life of ours] is so uncertain/confused today . . . but back in the past it seems like they knew things in advance, however life was going to be, right up to the present). From this perspective a resistance to interpretation can be seen as a sign of openness toward the future and future interpretive possibilities—a belief that meanings are not yet known and cannot yet be known. It can also be seen as a sign of humbleness about one's own ability fully to understand the past, the present, or the future.

The Titles of the Texts

Wherever Arapaho titles for the various texts exist in the manuscripts, these have of course been used, in Arapaho and/or English. Many of the texts lack titles in the original manuscripts. For texts lacking titles, they have been supplied by C'Hair and Moss.

The Translations and the Format of the Texts

Cowell has sought to produce "smoothly faithful" translations. By "faithful," we mean that the translations stay fairly close to the original language. In particular, where a given Arapaho verb stem is repeated on multiple occasions, we have tried to repeat the same English gloss for that stem. Of course, a given word in one language may have multiple possible translations in another language, depending on contexts, so it would be absurd to try to maintain complete one-to-one translations across an entire collection. Nevertheless, we have sought to avoid what could be called "stylistic variation" simply for the sake of variety. Thus the verb *hiine'etii-* is consistently translated 'live' rather than varying 'live', 'dwell', 'reside', and other possibilities. Brackets are used where elements are included in the translation that are not specifically in the text. This is partially a subjective judgment, of course; virtually every line of the translation could have brackets, but we have tried to avoid this. Most importantly, when nouns are referenced inflectionally on the verb in Arapaho (and thus need not be stated explicitly in the language), we have often added the explicit noun in the translation for clarification, because English grammar does not permit referent-tracking in the same way as Arapaho. We consider those nouns to be part of the basic meaning of the Arapaho and fully accessible to the listener. Thus Arapaho verbal phrases like *hee3éihók* or *hee3oohók* are translated 'the skunk said to the rabbit' or 'the rabbit said to the skunk' rather than as a superliteral 'the other one said to him' or 'he said to the other one'. Due to the availability of inflectional markers, nouns are typically dropped in Arapaho, so the choice of whether to use an explicit noun or not is important stylistically. The type of translation used here washes out that stylistic feature for the sake of clarity in English, but of course the original can easily be consulted.

"Smoothly" means that we have tried to produce normal English in terms of word choice and word order. We could make major changes in English word order as part of an effort to capture the Arapaho even more closely. Arapaho has free word order, though with a tendency for the newest information to come first in the sentence. But this closeness in word order would come at the cost of often very awkward-sounding English. This level of literal fidelity has been avoided, because the texts are certainly not awkward-sounding in Arapaho.

We have used a fairly formal level of English, because the narratives themselves make use of markers and features that clearly give them a formal (and sometimes archaic) feel in Arapaho, as explained above. For example, the citational form *heehéhk* 's/he said' occurs only in formal narratives: where a noun or personal name for the speaker is given with this form, we translate 'said so-and-so' rather than 'so-and-so said,' because the former sounds more "literary" in English. Following the suggestion of Doug Parks (1991: 62), however, we have tried to translate direct speech in a more colloquial style. As explained above, the grammar of reported speech in the narratives is the same as that of everyday speech. When discussions of different translation possibilities occurred, C'Hair and Moss typically deferred to Cowell as the native English speaker. "We explained the Arapaho to you, now you fix up the English," they would often say. Nonetheless they were of course central to the entire translation enterprise.

A guiding principle of this volume has been to maximize the value of the bilingual format. Rather than simply publishing the Arapaho and letting it stand on its own, parallel to the English, we have been guided by the principle that the Arapaho should be made as revealing as possible through processes of intervention. While such interventionism in texts goes against principles of editing for widely spoken or well-understood languages, a very real possibility exists that no one in the future will have full access to the Arapaho language—though we of course hope that this is not the case. But we believe that those who do have full access to the language now, either as native speakers or as scholars working with such speakers, should intervene in editions and maximize the clarity with which the Arapaho versions of the narratives can be used, to gain the full benefit of the extra expense of the bilingual format.

We have done this in two ways. First, we provide detailed introductions to each text, which focus in particular on linguistic details of structure and content available only in the Arapaho versions. Second, we have formatted the Arapaho texts themselves in various ways, including dividing them into scenes and using graphic means to highlight certain linguistic features in the texts. Any such intervention naturally involves an element of subjectivity, so this is a form of interpretation. Nevertheless, full access to the original text remains, if the reader simply ignores these graphic features. Interpretations from those knowledgeable in the traditions may never be replicable or practicable in the future, however, so some interpretation is surely better than no interpretation. Embedding some of these interpretive analyses in the body of the texts themselves is intended to maximize clarity and transparency.

Additionally, for reading and grammatical analysis purposes, we have used the equals sign (=) to separate proclitics (Cowell and Moss 2008: 233–39) from nouns and verbs. We have used hyphens (-) to separate prefixes and suffixes from nouns and verbs. We have tried to do this for all affixes with the exception of the singular possession prefixes of obligatorily possessed nouns (Cowell and Moss 2008: 66–68). Also, where inflectional suffixes are suppletive (obviative -*o* replaces proximate -*e* and similar situations) we have not separated the -*o* from the noun stem. Such marking is fraught with problems in a language like Arapaho, which has complex sound changes within words and among different affixes. In addition, Arapaho has many shorter noun stems that occur on their own but have a longer underlying form that occurs when affixes are added. In such cases we have placed the hyphen after the longer form of the noun (for example, *hotíí* 'wheel' > *hotííb-e'* 'wheel-LOC'), except in the most common case of singular versus plural distinctions (thus *hotíí-wo'* 'wheels' rather than *hotííw-o'*). This is an imperfect system but should help serious students greatly in understanding the structure of the words, provided that they have read the Arapaho grammar. Such readers will want to consult appendix B for more guidance, including a list of abbreviations used.

Finally, we have sought to reproduce what the original speakers were saying rather than to reelicit what they were saying and then produce the modern Arapaho equivalent. This is true not just on the level of grammar and vocabulary but on the level of individual sounds as well. For example, the original transcriptions suggest that unaccented short vowels were often retained where they are now dropped in modern Arapaho, as in *hésinée-* 'hungry' > modern *hésnée-*. Another example is /e(e)/ following /o/ (with certain consonants intervening). Kroeber's transcriptions show this as being pronounced /e/ (*honóh'e* 'young man'), whereas modern speakers pronounce it /oe/ (*honóh'oe*). We try to stay as close as possible to the earlier transcription, not the modern equivalent.

Such a process necessarily includes subjective judgments. To take one common example, Kroeber frequently transcribes a final vowel plus a glottal stop with a repeat of the same vowel after the glottal stop. Thus he often writes *nähää* for *néhe'*. There is in fact a slight breath after the release of a glottal stop in modern Arapaho. This is purely a phonetic artifact of pronunciation, however, not an actual phonemic vowel, and thus we do not transcribe the third *ä* written by Kroeber in such intances. Kroeber in particular also used numerous diacritic marks on vowels, most of which mark fine phonetic distinctions rather than phonemic ones. With the exception of the three texts for which we include original transcriptions,[8] we have not tried to take account of these.

The issue of pitch accent has been especially problematic. Pitch accent is phonemic in Arapaho, though modern fluent speakers do not normally write it. Based on the best of the transcriptions used here, the pitch accent system does not seem to have changed to any significant degree since 1900. Where Kroeber and Gatschet indicate pitch accents on words they almost always correspond to the modern ones. They write fewer of them than actually exist, however, at least in the modern language. In Kroeber's earliest transcriptions in particular, he wrote very few (see the introduction to "Open Brain/Tangled Hair"). To put in all of the accents that he likely missed at this point would be to rewrite his Arapaho into the modern language, and that is what we are trying not to do. At the same time, most of what is missing probably really is "missing," rather than reflecting a change in the system. Taking a conservative approach, we have chosen to write in Kroeber's and Gatschet's pitch accents as they noted them, but not to add additional ones. The accents are marked with (´) both in their work and here, though we also sometimes interpret orthographies such as *ûû* as indicating *úu*, based on modern evidence. This approach provides useful information about the relative saliency of pitch accent for Kroeber and Gatschet, but readers should be aware that the transcription here does not necessarily represent the "true" distribution of pitch accents in Arapaho in 1900. Michelson also wrote pitch accents. In his case the accents he wrote in his early work in 1910 seem very inaccurate. They do not correspond with Kroeber or Gatschet or the modern system or even with Michelson's own later work. Because we believe that these accents would simply be misleading, we have not included them, although we do include his accents in later texts from the 1920s.

Note that where we cite and discuss Arapaho forms in notes and introductions we use the modern spellings and modern pitch accents for the sake of maximum accuracy. Thus there are minor differences between these forms and those attested in the texts in terms of spelling and pitch accent. We also use citation forms (noun and verb stems) rather than inflected forms in many cases in these discussions. These are marked with dashes before or after the form (*ciitéi-* AI 'to enter') where it would otherwise have an inflection. Be aware that Arapaho verbs and most verbal prefixes show "initial change" when they have no other element preceding them (thus *ceníitéi-noo* 'I am entering' [Cowell and Moss 2008: 73–74]). And morphophonemic rules apply (see Cowell and Moss 2008: 16–22), such as *nih-* PAST + *íine'étii-* 'live' (or any other vowel-initial form) > *nih'íine'étii-*, with a glottal stop inserted. Thus while appendix B should be helpful to serious readers, the forms listed there often vary in ways that are beyond the scope of this introduction.

Where an Arapaho element (normally single sounds or syllables) appears to be missing, we have added it in the Arapaho transcriptions, with square brackets around the added element, such as [n]. Where unexplained extra sounds occur in the Arapaho material, we have put them in curly brackets, such as {n}.

Notes

1. Certain families are especially prominent among both the Northern and Southern Arapahos in mediating between the tribe and the federal government in relation to the Sand Creek Massacre National Historic Site, which is a good contemporary example of this process. See Wiles 2011: 98–101, 179–89 for details of this process at Wind River.

2. "Carlisle Indian Industrial School" (http://home.epix.net/~landis/). All subsequent references to "Carlisle" and the Carlisle graduates in the introduction are from this source unless otherwise noted.

3. This is apparently the same name that Truman Michelson writes as *bitchea* (NAA, MS 3346), who is the subject of his autobiography of an Arapaho woman. That woman was born around 1855 and could easily have been the mother of Boynton, but Berthrong (1976: 166) reports that Boynton's mother was a Cheyenne (though in that case why she would have had an Arapaho name is unclear).

4. Doris Duke Collection, Jesse Rowlodge Interviews with Julia A. Jordan, MS T-205, T-220, and others.

5. Other Arapaho material is found in Gatschet MS 3027, but this simply cites forms from the other two manuscripts.

6. The following website has audio files of some of Mooney's Arapaho recordings: http://www.ghostdance.com/songs/songs-mooneyrecordings.html.

7. Doris Duke Collection, Jesse Rowlodge Interview with Julia A. Jordan, March 19, 1968, MS T-220, p. 3.

8. Gatschet, "The Myth of the Milky Way," Kroeber, "Yellow Bull Races the Horse," and Michelson, "Nih'oo3oo Loses His Eyes." The first two texts are versions of the same story, with some of the same words, in order to allow for maximum comparability. They were also among the last texts recorded by each collector, based on their dates and places in the manuscripts and thus probably among the best-transcribed texts. The text from Michelson is likewise among his last and best-transcribed texts. These three texts are intended to give an adequate representation of the orthographies used by each of the three major collectors, as well as the retranscription decisions faced by the editors.

Creation Accounts and Etiological Narratives

The Turtle Fetches Up
the Earth from the
Bottom of the Waters

Teller unknown, Oklahoma, about March 1893
Collected by Albert Gatschet
NAA, MS 231, pp. 268–70

This is the only creation story recorded in Arapaho. The title above is from Gatschet's manuscript. In principle, the creation story is only supposed to be told by certain ceremonial individuals and on certain special occasions—in particular, during the Rabbit Lodge ceremony prior to the Sun Dance. The full story was known only to a few old people, and its telling was said to last multiple days. Short, fragmentary versions have been recorded and published in English, however (notably Dorsey 1903). This version also is clearly very brief and fragmentary, so it seems appropriate to share this text here because it includes no new information per se. The "water snakes" are normally identified as garter snakes in other sources. The fact that the turtle is "red-headed" is important symbolically: red ceremonial paint (*hínow*) is the most sacred of all the paint colors for the Arapahos. One linguistic detail of the story that is significant is the use of the form *bix-* 'to appear'. It occurs in *bíxoúusee-* 'appear above the water [after diving]' and in *bixooyéítii-* 'stack s.t. up until it becomes visible'. The upward movement and appearance of the searching animals is rendered concrete and permanent through the upward movement and appearance of the stacked earth; rising up out of the water is a magical moment.

Finally, comments from William C'Hair illustrate some of the additional potential meanings in this text. On talking about the turtle, he told a story about when the Arapahos were given a turtle's shell long ago and told that it was the map to their homeland. They did not fully understand this, so they wandered the land, going to all four cardinal points (the four legs of the turtle) and trying to figure out how to use the map to locate home. Finally, on their fifth, decisive journey, they came to the mountains. They then looked at the turtle's back and realized that the bulge on top was the mountains, the line along the ridge of the back was the continental divide, and the other lines on the back were the rivers flowing down from the mountains. They knew that they had found their home. While none of this account is explicitly included in the creation story, it illustrates how much additional symbolic information could be attached to just one element of the story for knowledgeable listeners.

Heetíh-téi'oo-' bííto'owu' hóót-niitoh-úúne'etíítooni-',
In order that the earth where people would live would be strong,

hee3ei'-cee-ce'eseihí-3i' cese'ehíí-ho' nih-'o3í'eebeíhi-3i' hi3óóbe' néc-i'.
all the different kinds of animals were sent down under the water
[to look for earth].

Níítowuuhu' hoo3óó'o' nii'eihíí-ho' nih-'o3í'eebeíhi-3i' hót-notiih-óú'u[1]
bííto'owu' hi3óóbe' néc-i'.
First some of the birds were sent down under the water to look for
earth.

Heeyóúhuu hih-'óówu-no'úxotii-no' nóóxu3 néc-i'.[2]
They did not bring anything back to the surface of the water.

Wóóniihi' hee3ei'-yeiyóhtee-3i' cese'eihíí-ho' nih-'o3í'eebeihi-3i' hi3óóbe'
néc-i',
Later all the four-legged animals were sent down under the water,

heetih-ceeštíí-3i' bííto'owu'.
to get earth.

Hih-'óówu-utét-owuu.
They did not get to it.

Noh nih-cé'-bixouuséé-3i'.[3]
Then they came back up above the surface.

Nécii-šííšiiyei-no' nih-'ó3i'eebeíhi-3i', hótni-inówouséé-3i',[4] biito'ówu'
hot-notiih-óú'u.
The water snakes were sent to dive under the water to find earth.

Heeyouhuu hih-'óówu-cebi-nouutíí-no'.

They did not bring anything back out of the water.

Be'enoo nih-'o3i'eebeíhi-t hótni-inówousee-t.

The turtle was sent to dive under the water.

Nenééni-t nii-bee-be'é'ei-t be'énoo nih-'inówousee-t, toh-nii3-notííh-o' bííto'owu',

It was the red-headed turtle who dove under the water, who took part in looking for earth,

hótn-ii-niišihi-' biito'ówu', hoot-níítoh-'uune'etíítooni-'.

so that the earth could be made, where people would live.

Toh-ce'-ihcí-bíxouuseet, bííto'owu' hikóób-e' nih-'eíbi-ni'.

When he popped back up above the surface of the water, earth was stuck on his back.

Be'énoo he'=iiš-no'úxotii-t biito'ówu'.

Somehow the turtle brought back earth.

Hóno'ut nii3éí'i-hiine'etíí-3i' néc-i', ne'-[n]oo-notíxotíí-3i'.

All the creatures that live in the water then went looking for mud to bring up.

Noh tohúú-co'ooyéítii-3i' ce'-tee-teešííhi',[5]

And after they stacked [the globs of mud] one upon the other,

heíhii hé'ih-'ihci-bixooyéítii-no' néc-i'.

soon they had stacked it up until it appeared above the water.

Noh nenéé-' biito'ówu' héni-nííšihi-'.

And that is what the earth is made of.

Notes

1. The verb is aberrant. One would expect *notíítii-* (AI.T) or *notíít-* (TI). The verb used here is TA *nótiih-*, but the ending is TI 3PL. This occurs throughout the text.

2. *Nóóxu3-* is apparently related to *hóóxu3-* 'right up next to, in contact with'.

3. The Gatschet manuscript has *bixóuu3ee-3i'* rather than *bixóuuséé-3i'.*

4. The verb again is *3éé-3i'* rather than *séé-3i'.*

5. *Teesiihi'* means 'above, on top of'. The initial element of the adverbial particle is unclear. While the manuscript gives *ce'-teesiihi'*, in his notes after the text, Gatschet records *co(o)-tee-teesiihi'*, which could be *co'-tee-teesiihi'* 'round/spherical/lump-REDUP-on top', though one would expect *ce'-* rather than *co'-*. This form would be fitting, roughly describing the shape of a turtle's back: the round mound of mud piled up to form the earth would then replicate the turtle's back.

The Creation of the Earth

Told by White Breast, John Goggles, interpreter,
Wyoming, September 1910
Collected by Truman Michelson
NAA, MS 2708, 11 pp.

This text is untitled in the original manuscript. The title was supplied by C'Hair and Moss. The text was taken down only in English. The original Michelson version is presented here, with added editorial guides (in brackets).

The most interesting aspect of this story is the presence of Mexicans. The Arapaho word for Mexican is *co'cóónii-nén*, meaning literally 'bread-man'. Allan Taylor has shown that the Gros Ventres originally used this word for the French before it later was used for the Spanish and Mexicans (Taylor 1996). The same is probably true for the Arapahos. The name for St. Louis in Arapaho is *có'coo-ííteen* meaning 'bread people's tribe/camp'. St. Louis was of course primarily a French city. The Arapahos, who stayed mostly on the northern plains in the eighteenth century, would have had much more contact with French traders and trappers during that time than with Mexicans in New Mexico. It is well known that these French traders did indeed tend to live with the Indians, sharing their way of life and often marrying into the tribes and fathering children. They were also the earliest source of trade beads, as mentioned here.

The connection of the "Mexicans" with corn, Navajo blankets, and dark skin does seem to refer to the New Mexico settlement area, with which the Arapahos would have had a contact in the later eighteenth and early nineteenth centuries as they shifted farther south on the plains. This was especially the case after 1825, when the Santa Fe Trail opened and commerce greatly increased around places such as Bent's Fort. Thus this account seems to amalgamate two different geographical and historical eras and two different versions of "Mexican" into a single identity as non-Anglo-American.

Note finally that a number of Hispanic families married into the Arapaho tribe, some quite early. This account clearly establishes a special closer relationship between early Hispanics and the Arapahos as compared to Anglo settlers and perhaps reflects this process of intermarriage.

[The Time of Only Water]

The beginning of the Arapahoes was from the Sacred Pipe; there was all water, the pipe was on the water. The pipe was unbared [uncovered], not tied up. The first thing the pipe did was to get all the animals that lived in the water in order that he might choose one to get the dirt under the water. He sent most of them but they did not get it, they came up drowned.

[The Creation of the Land]

But there were two, a duck and a turtle. They were both coming up with a little piece of mud from the bottom and the man commenced to pack the mud up in his hands, to dry it. He took off his moccasins and let the dirt on the soles. After it was dry he took it in his fingers and began to sing. He threw it all around while singing and turned into land: He sang again, the land grew bigger. The third time he sang the land grew as far as he could see. The fourth time he sang there was more land than water.

[Creation of the Different Races]

When he finished making the land, the first Indian was a Mexican, the second a white man. The Mexican was asked how he was going to be made—he said "out of mud." The white man was asked how he was going to be made—"out of lime, white paint." The way the Mexican was going to make a living was this way. He asked for corn—the white man when asked how he was going to make a living—asked for everything. That is why the white man is better off than anyone else.

[Origin of Death]

The Indian who made all, when he said how the Indians were to be when they died. He threw animal dung into the water. It sank but floated. They were to die and then live again. White man said—picking up a rock, throwing it into the water; it sank. He said that they should die forever, if they came back after they died there would be too many: they might crowd the land.

[The Arapahos Are to Occupy the Center of the Lands]

White man said he was going to be more numerous than the Indians. The Indian placed the white man on the other side of the ocean, because there were going to be many of them. He placed all the Indians all, crowds. He placed the Arapahos who were to be few, not many, in the center. He then named all the trees, grass, rivers, that were on the land. This is why the Arapahos are living in the middle of all the tribes.

[Medicines and Paints]

The first Indian said they should live at least 100 years. He then gave rules how the other tribes should live. [The] Indian and the white man were asking for paints. The white man asked for all kinds of paints; also the Indian; at the same time asked for medicines, the white man one way and the Indian another. The reason why the Mexican[s] got the corn was that as long as they had corn and the sacred pipe they would stay with the Arapahos.

[Wrapping and Hanging the Sacred Pipe]

After the animals were all named, the best were picked out, he picked out a wild fox. He took off the hide and wrapped it around the sacred pipe; at the same time the Mexican gave a Navajo blanket to wrap the sacred pipe in order that he (the Mexican) might be more like an Arapaho. The man who made all said—"the way they should keep the sacred pipe should be four sticks tied together that they might hang the sacred pipe; that they must not let the sacred pipe lie on the ground.["]

[Origin of Moccasins (and Human Clothing)]

He made a man of mud and a woman of mud. There was a woman then, and a man. He told him he might have moccasins. He told her, "What kind of moccasin are you going to make?" The woman did not know. The man said she had better make it out of white buffalo hide, with hair on it. The Mexican said he had beads, [and] gave them to the man. This man gave it to his wife to put on the moccasins. The Mexican said he gave the bead[s] [so] that he might live with the Arapahos a long time.

[Origin of Hide Tanning (and Blankets and Lodges)]

The man said he wanted a blanket. He told his wife to get it. She started in some direction. She found a white buffalo hide nearby. She brought it to her husband. He told her to make a blanket out of the hide. This man took it and spread [it] on the ground at the foot of the pipe. He called his wife to stand close to that hide. He got a sagebrush and stuck it on the back of his head and around each wrist, and some on the soles of each foot. Then she began to tan the hide. When she had it already she spread it on the ground, and sat on the middle and it was done.

[Beginning of Moving Camp, with the Sacred Pipe Wrapped in Buckskin]

The man and woman were then parents. They had kept the sacred pipe. When they wanted to move some distance they said "How are we going to move"—the woman said that they would pack the pipe, the man said he would carry the four sticks. The man started on, the woman behind. They stopped. The man stuck up the sticks and the woman hung up the pipe. The woman asked her husband how they were going to tie up the pipe. They had nothing. He pointed to the hide and said "go get that hide." She stepped a few steps and went ahead. There was a hide of buckskin. She said—"how shall I cut it?" the man said: "look under the hide." There was a knife of rock under the hide. Then she began to cut the strings. She wrapped them around the sacred pipe. Now he told his wife that they might move again.

[Horses Are Obtained]

The woman commenced to pack the pipe; the strings were then half tied. They camped. They put up the sticks and then the pipe. The man carried the sticks and the woman the pipe. Where they camped she asked her husband (they had a horse then) how this horse might carry the pipe. The man said the horse was going to carry the pipe. While they camped they talked [about] how they were going to get horses. This man told his wife to get a stick a ways from them. He gave his wife a stick to take it over to the other stick and tie them together. The other stick became a rope, the other one a horse. So she brought the horse which was a mare to him. She went back there was a stick there. She did as before. There was a stallion there. She told her husband that he might own the horse and she the mare.

[The Arapahos Reach the Middle Place]

They moved camp again. The man told his wife to cut some tall slough grass, to cut two, to tie them on each side of the horse and lay the pipe on it. They started—the man went ahead leading the horse, the woman the mare. Ropes were made of horsehair. When they camped they got in the middle of the land they were going to stay in. That is why the Arapahos are living in the center of the land now and why the pipe is here.

[Added Note]

White Breast says for a long time the Arapahos used dogs as burden bearers even when he was quite a boy.

The Myth of the Milky Way

Teller unknown, Oklahoma, March or April 1893
Collected by Albert Gatschet
NAA, MS 231, p. 285

We include Gatschet's original transcription of this narrative (in italics, as for one narrative collected by Michelson and one by Kroeber). Note that the symbol (´) indicates an accent mark on a syllable, while (') indicates a glottal stop. The title is from his manuscript.

This is a well-known narrative across the plains and is still known today among the Arapahos. This particular untitled version, though short, contains more specific words for the two animals than any other Arapaho version. While modern versions often simply talk of a horse and a buffalo, and more specific variants mention a bobtailed horse (*wo'os*), this is the only version that specifies a *black* bobtailed horse and a *young* buffalo bull. Youth is strongly associated with impetuousness and poor decision-making in traditional Arapaho culture, so this detail is certainly appropriate. Conversely, black is the color of paint used in victory dances after successful raids or battles, again making the detail meaningful. Neither Moss nor C'Hair had heard the term *wo'os* used in this sense, but both note that it sounds to them like *wo'ót*, meaning 'coal'; Moss said that he has heard *wo'ós* used for 'coal' as well, so the detail of blackness seems embedded in the word. This particular version lacks the specific detail that the Milky Way is made up of the dust raised by running hooves but does use a unique word to describe the result: a long 'white cloud extending along' (*ceb-nook-ó'eti-*, along-white-cloud-). 'Cloud' has a greater semantic range in Arapaho than in English: the glow around the moon that occurs on some nights, for example, is called a *hiisiisínoonó'et* 'moon cloud'.

Ni'hwatä´n washî´nit hiwa´xāx ni'hnanü'hti´wat waxathöü.
Nih-wo'téén-wo'ošííni-t hiwóxhoox nih-nonouhtííw-oot wooxo3ou'u.
A black bobtailed horse raced with a young buffalo bull.

Nihî-îthi-ihî´thine´nna nähä-i´theinan haye´hak hatetcha´nibinît
hithēina´n.

Nih-'ii-3i' hihíí3inén-no', nehe' híí3einoon hoyéí-hok, hoot-tecó'oni-
biini-t hii3einóón.[1]

The Indians[2] said, if this buffalo wins, the horse will always be eaten.

Na'hwotä´nwash haye´hak hi´thena atna´tawit.

Noh wo'téén-wo'oš hoyéí-hok, híí3einoon hootnó-ótoowu-t.

And if the black bobtailed horse wins, the buffalo will be consumed.

Watä´nwash ni'ha-a´yēt.

Wo'téén-wo'oš nih-'óyei-t.

The black bobtailed horse won.

He´nni ä´ya nitchä´binaka´-eti nänihīthkāt,

Híni' hééyoo-' nii-cébi-nookó'eti-', ne'=nih-'ii3koohu-t,

That long white streak across [the night sky] is where he came running
through,

nahě´ni nitchäbä tcheneiwa´tä nä-ni-î´thikahĭt hi´theino.

noh híni' hihcebe' ceneiwóótee-', ne'=nih-'íí3ikoohu-t híí3einoon.

and that [streak] above that turns off to the side, that's where the buffalo
came running through.

Tiha-ayathät ni'htchebixtchähit.

Tih-'oyoo3ee-t, nih-ceibíhcehi-t.

When he was beaten, he ran off to the side.

Notes

1. Based on the content 'buffalo' here must be an error, with 'horse' the intended word.
2. *Hihíí3inénno'*, meaning literally 'the men from here'.

Yellow Bull Races the Horse

Teller unknown, Oklahoma, 1899
Collected by Alfred Kroeber
NAA, MS 2560a, Notebook 13, pp. 11–12

We include Kroeber's original transcription for this text. Notice that he only rarely indicates glottal stops. Among the symbols that may be unfamiliar are *c* for modern *s* and *ç* for modern *3*. The title here was supplied by the editors.

This is a widely known Arapaho myth, recorded first by Gatschet in Oklahoma in the 1890s and still told today at Wind River. This is the only version that describes the buffalo specifically as *woxo3ou'* 'yellow bull' (an archaic word meaning a young buffalo bull). The description is appropriate in that the bull shows a kind of youthful impetuousness in the race. At one point, Kroeber actually glosses the word as 'Young Bull'.

Another interesting linguistic detail is the description of the way in which the buffalo runs off the circular path on which he is traveling *(ceib-ko'ei-'oo-AI* off to the side-circle-going-). Other versions of the myth say that the bull simply ran off the path, without the detail of the circle. William C'Hair noted that the race was supposed to circle the entire sky. This would make the path of the race at night parallel to the path of the sun during the day and also suggests the motif of the Sacred Wheel (an important Arapaho religious object) as well as other circles such as the Sun Dance lodge. This information raises the horse from being simply the winner of the race to a ceremonial actor, completing a sacred circle central to Arapaho cosmology, and of course gives added meaning to the Milky Way as well.

Waxaçō´û năⁿ´ wă´ôc häⁿĭxnanû´xtĭnaⁿ hôtănīī´hĭi

Woxo3óu' nóh wó'os[1] he'ih-nonóúhti-no', hoton-neh'eih.[2]

Yellow Bull and Bobtail Horse raced each other, to see who would be killed.

Häⁿt nä´äsăā´n nāⁿçĭä´äbĭnä´xk^u

"Hootné-eso'óó-n noo3i'éebi-néhk,

"If you win the race, you will be swift,

52

hāⁿtnīhāⁿwûûnäh'ä´ ä häⁿçē´ihäxk^u wax̌äçō´û
"ho-otn-eihoowu-neh'ée," hee3-éihok woxo3óu'.
"you will not be killed," they said to Yellow Bull.

Ăh^a bīītĭ wă´ óc nāⁿçĭäⁿbä´xk^u hôtnī´ihāⁿwûûnî´hii̧
"'oh bíiti' wó'os noo3i'eeb-éhk, hotn-éíhoowu-néh'eih.[3]
"But if on the other hand Bobtail Horse wins the race, he will not be killed.

Hāⁿtnīinä´nĭn tīitäx^akûûtānī´nĭn bä^jhī´ĭhĭ häⁿçä´ äⁿtäxk^u
"Hootnii-nééni-n tih'ii-teexokuutonííni-n,[4] behíihi'," hee3ée-tehk.
"You will be the one who will be ridden, by everyone," he was told.

Hä'nää'ä'ctcĭxtcĕçĭkāⁿ´ hûç̧_i
He'=nee'ees-cih-ce3ikóóhu-3i'.
Then they set off like that running toward the finish line here.

Tcĭxkāⁿō´ūtāna tcēiçīī´hi
Cih-koo'óuuto'oo-no' cei3iíhi'.
They ran this way, making a cloud of dust.[5]

Täⁿ´bä nähīiçē´ĭ hä'nää'ēikāⁿ´hûçi, wax̌açôû häⁿix tcē´ibⁱ kă´ēiăⁿ
Téébe neehii3éi' he'=nee'ei'kóóhu-3i', woxo3ou' he'ih-céibi-kó'ei'oo.
Just when they had run to the halfway point, Yellow Bull went off the course.

Nähää wă´ óc häⁿ´ ix nī´ icⁱ sê´ h^anăak̲āⁿ´ çīäyā´anä´a̲
Nehe' wó'os hé'ih-níisi-séh-no'ukóó 3i'eyóon-é'.
Bobtail Horse arrived over there at the finish line all by himself.

Wô´t nû´hûû nä^änī´ i tcäⁿê´sāⁿhôk hīiçē´inān
Wót=núhu' neenéi'i-ceéso'oo-hok hii3éinoon.[6]
This is when the buffalo was doomed to be slow ever afterward.

Näⁿ´nĭh^jī´ ihīināⁿnăă´xk^u
Noh nih'íi-biin-oono'óhk.
Ever since then, we eat the buffalo.

Āⁿxûhäⁿnī´ĭhĭ bätĭ´hīī häⁿyāⁿ´nı̣ bī´ĭ´nāⁿ wăŏc

Hooxoheeníihi' betíhii heeyóó-ni' bíínoo[7] wó'os.

In return [for his victory], Bobtail Horse received a long tail.

Nääh'tcĭ'bääçīităwᵘ tănō´û-nē´ĭhĭt hīwăxŭhāⁿx

Nee'ee-cih-bee3itowu-tonóunéihi-t hiwóxuhoox,[8]

And thus the horse was used from that point on,

Häⁿt'täⁿtcēiçīī´hı̣

heetee cei3iíhi'.

from the ancient days up to the present.

Notes

1. *Wo'ós* 'bobtail horse'.
2. Kroeber glosses this form 'for the right of carrying burden'.
3. Note in this sentence that the Arapaho for 'killed' occurs as a middle voice form the first time but a passive form the second time.
4. Use of the past habitual form *tih'ii-* seems anomalous here. The literal translation is 'you will be the one who was habitually ridden': *téexokúútoníini-* AI 'to be a thing which is ridden'.
5. This is the Milky Way (*bóoó* 'path') that we see today.
6. Literally, 'that was when the buffalo was not swift' (meaning that was the decisive moment after which he would not be swift).
7. The verb for 'give' is a middle voice form, but with the ending /-oo/ rather than modern /-ee/. This is common in texts of this era.
8. *Bee3itowu-* is an old/archaic form, meaning 'from then on, from that time on'.

The Arapaho Migration across the Missouri River to the . . .

Told by Jesse Rowlodge, Oklahoma, 1929

Collected by Truman Michelson

NAA, MS 1791, 3 pp.

This is one of the most famous traditional Arapaho narratives, not only within the tribe but also across North America. The narrator here gives a very simple account, which focuses on the main action: the breaking apart of the ice. It does not explain that this led to the splitting of the formerly unified Arapaho or Arapahoan people. Exactly which peoples were split varies according to the narrator. The editors have heard this story referred to in relation to the splitting of Northern Arapahos from Southern Arapahos, but it is most commonly invoked to account for the separation between the Arapahos and Gros Ventre/White Clay people. It is also used to refer to the crossing of the Bering Strait and is probably used in reference to other separations as well. The title here is the one found in the manuscript, offering no final destination.

Linguistically, the remarks made by the grandmother to her young companion when she is asked to obtain the horn are the highlight of the story. The particle *wo'úú3ee3éin* could be translated in a number of other ways, including 'why do you have to bring that up now?!' or 'this is a heck of a time for that!?' It indicates strong exasperation and condemnation on the part of the speaker as well as the suggestion that normal proprieties are being violated. The following remark by the grandmother is also quite colorful and expressive and could be translated 'I'm always having to provide things for you!' or more loosely 'you're always wanting something else!' The phrase suggests selfishness, self-centeredness, or an excessively demanding request on the part of the girl. Thus the splitting of the tribes is not an accident but is specifically attributed to the girl's mistimed and inappropriate request, at least in this version of the narrative.

Other versions of this narrative suggest that the monster in question is the Water Monster (*hííncebiit*).

Téécixo' hinee teebe hinóno'éí-no' tih-cih-'ihciniiho'óó-3i', hé'ih-'itét-owuu niiciihéh-e'.

Long ago as the ancient Arapahos were moving upstream, they came to a river.

Hé'ih-béésoo.

It was big.

He'ih-ceciniin, noh wó'ow-ú' he'ne'-tees-okeeekóni-'.

It was wintertime, so they crossed over on top of the ice.

Beeseis wóów he'ih-'iixokeéékon.

The greater part had already made it across.

Noh toon=hiseihíhi' noh hinííwoho' toh'ét-sii'ihisee-3i', nehe' híseihíhi' he'íh-noohoot hiníínis.

And just as a certain girl and her grandmother were set to walk out onto the ice, the girl saw a horn.

He'ih-'óówoh-bisisé-n wo'ów-u'.

It was barely protruding from the ice.

"Neiwoo, hinee hiníínis cih-tebe3eihowúún-i heetih-'iwoo-'úúni3ébi-noo," heeh-éhk.[1]

"Grandmother, chop that horn off for me so that I'll have a nice horn for the end of my dart-game stick," said the girl.[2]

"Wo'úú3ee3ein![3] Yohohúú-céé'iyei!"[4] heeh-éhk néhe' betebíhehihi'.

"This is really not the time! I always have to get things for you!" said the old woman.

He'né'-oowúhcehi-t.

Then she quickly got off her horse.

He'ne'-tebe3eih-o' núhu' hiníínis.

Then she hacked off the horn.

Teebe he'=iitox-to'óót-ou'u, he'ne'i-bisii'oonóó'oo-ni'.

She had just finished striking it a few times, and then blood started coming out.

"Neiwoo, he'=bisii'óónoo'oo!" heeh-éhk nehe' hiseihíhi'.[5]

"Grandmother, it looks like it's bleeding!" said the girl.

Noh nóónonox, xonóú núhu' wó'ow-uu, he'ne'i-níh'éí-koo-koh'u-xóuuwó'oo-'.

And to their astonishment, right away all the ice, then it rapidly split apart in every direction from that point.

Heihii he'ne'i-noo-nóxowu-noehi-t heebe3-nenítee.

Not long afterward then a great being suddenly burst forth into view.

Béébeet hees-koxúnoo'oo-', he'i=nee'eetox-uuxokeeekóni-'.

Due to the cracking of the ice, only those already on the other side made it across the ice.

Notes

   1. The meaning and exact spelling of the element '*iwoo-* are unclear.

   2. See Michelson 1933 for an explanation of this game and the implements.

   3. The (or at least a) modern form of this word is *wo'úu3óo3oonón.* It indicates an importunate request. Rowlodge and Michelson gloss it here as 'during such confusion'.

   4. Modern *yohou=* is a proclitic that indicates excessiveness and can have many glosses depending on the exact context in which it is used. Here Rowlodge and Michelson gloss the phrase *yohohúú-céé'iyei* loosely as 'you have so much to say!': AI.O *cee'iyei-* literally means 'give gifts to people, distribute things'.

   5. Because Michelson did not record many glottal stops and preconsonantal /h/, this form could also be *heh=biisii'óónoo'oo-',* meaning 'wow, it surely is bleeding!'

Naming the Earth

Teller unknown, Oklahoma, 1899
Collected by Alfred Kroeber
NAA, MS 2560a, Notebook 2, p. 65

This brief text is related to the creation of the world and its naming, with the title supplied by the editors. One interesting feature, which shows possible Christian influence, is the concept of the Creator naming the earth. In no other account of creation in the Arapaho tradition does the Creator "name" things—they are simply created. The word for 'earth' literally means 'bare' (*biito'-*) 'ground' (*-owu'*). The same root appears in the story in *koh'ówu'* 'creek' (literally 'split ground [where the water has eroded it]') and *no'ko'ówu'* 'down below' (literally 'on the surface of the ground, at the bottom of a container'), so the narrator seems to have been concerned with the name for earth itself and its variant uses.

Hihcebe' Nih'oo3oo nih-'ii-hok, hoton-iine'etiitooni-ni' nuhu' no'ko'owu-u' hinenteeniit.

White Man Above commanded that the people should live down below on the earth.

Nee'ee-hiine'etiitooni-'ehk.

That's why people live here.

Noh niistii-hok niiciiho-ho, koh'owu-u, noh hoh'en-ii.

And he made rivers, creeks, and mountains.

Nee'ee-beh-eenitou'u-'.

That is the reason these things are all here.

Ne'i-nihiit-o'ohk nuhu' biito'owu'.

Then he called this place "earth."

Hoton-niihihi-'.
It should be called thus.

Noh ne'=nii'-niisih'i-' nuhu' biito'owu'.
And that is when this earth was named.

Ne'=nih-'iisi-nihiit-o'ohk Hihcebe' Nih'oo3oo.
That's what White Man Above called it.

Trickster (Nih'oo3oo/"White Man") Stories

The Sun Dance Cycle

Nih'óó3oo tih'esooku'oot hóseihoowú'/When Nih'oo3oo Witnessed the Sun Dance

Told by Cleaver Warden, Oklahoma, August 22 or 23, 1899

Collected by Alfred Kroeber

NAA, MS 2560a, Notebook 10, pp. 11–13

English version published as "Nih'oo3oo and the Mice's Sun Dance" in Dorsey and Kroeber [1903] 1997: 107–108

This is another widespread and classic story, linked to elements of the Sun Dance. Kroeber writes in his notes to this text that "the cotton-wood + esp. willow are used for shade in sun-dance, have connection here." In reality, both trees are intimately connected to the ceremony in construction of the lodge and in the altar.

More generally, this story explains the origin of the Sun Dance itself and how it was brought to the Arapahos from the mice. A key word in this version of the story, for example, is the element *cécih-*, meaning 'soft'. It occurs as a description of the drumming sound that Nih'oo3oo hears: *cééciheinóóni'* 'there is the sound of soft drumming'. William C'Hair notes that this word is also used to describe the sound of prairie chickens and sage grouse calling on their leks (dancing grounds). Moreover, the Sun Dance drum, singers, and dancers are all linked to the prairie chicken and/or sage grouse. Sun Dance singers are called *céneeno'* 'grouse', and singing Sun Dance songs is called *céneeni-* 'acting as grouse'. The traditional call for the drummers to come to the lodge is *cíi3íh'ohu* 'fly in here!' This linkage of grouse and singing/dancing is specific to the Sun Dance. Thus the single word *céciheinóóni-* evokes a whole constellation of symbolic connections.

This narrative is part of a cycle of Nih'oo3oo stories that all relate to elements of the Sun Dance. "Nih'oo3oo and the Mice's Sun Dance," "Nih'oo3oo and the Burrs/The Elk Skull," and "Nih'oo3oo Cuts His Hair" are central to the overall Sun Dance origin myth and could be told as a single narrative (see Dorsey 1903: 210–12). The leafy small trees and branches that are placed around the Arapaho Sun Dance lodge are made especially thick at the west side of the lodge: according to legend, this is where Nih'oo3oo tries to stick his head in (as he did with the Mice's Sun Dance) and thus needs extra protection (Dorsey 1903: 113).

This story also contains an ecology lesson. Nih'oo3oo encounters six plants: milkweed, blackjack oak, dogwood, hawthorn, cottonwood, and willow, before finally reaching the river on his seventh groping encounter. These plants have increasing moisture requirements that in fact match the sequence in which Nih'oo3oo encounters them. The number seven is also sacred in Arapaho.

Kroeber writes in his notes in the manuscript:

> At night, moonlight, children lie in row on ground, + one comes along touching them in middle of forehead, asking them what kind of bush they are. Or "who was your gr. father," etc. + other relations. Also what is your food, what is your clothing. The child representing wh. Man carries another representing deer on his back, + lays down, saying "here is my meat, my marrow from bones, etc."
>
> Also lie down in row + pull each other up, bracing feet. If come up straight are O.K., new again; if bend while pulled, are bobtailed [*wo'os*], like deer or antelope. All these games "contain" or refer to this story.

Very similar information is provided by Dorsey (1903: 189–91).

Hi3o'owu-u' Nih'oo3oo.
Nih'oo3oo was on the prairie.

Hoseihóówu' he'ih-'itét hee3e'éitee-'.
He reached the front of a Sun Dance lodge [inside an animal skull].

He'ih-yihóó.
He went over to it.

Ho'éiihi' ceciheinóón.
The drum was making a soft sound as it was played.

He'ih-niitówoot tih'ii-xounóó-ni'.
He heard yelling/cheering.

"Yeh! hi3í=heetih-'esookú'oo-noo," heeh-éhk.
"Gee! let me watch on," he said.

He'ih-noxho'oowoo-xounóotiin.[1]
Everyone was shouting/cheering.

He'ih-ciite'éin hisó'ooteeb-e'.
He put his head inside at the front entrance.

Tih-'iis-ciite'ein[i-t], he'ih-nééni-no' nuhu' hookuuhúh'-o' nih'ii-
só'ootehí-3i',[2] beh-nóuuhcehí-no'.
Once he put his head in, these little mice who were horsing around in
there, they all ran outside.

Nih'óó3oo he'ih-'ote'éikoo.
Nih'oo3oo discovered that he had gotten his head caught [inside the
skull where the mice had been dancing].

Kookón he'ih'ii-notii'éyei.
He was just groping about for things, wherever his hands happened to
land [as he stumbled across the prairie].

"Ho-tohuu3i-bíísiin?" niít-o'óhk hi-bíisiyóo-no.
"What kind of bush are you?" he said to whatever he felt.

Noh "hé3ebiis," nii3ée-tehk.
And "dogbush," he was told.[3]

He'ih-cé3ei'oo.
He set off again.

"Neehéé, ho-tohuu3i-bíísiin?"
"My friend, what kind of bush are you?"

Noh "beetéibiis."
And "bow-wood," [he was told].[4]

"Hih'óó!"
"All right!"

"Neehee, ho-touhúu3i-bíísiin?"
"My friend, what kind of bush are you?"

Noh "hooxéíhiineniiwoheét."
And "Pawnee clan bush."[5]

"Wohéi, woowuh nii'óotee-'," nii-hók.
"Well, now the river is close," he said.

"Nééhee, ho-tohuu3i-bíísiin?"
"My friend, what kind of bush are you?"

"Howoh'uubíis."
"Praying bush."[6]

"Hih'óo!"
"All right!"

Koox=he'ih-cé3ei'oo, hiiyoh=notii3íyei-n.
Once again he set off, carefully and thoroughly groping about for things.

"Neehéé ho-tohuu3i-bíisiin?"
"My friend, what kind of bush are you?"

Noh "hohoot," hee3éih-ehk.
And "cottonwood," he was told.

"Nooxow-uu'óotee-' wóów," níí3et-ehk.
"The river is really close now," he said to himself.

Ceneeyohwúsee.
He kept doggedly moving onward.

"Neehee, ho-tohuu3i-bíísiin?"
"My friend, what kind of bush are you?"

Noh "yóokox," hee3ée-tehk.
And "willow," he was told.[7]

"Wohéi, wóów nooxow-úu'ootee-'," heeh-éhk.
"Okay, now it's right here," he said.

He'ih-beh-nóo-noobée.
There was sand all over.

Tousi-tébi-n!
Boy, was [the river] deep!

Wot=xonóu he'ih-'oowuniihou'oo.
Before you know it [after falling in], he was floating downstream.

Hoowúniihiihi' hísei-no' he'ih-tousébi-no'.
Downstream some women were bathing.

"Bééyoo 3oonitéec hooxebi'ón-e'," nii-hók.
"[Hit me] right smack in the middle of the face," he said.

Hiitouúk, he'í=néé'eeti-to'óot-owuní3i.
Sure enough, that was where they hit [his forehead].

Koh'e3éih-owuu.
They split it open.

"'oh konóuu[8] heetih-'iwoonétini-noo,"[9] hiséi-no' nií-hohkoni'.
"For me I'll take it for the handle of my scraper," the women said.

Hii3ikuuton-óó3i' hiniini3-o, bih'ihíini3-o,
[Once] they have seized his horns, deer horns, [they said:]

"Nih'óó3oo yóhou=cee-cee'í3ei."
"How wonderfully Nih'oo3oo provides things for us!"

Notes

1. The meaning and exact spelling of *noxho'oowoo-* is unclear. The preverb *howoh-* means 'lots, many' and would make sense in this context, but the transcription makes such a reading unlikely and leaves the *nox-* still unexplained. Kroeber glosses the form as 'continual' yelling.

2. William C'Hair notes that *só'ootehí-* means to play around in an unorganized or childlike way. It is hardly a good description of the Arapaho Sun Dance but does seem to fit the image of mice.

3. According to Kroeber's notes: "bushes that grow farthest out on prairie from river, has [*sic*] whitish leaves, much pith. These are common milkweeds (*Asclepia speciosa*). The pods are called *he3ebéíhtoono*, 'dog's feet' in Arapaho."

4. This is identified as blackjack oak in the manuscript.

5. Identified as what "white people" call "dogwood" in the manuscript. Kroeber adds, however, that it has "small green berry-like flowers," which does not match most dogwood flowers, though they do have clusters of green berries later in the spring once the flowers have bloomed.

6. This is identified as hawthorn in the manuscript ("dark red bark, edible berries, haws").

7. The manuscript notes that it "also grows nearest river."

8. The exact meaning of this form is unclear: *(h)ohkonouu* is glossed here as 'for me' in Kroeber's manuscript.

9. *Hiwoonétini-* is an AI possession verb, derived from the archaic word *wóonét*, an elk horn scraper (Kroeber NAA, MS 2560a, Notebook 7).

Nih'oo3oo noh [Hi]woxuuhookuhu'ee/Nih'oo3oo and the Elk Head

Told by John Goggles, Wyoming, September 24, 1910
Collected by Truman Michelson
NAA, MS 2708, 5 pp.

This is the central element of the myths surrounding the Sun Dance. Other versions are Dorsey and Kroeber narratives 52 and 53. This is a relatively spare version: the narrator does not indicate initially that the Sun Dance is occurring inside an elk's skull. He also does not provide the detail that it is young women who are bathing in the stream, though this occurs in other versions.

Nih'oo3oo he'ih'ii-'oowuniihisee niicii.[1]
Nih'oo3oo was walking downstream at a river.

He'ih-'itet he'ih-no'otoo'oe-n.
He reached a spot where there was thick brush.

He'ih-niitobee, he'ih-niibootiini-n.
He heard singing.

Hoseihoowu' he'ih-neeni-n.
It was a Sun Dance going on.

Noh he'ih-yihoo.
And he went there.

He'ih-noohoot hoseihoowu'.
He saw a Sun Dance.

He'ih-yihoo.
He went there.

He'ih-no'usee.
He arrived at the spot.

He'ih-no'o3nenitoohu-n.
There were a lot of folks about.

He'ih-cii-ni'-itetooku'oo.
He couldn't manage to see what was going on.

He'ih-nihi'nee-3ei'ein.
He shoved his head inside.

He'ih-'iis-3eiikoo, he'ih-cii-noohoo3ei.
After he thrust his head inside there, he couldn't see anything.

'oh hookuuhuh'-o he'ih-nih'eikoohu-nino.
But the little mice inside there scattered frantically in every direction.

'oh he'ih-3eiikoo.
And he had plunged his head inside [an elk's skull, so that it was stuck].

Wohei hookuhu'ee he'ih-'ote'eikoo.
Well, he had his head stuck in the skull.

He'ne'-no'oeteisee-t.
Then he went toward the river.

He'ih-bii'iitii niiciihehe'.
He found a small stream.

He'ih-cenis nec-i'.
He fell into the water.

He'ih-ce3i3ou'oo hoowuniihiihi'.
He floated off downstream.

Kou3iihi' he'ih-niitobee heeh-ehkoni', "Hiwoxuu, hiwoxuu ceneitou'oo-t!"
heeh-ehkoni'.
After a while he heard some people saying, "An elk, an elk is floating
this way!" they said.

He'ih-no'ou'oo heetoo-ni3i.
He floated to the spot where they were.

Noh heeh-ehk, "3oo3ooni3-e' hii-to'ow-u'," heeh-ehk Nih'oo3oo.
And he said, "You must hit me right between the horns," said
Nih'oo3oo.

Tousebeihii-ho he'ih-to'ob-e' noh 3oo3ooni3-e'.
The ones bathing in the stream hit him, right between the horns.

He'ih-bexoh-owuu.
They hit the skull [with a rock].

He'ih-koh'unoo'oo-n beeyoo.
It split in half right down the middle.

Noh he'ih-kohei'i Nih'oo3oo.
And Nih'oo3oo stood up.

Noh heeh-ehk, "Nohtou he'i=koh'e3eihowuun-e'?"[2] heeh-ehk
Nih'oo3oo.
And he said, "Why did they crack [my skull] in half?" said
Nih'oo3oo.

He'ih-nouusee.
He came out of the water.

He'ih-ce3ei'oo hoowuniihiihi'.
He set off downriver.

Nee'ei'ise-'.

That's how the story ends.

Notes

1. One would expect locative *niiciihehe'* here.

2. *Koh'e3éíhowuun-* TA 'crack s.t. for s.o.' with nonaffirmative inflection *-e'*, 3/1S. Dubitative *he'i=* can be followed by either conjunct iterative or, less commonly as here, nonaffirmative inflections.

Nih'oo3oo noh Woniseineehiisii/ Nih'oo3oo and the Burrs

Told by John Goggles, Wyoming, September 24, 1910
Collected by Truman Michelson
NAA, MS 2708, 4 pp.

orsey and Kroeber narratives 54 and 55 are versions of this story. It is a central element of the Arapaho Sun Dance myths and is often told as a follow-up to "Nih'oo3oo and the Elk Skull." Nih'oo3oo meets the girls when his head is still in the elk skull; they break the skull apart for him then proceed to nurse his injury, only to put burrs in his hair. As with all the stories collected by Michelson, this is a fairly spare and straightforward recounting. An interlinear analysis of this story is presented in appendix B. Alonzo Moss notes that the verb for 'delouse' also can connote playing with someone's pubic hair, so that the girls' offer to delouse Nih'oo3oo has clear sexual connotations. This explains his eagerness to be deloused and his reticence to reveal the incident to his wife.

The ending of the story plays on the fact that *nih'óó3oo* means both the traditional trickster and also 'white person'. Sometime after contact with Euro-Americans, when this extension of the word for trickster occurred, the trickster stories began to be reinterpreted in this way, as stories in part about white people and their characteristics. Such interpretations are not a required element of the story but can be added (often at the end). If the story is told as part of educating a younger person about the Sun Dance, the detail would not necessarily be added; but if told (especially in English) for an audience including whites, it is typically added. Thus these narratives, like all oral ones, can change to respond to the context of their telling. Some contemporary versions have Nih'oo3oo ending up completely bald. Then the teller adds: "And that's why white people go bald."

Nih'oo3oo he'ih-'oowuniihisee niihiihi' niiciiheh-e'.
Nih'oo3oo was walking downstream along a river.

He'ih-noohob-ee hiseihih'-o hooxono'o.
He saw some girls on the other side of the river.

He'ih-'okeee he'=iitoo-ni3i, noh hee3-eihok,
He crossed over to where they were, and they said to him,

"Nih'oo3oo heh-'i3ooxuh-ee,"[1] hee3-eihok.
"Nih'oo3oo, let us delouse you," they said to him.

"Hih'oo," hee3-oohok.
"All right," he said to them.

Noh he'ne'i-cesisi-i3ooxuh-eit.
And then they began to delouse him.

Noh beenihehe' hoo3-iihi' he'ih-nokohunoo'oo.
And a little while later he fell asleep.

Kou3-iihi' he'ih-'owoto'oo.
After a long time, he woke up.

Noh he'ih-bii'in-ee woniseineehiis-ii hinii3ee'een-e'.
And he found burrs in his hair.

He'ih-beh'eibi-nino.
They were stuck all over his hair.

He'ih-cii-noohob-ee hiseihih'-o.
He didn't see the girls.

'oh heeh-ehk, "Heet-3iiyouheti-noo."
And he said, "I will cut my hair."

He'ne'i-hiten-o' wooxe.
Then he got a knife.

He'ne'i-3iiyouheti-t.
Then he cut his hair off short.

Hei'iisi-3iiyouhu-t, he'ne'i-heecikoohu-t.
Once he had cut his hair off, then he went home.

Noh he'ne'i-ce'-no'eecikoohu-t, noh hiniin hee3-eihok,
"He-ih-tousitoo?"
And then he arrived back home, and his wife said to him, "What have you done?"

Noh heeh-ehk Nih'oo3oo, "Nih-niitobee-noo nih-'iiyohoote-ninehk," hee3-oohok.
And Nih'oo3oo said, "I heard that you were dead," he said to her.

"Nee'ee-3iiyouhu-noo."
"That's why I cut my hair."

Noh nih'oo3ou'u, ne'=nii'i-3iiyouh-ehkoni' nih'oo3ou'u.
And the white men, that's why the white men cut their hair.

Nee'ei'ise-'.
That's how the story ends.

Note

1. This verb occurs as both *hii3oox-* and *hii3ooxuh-*.

Nih'oo3oo Cuts His Hair

Told by Cleaver Warden, Oklahoma, ca. August 11–14, 1899

Collected by Alfred Kroeber

NAA, MS 2560a, Notebook 6, pp. 91–95

English version published in Dorsey and

Kroeber [1903] 1997: 110–11

There are a number of versions of this story, which is part of a longer cycle of trickster stories related to the Sun Dance (see Dorsey 1903: 66), where the burrs are one important ceremonial plant. In some versions Nih'oo3oo encounters young girls by chance, but in this version he meets sisters-in-law. The brother-in-law/sister-in-law relationship is a joking one in Arapaho, with sexual teasing expected, and this story fits into that social framework. Picking out lice can often be understood as a sexual metaphor in other Plains traditions as well (Rice 2004).

Part of the punch line of the story, so to speak, involves the burrs, which are called *woníseineehíís* in Arapaho. The initial part of this word looks like *won-hísei-* 'go to-woman' and the word is folk-etymologized in Arapaho as 'go-look-for-women bush'—thus the irony of Nih'oo3oo's ending up having burrs from this bush stuck in his hair due to excessive pursuit of women.

Hair was traditionally cut for mourning, which explains Nih'oo3oo's excuse to his wife (he does not want to admit either that he was sexually molesting his sisters-in-law or that they got the best of him). The most humorous part of this particular version is Nih'oo3oo's completely over-the-top mourning performance, combined with his wife's eye-rolling knowledge that once again he has been up to something. She is not fooled for a second. Her final prosaic reply puts an end to both his false hysterics and his false joy at discovering his supposedly dead wife alive again.

A final notable stylistic feature of this version is the use of characters in the story to view Nih'oo3oo, rather than the narrator describing him. In particular, the characters think to themselves or comment to themselves about Nih'oo3oo, rather than talking to him. This allows the narrator more easily to couch the vision of the trickster in more colorful language than if speaking strictly as a narrator, because the other characters can make extensive use of dubitative types of expressions, emphasizing the puzzlement that Nih'oo3oo causes in all around him. The dubitatives are underlined in the story. Of course Nih'oo3oo is equally dubious about his own actions, condition, and circumstances.

Nih'óó3oo hiitéén he'ih-no'ús.
Nih'oo3oo arrived at a group camp.

Céée3i' hiséi-no' heh-niisí-3i' he'ih-'oonóxuyei-no'.
Outside, two women were sewing.

Cebisee-hek Nih'oo3oo hee3e'éici-ni3i.[1]
Nih'oo3oo walked past in front of where they were sitting.

"Níhii, Nih'óó3oo, toot=(h)éi-ihoo?" hee3-éihok.
"Well, Nih'oo3oo, where are you going?" they said to him.

"Nehéicóó, heh-'i3óoxuh-ee.
"Come here, let us delouse you.

"Heh-'i3ooxukúu3-ee."
"Let us give you a quick delousing."

"Hehnee=noohohouhu-noo, nei3ebóó-no'."
"I am really in a hurry, my sisters-in-law."

"Hiino3óón[2] Nih'oo3oo: cíhnee!
"We mean it, Nih'oo3oo: come here!

"Heh-'i3óóxuh-ee tótoos beenihéhe'; nó3=neeciihí'."
"Let us delouse you even if it's just a little bit; you know it would be good, just for a short time."

"Wohéi, hiikookónoo'," nii-hók Nih'óó3oo.[3]
"Okay, if you insist," said Nih'oo3oo.

"Ke-i3oobei-be, nei3eboo-no'?
"Are you telling the truth, my sisters-in-law?

"Koo=no-ot-teese'éisin ho-coow-únoo?"[4]
"Should I put my head in your laps?"

"Hohou, nei3ebóó Nih'óó3oo, neniihenéíhi-n.[5]
"Yes, my brother-in-law Nih'oo3oo, it's your choice.

"'inehóus, cih-ceenóku, cih-teese'éisii."
"Well now, sit down here and put your head on our laps here."

Nih'óó3oo ces[is]-i3ooxuhee-téhk.
Nih'oo3oo began to be deloused.

Wot=Nih'óó3oo heeneet-teexóhee-3i, "Yohou=koxcéí'i!"[6]
I guess wherever Nih'oo3oo rested his hands, "Oh you're so soft and
plump!" [he said].

"Ne-ih-'íni, ne-ih-woowó3-oo."
"I wish I could have intercourse with her."

"Hiiyohóu=wóówosei!
"Oh how dirty you talk!

"Yohóu=nee-ni'etéébet Nih'oo3oo," nii3-éihok.[7]
"Oh what wild fantasies you have, Nih'oo3oo," they were saying to him.

He'ne'-i3ooxuhee-téhk, héíhii hé'ih-nowone'éicí3-e' Nih'óó3oo.[8]
Then he was deloused, and soon their picking at his head made
Nih'oo3oo drowsy.

Toh-3íí'oobe-' Nih'oo3oo, tih-'ee3nee-nókohu-t,
After Nih'oo3oo was snoring, when he was really asleep,

"'inehóus hisée,[9] neh-cíh-won-ko'un-ín woniseineehíís-ii," hee3et-ehkóni'.[10]
"Well, girl, you better come and pluck some burrs," the women said to
each other.

Nih'oo3oo nosou-3ii'óóbe-'ehk.
Nih'oo3oo was still snoring when they returned.

"Hei3ebíh-in, heetih-'itéibi-t.
"Our brother-in-law, let's have him have some lice.

"Noh wo'éi3 heetih-ciitéibi-t," nii-hohkóni'.
"Or let's have him not have any lice [if he would prefer]," they were saying.

Né'-eibton-óóhkoni' woníseineehíis-ii hinii3e'één-e'.
Then they stuck burrs in his hair.

Toh-'úus-beh-eibíh-ooni3i, he'ih-nóo3-e' beh'eihíinen.
Once they had stuck all the burrs on his head, they went off and left the old fellow.

Kou3íihi', "uuú," Nih'óó3oo he'ih-'owóto'oo.
After a long time, "uhh," Nih'oo3oo woke up.

Cee-cesicé'ein.
He scratched around on his head.

"'oo'hó," nii-hók.
"Ouch!" he said.

"Heeyóuti'?"[11]
"What is this?

"Híiwo' yohou=tóxu'oo?!
"What in the heck is so sharp?!

"'oo'hó," nii-hók, ceesicé'eini-3i.
"Ouch!" he was saying, whenever he scratched his head.

He'iisóú'u, hí'ii nih'ou'éi'oo-'[12] woníseineehíis-ii.
No matter what he did, the burrs made his face tighten up from pain.

Kóhei'i-hok Nih'oo3oo.
Nih'oo3oo stood up.

"No-hohookeeníit!

"I am so crazy!

"Híiwo' cih-'iistoo-nóóni?" nii-hók.[13]

"What in the heck am I going to do now?" he said.

Toh-kóhei'i-[t], kookuyón hoowuniihiíhi' he'ih-cé3ei'oo.

After he stood up, he just set off aimlessly, headed downstream.

Hitét-o'ohk níiinon.

He reached a tipi.

"'oohé' Nih'óó3oo, <u>he'=iisi-ihoo-3í</u>?"[14]

"Well, here's Nih'oo3oo, where could he be going?" [the owner said].

"Ceebíin-bebée'ei-n."[15]

"You have filthy curly hair."

"Hee, beebée'ei-noo.

"Yes, I have curly hair.

"Hoowuhtéíbee-noo!

"I have a head full of lice!

"Nih-í'-coo-noo," heeh-éhk Nih'óó3oo, "hot-3iiyoh-únee."

"The reason I have come," said Nih'oo3oo, "is so that you can give me a haircut."

"<u>Nohtóus wo'úukoo'eeníihi'</u>,[16] Nih'óó3oo?"

"Why should we do anything for you, Nih'oo3oo?"

"Neniitóbee-noo netesíh'e hiiyoote-'éhk.

"I have heard that my wife is dead," [he replied].

"Nee'éé-béet-3iiyouhú-noo."

"That is why I want to get a haircut."

Nih-bii-bixoninoo'oo-hók Nih'óó3oo.
Nih'oo3oo began sobbing pitifully.

Nih-nii'iibee-hék heenei'í3ecoo-3i.
He blew his nose whenever he happened to think about it.

"'inehóus Nih'óó3oo," hee3-éihok.
"Well okay, Nih'oo3oo," he said to him.

Nih-coon-too-tou'ucí3et-ehk.[17]
[Nih'oo3oo] kept trying to contain himself but couldn't.

"Nohuusóho'!"
"That's it!"

"Wohéi konoo' nehínee," nii3-éihok, nii3ee-tehk Nih'óó3oo.
"Okay already, that's enough!" they were saying to him, Nih'oo3oo was
told.

Tih-'iis-3íiyouhu-t, cé3ei'oo-hok.
After he got his hair cut, he set off for home.

Toh-ce'eeckóóhu-t, toh-neehéyeisee-t hiyeih'ín-e', nii3éi'[iinit].[18]
When he got back home, when he got near his lodge, then with all his
might he began to cry.

He'ih-coo-cooníitoo.
He was prostrate with sorrow.

"Toh'uni bíxoo3-o', toh'uni bixoo3-óú'u neníisoo-no'," neenei3óteib-ehk
Nih'óó3oo.
"The one I loved, my children whom I loved," was what Nih'oo3oo was
sobbing.

"Koox=hohookéé!
"There goes that crazy guy yet again!"

"He'=ii3i-níisitoo-3i," nii3-éihok hiníín.

"What has he done now?" his wife said about him.

"Netesih'ówuh,[19] toh-ni'-bíxoo3-o'!

"My wife, whom I loved so much!

"Neníisoo-no' toh-ni'-bíxoo3-ou'u!

"My children, whom I loved so much!

"Nóónonox," neeneih-óhk, heecisísee-t.

"How could this have happened?" he was saying over and over, as he was walking along.

"Nohoni koo=wó'ooto'[20] Nih'óó3oo heesi-3íiyoohu-t?

"Why just now would Nih'oo3oo have gotten his hair cut that way?

"Koox=he'=íistoo-3i."

"He must have gone and done something yet again," [his wife was saying].

Nih'oo3oo no'usee-hok híyeih'-e';

Nih'oo3oo arrived at his lodge;

hiníín he'ih-noohób-ee noh huníisoo-no.

he saw his wife and his children.

"Netesih'ówuh yo'oh=n-eeyéíh-ce'-noohów-oo{woo}!![21]

"My wife, it's so good to see you again so unexpectedly!

"Nih-niitóbee-noo tih-'iiyohoote-néhk.

"I heard that you were dead.

"Ne'=nih-'íis-3iiyoohu-noo," hee3-oohok huníín.

"That's why I got my hair cut," he said to his wife.

Nih'óó3oo he'ne'í-iten-oohok.

Then Nih'oo3oo held/hugged his wife.

Nih-nii-niiten-oohok.

And gave her many kisses.

"Yo'oh=n-eeyéíh-ce'-noohów-oo netesíh'e!

"It's so good to see my wife again!

"Wo'úunoononóx."

"I am so astonished [to discover you alive]."

"Hé'ih-ceyotów-oo3ítouh nées," hiníín hee3-éihok Nih'óó3oo.

"My husband was apparently told a false story," his wife said to Nih'oo3oo.

Notes

1. Kroeber transcribes *heece'éi3i-ni3i*, but what was intended must have been *hee3e'éicini3i*. He has transposed two consonants.

2. *Hiinó3oon* is a woman's word, indicating extreme insistence. But cf. *hiino3óón* 'instead'.

3. *Kónoo'* literally means 'anyway,' as in 'I'll do it anyway, even though I'm not particularly interested'. *Hiikóokónoo'* could also be translated 'might as well, what the heck'.

4. *Ho-coow-únoo* means literally 'your thighs'.

5. Kroeber gives a translation 'yes' for *hohóú*.

6. William C'Hair says the modern form of this word is *yohúu-*. Note that nonaffirmative inflections follow this preverb.

7. *Neení'etéébeti-* AI.REFL means 'to wish out loud', with the implication that the wish is just idle talk and will not be realized. Colloquially it could be glossed 'in your dreams'.

8. The final verb is transcribed as *ci3-oo* by Kroeber, but the ending must be *ci3-e'*.

9. *Hiséé* is the vocative form of *hísei* 'woman'.

10. Burrs are treated as animate here. Normally they are inanimate.

11. *Heeyóu* means 'what is it?' *Heeyóúti'* is archaic.

12. *Nih'óú'oo-* II 'stinging pain' *nih'óú'ei'oo-* II 'face tightens up'.

13. *Cih-* can be used in place of *he'=* as a dubitative proclitic. Note that conjunct iterative inflections follow.

14. William C'Hair says that *'oohe'* is a variant of *'oh* 'and, but' but translates it as 'well' or 'so here's'.

15. Cf. II *cebííni-* 'soiled, dirty, needing washing'.

16. *Modern Nohtóu wo'úukóó'oenííhi'* can generally be glossed 'why should we do it?', carrying a dubious or antagonistic implication.

17. Kroeber transcribes *-3ícet-ehk*, but this must be *-ci3et-ehk*. As in the case cited in note 1 above, he has transposed two consonants (the same two, in fact: /c/ and /3/).

18. William C'Hair notes that *nii3éí'nee-hehk* means 'with all his might' in modern Arapaho. In this volume the form is usually *nii3éí'iinit*.

19. C'Hair says that *netesih'oówuh* is a vocative form. Cf. *netesíh'e* 'my wife'.

20. *Nohoni* means 'why?', with an implication that the speaker has a thought or opinion contrary to or at least far removed from that of the addressee (it also occurs in "The Skunk and the Rabbit," where it is used to mean 'why don't you' when the addressee is hesitant or disagrees).

21. *Yó'oh*= 'I see it, but I don't or can't believe it's really so'. *Ne-* (1S)+*ééyeih-* 'it is good that'>*nééyeih-*. The combined expression indicates something like 'I never would have believed, or still can't believe, that something so good has happened'. The same expression occurs in the "Speech of Woman's Father at Marriage" in this collection. Here, of course, the expression is a good deal more ironic.

Other
Trickster
Stories

Nih'oo3oo and the Plums

Teller unknown, Oklahoma, August(?) 1899
Collected by Alfred Kroeber
NAA, MS 2560a, Notebook 6, p. 12

This is a very rudimentary version of this well-known story (title supplied by the editors). Salzmann 1956b contains a longer version. Nevertheless, this version does illustrate a pervasive theme in the Arapaho texts
in this collection: things are not always what they appear to be. The trickster
Nih'oo3oo is a common victim of failing to appreciate this (see "Nih'oo3oo
and the Deer Women"), but the need for careful perception and suspicion of
immediate surface appearances occurs in other stories such as "The White
Dog and the Woman," "The Skunk and the Rabbit," "The Turtle and the
Rabbit," and "The Porcupine and the Woman Who Climbed to the Sky."
Note that a number of different psychological or emotional states are
linked to the failure to look carefully and see the underlying truth: hunger
and appetite, sexual desire, egocentrism, impatience, and excessive self-
confidence. But what visual clue does Nih'oo3oo miss in this story? In one
sense the answer is obvious: water reflects things. More generally, water
seems to have special powerful properties in much of Arapaho mythology.
It is the home of the Water Monster. Crossing it can be dangerous and can
even lead to the permanent splitting of the tribe ("The Arapaho Migration
across the Missouri River to the . . ."); diving into it can also be dangerous
and tricky ("Nih'oo3oo Sharpens His Leg and Dives on the Ice"). It is the
place from which the earth itself is drawn at the time of creation. Sinking
into it not only can lead to death but recalls the very "Origin of Death":
because buffalo dung floats to the surface after being thrown into the water
by Nih'oo3oo, he is fated to live forever and/or be constantly revived. In contrast, because the Indian threw a rock into the water and it sank, he is fated
to die. In this particular story, Nih'oo3oo ties rocks to himself to stay under
the water so that he can look for the supposedly sunken plums but floats back
up to the surface despite this. As much as the story seems to mock Nih'oo3oo,
Cowell notes that from another perspective he seems to be mocking the
mortal, drownable Indian (or human): even rocks will not keep Nih'oo3oo
down. He may be a silly fool, but he is a protean fool, whose ability at least

to attempt to indulge his every desire with no ultimate harm is something that even well-socialized and cautious individuals must envy at some times in their lives.

Nih'oo3oo hoowuniihisee-hek.
Nih'oo3oo was walking downstream.

He'=itet-o'ohk hoxotóóno'.
He reached a steep bank.

He'=noohoot-o'ohk beesibi-no néc-i'.
He saw plums in the water.

Ne'-hinowousee-hek.
Then he dived under the water [but failed to get the plums].

Ce'-hinowousee-hek nec-i'.
He dived under the water again [but again failed].

Ne'-toukutoo-hok hoh'onookee-no hiicetin-e' noh hi'oot-e'.
Then he tied rocks onto his hands and his feet.

Ne'=ii'-inowousee-hék, toh-notoun-o' beesibi-no.
Then he dived under the water again, because he was looking for plums in the water.

He'=cih-ce'-bixou'oo-hok hoo3i3iniíhi'.
Then he floated back up to the surface on his back.

Hihcebe' noohoot-o'ohk beesibi-no toh-'outé-ni'i.
Right nearby he saw plums hanging on a bush [above his head].

Nih'oo3oo and the Elk

Told by Benejah Miles, Oklahoma, July 15, 1899
Collected by Alfred Kroeber
NAA, MS 2560a, Notebook 3, pp. 33–34

This is a very short version of this narrative (title supplied by the editors), which leaves several details unclear—in particular, Nih'oo3oo knows that there is a cliff nearby when he proposes the race and plans it so that the elk will run over the edge of the cliff and be killed. Also, when the coyote arrives, Nih'oo3oo asks him over and over to clean the guts of the elk in a stream, but the coyote repeatedly eats them instead and then tells Nih'oo3oo that they were taken from him by the fish in the stream, so Nih'oo3oo gets fed up. Similarly, the implication at the end of the story is that the wind causes the branches to become entangled, trapping Nih'oo3oo. The detail about his ending up caught in the tree is unique to this version of the story.

Structurally, the story can be divided into three segments in which Nih'oo3oo comes upon/meets (TA *hites-*) someone new and a fourth segment in which he gets entangled in the branches. The segments track his gradual loss of agency: Nih'oo3oo does the walking and meeting in sections one and two but is met by the (obviative) coyote in section three and then finds himself completely immobilized in section four.

Níiinon he'=hoótee-'ehk, Nih'oo3oo 'oh hoowúniihisee-hék.

A tipi was standing, where Nih'oo3oo was walking downstream.

Tei'yoonóh'-o he'ih-'ités-ee.

He came upon some children.

"Nesihoo," hee3-éihok, "toot=(h)éí-ihoo?"

"Uncle," they said to him, "where are you going?"

"Noowúniihisee-noo."

"I am going downstream."

89

He'ih-nosóusee.
He was still walking.

He'ih-'ites-oo hiwóxuuh-uu.
He came upon some elk.

Ne'í-nonouhtiiw-oohók.[1]
Then he raced against them.

He'ih-3i'én-ee hit-ou-w.
He bet[2] his robe.

Ne'-ce3koohuuw-oohok.
Then he started to run with them.

"Beh-no'úusihcehi-'!"
"All of you shut your eyes quick!"

He'i=beh-nóxowusi-'ehkóni' hiwóxuuh-uu.
All the elk were killed when they plummeted to the ground [off a cliff].

Hé'ne'-ceniihei'i-t.
Then he skinned/butchered them.

He'ne'-oon-óokouhu-t.
Then he cooked a big meal for himself.[3]

Kóó'ohwúhu' hé'ih-'ités-e'.
A little coyote came along.

Hé'ne'-oon-o3i'ééw-oot hotn-een-ehiiseton-eit hi-bíi3iwoo-no.
He asked the coyote to wash the paunches[4] for him.

Cése' koo'ohwúhu' he'ih-no'kóó.
The little coyote came running back with nothing.

"Neisoh'oo nówo'-uu hootoow-uní3i."
"Older brother, the fish ate up everything I had."

He'ne'=nii'-biin-eit hi-bíi3iwoo-no.

Then he gave it some more paunches to clean.

He'ih-ciisibih-e'.[5]

[But after it came back with nothing,] he got fed up with the coyote.[6]

He'ne'-noxóbe3eih-oot.[7]

Then he bashed it with a club.

Hohootí-no he'ih-teicein-een-éesi-nino.[8]

The tree branches were snapping and scratching against each other in the wind.

He'ne'-ouuhu-t hohoot-í', tohuu-noonó'oon-oot.[9]

Then he climbed up into a tree, to get [the branches] to stop making all that noise.

He'ne'-kohyeibinoo'oo-t hohoot-i'.[10]

Then he was stuck fast in the tree.

He'ne'-otoowukuuton-eit hoséinóu, toh-nei'eibinoo'oo-t hohoot-i'.

Then the coyote gobbled up his meat, while he was stuck tight in the tree.

Notes

1. The manuscript has -*hoowok* rather than -*woohok,* as Kroeber reversed the syllables.
2. *3i'en-* TA, literally 'place standing, put forth or out'.
3. Literally 'cooked several things for himself'.
4. The *bii3iwóóo* is one of the stomachs of an ungulate, technically called the "manifold" or the "Bible" in Arapaho English, because it looks like the leaves of a book.
5. Literally 'it [coyote] made/got him [Nih'oo3oo] fed up, tired of him [coyote]'.
6. Because every time he gave the coyote something to clean, the coyote ate it instead.
7. *Nóxow-* 'intensely, hard' -*e3eih-* TA 'by collision, blow'. This could be translated as 'he smashed him to the ground' or 'he laid him out'.
8. The verb is *teic-éin-een-eesi-* II '???-noise-REDUP-by wind-'. Thus 'blowing all about making ??? kind of noise'.
9. *Nóonó'oon-* means 'get s.o. to change his or her mind or to do s.t. different'. Cf. Gros Ventre TA *nyoʔoob-* 'convince people to change their mind by talking to them'.
10. Cf. *kohy-óhoé* 'glue', literally 'thing for sticking things [together]'.

Céb toh'oowunííhou'oo'/Pemmican Floating Downstream

Told by Cleaver Warden, Oklahoma, August 22, 1899

Collected by Alfred Kroeber

NAA, MS 2560a, Notebook 10, pp. 6–10

English version published as "Nih'oo3oo Pursued by the
Rolling Stone" in Dorsey and Kroeber [1903] 1997: 69–70

This is one of the few texts in Kroeber's manuscript with an Arapaho title, but he published it with a different title. The manuscript title is used here. This text is analyzed in detail in appendix B.

The story has many nice examples of forms that subtly include speaker judgments in what are otherwise statements of fact—in particular, judgments that involve implied insults, a lower evaluation of the addressee than the addressee's own, and a very low speaker opinion of the addressee—all expressed through the voice of the trickster. This story also contains some good examples of direct derogatory statements and insults, again in the voice of Nih'oo3oo. These forms are explained in the notes but especially include the use of *yonó'oh=* (indicating that the speaker's view of a situation is far less favorable than someone else's) and future statements made with nonaffirmative inflection.

Such forms are all the more humorous in contrast to the examples of potential modality that Nih'oo3oo uses once the tables are turned, he gets in trouble, and he needs help: the prefixes *hi3=, hih-* 'if' or 'if only' or 'it would be good if'. We also find many examples of his own surprise and in particular the difference between actual events and his own expectations (involving idiomatic expressions with *wot=, koowót=,* and *keih-* or *keis-* as well as some lexical items). First Nih'oo3oo underevaluates those around him, then he discovers that he has overevaluated himself. Note the many examples of (excessive) politeness that he uses as well—particularly the many vocatives, which feature not the normal *be* 'friend' but rather *beh'éé* 'old man' and *neehéé* 'dear friend', which are clearly over-the-top uses in this case.

Overall, this story is truly a masterpiece in the use of what linguists call "modality." This involves expressions of speaker attitude toward events or people. As this discussion makes clear, the story centers around imbalances in these attitudes: first Nih'oo3oo's arrogant and dismissive undervaluation of those around him and second his shock and surprise when things are not going as he would expect or want. All of this is compounded by the imbalance between his verbal treatment of the nighthawk and the reality of the actual treatment that he imposes on it at the end of the story. Nih'oo3oo's speech, perspectives, and judgment always seem to be out of joint with the reality around him. Sometimes he suffers because of this, but sometimes others do.

Cowell notes that the poetic organization of the story also clearly seems based in these modal and other expressions of imbalance. The narrative can be broken into smaller sections based in part on the sentence-initial occurrence of these modality markers. We have divided the narrative in this way below.

Mixed with this focus on modality are many uses of vocabulary and grammatical structures that highlight the ironic reversals or echoes in this story. We have italicized a number of these, including a few quite subtle ones such as echoes of *houun-*, 'superlative'; *ceb-/cow-* 'past, by'; *ce3i-* 'away'; and *cen-* 'down'. Note that many of these echoes are spatial in nature and quite different from the play with modality. Nevertheless the repeating spatial orientations, combined with the different actual events and different perspectives of Nih'oo3oo, further reinforce the overall ironic effects of the story.

Kroeber's notes at the end of the text add: "The moral lesson of this myth is not to be greedy." Perhaps a more interesting feature of the ending to a modern reader is that the description of the rock going to pieces (or more literally 'losing parts') uses the word *ko'únoo'oo*, which is also a word for a male orgasm, as Alonzo Moss notes. The same root is echoed in the verb *kó'ob-* (TA), *ko'óót-* (TI) 'bite off a part', which is used multiple times at the beginning of the narrative. We can also compare this narrative to "Nih'oo3oo Pursued by the Rolling Skull": in both cases he wishes for "a hole" where he is running—and the latter narrative also notes a deep fissure in the earth. With these facts in mind, we can better appreciate the humor and various resonances of interesting sexuality or eroticism in the ending and indeed the entire text.

Cowell notes that one could see this narrative in general as a reflection on life and the valuing of life. Within traditional Arapaho culture, it was believed that the life spirit of an animal that was killed ceremonially was transferred to the animal's hide (Dorsey 1903: 62, 71). In connection to this, the Arapaho word *hou* is animate when used for 'animal-hide robe' but inanimate when used for 'cloth blanket'. The rock (also animate in Arapaho) seems to come to life when the robe is placed upon it, seeming to echo the ceremonial attitude about the life force. Conversely, the cavalier way in which Nih'oo3oo treats all life—the pemmican (a food made from crushed dried meat, crushed dried berries, and lard), normally inanimate but treated as animate here; the robe; and the helpful nighthawk—is typical of his role as mirror inverse of proper Arapaho values. And in relation to the sexual themes, note that Nih'oo3oo is highly sexually oriented in Arapaho narratives but completely nonreproductive.

Nih'óó3oo hoowúniihisee-hek.
Nih'oo3oo was walking downstream.

Céb he'ih-*ców*ou'oo.
Some pemmican floated by.

He'=iis-ooyeikóó.
He managed to run around ahead of it and caught up to it.

"Hei-tohuu3éí'-ko'ób-ee?"[1]
"How much of you can we bite off?" [he asked the pemmican].

"Béénihehe' nii'-ko'ób-een."[2]
"You can bite off a little bit."

Koox=he'ih-ce'-no'o'ús.
[After doing this, Nih'oo3oo] got back out of the water again.

He'ih-'óóyeikoo.
He ran around ahead of it again.

"Hei-tohuu3éí'-ko'ób-ee?" niit-o'óhk céb.
"How much of you can we bite off?" he said to the pemmican.

"Beénihehe'."
"A little bit."

He'=iis-ooyei-kó'oot konóhxuu.

Despite [what the pemmican said], he managed to bite off most of it.

Koox=ci'=he'ih-'óóyeikoo, beebéi'on.

Then yet again he ran around ahead of it, way on downstream.

"Hei-tohuu3éí'-ko'ób-ee?" Nih'óó3oo nii-hók.

"How much of you can I bite off?" Nih'oo3oo said.

"Béenihehe'," nii3ée-tehk.

"A little bit," he was told.

He'ih-bees-ko'óót konóhxuu.

Despite what he was told, he bit off a big piece.

He'ne'-*ouu-cén*ooyeikoohu-t.

Then he ran way on down around ahead of it as fast as he could.

"Hei-tohuu3éí'-ko'ób-ee?" nii-hók.

"How much of you can we bite off?" he said.

Béeyoo he'ih-ko'óót.

He bit some off right in the middle.

Hiiwóonihehe' he'né'-*béneebe3*,[3] bees-ko'óót-o'.

Now he took a big bite and got the whole thing.

"Howóh[4] heenee3éhtoneihí-3i Nih'óó3oo!"

"Who would have imagined how clever/tricky Nih'oo3oo is!"[5]

[he said about himself].

He'ih-*ce3í*kotii hookoo3íihi'.

He set off for home.

Biikóó, toh-nókohu-t, hit-óu-w he'ih-bíi-bii3í3-ee.[6]

That night, when he was sleeping, he crapped on his buffalo robe.

He'ih-nohk-*ce3íkotii.*
He set off with it.

"Néhe' hóu, he-eti-itóuw[7] béh'ee," *héét-o'ohk*[8] *hih-noohóo3oo.*
"This robe, it can be your robe now, old man," he said to whatever thing he saw.

Neenowó', teebe *toh-ceníisee-t,*
Rushing along, once he had gone a good distance,

he'ih-ce'é'ein, nih-'íitoh-bei-t hit-óu-w.
he looked back, where he had given away his robe.

Wot=kéis-iiyootéíhi-n![9]
He was amazed to see that it was all clean!

"Ceis-ín ce'íihi', *yonó'oh*='itóuwú-n?"[10] heeh-éhk Nih'óó3oo.
"Give it back to me, what in the heck are *you* doing with a robe?" said Nih'oo3oo.

He'ih-nohk-*ce3í*kotii.
He set off with it.

Kóox=he'ih-ce'-beeníin.
Then once again it was covered with crap [after he slept on it].

"Béh'ee, núhu' he-eti-itóuw," nii-hok, tih-yihkúutii-t heeyóúhuu.
"Old man, this can be your robe," he said, when he tossed it away toward something or other.

Heet-3i'ookuu-ní' wot=nehe'=nih-'íístoo-hok.
Wherever something was standing, that's what he would do.

Cee'-beeniini-ní3i[11] hówoh'uuhu' . . .
Whenever it got all covered with lots of crap again . . . [he would do the same thing].

Koox=hit-ou-w, he'ih-ce'i-soo3íh-ee hit-óu-w.
Then once again his robe, he soiled his robe again.

Noosousée-t, he'ih-cih-'ités-ee {no}hoh'onóókee-n.
He is still walking [with his robe dirty again], and he came upon
a rock here.

"Béh'ee, nuhu' he-eti-itouw," hee3-oohók.
"Old man, this can be your robe now," he said to it.

Toh-ceníisee-t, he'ih-ce'é'ein.
When he had walked a good way, he looked back.

> *Koowót=*nehe' hóu hé'ih-'iis-iiyooteih!
> To his surprise, this robe was all clean!

Ce'íkotii-hok.
He hurried back.

> *"Yonó'oh=*'itóuwu-n," hee3-oohók.
> "What is someone like *you* doing with a robe?" he said to the rock.

Ce'-ítenowuun-oohók, he'i=néé'ees-*cé3*ei'oo-t.
When he took it back from the rock, he set off again.

Toh-ceníisee-t, heeyóuti'[12] hé'ih-'étei'oo.
When he had gone a good way, there was a rumbling sound from
something.

Nih'óó3oo *he'ih-ce'é'ein.*
Nih'oo3oo looked back.

> Noononóx, hoh'onóókee béeyoo héetoo-t he'ih-ceitétei'oo.
> To his astonishment, the rock was rumbling right toward where he was.

Cih-nóo-noh'uhcehisíne-'.[13]
It was tumbling and bouncing along toward him.

Xonóu he'ih-*ce3i*kóó.
Right away he took off running.

Hoh'onóókee he'ih-cih-3ooku-koo'óuuto'oo.
The rock was following behind him, kicking up clouds of dust.

"Hih-tónot,[14] hehkúhnee-noo.
"If only there was a hole in the direction where I am running.

"He[i]h=nó'o3oo hehkúhnee-noo," nii-hók.
"[I wish there was] a strong/powerful place [for protection], where I'm
fleeing," he said.

Hé'ne'=ii' . . . , he'ne'-*houu*-nihi'kóó, toh-to3ih-éit,
Then . . . then he was running as fast as he could, because it was
following him.

"'uuh beh'éi."
"Uhh, old man," [Nih'oo3oo said].

Hei'-néetikoohu-t, kotóukoo.
When he was tired from running, then he ran under the cover [of a
stream bank].

"Hí3=heet-*ceb*kóóhu-t," heeh-éhk.
"It would be good if it would go past," he said.

He'ih-koxó'-tées-tee-teco'oo hikóob-e'.
The rock slowly rolled on top of his back.

"Béh'ee, toh-'ooben-ín," *nii3-oohók hih-noohowóo-no* cése'ehii-ho.
"Old man, take it off me," he said to the animals he saw.

Koowót=hé'ih-ceh'e3ih-e'.[15]
To his disappointment, they did not listen to him.

Císihí' he'íh-cih-noononóó'oo.
A little nighthawk came soaring around this way.

"Neehéé, cih-'ooben-ín nehe' hoh'onóókee-n," niihók.
"Friend, take this rock off me," he said.

Kou3íihi' cisihí' *cen*ih'ohuukóó beenihéhe'.
Eventually the little nighthawk dove down a little bit.

He'ih-ko'oxóuh-uu.
He blasted off some of the rock [by farting/with his anus].

Heeyów=*ceen*ih'ohuukóohu-3i, ceneetí-3i,
Every time he dove down, when he farted,

nóónoxoo[16] he'íh-ko'únoo'oo nehe' hoh'onóókee.
gradually, bit by bit, this rock was getting chipped away.

Béneebe3 hé'ne'-hihci-noononóó'oo-t beebéi'on.
One final time, he soared way up high far away.

Nii3éí'iinit cenih'óhuukoo hetebíihi'.
He dove down at the rock on a collision course, with all his might.

Ceetí3-ee, behis-3ó'oh-oe.
He farted at it and shattered it all to bits.

Nih'óó3oo he'=kóhei'i-hok.
Nih'oo3oo jumped up.

   "Nééhee, nehéic, hot-nii-ni'ib-é3en," hee3-oohók cisího'.
   "Friend, come here, so I can share some good words with you," he
   said to the nighthawk.

"Neiteh'éi, yóhou=hiixonéíh het-ówouuyoo{n}.
"My friend, how helpful you have been, in taking pity on me.

"Hi3í=tee'etínee-n,"[17] hee3-oohók.
"Will you open your mouth?" he said to him.

He'ih-koxo'etinée-n.

The nighthawk got his mouth stretched apart.

> *"Yonó'oh=*'uuxonéíh,[18] wottowuuhuu!"[19] hee3-oohók.

"You thought you were so useful/helpful, you dirty scoundrel!" he said to him.

> "Béébeet heet[n]ii-néé'eenii[ni] béesetinéé-nee."

"You [nighthawks] will just have a big mouth like this from now on."

Notes

1. Note use of 1P for 1S here. This is commonly done by Nih'oo3oo in trickster stories.

2. Note again 1P for 1S.

3. *Béneebé3* means 'everything [finally]; the last time; one last time; all gone now'. Note that the same word is used toward the end of the story to describe how the nighthawk finally cracks apart the rock under which Nih'oo3oo is trapped.

4. *Howóh* sentence-initially before a verb serves to indicate that whatever is described in the verb has turned out to be unexpectedly wrong or contrary to expectations and moreover that in retrospect one should have known better or not made excessively hasty or arrogant assumptions. (See "The White Dog and the Woman," where several examples of this construction occur.) Here the entire construction is used ironically.

5. Kroeber translates this as 'How lucky you are, Nih'oo3oo!' The phrase is obviously used in an ironic sense, as the translation tries to make clear.

6. Note that the robe is animate, object of the TA verb *bíibii3i3-* 'to shit on'. A buffalo robe is animate in Arapaho, while a blanket is inanimate. The word for both is *hou*.

7. *He-eti-itóúwu-* 2S-FUT-have robe (AI)-. Note the nonaffirmative inflection. The construction means 'you might as well/should have a robe', with the implication that the item in question is of minimal value.

8. *Héét-* TI 'say s.t. to s.t. (inan.)'. Cf. vta *hee3-* 'say s.t. to s.o.'

9. The verb derives from *koo=hi-iis-hííyootéíhi-n,* INTERR=3S-PERF-clean(AI)-4S. The combination of *wot=* with *keih-* or *keis-* forms an idiomatic expression indicating astonishment, amazement, and something completely the opposite of expectations or desires. Perhaps the closest idiomatic English gloss would be 'can it really be?!'

10. Here *yonó'oh=* is used with nonaffirmative inflections (contrast the usage at the end of the story). It indicates negative or contrary judgement of a fact on the part of the speaker and could be glossed 'who would have thought!' or 'I never would have imagined'.

11. The inflection here is 4S.ITER.

12. *Heeyóu* means 'what?' The form *heeyóúti'* occurs elsewhere in texts from Oklahoma.

13. We interpret the verb as *-ihcehísin-* TA. Normally the form would be *-ihcehísib-,* which implies intentional action. A rock generally does not seem to have intentionality, which would thus lead to the former form.

14. *Hih-* is a contrary-to-fact prefix.

15. The manuscript has *3eh'e3ihe'.*

16. *Nóónoxóó* 'gradually, bit by bit'.

17. *Hi3-* is used here with its now-archaic future potential meaning: 'if' or 'if you should'.

18. *Yonó'oh=* (or *yó'oh=*) can be used dubitatively, as 'it's supposedly so, but I don't think so/it doesn't seem so', or in more direct contrary judgments: 'you/they may say it's so, but it isn't'. This is an example of the latter usage. Note that nonaffirmative inflection occurs here with these dubitative usages.

19. *Wóttowúúhuu* is a general insult term, particularly used for people who are disloyal, do not live up to what they promised, criticize people behind their backs, or are otherwise deceitfully harmful. It is often glossed by speakers today as 'you son of a bitch'.

Nih'oo3oo Pursued
by the Rolling Skull

Told by Philip Rapid/Rabbit, Oklahoma, August 17, 1899
Collected by Alfred Kroeber
NAA, MS 2560a, Notebook 9, pp. 57–61
English version published in Dorsey and
Kroeber [1903] 1997: 70–71

This story is untitled in Kroeber's manuscript: he supplied the title at the time of publication. This particular story should especially be appreciated for the fine detail used in the descriptions, featuring many less common, colorful, and very precise motion verbs. For example, rather than just using the verb *hotíiwo'oo-* 'to roll', we find also:

kohkotíiwo'oo- 'to penetrate through something by rolling'
nóh'otíiwo'oo- 'to roll uphill'
hóówotíiwo'oo- 'to roll downhill'
ce'óówotíiwo'oo- 'to roll back down'
no'otíiwo'oo- 'to reach a place by rolling'
toyoni'oxúúnotíiwo'oo- 'to roll along as nice and smooth as can be'
hoowohcé3i3o'oo- 'barely moving/rolling forward'

Similarly, the narrator employs a rich variety of terms indicating crossings and obstacles to crossings as well as an extensive set of terms for the motion of the trickster and other figures, making much use of directional prefixes *cih-* 'in this direction' and *seh-* 'from here over to there', as well as the base morphemes *kóóhu-* 'to run'; *o'oo-* 'to go/move' (seen above); and *(n)oo'oo-* 'inchoative, ongoing, evolving', combined with numerous modifiers. Note, for example:

hoowohkox3ínoo'oo- 'barely making it over the top of a hill, to the other side'
bixoúnoo'oo- 'rising into view from below the water/ice'
bisínoo'oo- 'coming into view'
nóh'néetinoo'oo- 'getting tired from going uphill'

102

ho'wúnoo'oo- 'closing quickly'
hesíino'wúnoo'oo- 'slamming shut violently'.

The frequency with which the base morphemes occur, combined with the constant variation in the modifying forms to which they are attached, produces a kind of theme and variation effect that could be compared to the effect of meter and rhyme in Euro-American classical poetry. We have boldfaced and italicized the morphemes in question where they occur in the text.

On a larger scale, the way in which the narrator varies the rhythm constantly from slowness, slight motion, and being stuck to moments of great rapidity of motion and headlong flight produces another abstract rhythmic pattern of stops and starts across the text, which is intricately interwoven with the various motion morphemes. We have marked what we consider to be the varying slow and fast sections of the text.

SLOW

Nih'óó3oo he'ih-noonóyei.
Nih'oo3oo was fishing.

He'ih-tónoti-n wo'ów-u', nih-'íitoh-nóyei-hok.
There was a hole in the ice, where he was fishing.

Toh-nosóu-noonóyei-t, he'ih-cíh-koo-koxo'einóó-n wo'ów-u'.
When he was still fishing, the ice could be heard cracking apart at various spots.

Hei'-íini he'íh-ce'-wóteinoo-n núhu' wó'ow.
Every once in a while you could hear the ice cracking again.

"Hiiwo' he'íi3óu'u," nih-'iisi3ecoo-hok.
"I wonder what that is," he thought to himself.

He'ih-seh-nei'oohóo3ei niit-woteinóó-ni'.
He looked over there where the sound was coming from.

He'ih-cii-noohóót teesííhi' wo'ów-u'.
He could not see anything on top of the ice.

FAST

Ceeciis heet-tónoti-ni' núhu' wo'ów-u', he'ih-cih-bixou*nóó'oo* 3iikonóokuhu'ee.

Suddenly, where the hole in the ice was, a skull rose into view above the water.

Wot=nih-too-néetineih-ehk[1] nehe' Nih'óó3oo.

Nih'oo3oo was almost scared to death.

Kookón nii3ei'iniit he'ih-tóko.

He just ran away as fast as he could go.

"Hóót-neh'-é3en," hee3-éihok nuhu' hookuhú'ee-n.

"I will kill you," the skull said to him.

Ceece3ó'oh he'ih-'iiní-to3ih-e'.

All of a sudden it was coming after him no matter where he went.

Kookuyón cee-ceceibkoh-ee, koo-kox3ííhi', hohóot-i' noh coobéi-'i.[2]

He just fled from it on this side and that, over hill and dale, among trees and in the sand.

Heénoo he'ih-'iiní-to3ih-eihók.

Still inevitably it was following him everywhere he went.

"Heih=conoobéet," heeh-éhk nehe' Nih'óó3oo.

"I wish there was a sandy patch," said Nih'oo3oo.

Híitouuk he'ih-conoobéet.[3]

And sure enough there was a sandy patch.

SLOW

He'ih-'óówoh-cé3i3*o'óó* núhu' hóókuhú'ee.

This skull was barely moving forward now.

Hoonii he'ih-kohk*otiiwó'oo*.

After quite a while the skull rolled through the sandy spot.

FAST

"Heih=cee-cétoo'ee," nii-hók néhe' Nih'óó3oo.
"I wish there was thick brush with lots of branches," said Nih'oo3oo.

He'ih-cee-cétoo'ee-n.
Then there was thick, many-branched brush.

SLOW

He'ih-nóus núhu' hóókuhu'ee.
This skull got stuck there.

Néyei-kohk*otiiwo'óó*.
It was trying to roll through the brush.

'oh wóów hé'ih-'óxon*ikoo* nehe' Nih'óó3oo,
And now Nih'oo3oo had run really hard [and gotten far away],

hónoot he'ih-'íin3*ikoohu*-n[4] núhu' hóókuhu'ee.
until this skull rolled around the edge of the brushy area.

FAST

Hei'-íis-kohk*ó'oo*-n, 'oh he'né'-ce'-yih'oon-éit néhe' Nih'óó3oo.
After it managed to get through there, then it started pursuing Nih'oo3oo again.

Kóóx=hé'ih-'éyeih-'etéb-e'.
Once again it had almost caught up to him.

"Heih=co'óteyoo," heeh-éhk.
"I wish there was a hill," he said.

Koox=hé'ih-co'óteyoo.
And once again, there was a hill.

SLOW

He'ih-nóh'-neetí***noo'oo*** núhu' hookuhu'éé.
This skull was getting tired from rolling uphill.

He'ih-noh***'otíiwo'oo***.
It was rolling uphill.

Neehii3éi', he'ih-ce'-óów***otiiwo'oo***.
Halfway up, it rolled back down again.

Koox=wóów he'ih-'oxón***o'oo*** néhe' Nih'óó3oo beebei'ón.
Once again now Nih'oo3oo had run very hard and gotten far away.

Néeso he'íh-ce'óów***otíiwó'oo***.
The skull rolled back down the hill three times.

Yeneini'owóó-ni', hé'ih-'óówoh-kox3i***nóó'oo***.
On the fourth time, it just barely made it over the top.

FAST

Hii'oohówun, he'ih-'iis-iixow-óówukuuh.
Once it had gotten over, it was as if it had been hurled down that slope.

Wóów koox=hé'ih-'eyeih-'etéb-e'.
Now yet again it had almost caught up to Nih'oo3oo.

"Hoo," heeh-éhk, "heih=heebé3-kóh'ot biito'ówu-u' nuhu' hee3i***kóohu***-noo," nii-hók nehe' Nih'óó3oo.
"Ohh," he said, "I wish there was a big crack in the ground where I'm running," Nih'oo3oo said.

Huutouúk, he'ih-'eebé3-kóh'ot biito'ówu-u' núhu' téébe hee3i***kóohu***-t.
And sure enough, there was a big crack in the ground just where he had come running from.

SLOW

Koox=hé'ih-noono'oo'es{i}[5] núhu' hookuhu'*ée*.
Yet again the skull was impeded.

He'ih-bii-biibi3itón-e'.
It pleaded to him.

"Wohéi," hee3-eihók, "hiis-ooxúun*o'oo*-noohók, ho-otn-éihoowu-
kóhtowuh-e3," hee3-éihok.
"Okay," it said to him, "after I have crossed over, I will not do you any
harm," it said to him.

"'oh cii-hóoxúún*o'oo*-nóóhk, hootn-esínih-ín,
"But if I don't get across, I will be angry at you,

"noh héét-neh'-é3en," nii3-éihok núhu' 3iikonookuhú'ee-n.
"and I will kill you," the skull said to him.

"3íh=cih-'ooxuu-3iiwonóoon,"[6] hee3-éihok.
"Why don't you make a bridge across for me," it said to him.

"Wohéi," hee3-oohok, "cih-'ooxúús."
"Well," he said to it, "come on across."

He'ih-seh-'ooxuu-3iiwonóoon-ee[7] bésehe'.
He made a bridge for the skull with a small stick.

"Néi'en-óo," nii3-éihok.
"Hold it tight," the skull said to him.

Hé'ih-néi'enowúún-ee.
He held it tightly for the skull.

FAST

He'ih-toyóni'oxuun*otiiwo'oo*.[8]
The skull was rolling along just as nice and smooth as can be.

Neehii3éi', toh-no'*otiiwo'óó*-[t], he'ne'-i3ecikúutii-t núhu' bésehe'.

But when it reached the middle, then Nih'oo3oo flipped the little stick over.

Núhu' nih-'íitoh-*'otiiwo'oo*-n núhu' hookuhu'ee-n, he'-seh-cenis[9] béébeet núhu' héet-koh'oti-ni'.

From the place where this skull had rolled to, it just fell from there down into the crack.

Noh xonóu toh-'uus-cénise-', núhu' biito'ówu' xonóu he'ih-'o'wu*noo'oo*.

And immediately after it had fallen, the earth immediately closed up.

Béébeet hesiin-o'wú*noo'oo*.[10]

It just slammed shut.

SLOW

He'ih-cii3o'-cih-ce'-bisí*noo'oo*,

The skull never reappeared again,

noh wo'éi3 keih-cooh-nóóhow.[11]

or at least it was never seen anymore so far as is known.

Nee'ees-néhtoni-ce'-íine'etii-hok[12] nehe' Nih'oo3oo.

That is how Nih'oo3oo survived through trickery/cleverness.

Notes

1. One would expect *nee3i-neih-* here.
2. *Cóóbe'* 'a roughly circular sandy spot' LOC *coobéí'i*.
3. *Cóóbeeti-* II 'to be a sandy patch'. The initial changed form *conoo-* is aberrant here.
4. Kroeber has *-koohuno*. Perhaps the verb was actually *koohúúno'oo*, 'in the process of moving quickly', but more likely he simply heard a release between the final *−n* of the verb and this initial *n-* of following *núhu'*.
5. The most likely word here is AI *hé'ih-nóonóús* 'it was completely stuck'. This may be what was intended. Alternately, more closely matching the transcription would be *hé'ih-nóonoo'óees* 'it went around'. This does not really make sense in the context, however.
6. *3iiwonéee-* AI 'make a bridge' > *3iiwonóoon-* TA 'make a bridge for someone'.
7. Kroeber transcribes *-sii-* in the first verb, but there is no obvious reading for this, whereas the deictic *-seh-* 'from here to there' seems quite appropriate.

8. *Tóyoní'oxúúnotíiwo'óó-* 'rolling along nice and smooth, as if perfectly round'. The prefix *tóyoní'oxuun-* means more generally 'working just like it is supposed to, things are going just as they are supposed to'. Cf. AI *ni'oxúuní-* 'to work well'.

9. The manuscript has *se3-* rather than *seh-*.

10. *Hesíin-* 'quickly, rapidly, fast'.

11. *Keih-cooh-nóóhow* means literally 'did you-not any more-see me?' The use of negative questions of this type forms an idiomatic expression meaning 'as far as is known, it was never seen anymore'.

12. *Néé'ees-néhtoni-ce'-ííne'étii-* = thus-trick-again-live (AI)-.

Nih'oo3oo and the Deer Women

Told by Cleaver Warden, Oklahoma, August(?), 1899
Collected by Alfred Kroeber
NAA, MS 2560a, Notebook 6, pp. 43–44
English version published in Dorsey and
Kroeber [1903] 1997: 56–57

The title of this text was supplied by the editors. The text makes amusing use of evidential particles and prefixes. William C'Hair noted that "good words" in the text include *cobóuu* 'no way! it can't be!'; *híixowúh-* 'it sure looks like . . . but I don't think it is' or 'it sure looks like it to me, though others say it is not so'; and, *yóhuhoh=* 'it supposedly is, but I don't think it really is'. These lexical elements underline the more general issue of judgment for the trickster. Nih'oo3oo is understood as chronically lacking in proper judgment and social understanding among the Arapahos. In this story that same inability properly to determine and read situations is highlighted by the various evidential forms, all of which indicate uncertainty, hesitation, or judgment contrary to general opinion. Even more importantly, in such situations of uncertainty, where the "ideal" traditional Arapaho behavior would be to resist action until further certainty is attained, Nih'oo3oo takes exactly the opposite approach, as best indicated by the word *hiikóokónoo'* 'anyway, whatever, might as well'. Thus Nih'oo3oo first faces difficulty reading the situation that he confronts in the story then has a secondary level of difficulty in determining how to act in the face of the uncertainty that he is experiencing. The nominalized verb forms 'craziness' and 'nosiness' at the end of the story are typical expressions used by Nih'oo3oo at the end of trickster stories and further underline his two levels of "uncivilized" behavior.

Nih'óó3oo he'=oowún[iih]isee-hok.
Nih'oo3oo was walking downstream.

Toh-nosoun-oowuniihísee-t, hísein-o' heh-niisi-3i' he'ih-tousebi-no'.
When he was still walking downstream, two women were bathing.

He'ih-noohób-e'.
They saw him.

Xonóu he'ih-no'o'úhcehi-níno.
They immediately jumped out of the water.

Koxéciihi' he'ih-tee-tecihcehí-no'.
They quickly rolled all around in the sticky mud.

He'ne'-hiiton-3i'ookuu-3i'.
Then they stood on each side of where he was walking.

Nih'oo3oo he'ih-'ites-ee cééxoon.
Nih'oo3oo came upon one of them.

"Cobóuu[1] nénee-' tebí3is!
"Surely that's not a tree stump!

"Hiixowuh-tónoti-'.[2]
"There appears to be a hole in it.

"Hiixowuh-'iso'oníinoo-'.
"It appears to have an anus [too].

"Tebísis; yohuh=nénee-'[3] tebí3is.
"A stump; that's supposed to be a tree stump, [but I don't think so].

"He'=ni'-woowótowoo.
"Maybe I could have myself some good sex.

"Noh neeyou ceese'!
"And there is another one!

"Ci'=yohuh=nénee-' wo'tee[n]-tebí3ixoo.[4]
"That doesn't look like just a black tree stump to me.

"Hi3í=wohee'-cii-céyoox.[5]
"I wonder if it might not have a vagina . . .

"Wohei hiikookónoo' toh-nenee-' tebí3is."

"Well, I might as well go ahead, because it's just a tree stump."

Nih'óó3oo he'=yii3i'éin-o'ohk.

Nih'oo3oo had his penis pointed that way, [just ready to enter].

Teebe, bíh'ih he'=ce3-céno'oo-hók.[6]

Just as he did that, a deer leaped away.[7]

"Uuúh! beh'éi!"

"Ohh! Old man!"

Nih'óó3oo he'=neeseekuu-hók.

Nih'oo3oo was left behind standing there.

"No-hohookeeníit!

"How crazy I am!

"Nei-ciikóyoniihíit!

"How nosey I am!

"Nee'ees-iini hi3etí-ni'."

"Oh well, I guess it's okay for now—[maybe later]."

Notes

1. The particle *cobóu(')u(h)* means 'no way, it can't be.'

2. The pitch pattern here is *híixowúh-*.

3. The proclitic yohuh=4 AFF inflection means 'supposedly, but not really'. It is used in sarcastic expressions such as 'you're supposed to be so . . . [but you're not really . . . at all]'.

4. The form *tebi3-íse'* is verbal, 'it has had the top cut off'. The form *tebi3-ixoo* is a derived nominal form, 'object that is the result of cutting the top off'.

5. *Hi3í=* is used here in the archaic sense of 'if [potentially]' or contrary-to-fact. This usage is well documented in the early 1900s translation of the Gospel of Luke. The form used for 'have a vagina' is not recognized with that meaning by modern consultants and appears to be either a slang or joke word. *Céy-oox* means 'a deep hole'. Cf. II *cey-oxesnoo-* 'to be deep mud'; and *tonoox-ohei* AI.O 'dig a round hole by instrument'; *noox-citii-* AI.T 'dig a hole in the ground by hand', with noninitial form *-oox*.

6. Kroeber records *cešcéno'oo-* rather than *ce3céno'oo-*.

7. The white-tailed deer, in particular, is believed to turn into a woman. If a man falls for this deer woman (which always turns back to a deer at the last minute), then he will go crazy. It is said that the deer *he'ih-'inéniiwóón-e'* 'drove the man out of his mind'.

Nih'oo3oo and Whirlwind Woman

Teller unknown, no date (but other texts from the
same MS dated July 1926)
Collected by Truman Michelson, Charles Crispin, interpreter
NAA, MS 2994, pp. 46–48

V ersions of this story appear in Dorsey and Kroeber [1903] 1997, narratives 47 and 48. Because Michelson's manuscript gives no title, we
use the title from Dorsey and Kroeber. Whirlwind Woman is a mythological character, associated with the creation of the world and also in particular with Arapaho women's sacred quillwork (Anderson 2013). The ending of this story is quite terse but signifies that people should not get
married quickly, due purely to physical attraction, without going through
the proper period of preparation and cultural ritual—a theme of general
importance in Arapaho society (see Fowler 2010: 45–51). Furthermore, the
story suggests that a suitor should not have to talk the bride into the marriage and should be aware of fundamental differences between the part-
ners. As with all trickster stories, what happens here is exactly the opposite of what should happen in normal society. At the same time, the story
offers an etiology of divorce as an acceptable practice. Women had the
right to institute divorce in traditional Arapaho society and often did so
(Hilger 1952: 211–16).

The ending at the river echoes important mythological themes. First, the
tribe itself was once split up when some people failed to cross a river (see
"The Arapaho Migration across the Missouri River to the . . ."). Second,
crossing big rivers was seen as dangerous not only in practical terms but
because Water Monsters often dwelt there and would drown people (the
Water Monster appears in the migration story as well). Thus, Cowell suggests, in this story marriage and divorce and wives are elevated from merely
social phenomena to powerful supernatural ones, which may have implications for the larger tribe and not just the individuals involved. Recent work
by Loretta Fowler (2010) and Jeffrey Anderson (2013) underlines the powerful social and ceremonial role of Arapaho wives generally and the elder
quill workers associated with Whirlwind Woman in particular, both in

conjunction with husbands and independently of them. This story does not directly engage with all of those elements, but they are evoked and contained in the image of Whirlwind Woman, which is itself a reminder of the social and supernatural power of women. This image is discussed more fully in Anderson 2013: 112–13.

Linguistically, the second line is quite amusing in that it piles superlatives one on top of the other. The basic verb is *bébeenéíhi-* meaning 'beautiful' or in everyday modern Arapaho 'a buckskin beauty'. The addition of dubitative *he'=* and *iis-* 'how' leads to a meaning something like 'you just can't believe how beautiful she was'. The addition of the compound proclitic *koowót=* adds a further meaning of contrary to expectation or intention, as in 'he never could have imagined that there could be someone that unbelievably beautiful'. Obviously the exact translation of this extremely complex and colorful phrase is quite a challenge.

The trickster's punch line to his now ex-wife is also tricky to translate. It could be paraphrased as 'we're through, you'll have to find someone else to marry [again], but I don't think you'll find anyone to keep up with you, so you'll just have to be your own best company' or more briefly 'I doubt that *you'll* find someone else to marry you again!' The line captures the sense of the bitter failed husband, who tries to blame his wife for his failings. Of course Whirlwind Woman does not bother to reply.

Nih'óó3oo he'ih-'ités-ee hísei-n.
Nih'oo3oo came upon a woman.

Koowót=he'=íís-bebeenéíhi-n.
She was a real one-of-a-kind buckskin beauty beyond his wildest imaginings.

"Wohéi," heeh-éhk Nih'óó3oo, "neneeni-noo toh-'éso'óó-noo,
"Well now," said Nih'oo3oo, "because I'm a fast runner,

"hoot-niib-é3en," héé3-oohok Neyóóxetíísei-n.
"I'll marry you," he said to Whirlwind Woman.

"Hííko," hee3-éihok.
"No," she responded to him.

'óh he'ih-níhi'nei.
But he insisted.

"Toh-cii-beesíii-noo," nii3-éihok.
"Because I don't camp for long in any one place," she would respond
to him.

'óh he'ih-níhi'nei.
But he insisted.

"Hih'oo," hee3-eihok.
"All right," she said to him.

He'=nee'ees-nííw-oot.
And I guess that's how he came to marry her.

He'ih-koheisíhce nehe' Neyóóxetíísei.
Whirlwind Woman jumped right up.

Nih'óó3oo he'ih-'ouneetii[1] toh-'úniini-t.
Nih'oo3oo ran along beside her because she was his wife.

Kóóx=he'ih-koheisíhce.
Once again she jumped right up.

He'ih-sii'ihéíhce heebe3-niicííheh-e'.
She ran right into a great big river.

Nih'óó3oo he'ih-tou'úhce.
Nih'oo3oo stopped dead in his tracks.

"He3éb-ce'-nííbeti," héé3-oohok.
"Get married again to yourself over there," he said to her.

Nee'ei'íse-'.
That's how the story ends.

Ne'=nii'-cii-niibetíítooni-'.

That's why people don't stay married sometimes.

Note

1. *Houneetii-* AI.T 'run alongside' containing the root *hoy-* 'next to'. Cf. *hoyoku-*, 'sit next to'.

Nih'oo3oo and the Ducks

Told by Cleaver Warden, Oklahoma, July 8, 1899
Collected by Alfred Kroeber
NAA, MS 2560a, Notebook 6, pp. 27–28

This is a very rudimentary version of this common story (title supplied by the editors), more a plot summary or description of the story than an actual full recounting. It is also poorly transcribed: in some cases verbs or whole phrases seem to be missing. Despite this, it contributes to a fuller appreciation of the variations in this story. For example, this is the only version where the 'hero duck' is described as a *síisiicéhe'* 'little duck', using the diminutive. It is common in Arapaho stories of all types for heroes to be young and precocious, and these qualities are often emphasized by describing how small and inconsequential the young hero seems. Thus the use of the diminutive with the little duck serves to link him to a more general heroic motif in a way that does not occur in other versions of the story. The theme is further emphasized in this version by the fact that he is dancing *ho'oox-* 'at the end/at the edge' and also *nóko3ee* 'off to the side, out of the way', emphasizing his seemingly marginal position. This is another key motif in stories of Arapaho heroes of all genres. Thus the little duck receives much more attention even in this rudimentary telling than he does in many fuller versions.

This version does not appear in Dorsey and Kroeber, but two others do (narratives 26, 27).

Nih'óó3oo he'=hoó'eineeti3-oohók síisiik-o hot-betoóóh-oot.
Nih'oo3oo called together some ducks in order to make them dance.

Nee'ee-wóóhoyookuu-hohkóni' síisiik-o'.
The ducks all stood together in a group.

"Wohéi," Nih'oo3oo heeh-éhk.
"Okay," Nih'oo3oo said.

"Heetnii-no'uusi'óó-nee[1] beeteee-néi'i.

"You all close your eyes when you are dancing.

"Heetnii-neceí-'i nii-koonookuhcehí-3i'," heesineee-hek[2] Nih'óó3oo.

"The ones who open their eyes will die," sang Nih'oo3oo.

Heetox-ce'inéé-3i, nii-tebe'eis-eihohkóni' heh-níiséihi-ni3.

Every time he repeated his song, he cut off the head of one of them.

"Heetnii-necé-nee nii-koonookuchehí-3i'," nii-hok Nih'óó3oo.

"You will die, the ones who open their eyes," Nih'oo3oo would say.

Toh-'uuyéini-t[3] ceesé' síisiicehé' ho'óox[ohwoo-t], nóko3ee.

One little duck was still alive, dancing at the end/edge of the group, off to the side.

He'ih-cii-cíínooku'oonówoo.[4]

He did not keep his eyes down/shut [like the others].

"Hotnii-néce-no' nii-kóónookuhcehí-3i'," nii-hók Nih'óó3oo, toh-betoooh-oot síisiik-o.

"They will die, the ones who open their eyes," Nih'oo3oo would say, when he was making the ducks dance.

"Ho-nóo3ih-éibe,"[5] Nih'óó3oo heeh-éhk,

"I guess he abandoned you all," Nih'oo3oo said,

síisiicehé' ho'oox[ohwoo-t], toh-koyíh'ohukóóhu-t.[6]

when the little duck dancing at the end of the line quickly flew off and escaped.

"Howóh, he'ne'-siiyei-ní3!" Nih'óó3oo.[7]

"And he was the best one!" [said] Nih'oo3oo.

Notes

1. The manuscript has *no'uusi'éénee* rather than *no'uusi'óónee*.
2. The final *-ineee-* means 'sing'.
3. The reason for the use of *toh-* 'when, after' is unclear here.

4. *Ciinookú'oo-* literally 'keep the gaze down'; by extension 'keep eyelids down/closed'. Here the derived form *ciinookú'oo-n-owoo-* AI.SEFB means 'keep eyes closed for oneself'.

5. Kroeber gives the gloss 'you all got word of it'. The verb is unclear: we chose to assume that it is *nóo3-* TA 'abandon', but it could be *nó'o3ih-* TA 'treat harshly, cruelly, kill', in which case the gloss would be something like 'Well, I guess [the little duck] didn't do much for the rest of you [dead ones]'.

6. *Koyíh'ohu-* AI 'fly off/away', specifically in the sense of escaping from danger or evading capture. *Koyíh'ohu-kóóhu-* means 'escape by flight/fly off very quickly'.

7. *Howóh* in initial position usually expresses surprise that something is not the way it was expected to be. Thus the line could be glossed as 'and I was just so looking forward to tasting that nice little one at the end [that it turns out is gone now]!'

Nih'oo3oo and the Dancing Ducks

Told by Philip Rapid/Rabbit, Oklahoma,
August 18 and earlier, 1899
Collected by Alfred Kroeber
NAA, MS 2560a, Notebook 9, pp. 62–64, 77–82
English version published in Dorsey and
Kroeber [1903] 1997: 59–60

Numerous versions of this story have been recorded in Arapaho. This version is not particularly detailed, but it has a number of nice moments of humor, using interesting linguistic forms. The ducks, for example, get to dancing very intensely or 'furiously' (*níhi'neen-*), without realizing that Nih'oo3oo is killing them, nicely capturing their obliviousness. Once he has cooked and eaten them, he sleeps until noon 'scarcely stirring' (*howo3ínoo'oo-* means literally either 'in the process of waking up' or 'waking up quickly', so the negative of this used in the story means that he slept soundly and continuously). On waking, he thinks of cooking more for himself 'slowly and enjoyably, in a leisurely way' (*kóó'oen-*), with this mood reinforced by the reduplication *heeneesí3ecoo-* 'he was thinking this over, reflecting on it'.

Immediately after this, the mood of leisure and languor is interrupted by the use of *wot=keih-noohóót* 'he was very surprised not to see, to his consternation he did not see' *tótoos níiseti'* 'even a single one' of his pieces of meat. He is then described as *néetéteehee-*'so angry he couldn't even speak', 'beside himself with rage', or more literally 'dying from an angry heart'.

Another very humorous moment is when the bear describes his encounter with the skunk. Very detailed and relatively uncommon words are used again, often in reduplicating and polysynthetic combinations: the skunk comes out *ceecíís* 'all of a sudden, completely by surprise' and then attacks him (*kouso'óóton-*), with the verb here specifically meaning attacking in a very aggressive manner, full of fury, ready to raise hell, or, as Cowell chooses to translate for the sake of the cross-linguistic pun, 'loaded for bear'. The verb *hiisib-tée-tec-íhcehí-* means 'to bed/onto ground-REDUP-roll-quickly-', thus 'rolling rapidly all over the place on the ground'. The verb *heen-éh-i'ei-síb-etí-* means 'REDUP-wipe-face-to ground-REFL-', thus 'wiping one's face back and forth against the ground'.

This episode of the skunk and the bear, though brief, can be connected to Arapaho ceremony. In particular, the ceremonial practice of spitting on the hands, which is very common in the Sun Dance, is linked to the skunk "charging" the bear (Dorsey 1903: 17) in narrative. The act of spitting itself is rich in symbolic significance, representing such things as "information given by the Man-Above," "the breath of a person, or . . . life," and an imitation of "scattering clay to the four directions" at the time of creation (Dorsey 1903: 43). The story does not elaborate on these elements, but they are all present in the simple image of the skunk suddenly charging at the bear and spraying it.

Returning to the main events of the story, it is clear that the bear, like the ducks, is completely unwary and oblivious and falls for Nih'oo3oo's trick. The uncommon word *wo'úunénii3é'*, as explained in the notes, captures the bear's gullible and unreflective response to Nih'oo3oo's suggestions, as he figuratively 'falls right into the middle of the trap'. This is reinforced by the sarcastic comment meaning literally 'how smart the bear was!'

More subtly, Nih'oo3oo himself seems obsessed with vengeance after his ducks are stolen. This is encapsulated in the repeated occurrences of the root *no'ot/no'o3-* meaning 'a lot, intensely'. He uses the word *nó'o3ih-* 'do great harm to' on multiple occasions. He talks of *nó'oteecí-* 'a lot of snow' coming and *nó'oto'úxoo-* 'a lot of clouds building up'. Nih'oo3oo says that he must 'make it hard on' the bear (*nó'o3íton-*). It seems as if he can only think of intensity and harshness. Similarly, as explained in the notes, the reduplicated form *heenee3-* 'say over and over' occurs in multiple variants throughout the texts and further emphasizes Nih'oo3oo's obsessive nature.

Other examples include the multiple uses of the TA abstract final *-kuu3-* 'to act rapidly, strongly violently'; the AI final *-kóóhu-* 'to run'; and less common lexical items such as *nókoo3óó-* 'bitterly cold' and *céece3ó'oh* 'quick as a flash, before you know it'.

Finally, the violent intensity of the story is both underlined and ironically dissipated in the scattering flight of the wolves at the end of the story. Two similar complex polysynthetic verbs describe this: *nohk-níh'ei-ce3i-kóóhu-* 'with[food]-scatter-away-run-' and *níh'ei-nonii-koh-* 'scatter-lost/disappear-flee from-'. Similarly, the description of how the wolves *cihi'kuu3-* 'tear to little bits' the bear reinforces the same motif. Cowell suggests that *níh'ei*- 'scatter' and *cíhi'*- 'small bits/pieces' both symbolize what Nih'oo3oo's grand plans have come to, while also capturing his frantic, violently intense, and unfocused nature (and echoing the scattering escape of the ducks at the end of the first episode of the story).

Nih'oo3oo he'ih-'oowúniihísee.
Nih'oo3oo was walking downstream.

Noobéi-'i he'ih-'ités-ee síisiik-o.
On a sandbar he came upon some ducks.

"Toot=(h)éi-ihoo Nih'óó3oo?" hee3-éihok.
"Where are you going, Nih'oo3oo?" they said to him.

"Kookuyón niinixóó-ni',"[1] hee3-oohók.
"I'm just wandering around wherever," he said to them.

"Cih-betoooh-ei'ee=hi3í!" hee3-éihok.
"Maybe you could play for us so we can dance!" they said to him.

"Wohéi, wohéi!" heeh-éhk.
"Okay, okay!" he said.

He'ih-'itén-ee ho'eiího'.
He got a drum.

"Neehii3éi' heet-3i'ookuu-noo.
"I'll stand in the middle.

"Noh héti-noo'eenohwooton-íbe
"You must dance around me in a circle.

"Honóóyoo, ciibeh-koonóoku-'; toon=konoonóoku-t heet-néce-'.
"Don't you dare open your eyes; whoever opens his eyes will die.

"Hónoot hei'towuun-e3énehk, cih-nee'ee-koonookú-nee,"
hee3-eihohkóni'.
"[Wait] until I tell you, then you can open your eyes," he said to them.

He'ne'-ce3i3ohwooh-éi3i'.
Then he had them start dancing.

Hokóo3iihi' he'ih-cei'soo-nino hih-biso'oo3oo-no nehe' Nih'óó3oo.
From time to time the songs that Nih'oo3oo came up with changed.

Hokoo3iihi' he'ih-nih'ootohonkuutón-ee.[2]
He kept changing [the tunes] to make things good for them.

Toh-nosou-nihi'neenohwoo-ní3i, he'ih-nonih'ii3itón-e'.
While they were still dancing furiously, the ducks forgot about him.

He'ih-'iten heebe3í-bes.
Nih'oo3oo took a big stick.

He'ih-niito'-one3eih-ii neniitowohwoo-ní3.
First he knocked the lead dancer dead.

Béébeet he'ih-niitein-one3eih-ii.
He just knocked them dead all in a row, one by one.

'oh céése', nehe' hiitooxóhowoo-t, hé'=néhtoneih.
But one of them, the one dancing last, he was tricky/clever.

He'ih-kóónook beenihéhe' núhu'.
This one opened his eye just a little bit.

Hei'-nó'ooku-t,[3] wóów, woowuh hé'ih-niisóo' yoo3óniini' he'ih-neh'-ee núhu' síisiik-o, hee3éi'-cii-koonooku-ní3i.
When he managed to see, already, already he [Nih'oo3oo] had killed twenty-five of these ducks, all the ones who had not opened their eyes.

Nehe' nih-'itooxóhowoo-t he'ih-noohób-ee tóh-nosoun-one3eih-éini3i.
The one who was dancing last in line saw Nih'oo3oo as he was still knocking them dead.

Xonou he'ih-noh'úh'o.
Right away he flew upward.

"Nenehtonih-éinee Nih'óó3oo.
"Nih'oo3oo is tricking you.

"Nóóne3eih-íinee," hee3-oohók nehe' nih-koyíh'ohu-t.
"He's knocking you all dead," the one who had flown away said to them.

Hee3éi'-wonoh-'úune'ítii-ni3i, hee3ei'-ci'íisisí-'i
he'ih-behí-koyih'ohú-no'.
All the ones who were still alive, all the ones who were left, all flew
away and escaped.

Benii'ón-nee'eesi-niiyei-hohkóni'.[4]
They escaped with their lives thanks to the fact that the one duck
happened to open his eye at the right moment.

Xonóu he'né'-wo'oten-óot hih-noxowoh-éeeno.
Right away he [Nih'oo3oo] gathered up the ones he had killed.

Toh-'uusi-wo'otén-oot, he'ne'-beh-ko'e3éin-oot.
After he had finished gathering them up, he cut them all open.

Tih-'iis-kó'e3éin-oot, hé'ih-see-se'és-ii.
When he had finished cutting them open, he sliced the meat flat.

He'ne'-ouutéyoonée-t.
Then he hung the meat to dry.

Heh-niisi-ní3i he'ih-'óókouh.
He cooked two of them for himself.

Toh-'ótoow-oot, he'ne'-no'uyóóhu-t.
After he ate them up, then he got his bed ready.

Xonóu he'ih-cesis-nóko.
Right away he went to sleep.

He'ih-cii3o'-owo3inoo'oo hónoot he'ih-'éyeih-koh'uusiiní-n.
He never even stirred until it was almost noon.

Xonóu toh-'owóto'oo-t, "'oh heetih-kóó'een-ookouhú-noo,"
heeneesi3ecoo-hók.

Right away after he woke up, "I should cook some more for myself, nice
and slow," he thought to himself.

'ohwóo' wóx-uu he'ih-cih-'otoowúún-e'.

But then a bear had come over and eaten up his food.

He'ih-yii3é'ein nih-'iitoh-'óuuteyoonee-t.

He looked over there to where he had hung up the meat to dry.

Wot=keih-noohóót[5] tótoos niisetí-ni' hoséino'.

He was stunned to see not even a single piece of meat.

He'ih-'eyeih-neetíteehee toh-'ebiitebée-t hit-oséinóu.

He was almost beside himself with rage because his pieces of meat had
been stolen from him.

"Hóéii, toon=no-otni-ites-éiit, níito' heet-nééni-t ne-ebiiteb-eiit,"
heeh-ehk nehe' Nih'óó3oo.

"Hey, whoever meets up with me, the first one will be the one who
robbed me," said Nih'oo3oo.

"Heih=neniinook toon=nehe' ne-ebiitookob-eiit."

"Let him become blind who stole my meat from me."

Hiitouuk he'ih-'ités-e' heebe3i-wóx-uu.

And sure enough a big bear came along and met him.

"Hóó3o' biiti' heet-no'o3ih-é3en," heeneesi3ecooton-oohok, tih-'ites-éit
núhu' wox-úu.

"Now it's my turn to harm you," he was thinking with regard to the
bear, when this bear met up with him.

'oh he'ih-neniinóok nehe' wox.

And this bear was blind.

"Wohéi, toot=(h)éi-ihoo?" hee3-oohók.

"Well, where are you going?" Nih'oo3oo said to him.

"Ooo, niiyohóu-' niisi-xóuuwúsee-noo," hee3-éihok.

"Oh, there's no way for me to walk a straight path," the bear said to him.

"Ko(o)-ot-cii-cih-'ówouunon?" heenee3-éihok.

"Could you please take pity on me?" the bear pleaded to him.[6]

"Nohowóh[7] he-ih-tous-neníinook?" hee3-oohók.

"Now how did you get to be blind?" Nih'oo3oo said to him.

Noh, "Nih'ii-3éi'einí-noo nuhu' nih-ko'eitonotí-', tih-'ésinéé-noo.

And [he said], "I put my head inside this round hole since I was hungry.

"'oh céeciís heh-cih-bís-kóuso'óoton-éinoo xouhu'.

"But I was surprised by a skunk that appeared and came at me 'loaded for bear.'

"Xonóu heh=cih-césis-woxu'óotii-t nesíisei.

"Right away he sprayed his medicine in my eyes.

"Xonóu heh=césis-nih'oo'óú-'u.

"Right away they surely did start burning/stinging.

"Ne'-íisib-tée-tecihcehí-noo.

"Then I lay down and desperately rolled all around.

"Nih-'een-éhi'eisibetí-noo.

"I rubbed my face all over on the ground.

"Konoonooku-nóóni, nih-nih'óó'ou-'u nesíisei," hee3-éihok.

"Whenever I opened my eyes, they burned/stung," the bear said to Nih'oo3oo.

"Wohéi cih-3ookúh-u!

"Well, follow me!

"Hootne-e'ineexoh-é3en," hee3-oohók núhu' wóx-uu.

"I'll guide you around," he said to the bear.

"Heh=síiyeih=hoot-nó'o3oo-' híni' no'oto'úxoo-'.
"There will be a really terrible storm from those thick clouds building up.

"Hihíi3iihi' nenéb-e' hoot-no'otéeci-'.
"There will be a lot of snow from the north.

"Hiit 3ei'is[ii] núhu' heetoh-co'ooyeitei'-i béx-o noh woxú'-uno.
"Go inside here where sticks and grass are piled up.

"Heet-néi'-kotoyoh-u3en.
"I'll cover you up nice and tight.

"He-ebeh-totóuutoo,[8] toh'et-no'o . . . toh'et-nókoo3oo-'."
"You might really have a hard time of it otherwise, because . . . because it's supposed to be bitterly cold."

Wo'uunénii3e' he'ih-3ei'iní[s] néhe' wox.[9]
The bear went right straight inside there.

Toh-'úus-nei'-kotoyoh-uut, "Ciibeh-noh'oówusíi."
After he had covered him up nice and tight, "Don't move around!" [he said to him].

"Xonóu nókohu.
"Go to sleep right away.

"He-etn-eihoowu-tóe," hee3-oohók.
"You won't be cold," he said to him.

Xonóu he'ne'-nóóh'-o' núhu' woxú'-uno noh bexóh'-o nooxutootée-ní'i.
Then right away he set fire to the grass and little sticks lying right up closest against the bear.

Céece3ó'oh wot=hih-tou3ei'e3ee.
Before you know it, what a big fire there was!

Hih-tou3e'íyei nehe' wóx!
How brilliant this bear was! [i.e., 'How dumb could it be?!']

'oh wot=héetee he'ih-'oo'éinéeti3-ée hooxéíhi-no.

And Nih'oo3oo had called together some wolves beforehand.

"Xonóu het-i3ikuu3-oobe [n]eyeih-ce3ikooh-ehk," hee3-oohók.

"Seize him right away if he tries to run away," he said to them.

"Noh hóot-koo-koh'ookéi-no', toh'et-no'o3íton-o' toh-no'o3ih-éinoo.

"And we'll split up the meat, because I should make it hard on him, because he caused me harm.

"Nih-'otóówuun-einoo not-oseinóu," heenee3-oohók.

"He ate up all my pieces of meat," he explained to them.[10]

Wot=núhu' hooxéíhi-no', nenééni-yohkóni' hih-'oonotoowuun-éiitono, koo-he-e'ín?

But in fact these wolves, they were the ones who had eaten up his meat, you know?

Toh-'e3ebi-no'oxúh'u-t néhe' wóx, xonóu he'ih-neetoxúhu'.

When the fire burned over there to where the bear was, he was immediately burned to death.

Teecixo' he'ih-kohooné'ei.[11]

The hair burned for a long time.

Hei'-beexu-ceene3ee-', xonou he'ih-wotikoohu-nó' nuhu' hooxéíhi-no'.

Once the flames had sunk down a little, right away the wolves ran into the fire.

Xonóu he'=cihi'kuu3-oohohkóni'.

Right away, they tore the bear to pieces.

Béébeet he'ih-nóhk-nih'ei-ce3ikóohu-no'; koowot=he'ih-koh'ookei.

They just ran away in every direction with the meat; Nih'oo3oo didn't get a thing.

Heenóo hiniiteh'eih-ínoo béébeet he'=nih'ei-noníikoh-oohohkóni'.[12]

As always happened, their [other wolf] friends just ran away from him in every direction.

"Cobóu-hohookéeni-n Nih'óó3oo," hee3-eihók.[13]

"No one could be as crazy as you, Nih'oo3oo," they said to him.

"Wóów níis heebiitebéé-n hot-oséinou," hee3-eihók, tih-'inowukoohu-ní3i heet-co'oo'ee-' nuhu' hooxeihi-no'.

"You've now had your pieces of meat stolen from you twice," they said to him, when the wolves were disappearing into the brush.

"Hookóh no-no'o3ih-e',[14] hookoh hoohookéeni-noo," heenee3et-ehk néhe' Nih'oo3oo.

"Maybe the reason they so abused me is because I'm crazy," Nih'oo3oo kept repeating to himself.[15]

Notes

1. Note that 1PL is used here rather than 1S—a fairly common feature in narratives (see "The Skunk and the Rabbit"). This makes the person speaking seem self-effacing—a good strategy for Nih'oo3oo in this case as he prepares his trick.

2. The element -'ootohon- is unexplained.

3. *Nó'ookú-* literally means 'his eye arrives at a place'. More loosely, he partially opens his eye so that his vision reaches the place he wants to see.

4. The MS has *eyei-* rather than *iiyei-*.

5. *Wot=keih-* forms a single unit, meaning 'very surprised not to' or more emphatically 'not a single' or 'not any at all'.

6. Literally 'said to him multiple times'.

7. The manuscript actually has *nohoowehe'* but the /we/ sequence does not occur in Arapaho within phonological words.

8. *Totóuutoo* 'have a difficult or hard time with things, be down and out'.

9. *Wo'úunénii3é'* means 'right to the center', 'right on target'. The implication is that the bear 'plunges right straight ahead' without thinking about what tricks Nih'oo3oo might be up to.

10. Literally 'said to them over and over'. Beyond simply 'explaining', the verb captures the extent to which Nih'oo3oo is obsessed with having lost his ducks and seeking vengeance, like the function of the root *nó'ot-* discussed in the introduction to this story.

11. Cf. *kohóóxoe-* II 'burn'. The form here seems to be *kohóon-é'ei-(ni?)*, burn-hair-(II?).

12. The Arapaho text actually says 'their friends'.

13. Literally 'there is no way that you can be that crazy'.

14. The verb has the NONAFF inflection *-e'*, 3/1S, thus the translation 'must be'.

15. Literally 'saying over and over'. Note that this is the third variant on reduplicated *heenee3-* 'say repeatedly' in the text.

Nih'oo3oo noh Siisiikou'uu/Nih'oo3oo and the Ducks

Told by John Goggles, Wyoming, September 23, 1910
Collected by Truman Michelson
NAA, MS 2708, 6 pp.

Many versions of this famous story have been recorded, and it is widely known by contemporary Arapahos as well as being widespread on the plains generally. Other versions are Dorsey and Kroeber narratives 26 and 27 and the two others in this volume. This version makes nice use of shifting perspectives, particularly on the race between the coyote and Nih'oo3oo. Once the race starts, we see the coyote from Nih'oo3oo's perspective 'way far away' (*beebéi'on*) 'over that way' (*hé3eb-*). The particle *wootii* 'it seems like' comically understates Nih'oo3oo's shock and dismay at seeing his opponent fit as a fiddle. The perspective then switches to the coyote, who has left Nih'oo3oo far behind him and sees him running 'this way' (*cih-* 'to point of view') but again 'way far away' (*beebéi'on*). The ironic reversal is heightened by the final view of the coyote, 'laughing it up' (*hóon-oxóoni-*), just as Nih'oo3oo was 'laughing to himself' (*hoxóoh-etí-*) earlier in the story; once again coyote is *beebéi'on* 'way far away'. Note that the narrator carefully places the word for 'way far away' in exactly the same place prior to the verb with each usage, to underline the ironic parallels. Arapaho has free word order, so this is a deliberate choice. These carefully managed reversals of perspective and ironic parallels in language are where the joke turns on the trickster. Of course, this reversal is hinted at earlier when the duck opens its eyes—there as well the perspective shifts from Nih'oo3oo's point of view to his opponent's, and the immediate result is an escape. Note that all full versions of this story feature a two-part structure, with the episode of the killing and escape of the ducks followed by a second episode that shows a great deal of variety.

130

Note also that the verb *betóooh-* literally means 'to make someone dance'. It is difficult to translate succinctly, because its actual meaning is that someone is singing and drumming in order to give someone else music to dance to. It does not include a sense of 'forcing' someone to dance. In other versions of the story, the ducks' eagerness to dance (and fall into Nih'oo3oo's trap) is underlined more clearly.

Nih'oo3oo he'ih-'oowuniihisee niicii.[1]
Nih'oo3oo was walking downstream by a river.

Noh he'ih-bii'iih-ee siisiikou'-uu.[2]
And he found some ducks.

"Wohei neiteh'eiho-ho'," hee3-oohok siisiik-o, "heet-betoooh-e3enee," hee3-oohok.
"Well, my little friends," he said to the ducks, "I'm going to put on a dance for you," he said to them.

"Hih'oo," heeh-ehkoni'.
"All right," they said.

Noh he'ne'i-cesis-betoooh-oot.
And then he started drumming so that they could dance.

Noh hee3-oohok, "Toon=nii-koonooku-3i,[3] hootnii-necenoo'oo-[t].
And he said to them, "Whoever opens his eyes will be struck dead."

Noh heecisi-betoooh-oot he'ih-niiwouh'un bes.
And as he was having them dance, he had a stick in his hands.

"No'uusi'oo-'!" hee3-oohok.
"Close your eyes!" he said to them.

He'ih'ii-noxowuh-uu.
He was knocking them dead.

Noh ceese' siisiic he'ih-koonook.
And one duck opened his eyes.

He'ih-noohob-ee tih-noxowuh-eini3.
He saw that Nih'oo3oo was knocking everyone dead.

"Heii, Nih'oo3oo he'=besiite'einei-t!" heeh-ehk ceese' siisiik-o'.
"Hey, it looks like Nih'oo3oo is striking folks on the head!" said one of the ducks.

Beenihehe' he'ih-koyih'ohu-no'.
Only a few of them managed to fly away and escape.

"Heehee," heeh-ehk Nih'oo3oo.
"Hee hee," said Nih'oo3oo.

He'ih-'eeneiten-ee.
He gathered up all the dead ones.

He'ih-'oxoohet.
He laughed to himself.

He'ne'-ce3ei'oo-t.
Then he set off.

Beenihehe' wo'wuuhu' he'ih-nooxoh biito'owu-u'.
A little bit farther [down the stream] he dug a hole in the ground.

He'ih-wotitonee toh-'ookouhu-t.
He started a fire so he could cook the ducks for his dinner.

Noh hei'-iixookouhu-t, he'ih-noohob-ee koo'ohw-uu he'ih-coo-n.
And once he had gotten his dinner all cooked to perfection, he saw a coyote coming this way.

He'ih-'ites-e' noh hee3-eihok, "Nih'oo3oo, nih-niitobee-noo heso'oo-ninehk," hee3-eihok.
The coyote came along and said to him, "Nih'oo3oo, I heard that you're a fast runner," it said to him.

"Heetih-nonouhti-no'," hee3-eihok.
"Let's have a race," the coyote said to him.

"Hee," hee3-oohok.
"Yes," said Nih'oo3oo to the coyote.

"Neneeni-noo ceni'eihi-noo," heeh-ehk koo'oh.
"I'm lame," said the coyote.

"Ne-ihoowu-nihi'koo," hee3-eihok.
"I can't run," it said to him.

He'ne'i-nonouhtiiw-oot.
Then Nih'oo3oo was ready to race him.

Noh yein he'ih-neyei3ei.
And he counted to four.

"Ceesey niis neeso yein," he'ih-cesisihcehi-no'.
"One two three four," and off they went.

Noh koo'oh *beebei'on he'ih-'e3eb*koo.
And the coyote was running way out ahead over there.

Wootii he'ih-cii-kohtobee!
It seemed like he didn't have anything wrong with him at all!

He'ih-noo3ib-ee.
He left Nih'oo3oo behind.

Nih'oo3oo *beebei'on he'ih-cih*-3ookkoo.
Nih'oo3oo was running after him way far away back there.

Noh nehe' koo'oh he'ih-konoh-'iisiiten-ee siisiik-o.
And this coyote got every last one of the ducks.

He'ih-nohk-ce3koo.
He ran off with them.

Noh Nih'oo3oo he'ih-cii-bii3ih.

And Nih'oo3oo didn't get any dinner.

Koo'oh *beebei'on* he'ih-seh-'*oxoon*.

Coyote was laughing it up way far away over there.

Nee'ei'ise-'.

That's how the story ends.

Notes

1. One would expect locative *niiciihehe'*.

2. This text uses the archaic singular *siisiic* for 'duck' and archaic plural *siisiik-o'*. The archaic plural has become the modern singular, with a reformed modern plural *siisiikou'-uu*. The manuscript is ambiguous, however, in that in two locations Michelson records *siisiiku'(u)*. He often records final devoiced vowels after glottal stops and sometimes records /u/ for /o/, so we assume that the form is intended as *siisiiko'*, in line with the other unambiguous cases of that in the manuscript.

3. The manuscript has *too3-* rather than *toon-* here.

Nih'oo3oo and the Bears

Told by Benejah Miles, Oklahoma, July 15, 1899
Collected by Alfred Kroeber
NAA, MS 2560a, Notebook 3, pp. 35–37

The title here was supplied by the editors. In Arapaho stories Nih'oo3oo is always tormenting bears, who often appear as hapless victims. This story is interesting in the way it personalizes the bears. The female bears are *woxúúsei* 'bear women' and later are simply called *húseino'* 'women'; and the cubs are not *wóxuusóóno'* 'young bears' but rather *hi-níisóóno* 'his/her child', a word normally used for humans. When they discover that their children have been killed, the bear women do not 'howl' or 'growl' as animals normally do (*niitóuuhu-* AI), but rather 'yell' or 'scream' (*néeneyéit-* TI), in a specifically human way. This does not make the bears more sympathetic characters, however. Rather, it works ironically to underline the great distance between their gullible and slow-witted bear behavior and the words used to describe them as 'persons'. Thus the comic nature of the narrative is increased, and the bears are all the funnier because of their immense *lack* of human ingenuity.

Note also the focus on the bears' appetite as their downfall—they rush off to get berries, leaving their children behind, and then keep eating and eating rather than checking on the children when they return. Finally, the concluding wordplay further mocks the bears: from the participle *heteiné3oó* 'the specific noise that is being made by someone' Nih'oo3oo creates the unique NA agent form *heteine3ééhii* 'one who makes that specific noise'. Not only is the word comically bizarre, but his answer to 'who is making that noise?' is 'the ones who make that noise are making that noise'. Nih'oo3oo is the arch inventor in this narrative, always "cooking things up" (including the bears themselves at the end), but all his inventions are either lies or meaningless and empty (like the hole where he is supposedly located).

Nih'oo3oo he'=hoowuniihisee-hek.
Nih'oo3oo was going downstream.

Níiinon he'=hootee-'éhk.
There was a tipi set up.

He'ih-cíitei.
He went inside.

Woxúúsei-no' hiniisoon-ínoo he'ih-níi-niitokúb-eeno'.
Some bear women were sitting with their children.[1]

"Neh-won-ko'úyei-'; beesibi-no wonoo3ei-'i," hee3-óóhok.
"You'd better go pick berries; there are a lot of plums," he said to them.

"Nóó-noo3-e' heniisóó-no'."
"Leave all your children here with me."

He'ne'-tee-tebe'eis-oot hiniisoon-ínoo.
Then he cut off their children's heads.

He'ne'-céenóutii-t neeneecihiit-óno.[2]
Then he hung the heads back down in the rocking cradles.

Neene'-sii'ihéitón-oo[t][3] woxúúsei-no hiniisoon-ínoo.
He boiled the bear women's children for them.

He'ih-no'úsee-no' nuhu' woxúúsei-no'.
The bear women arrived back.

"Ciibeh-'iten-e' heníisoon-ínoo," hee3-óóhok.
"Don't go get your children," he said to them.

"Niito'-uusi-bii3ihi-'.
"Finish eating first.

"Hi3=het-won-eenéiten-oobe heniisoon-ínoo, hiisi-bii3ihí-neehek."
"You must go get your children later, after you have finished eating."

He'ih-'eyein-otoowoo-no'.
They had almost eaten their food up.

Nih'oo3oo he'ih-seh-yihoo.
Nih'oo3oo went off over there.

He'ih-ceniikóó.
He ran a long way away.

"Keih-nehtiicow-oobe heniisoon-ínoo?
"Did you recognize the taste of your children?

"Nih-sii'iheiton-e3énee."[4]
"I boiled them for you."

He'ih-neeneyeit-owuu hisei-no'.
The women were screaming/yelling.

He'ne'í-yeihon-oo3i'.
Then they chased after him.

"Heih=tonot hehkuhnee-noo," heeh-ehk Nih'oo3oo.
"I wish there was a hole where I'm fleeing," said Nih'oo3oo.

He'ih-tonotí-n.
There was a hole.

He'ih-3ei'íhce.
He jumped inside it.

He'ih-xook-tónoti-n.
It was a tunnel.

He'ih-nouuhce.
He came out the other end.

He'ih-kó'ookunéibitoo.[5]
He stuck something on his face so that it looked like he had only one eye.[6]

He'ih-cih-bisís.
He appeared back this way.

He'ih-'ités-ee nuhu' huséi-no.
He came upon these women.

"Heeyou?" hee3-oohok.
"What is it?" he said to them.

Noh "Nih'oo3oo 3eneiikoh-eino'ohk héet-tonoti-ni'.
And "Nih'oo3oo appears to have escaped from us inside a hole.

"Neníísoo-no' nee-néeton-eino'.
"He killed all our children.

"Ne'-3eiisee-t.
"Then he went inside the hole.

"He'i=koo-kou'einet.
"Apparently he scratched up his face.

"He'ih-cih-ce'i-nóe."
"Apparently he came out again."[7]

"3éneiisi-', ciitei-'!" hee3-oohok.
"He's inside there, go in!" he said to them.

He'ne'-ciitei-3i'.
Then they went inside.

He'ne'-wotitónee-[t] heet-tónotí-ni'.
Then he set fire to the place where the hole was.

"Cobou'u heteine3oo?"[8]
"Who could possibly be making a noise like that?" [the bears said].

"Heteine3eehii-ho' ceebih'ohu-3i'."
"Noise-making birds are flying past," [he said to them].

He'ih-nee-neetookuuh-úu.
He caused them all to be cooked to death.[9]

Notes

1. Kroeber translates the verb as 'nursing'.
2. *Nééneecihíít* is a children's swing in modern Arapaho.
3. Kroeber transcribes only *-oo*.
4. The manuscript has final *-noo* rather than *-nee*.
5. *Ko'ookún-eibitoo* AI.SELFB = one eyed-stick/attach s.t. inanimate to self.
6. This is a sly allusion to the fact that one of Nih'oo3oo's other names (or other variants) is One-Eyed Sioux.
7. This is why Nih'oo3oo stuck something (probably mud) over his face and one eye—to cover up the scratch and disguise himself.
8. *Hetéínetii-* AI.T 'make a specific noise' > NI.DEPPART *heteiné3oó* 'the specific noise [s.o.] is making'. *Cobóú'u(h)* means 'there is no way, it can't be, it's not possible'. Thus the whole sentence reads most literally 'there is no way someone could be making a noise like that', with the implication that 'there's no way someone could be making a noise like that without it being a bad thing for us'. Kroeber translates this as 'who is making that noise?'
9. Kroeber glosses 'he smoked them to death inside'.

Nih'oo3oo Sharpens His Leg and Dives on the Ice

Told by Philip Rapid/Rabbit, Oklahoma, August(?) 1899

Collected by Alfred Kroeber

NAA, MS 2560a, Notebook 6, pp. 47–54

English version published in Dorsey and Kroeber

[1903] 1997: 112–13

This trickster narrative focuses very heavily on one key element of Nih'oo3oo's behavior—his constant desire to imitate power that he sees in others and, ideally, to exceed them. He is always acquisitive and always in competition with others; but his vision and learning are imperfect and cursory and his imitation is unknowing and simple-minded.

The element of imitation in the story is very clear—the two visitation scenes include many word-for-word parallels (italicized in the Arapaho); the language of the story itself verbally enacts the imitative, repetitive desire of the trickster. The final scene, where the visitor comes outside (*no'óéhi-*) Nih'oo3oo's tipi to save him, serves as an explicit ironic reversal of the course of the two preceding visitation scenes, in which it is the host who goes outside (*no'óéhi-*) to exercise his power. Another subtle moment of irony involves the fact that the friend is 'still' (*nosou-*) (carefully, completely) sharpening his leg when Nih'oo3oo sees him, while Nih'oo3oo is 'still' (*nosou-*) being dragged around by the buffalo, with his leg stuck in it, when the friend sees him at the end of the story.

The element of vision is also central (key words are boldfaced in Arapaho). Nih'oo3oo's curiosity is underlined by his secretly watching (*hííbineen-*) what his host does. Note that he merely 'sees' (*nóóhow-*). The host's superior powers are underlined specifically in visual terms. He 'catches sight of' Nih'oo3oo (*hihco'óóton-*), a verb often used to describe scouts or soldiers seeing an enemy or a hunter seeing game. The host then tells Nih'oo3oo 'carefully and properly' (*bebíis-*) to watch and 'learn completely' (*hiix-* PERFECTIVE), for himself (*-owoo*) how to do things. The entire verb, *bebíisiixoohóótowoo-*, serves to encapsulate the moral lesson of the narrative.

Along with this verb, the narrative also features another long and complex polysynthetic form at the culminating moment—a common feature of Arapaho storytelling. That verb is *nosóú-hiin-itoo3-kóóhu-uh-* 'still-aimless-drag-run-CAUSATIVE-', 'causing him to still be dragged all over at a run'. As noted, the verb is doubly effective because the element *nosou-* 'still' recalls an earlier moment in the story.

Finally, in terms of structure, note that the narrator commonly uses *toh'uus-*, *tih'iis-*, and *hei'iis-*, all perfective forms meaning roughly 'once [this had happened]', to initiate new segments of narration.

In summary, this story's power rests for the most part not in the use of unusual or colorful descriptive terms (unlike Dorsey and Kroeber narrative 114, for example). Rather, its effects are based on a plainness and relative flatness of description, with a large amount of exact repetition from scene to scene. This makes the few uses of descriptive adverbs and adjectives (such as 'secretly' looking, or 'still' sharpening his leg) stand out all the more. Similarly, when the complex polysynthetic forms ('dragged around all over running' and 'look properly and completely for yourself') do occur, they stand out clearly. Through their linkage to other words and themes in the text ('still', 'vision') they have an even more powerful comic or moral effect.

The second part of the text is a version of a narrative often told alone (see Michelson, Dorsey, and Kroeber narrative 58). It follows the same patterns and rhetorical style as the first part of the text, so we leave it to the reader to search out these patterns. In NAA, MS 2560a, Notebook 10, p. 9 (verso) Kroeber records the following notes about either this story or another version of it. They illustrate that the interpretations that consultants provided around 1900 are quite complex and also virtually impossible to derive from the explicit contents of the narratives. Of course, such interpretations would have varied from consultant to consultant, but the one below (exactly reproducing his orthography and punctuation) illustrates the kind of interpretive traditions that accompanied the actual "texts" and to a great extent are now lost:

> The white man is the creator [beehiniiheneiht "the owner of all," also gives "boss," "maker of all"]. The story about the diving through ice is about bald-headed eagle. He had a tent which was black in the middle, + white above + below, + the whistling he does is the cry of eagle [as in mescal]; he sits in a dead elm tree + dives for beaver. Wh. Man dived from cottonwood instead.
>
> Wh. Man is the creator and father. He tries the various powers of animals, wants to learn; though fails; he is pitied + restored to life by bird; but he really gets the best in the end, for he gets the food; he learns the power of the bird; + he becomes the bird, in the sky; the eagle becomes [and] remains man below.

"The eagle really was a man and not a bird." [the creator becomes the worshipped bird; the man becomes man; the wh. man thus gets the faculty wh. the other loses]

Nih'óó3oo he'ih-ceitóón-ee hiniiteh'éi-ho.
Nih'oo3oo visited his friend.

Tih-'e3eb-*no'úsee-t*, "Wúukohei, wúukohei," hee3-eihok hiniiteh'éi-ho.
When he arrived over there, "Welcome, welcome!" said his friend to him.

"Wohéi bé, neeníh'ee-3i'oku-n híit," hee3-eihok.
"Well, friend, have a seat here," his friend said to him.

He'ne'-*no'oehi*-ní3.
Then the friend went outside.

He'ne'i-híibineen-**oonoyoohów**-oot.
Then Nih'oo3oo secretly watched him.

He'ih-**noohób**-ee toh-nosóu-*toxu'oh*-owuní3[1] *hí'oo3*.
He saw him occupied in sharpening his leg.

Tih-'iis-toxu'óh-o' hí'oo3, kookón *he'ih-no'o'ús*.
After he had finished sharpening his leg, he just went wandering out away from camp.

Heneecée-no hé'ih-'ííso'on-ee.
He flushed out some buffalo bulls.

"Hoei, hoei, hoei, hoei," heeh-éhk nehe' honóh'oe.
"Hoei, hoei, hoei, hoei," this young man said.[2]

He'ih-*tó'oxon-ee* heh-niiseihi-ni3.
He kicked one of them.

He'ih-'one3ei'on-ee.
He kicked it down dead.

Ceexoon he'ne'-yih'óón-oot.
Then he pursued another one.

Koox=he'ih-'one3ei'-ee.
Once again he kicked it down dead.

Beebéet núhu' niis-one3ei'ón-oot, he'i=nee'éesitoo-t hónoot he'ih-
yoo3on-iisibíh-ei'i.[3]
Just this way in which he was kicking them down dead, he did that until
he had brought down five of them.

He'ne'-ce'í-coo-t.
Then he came back.

Toh-'úus-ceníihei'i-t, he'ih-'iiyéíh-ee hiniiteh'éi-ho.
After he had finished butchering them, he offered his friend Nih'oo3oo
a feast.

    Toh-'úus-bii3íhi-t, nehe' Nih'óó3oo he'=nee'ée-heecikóóhu-t.
    After he had finished eating, then Nih'oo3oo was about to go home.

"Wohéi be," heeh-éhk nehe' Nih'óó3oo, "biiti' hetí-coo neyeih'-é'."
"Well, friend," said Nih'oo3oo, "now it's your turn to come to my lodge
sometime later."

    Wóotii toh-'oote'éin,[4] he'=nee'ée-3ebísee-t néhe' hinén.
    Well, sometime soon after, then this man went over there to
    Nih'oo3oo's lodge.

Toh-cih-*no'úsee-t* hiniiteh'éi-ho híyeih'-ín, "*wohéi, wohéi, wohéi, wohéi,
wohéi, wohéi bé*, ceenóku," hee3-oohok hiniiteh'éi-ho.
When his friend arrived at his lodge, "Well well well well well well,
friend, sit down," Nih'oo3oo said to him.

"*Wohei be*," heeh-éhk néhe' Nih'óó3oo, "*neeníh'ee-3i'óku-n hiit.*"
"Well, friend," said Nih'oo3oo, "have a seat here."

"Hoot-cih-ce'-ciitéi-noo," heeh-éhk.
"I will come back in here," he said.

Toh-'uus-*no'oehi*-t, he'ne'-ceenóku-t.
After he went outside, then he sat down.

Xonou[5] he'ih-césis-*toxu'oh hi'oo3.*
Right away he started sharpening his leg.

Tíh-'iis-toxu'óh-o', he'ne'-no'o'úsee-t.
After he finished sharpening it, then he went out of the camp.

He'ih-'íiso'ón-ee heneecee-no.
He flushed up some buffalo bulls.

Heh-níiseihi-ní3 he'ih-ko'ooyei'ón-ee.
He cut one out from the herd.

"Hoei hoei hoei hoei hoei hoei," heeh-éhk nehe' Nih'óó3oo.
"Hoei, hoei, hoei, hoei, hoei, hoei," said Nih'oo3oo.[6]

He'né'-*tó'oxon*-oot.
Then he kicked it.

Heh-níiseihi-ní3 núhu' toh-to'oxon-óot, he'ih-coon-koyei'íhce.
This one that he kicked, he couldn't pull out his leg.

He'ne'i-hiinítoo3koohuuh-éit.
Then it ran, dragging him all over the place.

Wóotii toh-koutonéíhi-t, "Yeh, hííwo' neiteh'ei, he'=ih-'iisitóó-3i!"[7]
hee3-éihok hiniiteh'ei-ho.
I guess because he was taking a long time, "Gee! I wonder what in the heck my friend has done!" his friend said about him.[8]

He'ne'-*nó'oehi*-ni3.
Then he went outside.

He'ih-**'ihco'ootón**-e', toh-nosóun-iinítoo3koohuuh-éit henéécee-n.
He caught sight of Nih'oo3oo, whom the buffalo bull was still dragging all over the place as he ran around.

Benii'ó[n]-eh-koyein-eihok[9] hiniiteh'éi-ho.
Luckily his friend went over there to pull out his leg.

Toh-'úus-koyein-éit, "Wohéi kóokon cih-**bébiis-iixoohóótowoo**," hee3-éihok hiniiteh'éi-ho.
After he had finished pulling his leg out, "Well, just watch carefully and learn for yourself," said his friend to him.

Wóotii toh-'uus-iixoohóo3ih-éit, kóox=he'ih-yoo3on-iisibéi-n.
After the friend had showed Nih'oo3oo how it worked, the friend put down five more [buffalo].

Noono'éet[10] he'='íiyeih-éihok hiniiteh'éi-ho.
His friend ended up providing him with food, rather than how it was supposed to be.

Hei'-íisi-bii3ihi-3i',[11] he'né'-no'oehi-ni3 hiyeih'-é'.
After they had eaten, then his friend left the tipi to go back to his lodge.

"Wohéi bé, biiti' hetí-coo," hee3ee-téhk nehe' Nih'óó3oo.
"Well, friend, now it's your turn to come to my place," Nih'oo3oo was told.

Wóotii bééxu-hóo3iihi', he'né'-yihóo-t hiniiteh'éi-ho.
I guess a little later, then he went over to his friend's.

"Wohéi cebísee bé," hee3ée-tehk.
"Well, walk on in, friend," he was told.

Toh-'úus-ceenóku-t, "3íh=cih . . . . 3ih=ceiten-ín biií-no'," hee3-oohok hiníin nehe' honóh'oe.
When Nih'oo3oo has sat down, "Why don't you . . . why don't you bring me some feathers?" said the young man to his wife.

He'=iis-iixów-nooxutóxu-no' biií-no'.
The feathers must have been right on top of the pile.[12]

"Wohéi 3íh=cih-ceiten-óo ho'óeet?"
"Well, why don't you bring my white paint here?"

He'ih-biín-e' hiníín.
His wife gave it to him.

"Wohéi cih-'íten-oo nót-ooxuu3icihiit," heeh-éhk, "noh ci'=ne-niitóu3oo."
"Well, get my shoulder belt for me," he said, "and my whistle too."

He'ih-biín-e'.
She gave it to him.

Toh-'uús-wóxesii-t, noh tih-'iis-ciito'ón-oot[13] be3é'i-no,
After he had painted ceremonially, and after he had put on wings,

he'né'-niisóho'-noehi-3i' hiniiteh'éi-ho.
then they both left the tipi, his friend and Nih'oo3oo.

He'ih-no'éeteisee-no'.
They went to the river.

He'ih-ko'ei-tónot wo'ów-u'.
There was a round hole in the ice.

"Wohei cih-'iixoohóotowoo kóókon bé," hee3-éihok hiniiteh'éi-ho.
"Well, just learn it by watching me, friend," his friend said to Nih'oo3oo.

He'ne'-cesis-3i'ookuu-ní3 hohóot-in.
Then he set off to where a tree was standing.

He'ih-nonouyookúu-ni3.
The tree was bent over [out over the water].

Yoo3ón he'ih-nebihce.
He motioned ceremonially four times, until he reached the fifth time.[14]

He'ih-ciitoo-níitouu3éi.
He blew on his whistle.

Koonow-nebíhcehí-3i, noh ci'=he'ih-noh'óówu3e'ineekóo.
Every time while he was motioning ceremonially, he flapped his wings.

Toh-yoo3oní'owoo-ni-', hé'ne'-cénonebeh'éee-t.[15]
When he got to the fifth time, then he plunged in headfirst.

He'ih-nohku-bíxouus nówo'-uu noh síisiik-o.
He appeared again above the water with some fish and ducks.

Nee'ees-iiyeih-oohók hiniiteh'éi-ho.
That's how his friend provided Nih'oo3oo with food.

Hei'-íis-**eeneiso'oo**-3i',[16] he'ne'-kohéi'i-t néhe' Nih'óó3oo.
Once they were satisfied, then Nih'oo3oo stood up.

"Wohéi bíiti' hetí-coo néyeih'-e'," hee3-oohok hiniiteh'éi-ho.
"Well, now it's your turn to come to my lodge," he said to his friend.

Koox=he'=íitox-úuus, he'ne'-bíiti'-ceitóón-oot híniiteh'éi-ho.
Once again, after a few days, then in his turn his friend went to visit Nih'oo3oo.

Nehe' honóh'oe tih-'é3ebi-no'usee-t hiyéih'-in,
When the young man arrived over there at Nih'oo3oo's lodge,

"Wúukohei wúukohei wúukohei wúukohei wúukohei wúukohei, cebísee be," heeh-éhk néhe' Nih'oo3oo.
"Welcome welcome welcome welcome welcome welcome, walk on in, friend," Nih'oo3oo said.

Toh-'uus-iicooh-óot hiniiteh'éi-ho,
After he had given his friend a pipe to smoke,

"3ih=betébi, ceíten-in né-biii-no', ne-níitou3oo noh ho'éeet, noh not-ooxúu3icihíit."
"Hey, old woman, bring me my feathers, my whistle and white paint, and my shoulder belt," [Nih'oo3oo said].

"Tóót=heinóotee-no?"
"Where is it all at?" [his wife asked].

"Nii-cii-bíi'iní-'i hei-niistootiw-ó," hee3-éihok hiníín néhe'
Nih'óó3oo.
"Your things aren't to be found," his wife said to Nih'oo3oo.

"Hiineenoxúhu! Niicíb-e' nóo-notin-ín!
"Hurry the heck up! Look around in back of the tipi for it!

"Néhe' yohóu=césoneih," hee3-oohok hiníín.
"I can't believe how uncooperative she is," he said about his wife.

Hooníi wóotii toh-bee3i-bii'iitii-ní3[17] hi-tonóunoo-no.
After a long time I guess she finally finished locating all his things.

Toh-behis-cii3ibii-t, hé'ne'-niiso'-no'éeteisee-3i' hiniiteh'éi-ho.
Once he had put everything on, then they both went down to the river,
his friend and he.

"Wohei bíiti', cih-'esóóhow-u bé," hee3-oohók hiniiteh'eí-ho.
"Well, now it's your turn, watch me here, friend," he said to his
friend.

He'ne'-koo'éé-teexóuuhu-t hohóot-in.
Then he slowly and carefully climbed up on top of a tree.

He'ih-nonóusine-n.
It was bent over [the water/ice].

He'ne'-césis-beebe3itoo-t.[18]
Then he started doing just as the friend had done.

He'íh-níitouu.
He whistled.

Konowuúhu' nii-noh'oowu3e'ineekooh-éhk.
At the same time, he was flapping his wings.

Kónow-niitóuu3eí, he'ih-nebíhce.

Each time while he was whistling, he motioned ceremonially as if to complete his action.

Wóów yoo3ón.

Now it's the fifth time.

Toh-niitootoxú'owoo-ni', he'ne'-nebeh'éee-t.

When it was the sixth time, then he plunged in headfirst.

Koox=he'ih-cebitoo néhe' Nih'oo3oo.

Yet again Nih'oo3oo had overdone it.

Toh-ko'úsi-' wo'ów-u', wo'úu-ceecii3owu', koh'e'éisíbee-t.

When he landed on the ice, he had not paid the slightest attention to what he should be doing, and he cracked his head open.

"Ne-ih-cii-nihii3-óo? koox=heesitoo-hok!" hee3-éihok hiniiteh'éi-ho.

"Didn't I tell him? Yet again he's done it!" his friend said about him.

Hoonii wóotii he'ih-'eecohoxúuh-e'.[19]

After a long time I guess his friend got him feeling better again.

Toh-'úus-ce'-e'ínooti-t, koox=he'ne'-bebiixoohoo3ih-eit hiniiteh'éi-ho.

Once he had regained his senses, then once again his friend showed him the right way to do it.

Kóóx=noono'éet he'ih-'iiyéíh-e' hiniiteh'éi-ho.

Yet again his friend ended up providing for Nih'oo3oo rather than the reverse.

Notes

1. Kroeber transcribes *toxu'owohu-*, but he must have intended *toxu'ohowu-*. The element *nosou-* 'still' here suggests slow and careful sharpening—something that Nih'oo3oo seems to fail to do.

2. The word used here, said four times, is used ceremonially in Arapaho (primarily in the Sun Dance) as both a greeting prior to asking for help and an expression of thanks. The

Arapaho AI verb *bíinonee-* means 'to say *hoei* four times, as a ceremonial action', illustrating the importance of this word and act.

3. *Hiisibih-* TA 'put down by shooting, shoot down'. The modern form is *híisiw-*.

4. *Hooté'ein* 'sometime soon after'. This word is used primarily or almost exclusively in Oklahoma, at least in this usage. Among modern Northern Arapahos, it has the more restricted meaning 'later, at some point [something will happen], and we hope you can be there/now at least you know about it'.

5. *Xonóu* 'right away' emphasizes Nih'oo3oo's haste (in contrast to his host, who apparently took a long time carefully sharpening his leg).

6. Note that Nih'oo3oo exceeds the normal four times that *hoei* is said.

7. *He'* = DUBIT plus *–ih-* PAST 'I wonder what he did' (note ITER inflectional suffix *-3i*). This looks like narrative past tense *he'ih-*, but the iterative inflection shows that it is actually dubitative past.

8. Note that unlike Nih'oo3oo, the friend feels no compulsion to see what is happening outside the tipi—thus he must say 'I wonder what is happening out there'.

9. TA *bíí'on-eh-kóyein-* 'fortuitous-from here-pull object out of s.t.-'.

10. *Noono'éet* is glossed by Kroeber as 'the opposite, the reverse'. It is not recognized today, but *nóono'óóntiini'* means 'I should have, but I didn't' or 'I should have done the opposite of what I did'.

11. The manuscript has *bii3ihi-ni'* rather than *bii3ihi-3i'*.

12. Gloss based on Kroeber. The main verb form *hiixow-nooxutoxu-* is not recognized today, though it seems to contain initial *hiix-* 'top, summit' and possibly the final *-toxu-*, related to number or quantity (cf. *héetoxú-* 'how many of them there are'). The implication is that the wife found the things right away with no trouble (contrast the behavior of Nih'oo3oo's wife later in the narrative).

13. Wings are treated as animate here—note the TA verb.

14. Kroeber corrects the meaning in the manuscript and the published translation to 'fourth' from 'fifth'. But in reality the verb *nebíhcehí-* refers to doing something four times before actually doing it the fifth time (like practicing a golf swing) for real, so the number five may be correct.

15. The same verb occurs in the name of the belted kingfisher, *níí-nebeh'éee-t* 'it dives in headfirst'. This is not an accident: other versions of the story of diving under the ice explicitly involve the kingfisher (see Dorsey and Kroeber narrative 59).

16. *Heenéisoo'óó-*, reduplicated form of *hiisoo'óó-* 'get to the point of satisfaction'. This is not used at present, but the basic root *hiix-* occurs in all modern forms of 'satisfied'. Cf. *híixowootéihi-* AI 'satisfied'.

17. The manuscript has *biicitii-* rather than *bii'iitii-*. But the former means 'bead s.t.', while Kroeber glosses the form 'found them'.

18. *Béebe3ítoo-* AI 'do it again just as before, as someone else did'. Cf. *benéebe3* 'one more time! [just like before]'.

19. *Heeceh-* 'recover health, strength, wellness' + *oxuuh-* TA final 'work on s.o.' > *heecóhoxuuh-* 'get s.o. healthy, well again by nursing, caring for'. The manuscript has *heecoxohúuh-*, but as elsewhere in this text (see note 1 above), Kroeber seems to have transposed consonants in his transcription.

Nih'oo3oo and the Coyote

Told by Philip Rapid/Rabbit, Oklahoma, August 7, 1899
Collected by Alfred Kroeber
NAA, MS 2560a, Notebook 6, pp. 24–26
English version published in Dorsey and Kroeber [1903] 1997: 56

Despite being so short, this text contains several lexical examples of features very characteristic of Nih'oo3oo: rapidity/intensity of action and violence more generally. The lexical elements expressing this include *cii-nei'éíhi-* 'unable to hold/restrain/control oneself'; *hi3kúu3-* 'seize by force, rape'; *nóxowu-* 'very, extremely, intensely'; *3óo3onóón* 'sudden surprise and disappointment' or 'of all the low-down dirty things!'; and *bis-ihcehí-noo'oo-* 'rapidly jumping into view', including both an inchoative (in process) ending *noo'oo-* and the form *ihcehí-* meaning 'run, jump, act rapidly'.

Koóx=Nih'óó3oo he'ih-'iinísee.
Yet again Nih'oo3oo was wandering around.

He'ih-noohób-ee hísei-n, tih-nosounó-oxuyei-ní3.
He saw a woman who was busy sewing.

Wot=héhnee=nih-noxoseih-éhk nehe' hiséí!
This woman sure was sexually desirable!

Nih'oo3oo he'ne'i-cenii-nei'eihi-t,[1] toh-ni'éenow-oot.
Then Nih'oo3oo could not keep control of himself, because he liked her.

He'ne'-neyeih-'i3ikuu3-oot.
Then he tried to seize her by force.

He'ih-noxowu-no'ús.
He got very close to her.

151

3óó3onoon hé'ih-bisihcehínoo'oo kóo'ohwúhu'.

Then to his great surprise and disappointment, she jumped up as a coyote.

Note

1. Normally one would expect *cenii-* only word-initially, with *cii-* after prefixes. Perhaps the speaker said *he'né'i-* then stopped and restarted as if the prefixes were not part of the word.

Nih'oo3oo Sends His Penis across the River

Told by Cleaver Warden, Oklahoma, August(?) 1899
Collected by Alfred Kroeber
NAA, MS 2560a, Notebook 6, pp. 28–32
English version published in Dorsey and
Kroeber [1903] 1997: 63–64

This text stands out for its use of what might be called "emphatic dubitative" forms. These grammatical constructions feature the dubitative markers *he'=, wot=,* and other forms that indicate both astonishment and wonder on the one hand but a sense of disbelief or exceeding of normal experience on the other. The markers all are followed by verbs that have nonaffirmative inflections (or in one case iterative inflection), all of which reinforce the sense of nonreality and uncertainly associated with the statements. Combined with the various statements meaning 'you might be lying' and 'no, I'm telling the truth' and the amusing uses of *hee* 'yes' in the hesitant sense of 'yeah, so you say, but . . .', these forms strongly reinforce the farcical, unbelievable, and over-the-top nature of the text. Examples include

he'=ii3óú'u-ni'éíhi-n 'have you ever seen one so pretty?!'
yóhou=hówootowóobéíh 'one can't imagine how wonderful this feels!'
wot=hih-tóusi-bee3íh-ee 'just see how he wants her!'
hih-tou3éí'-no'úutee 'just see how far it stretches to!'
he'=iíciteihí-3i 'how long can it be!?'

Further adding to the farcical, slapstick nature of the text are the many forms of hurrying used by the various characters—the text is a virtual dictionary of urgent commands. Examples include:

hóóho' 'hurry!'
néénowo', hiinéénowo' 'hurry, it's urgent, the situation is dangerous!'
yeeyi' 'hurry! (?)'
neníh-nehéíc 'just come here and don't think about quibbling over it!'

nóhoon-nehéic 'come here quickly!'
noxúhu 'hurry, act quickly!'
neh- 'you had better . . . !'

In Arapaho the overall effect is of a frenetic Three Stooges or Laurel and Hardy atmosphere. Note also the ironic use of 'old fellow' (*beh'ee*), as in "The Skunk and the Rabbit." Finally, Alonzo Moss noted in passing that the old stories "have real strange birds in them" and that you can tell stories are *heetéétoono* when such birds are present. Certainly the chickadee (?) in this story has its own strange experience.

Nih'oo3oo he'=no'usee-hek hiiteen.
Nih'oo3oo arrived at a camp.

He'ih-noohob-ee hisei-n, hiseitéi'yoo-n, he'=ii3óu'-ni'éíhi-n.[1]
He saw a woman, a young girl, the prettiest you've ever seen.

Wot=hih-tousi-bée3ih-éé xoo-xonou.
Well, right away, he wanted her more than anything in the world.

Nih-'iiyohou-' niis-e'inon-oohok.
But there was no way for him to make her acquaintance.

"Beh'ee,[2] neníh-nehéic!" nii3-oohok hih-noohow-óoono cese'eihíi-ho.[3]
"Old fellow, why don't you come here!" he said to all the animals he saw.

"Hoowúuni," nii3-éíhok.
"No," they said to him.

"Kon, hiiwo' cih-'íístoo-nóóni," nii-hok Nih'óó3oo.
"I wonder just what in the heck I'm going to do," Nih'oo3oo was saying.

Hó'ooto'[4] hé'ih-cebihkóókuu[5] hookuu.
Just then a mouse popped into view.

"Beh'ee, nóhoni-nehéic!" hee3-oohok Nih'oo3oo.
"Old fellow, why don't you come here!" said Nih'oo3oo to him.

"Hootn-ooxuuwutíí-n nei3oo."
"You will take my penis across the river."

"Hee, tih-'íheyoti-'."
"I hear you, but it's too heavy."

"Hííko, hii-hoowu-uhéyot!
"No, it's not heavy!

"Hiinó3oon noh hooxúuwutii-n, béh'ee."
"Instead of refusing, just take it across, old fellow."

Hookúuhuhu' ne'-ooxuuwutii-hók.
The little mouse started taking it across the river.

Neehii3éí' 3oonó'oo' he'=nohk-neetih'eb-éhk.
In the middle of the stream he was drowned with it.

"Sesiicenihiin![6] heeyeih'oow[7] béh'ee?
"Chickadee! Would you be kind enough [to help me out], old man?

"[Ne]nééni[n], howóh?
"You will do it, right?

"Hínee heetoh-ni'éihi-t hísei, het-xóuuwúxotii.
"That place where the pretty woman is, you must take it straight there.

"Beeyoo héetoh-tonoti-', heti-3eiín.
"Right where the hole is, you must put it inside there.

"Hoot-nohk-o3i'eeb-é3en."[8]
"I will pay you to do it for me."

"Hee, hé-ebeh-cií3oobei," sesiiceníhi' heeh-éhk.
"I hear you, but you might not be telling the truth," said the Greasy Bird.

"Híí3oobei-noo, beh'ée, sesiiceníhi'."
"I'm telling the truth, old fellow, little bird."

Ne'-ce3ixotii-hók Nih'oo3oo hinii3óón-in.
Then the bird set off with Nih'oo3oo's penis.

"Bééyoo[9] heetoh-tónoti-', xouuwuuhu', béh'ee.
"Right there where the hole is, straight in there, old fellow.

"Honóóyoo."
"Don't you dare [make a mistake]."

"Heehee," heeh-éhk sesiiceníhi-n.
"No problem," said the little bird.

Toh-ce3íxotii-t ho3oon,[10]
While he was carrying Nih'oo3oo's penis,

"Héii heti-nóówootóuuh.[11]
"Oh my, it's going to feel good," [Nih'oo3oo was thinking].

"Heet-[y]íis-ee3íhcehí-noo.
"I will push in that direction real quick.

"Héii kookón heet-[y]iis-éh-cii3-ciinohóu'u-noo."[12]
"Oh boy, I will just plant my seeds inside over there."

Hé'ii=nooxeihi' wó'wu-hihcebe', kon nohuusóho' . . .
I guess maybe now he was close, and then just this way . . .

"Howóh'oe, hii-hóówu-nokohú-no'," heeh-ehk sesiiceníhi'.
"Wait, [the people in the camp] are not yet sleeping yet," said the little bird.

"Wohéi wóówuh cih-'ee3íhcehi!
"Well, go ahead now, shove it on in!

"Héii yohuh=howootowobéih!"[13] heeh-éhk Nih'óó3oo.
"Ohh, this feels so good!" said Nih'oo3oo.

"Nenée-' hii3éti-', beh'ée, hei-notii3oo."
"This is the good thing, old fellow, that you've been looking for."

He'=tóo-to'oot-o'óhk hinii3óó.
He was patting his penis contentedly.

"'ií, he'ii3óú'u ne-bíisi3óó.
"Gee, there is something here that I am feeling," [said the girl].

"Hi3í=noh'ooséeyei!
"It would be good to get some light in here!

"Nooxeihi' siisiiyéi.
"Maybe it's a snake!

"Hóóho' noxúhu!" heeh-ehk nehe' hiseitéi'yoo.
"Oh my gosh, hurry!" said the girl.

Hiinóónonóx hih-tou3ei'-no'úutee.
They were all greatly astonished to see how far it extended.

"Heeyóuti'?[14] heebe3-síísiiyei, heebe3-siisiiyei!
"What is it? A big snake, a big snake!

"Hi3í=he'=iiciteihí-3i."
"We should see how long it is."

Ne'i-3ookutii-hohkóni'.
Then they followed where it led to.

"Héii, cih-'iten-ówu' hoh'onóóx.
"Hey, bring an axe here.

"Yeeyí'.[15]
"Hurry.

"Cih-'iten-owu' hoh'onoox.
"Bring an axe here.

"Cih-nihi'kóóhu-', hoohó'!"
"Run here, hurry!"

Hiinoononox, Nih'oo3oo he'=3i'ok-éhk heet-no'ooceise-ni' nuhu'.
To everyone's astonishment, when they got to the end of this thing,
Nih'oo3oo was sitting there.

"Kohéi'i!" nii3ee-téhk.
"Stand up!" he was told.

"Hii-hoowuuni," níi-hok Nih'óó3oo.
"No," Nih'oo3oo kept saying.

"Hiineenowo' neh-kóhei'i!" nii3ee-téhk.
"You better stand up this instant!" he was told.

"Nei-hoowu-néén.
"I'm not the owner of that thing.

"Hii3oobei-noo, nei-hoowu-neen," nii-hok Nih'oo3oo.
"I'm telling the truth, I'm not the owner," Nih'oo3oo kept saying.

Toh-nówono'usi-', hóónii hé'ih-kóhei'i.
Because he had become drowsy [from sex], only after a long time did
he stand up.

Híitouuk, he'ih-nééni-n.
Sure enough, he was the owner.

"Hooho', het-ceikoohuutii hoh'onóox!"
"Hurry, you must come running here with an axe right away!"

Nih'óó3oo he'=ce3ikuhnee-hék[16] xoo-xonóu.
Nih'oo3oo tried to escape from there right away.

He'=beh-'iisiiteniyei-hehk hinii3óó.
But all the length of his penis was being held by everyone.

Tebeseihi-yéhk.

It was cut off.

Niiheyoo he'i=neetii-3i.[17]

Maybe Nih'oo3oo bled to death for his wrongs.

Nih'óó3oo 3iík.

Nih'oo3oo ended up dead as a ghost.

Notes

1. The manuscript has /s/ rather than /3/ here.

2. This is a vocative form, pronounced *beh'éé,* literally meaning 'old man'.

3. The manuscript has a final /k/ on this word.

4. *Ho'óóto'* 'right then, just at that very moment'. More common is *wo'óóto',* with the same meaning.

5. Kroeber glosses this word as 'came by', but it actually appears to be *ceb-ihk-óókuu-* AI past/along-upward-stand- 'stand up on hind legs while moving along'.

6. Kroeber glosses this as 'greasy bird'. It has final *-Vn* vocative ending. This may be a folk etymology for the word 'chickadee' (though the basis is not apparent) or else an alternate name used for the bird in the past (though there is some confusion as to whether the American goldfinch was called 'greasy bird' due to the prominent black mark on its head while the rest of its body is bright yellow).

7. This form is not recognized today. It is glossed by Kroeber as 'will you be kind'. It may contain the preverb *heeyei(h)-* 'it is good that . . .'

8. *Nohk-o3í'eeb-* TA 'ask someone to do something for you, with [a gift or pay as] extra inducement'.

9. *Bééyoo* means more specifically 'right on, dead on, right in the middle of the target'.

10. Kroeber does not gloss this word, but it appears to be a shortened form of *hinii3oon* 'his penis'.

11. One would expect *heti-noowootouubeih-* 'feel very pleasurable' (*noowoot* IM-PERF < *howoot-* 'fun pleasure'). Cf. *ni'ouubeihi-* 'feel good'.

12. The element *ciinohóú'u-* means 'farm/plant seeds by tool'. Cf. *ciinóú'u-* 'farm, plant things'. Kroeber glosses the form as 'my arrows will be gone', which must have been an Arapaho slang term for ejaculation (i.e., 'I will empty my quiver'). A modern Arapaho slang term for 'ejaculate' is 'shoot repeatedly' (AI *cóocobóó-*).

13. The manuscript has *yoohuh(u)-*, but this is an early notebook, with less reliable transcription than later.

14. Here and elsewhere the manuscript has *heeyóuti'* rather than just *heeyóu.* Cf. modern *tóusóóti'* 'what?' as an alternative form of *tóusoo.*

15. The form is glossed 'hurry' in the manuscript but is not recognized by modern Arapahos.

16. The manuscript has *he3-* rather than *he'-* initially.

17. The form *néetíitoo-* is more standard.

The Origin of Death

Teller unknown, Oklahoma, August 22 or 23, 1899
Collected by Alfred Kroeber
NAA, MS 2560a, Notebook 10, p. 14

This is a myth that is widespread on the plains. This version (title supplied by the editors) is obviously a brief account, though it still shows some rhetorical elaboration in the clear parallelisms between Nih'oo3oo and the Indian. This particular version was not published in Dorsey and Kroeber, but a longer version appears there as narrative 41.

He'ih-níisi-no' hinenítee-no' hoot-nóo3ibéé-3i' hiine'etíít.[1]
Two people will hold a contest over life.

Híni'{hii} henéecei-biíhi3,[2] noh hóh'onóókee.
There was a piece of buffalo dung and a rock.

Wot=neen-ehkoni' nih'ii-hooxúwu-[3i'].
These two were the ones who were going to determine the future.

Nih'óó3oo he'ih-'itén heneecéi-biihi3, sii'ihkúutii.
Nih'oo3oo took the buffalo chip and tossed it into the water.

Hinówounoo'oo, he'ih-nonó3-ce'-bíxou'oo.[3]
It sank under the water but then quickly floated back to the surface.

"Hoot-né'-nii'-ce'-kóhei'i-noo," heeh-éhk Nih'óó3oo.
"That's why I will rise again from the dead," said Nih'oo3oo.

3ówo3nenítee hoh'onóókee-[n] bíiti' sii'ihkúu3-ee.
The Indian took his turn and tossed the rock into the water [and it sank].

160

"Béébeet hoot-ne'-nii'-iiyohóote-noo."[4]

"That's why I will just die," [the Indian said].

Notes

1. TA *nóo3ib-* means to defeat in a race or similar contest. *Nóo3ibéé-* is apparently an AI middle voice form, meaning 'to be challenged'.

2. *Híni'* means 'that one'. *Híni'íit* is an emphatic version of the same word. The /-t/ may have been omitted in the transcription. Otherwise the /hii/ is unexplained.

3. *Nóno3-* literally 'already', 'earlier', 'previously'. Here the suggestion is that the buffalo chip has already popped back up before anyone could even start looking for it.

4. For both Nih'oo3oo and the Indian, the sentences literally say 'that is when' as opposed to 'why'. A more literal translation would be 'that will be the decisive moment when henceforth I will . . .'

Nih'oo3oo Loses His Eyes

Teller unknown, dated July 22, 1926
Collected by Truman Michelson, Charles Crispin, interpreter
NAA, MS 2994, pp. 30–33

For this story we include Michelson's original transcription. It is one of the later stories that he collected, and the quality of the transcription is much better than his earlier work in 1910. Several symbols that he uses may be unfamiliar to modern readers: α for modern *o*, ω for modern *oo*, and ᵋ for the glottal stop ('). He also consistently notes glottalization and breathed release on final *t* and *k*. This is a distinctive difference between Arapaho and English pronunciation of final stop consonants (now as well as earlier).

Dorsey and Kroeber [1903] 1997 narratives 16 and 17 are versions of this story. Because no title is given in Michelson's manuscript, we include the title used by Kroeber. Although the "magical" word *3oo3ookoocei'i* that occurs in this story does not have any specific meaning, Alonzo Moss says that it sounds like 'following something closely' to him (*3ook-* means 'follow' while *-ook-* is a medial form meaning 'eye'). It also contains an element that sounds like 'rope' (*-oocei-*) or some other long, thin, stretched-out item, so it is actually rich in associative sound symbolism. The word *wu'oos* was not recognized by modern speakers but clearly has the meaning 'oh man!' or 'wow!' or something else indicating a combination of astonishment and admiration. The words spoken by Nih'oo3oo and the bird exactly replicate those of Nih'oo3oo and Whirlwind Woman in another of the stories: Nih'oo3oo 'insists' (*nihi'nei*) and his interlocutor finally says 'all right then' (*hih'óó*). Some versions of this story explain that Nih'oo3oo has small beady eyes because he was given the chickadee's eyes.

Nⁱᵋω'Өω häᵋ iᵋ āwu'nihisä
Nih'óó3oo hé'ih-'oowúniihisee.
Nih'oo3oo was walking downstream.

162

hä^εi^ε ite^{'ε}sä nī^εαhi^{'ε}o^ε

Hé'ih-'ités-ee nii'ehího'.

He came upon a little bird.

ne^{'ε}e^εe nī^εαh<u>i</u>^{'ε}i hä^{'ε}i^{'ε} ^αūΘku'ti isī'sēⁱ

Néhe' nii'eihíhi' hé'ih-'ouu3kúútii hisíísei.

This little bird threw his eyes up so that they hung [on a tree].

ΘωΘωkωtcēⁱ nī_ihα´k'

"3oo3ookoocei'i," nii-hók.

"3oo3ookoocei'i," he would say.

hä^εi^ε tce´ Θēⁱnωωnni´nǫ hisī'sēⁱ

He'ih-cé'-3eiinoo'oo-níno hisíísei.

His eyes went back into the sockets.

wu'ωs^ε ähe´k' nī^εω'Θω

"Wú'oos" heeh-éhk Nih'óó3oo.

"Wow!" said Nih'oo3oo.

betαhū nähä häΘωhα´k'

"Betooh-u nehe'," hee3-oohók.

"Bless me with this power," he said to the bird.

nänihäsī_ini niΘē´ⁱhαk' nu´hu^ε nī^εαhī´o^ε

"Nenih-'eesiini," nii3-éíhok núhu' nii'ehího'.

"Leave it be," the little bird says to him.

hα^ε häi^nīinēⁱ

'oh he'ih-nihi'nei.

But he insisted.

hi^εiω' häΘēⁱhαk'

"Hih'óó," hee3-éihok.

"All right," the bird answered him.

bi'ᵋyēn hät nī´sitω häΘē͡ihɑ´k'

"Bí'-yein het-níísitoo," hee3-éihók.

"You must do this just four times," it said to him.

hähixtce´Θïy̨ǫ

He'ih-cé3ei'oo.

He set off on his way.

nääeᵋ ni'ᵋω´Θω hä´nä´eᵋ nī´stωt'

Nehe' Nih'óó3oo hé'=néé'ee-níístoo-t.

Then this Nih'oo3oo did just as he had seen.

tcätce´Θωω hä´i bäΘtω

Ceecé3o'oh hé'ih-bee3too.

Before you know it, he had finished doing it [more than four times].

nä´nawɑᵋ hä̈ᵋi´Θi^ɑk'ᵋɑ´ hisī´sī͡ hä̈ᵋūt'e´ninǫ

Néénowo' he'íh-3i'ok,[1] 'oh hisíísei he'ih-'ouuté-nino.

He sat there expecting his eyes to come back any second, but his eyes were stuck up in the tree.

ΘωΘkωtcē͡i nī̧hɑ´k'

"3oo3ookoocei'i," nii-hók.

"3oo3ookoocei'i," he was saying.

ohä̈ᵋĩᵋtcūtceᵋ Θȩ̄nwon-ni´nǫ hisī´sē͡i

'oh he'ih-cii-ce'-3eiinoo'oo-níno hisíísei.

But his eyes wouldn't go back in.

nu´uu nī´ɑhī´hoᵋ häi ite´seᵋ

Núhu' níí'ehího' he'ih-'ités-e'.

The little bird came upon him.

bi̧ᵋyē͡in he´t' nī´stω ni̧ᵋiΘe´Θen häΘē͡i'hɑk'

"Bí'-yein hét-níístoo nih-'ii3-é3en!" hee3-eihok.

"I told you to only do it four times!" it said to him.

nähä tcixtce'ᵋ Өē͐ʲnαwu'ni nesī'sē͐ʲ häӨωhαk'

Nehe', "Cih-cé'-3eiinowúún-i nesíísei!" hee3-oohok.

Nih'oo3oo, "Put my eyes back in for me!" he said to the bird.

hi͐ᵋiω häӨē͐ʲhαk'

"Hih'oo," hee3-eihok.

"All right," said the bird to him.

hä͐ᵋ nä'tce'ᵋӨē͐ʲnawunē͐ʲt'

He'né'-ce'-3eiinowuun-eit.

Then it put his eyes back in for him.

o'ᵋ häixnän se'si tcebihi'hi͐ᵋ

'óh he'ih-neen sésiicebiihíhi'.

And it was the chickadee who did this.

nä'ē'ise͐ᵋ

Nee'ei'íse-'.

That's how the story ends.

Note

1. *Néénowo'* is normally used as an imperative particle, meaning 'hurry up, it's urgent!' The usage here is less common but expresses the sense of waiting urgently and desperately for something to happen. The use of this particle seems to be an ironic contrast to the previous line, where *céece3ó'oh* 'quick as a flash, before you know it' occurs. Now Nih'oo3oo is waiting urgently for something that will *not* occur, no matter what he does or how long he waits.

Nih'oo3oo and the Man
Who Dove through the Ice

Told by John Goggles, Wyoming, September 21, 1910
Collected by Truman Michelson
NAA, MS 2707, 1 p., and MS 2708, 4 pp. but second page missing

Michelson's recording of this text became separated over time into two separate files. He normally recorded a text in Arapaho then rewrote the text line by line with interlinear English translations as he worked with his consultant. The original text, in Arapaho only, is in MS 2707. The interlinear version is in MS 2708. Though one page of the interlinear text is missing, the complete text is available in MS 2707.

The text is untitled in Michelson's manuscript. The title supplied here was agreed upon by C'Hair and Moss. The text can be compared with Dorsey and Kroeber [1903] 1997, narrative 59 in particular and narratives 57 and 58 more generally for the motif of diving through the ice. The story is an example of the theme of the "bungling host" who fails to treat his guest adequately. Other stories in this collection, especially those connected with Nih'oo3oo, illustrate the same theme, including "Nih'oo3oo Sharpens His Leg and Dives on the Ice" and "Nih'oo3oo Arrives for a Visit." The theme occurs in other Native American traditions as well (Valentine 2004). As Cowell and C'Hair went through this story, they arrived at the line "there is nothing here for you to eat." This prompted C'Hair to say that the Arapaho word used in this situation is the transitive verb *konóoyóó'onóó'on-in* 'you have caught me at a bad/inopportune time [when I am unable to fulfill my obligations to you]' and that it is deeply embarrassing to have to say this. Although the word does not appear in the story, its very existence illustrates the discomfiture that the host faces in such a situation; this story simply takes that emotion as a given for the audience.

Nih'oo3oo he'ih-'ootii too3iihi' niicii.[1]
Nih'oo3oo was camping near a river.

Hinen-in he'ih-no'usee-[n].
A man arrived.

He'ih-no'u-ceitoon-e'.
The man had come to visit him.

"Heebe."
"Hello, friend," [said the man].

"Hiiyohou-' he-bii3hiit," hee3-oohok.
"There is nothing here for you to eat," Nih'oo3oo said to him.

"Hee," hee3-eihok.
"Yes," the man said to Nih'oo3oo.

"Ceis-in he-niitou3oo."
"Bring your whistle," [the man said to Nih'oo3oo].

"Hee," hee3-oohok hiniiteh'ei-ho.
"Yes," Nih'oo3oo said to his friend.

Noh he'ih-biin-ee hi-niitou3oo-n, hixon-kokuy-on.
And he gave him his whistle, a bone whistle.

He'ne'-noh'ohouuhu-ni3 hohoot.[2]
Then the man climbed up a tree.

He'ih-'one'eekuu.[3]
It stood bent down over [a river].

Noh nehe' hinen he'i=nee-niitouu3ei-t.
And then the man blew the whistle.

Yein he'i=niitouu3ei-t.
He blew the whistle four times.

Noh yein he'ih-nebihce.
And four times he made as if to jump.

Noh he'ne'-oowu-ceno'oo-t nuhu' wo'ow-u'.
And then he jumped down on the ice.

He'ih-xook-tone3eih.[4]
He broke a hole through the ice.

He'ih-'inowukoo nehe' hinen,
The man quickly disappeared below the water.

Noh hoo3iihi', hoo3-itet . . .
And a while later he reached . . . [the hole] [again].

He'ih-cih-bisisee nohkuuhu' hebes-ii heh-niisi-ni3i.
He reappeared with two beavers.

Noh hee3-eihok, "Beenii, hiine'ee-no' hebes-ii!
And he said to Nih'oo3oo, "Friend, here are two beavers!

"Heh-['ii]yeih-e3," hee3-eihok.
"Let me do you a favor," his friend said to him.

"Tousoo?"
"How's that?" [asked Nih'oo3oo].

"Neh-ko'youhu," hee3-eihok hiniiteh'ei-ho.
"You better boil them," his friend said to him.

"Hoot-neecisee-noo," hee3-eihok.
"I'm going to go on," the visitor said to him.

Noh he'ne'-ce3ei'oo-ni3.
And then he set off on his way.

Notes

1. One would expect locative *niiciihehe'*.
2. One would expect locative *hohooti'*.
3. One would expect final *-n*, 4S inflection.
4. The manuscript has a final *-o* which we assume is simply a devoiced "echo" vowel rather than the TI 3S inflection *-o'*, which would be ungrammatical.

Nih'oo3oo tohno'céiteet/Nih'oo3oo Arrives for a Visit

Told by Cleaver Warden, Oklahoma, August(?), 1899

Collected by Alfred Kroeber

NAA, MS 2560a, Notebook 13, pp. 12–14

English version published as "Nih'oo3oo Imitates His Host"

in Dorsey and Kroeber [1903] 1997: 120

This story illustrates many of the classic attributes of Nih'oo3oo. He wanders around alone, stumbling upon all kinds of situations. He is constantly being surprised by events (notice the number of times he uses the particle *hííwo',* which indicates knowledge or events contrary to expectations or more generally confusing ['I wonder', etc.] as well as the use of *híínoonónox* at the end of the story). He always seems insecure and needy, trying to match others' powers. He is always in a hurry (note his use of *hóóho'* 'quickly' to his wife and that he 'runs' outside of his tipi). His relationships with his family are problematic (note that he tells his wife to load 'your' children, the term 'load' itself is more normally used in reference to animals, and he also uses three different imperative forms in a row when talking to his children, as if he already does not trust them). He is constantly trying to show off, as with the abundance in his lodge. He is always loud and lacking in social graces, 'yelling' his command for food rather than just saying it, and gets angry very quickly (*wóttowúsoo* is as close as one can come to a curse word in Arapaho). He is constantly finding his own image of himself undermined. And he is very violent, often gratuitously so, with the violence against others being a projection of his own personal frustrations.

William C'Hair noted that he especially appreciated the following colorful and older words: *honóoyóó* 'don't you dare . . .'; *wóttowúsoo* 'scoundrel'; *híínoonónox* 'to his consternation'; *hóóho'* 'get a move on!'; *hóonóxon-* 'with great speed, violence, or intensity'; and *nóonó'o3ih-* 'abuse and misuse'.

Kroeber adds a note at the end of the story: "the 1st man did not do it by his children, but by medicine." This feature links the text to a broader Algonquian tradition of magical food available in the houses of culture heroes (who of course cannot be imitated by everyday people). See Milligan 2005.

Nih'óó3oo he'ih-no'úsee níiinon heetoh-niixóotee-'.
Nih'oo3oo arrived at a tipi standing all alone.

"Wohéi Nih'óó3oo, toot=(h)éi-ihoo?" hee3-éihok.
"Well, Nih'oo3oo, where are you going?" the owner said to him.

"Hiiwo', neiteh'éi, yonóu=kooyoo'onoo'onee![1]
"Oh what a terrible time you've caught me at, my friend!

"Hiiwo' cih-'ii3oo-ní'i he-bii3híít.[2]
"I wonder what in the heck you're going to eat.

"Wohéi cih-cíítei."
"Well, come on in."

Cíitei-hok Nih'óó3oo.
Nih'oo3oo entered.

"Cih-'oowúnoo'oo bíi3ib!" nii-hók nehe' hinén.[3]
"Food come down!" this man says.

"Cih-'oowúnoo'oo bíi3ib!
"Food come down!

"Cih-'oowúnoo'oo bíi3ib!
"Food come down!

"Cih-'oowúnoo'oo bíi3ib!"
"Food come down!"

Yéin toh-nihíi-t, hoo'uwoníini-'i hee3e'eítee-' he'ih-ko'ús.
When he had said this four times, various types of jerked meat fell in front of the tipi.

"Wohéi Nih'oo3oo hetí-bii3iwóon-oo," hee3-oohók hiniin nehe' hinén.
"Okay, you must cook these for Nih'oo3oo," said this man to his wife.

"Wuhhó', hiiwo' heh=neneehii3eihi-no'óhk, neiteh'éi.
"Golly gee, I see that we are just alike, my friend," [said Nih'oo3oo].

"Hetí-coo niixoo néyeih'-e'," heeh-éhk Nih'óó3oo.
"You must come to my lodge too," said Nih'oo3oo.

Tih-'iisi-bii3íhi-t, cé3ei'oo yiisíihi' híyeih'-e'.
When he had finished eating, he set off toward his lodge over there.

"Hóóho' betébi, bii-biino3oon-in heníisoo-nó'.
"Quickly, old woman, load your children [with food]," [he said to his wife].

"Heet-no'úsee-t het-bii3íhi-t."
"He will arrive to eat."

Hiníisoo-no he'íh-'eeneiseinééb-ee, "Yéin nihii-nóóhok, hee3e'éitee-' heti-cih-beh-ciinooxú-be.
He explained to his children, "When I say it four times, you must all unload the food in front of the tipi.

"Honóóyoo; niitóbee-', toyou'úuwuu-' hee3-e3énee."
"Don't you dare [forget]; hear what I'm saying, remember what I have said to you."

Néhe' hinén, Nih'óó3oo híyeih'-ín, néhe' hinén heetoh-no'úsee-t.
This man, at Nih'oo3oo's lodge, that's where this man arrived.

Wot=hih-tóus-nii3óyeisoo!
Nih'oo3oo's goods and possessions were so very plentiful!

"Héii, bií3iwó ceixotii-'!" nii-hók Nih'oo3oo.
"Hey, bring food here!" says Nih'oo3oo.

"Héii, bií3iwó ceixotii-'!
"Hey, bring food here!

"Héii, bií3iwó ceixotii-'!
"Hey, bring food here!

"Héii, bií3iwó ceixotii-'!"

"Hey, bring food here!"

Toh-bee3i-niitóuuhut, he'ih-cii-cebíí'oo-nino hiníisoo-no.

After he finished hollering, his children had not made an appearance.

"Hííwo', wottówusoo-no', he'=íh-'eeneistoo-nóó3i."

"What in the hell, damned brats, I wonder what the heck they're doing."

Nouuhceh-éhk.

He ran outside.

Hiinóónonóx, tih'ii-betée3ecoo-t Nih'óó3oo, hiníisoo-no he'ih-beh-noo-nókohu-níno.

To his consternation, though he thought he was a holy man, his children were all lying around asleep.

Toh-bii'ííh-oot, noonóxon-nee-nó'o3[ih]-ee.[4]

When he found them, he beat the hell out of them.

Notes

1. *Konóoyóó'onóó'(o)nee-noo* means 'you have caught me at a very bad time, when I have nothing to offer you'. It could be used when someone visits and might expect food when there is none.

2. *Cih-* is used here in place of *he'=* as a dubitative form; note the Conjunct Iterative inflection.

3. This sentence includes an example of an Inanimate Intransitive verb used grammatically as an imperative form (note the lack of a final inflectional suffix). Functionally, this is a hortative construction. Such usages seem always to occur with deictic *cih-*.

4. Kroeber transcribes the last verb as *-neeno'o3ee*. What was intended, based on Kroeber's translation, must have been *-nóonó'o3ihee*.

Nih'oo3oo and the Seven Sisters

Told by Cleaver Warden, Oklahoma, August 19, 1899

Collected by Alfred Kroeber

NAA, MS 2560a, Notebook 9, pp. 87–95

English version published in Dorsey and

Kroeber [1903] 1997: 86–88

The text of this narrative is somewhat difficult from an editing stand-point. A number of verbs occur in nonaffirmative inflection but without the expected *hé'ih-* prefix. This is not entirely unusual in Arapaho, although it normally occurs when an earlier verb in the sentence did have that prefix. In this text the *hé'ih-* is missing where it would normally be expected to occur. The text also shows unusual placement of the perfective marker /*íix*/ in several instances as well as several apparent errors of inflection (OBV rather than PROX, affirmative rather than nonaffirmative). Given the num-ber of fairly obvious anomalies, it is even harder to resolve less transparent problems in the text with confidence.

In terms of content, note that the serial disappearances of the younger sisters are all treated in roughly the same language: the group 'set off', 'spent the night', and 'the next morning, one of them had vanished'. In con-trast, however, the remarks of the older sister after each disappearance are strikingly different in specific content, though broadly similar in tone, and function as a showpiece of different idiomatic ways of saying 'I told her so, I tried to warn her, etc.' in Arapaho, adding much to the story.

The theme of clothing is well developed in the narrative: the women are specifically described as packing their things on their backs (*híniinóoxú-* AI). Their clothing and possessions (*hi-tonóúnoon-ínoo*, literally 'the things they use') are mentioned over and over in relation to each woman's disappearance as well as eventual reappearance. After being rescued from the wolf, the women put on new clothes (*hókoo3cíi3ibii-* AI) and then later are told to dress nicely (*néyoo'úú-* AI). Praying Young Man's clothes (*hit-éixó'o-no*) and possessions (*hi-tounoon-inoo* again) are men-tioned prominently. Finally, Nih'oo3oo's trick involves the way Praying Young Man dresses (*niisínouhu-* AI) and Nih'oo3oo dressing the same (*néé'eesínouhu-* AI) by stealing his clothes (*hi-tonóúoon-ínoo* again). Note that even the sisters' tipi is specifically described as being nice looking. Finally, the older sister is able to save her younger sisters from the Black Wolf because she is not just properly dressed but also has the expected womanly accoutrements (the pounder) with her, attached to her clothing—another of the 'things she uses'.

The overall effect, Cowell suggests, is to show how clothes, personhood, and personal agency are intimately connected. In fact, when the sisters and their clothes are described as disappearing, the word used is *hiiyohóote-* (AI), which can mean both 'disappear' and 'be dead and gone'. Similarly, the clothes 'disappear' at the end of the narrative (*hiiyohóú'uni-* II). The root *hiiyoh-* 'disappear' is used in both verbs. And, of course, without his clothes, Praying Young Man is reduced back to a stick, essentially 'disappearing' as well.

Continuing with this perspective, Cowell offers the suggestion that the Black Wolf (see the note on the meaning of the term) represents a kind of nature force who tries to take not just people but their clothing and thus their personhood as well and that he is conquered symbolically by the tools and clothing of civilization. Finery—in clothing and lodging—is conversely linked to the power literally to create a person, in the form of Praying Young Man. But, once created, the full personhood and agency of that person need to be recognized, the story seems to suggest. If others attempt to control the person too much then personhood (his goods and clothing) risks being lost. All of these themes can be compared to the game of Grandmother against Wolf that Dorsey (1903: 190) describes in relation to the Arapaho Sun Dance. In that game one large girl wrestles with a boy representing a wolf, in an attempt to protect other children from being food for the wolf. If the older girl wins, this represents victory over the enemy.

Finally, the bringing to life of Praying Young Man closely echoes Arapaho ceremonialism. In ceremonies such as the Sun Dance an action is typically done four times in a preliminary "pretend" fashion then done "for real" on the fifth occasion. A specific word (*nebkuutii-* AI.T) describes this process. Here it is on the fifth command that Praying Young Man arises.

Part One: Departure

Niisootoxúsei-no' ce3ei'óó-no'.

Seven women set off on a journey.

Notíitii-3i' biito'ówu'.
They were looking for [a new] land.

He'ih-beh-'iniinooxú-no' hi-tonóunoon-ínoo.
They all loaded their goods on their backs.

'oh he'=etéi[ni]-yohkoni'.
They spent the night somewhere.

Part Two: One Sister Vanishes

Toh-nookéni-ni', céése' he'ih-'iiyohóót.
When it was light the next morning, one of them had vanished.

"Céniixóotee-' niisiséé-no'," nih-'oo3-íi3-o'[1] neehebéhe'.
"It's a long way to where we are heading," I said to my younger sister,
trying to be helpful.

"Neh-nee3ó'oo, nei-beex-úu3-e'," heeh-éhk nehe' beneesései-[t].
" 'Let me remain behind,' she should have said to me," said the oldest
sister.

Koox=hé'ih-cé3ei'oo-no'.
Once again they set off on their journey.

He'ih-'etéini-no'.
They spent the night someplace.

Part Three: A Second Sister Vanishes

Koox=toh-nookéni-ni', céése' he'ih-'iiyohóót, nohkúuhu'
hi-tonóunoo-no.
Once again when it was light, one of them had vanished, along with
her things.

"Noohowóhoo, nóno3=he-ih-nee3óóxuwu."[2]
"My younger sister, you should have decided earlier to remain behind,"
[said the oldest sister].

Koox=he'ih-cé3ei'oo-no'.
Once again they set off on their journey.

Cih-'iitiséé-hohkoni' hiisíihi', tih-'i3óu'oo-' he'ih-ceenóku-no'.
They walked this way all day long, and when evening came they sat down.

Tih-'iisi-bii-bíi3ihi-3i', ceeni-bíh'iyóó-ni-', he'ne'=nii'-iisibi-3i'.
After they had finished eating everything up, it was late at night, and that's when they went to bed.

Part Four: A Third Sister Vanishes

Toh-nohkuseicíini-ni', céése' he'ih-'iiyohóót.
When morning came, one of them had vanished.

"Téi'yoon, hóokoh nóno3=he-ih-ciin-iiseinééb,"[3] heeh-ehk beneesései-[t].
"Child, didn't I advise you against [coming along] earlier?" said the oldest sister.

He'ih-cé3ei'oo-no'.
They set off on their journey again.

Beníkotii-hohkóni'; yéini-no'.
They were walking in a tight bunch; there were four of them.

Koox=he'ih-'etéini-no'.
Yet again they spent the night somewhere.

Part Five: A Fourth Sister Vanishes

Toh-nookéni-ni', céése' hé'ih-'iiiyohoot nohkúuhu' hi-tonounóo-no.
When it was light, one of them had vanished along with her things.

"Téi'yoon, kóokon beneet-niihóbei-t,"[4] heeh-éhk beneesései-t.
"Child, she just had to come," said the oldest sister.

Nohkúseic he'ih-cé3ei'oo-no', hot-nihí'neesee-3i',[5] toh-nótiitii-3i'
hoot-niitoh-'úune'etii-3i'.

Early in the morning they set off on their journey, since they had to
travel fast, because they were looking for a place to live.

He'ih-'etéini-no'.

They spent the night someplace.

Part Six: A Fifth Sister Vanishes

Toh-nookéni-ni' toh-'owóto'oo-3i', koox=céése' hiiyohóót.

When it was morning and they woke up, yet again one of them had
vanished.

"Kóokon téi'yoonoh'-o' nih-'oo3i-totóuw-ou'u, 'oh kookon nih-
nih'íneihi-3i'," heeh-ehk beneesései-[t].

"I just tried to warn these children for their own good, but they just
insisted on coming," said the oldest sister.

He'ne'-bi'-níisineníi-3i', toh-cé3ei'oo-3i'.

Then there were only two of them, when they set off.

He'ne'-kohtowú3ecoo-t tih-'iiyohóóte-ní3i hinoohowóh'-o.

Then the oldest sister thought it was funny/strange that her younger
sisters had vanished.

Koox=he'ih-'etéini-no'.

Yet again they spent the night.

Part Seven: Solving the Mystery

Bi'-niis-etéini-no'.

Just the two of them spent the night.

"Hiiwó' tóusooti?

"I wonder what is going on?

"Hiiwó' he'=ih-'íístoo-noo3i téi'yoonoh'-o'?

"What have these children done?

"Hi3í=heetih-'e'ín-owoo," nii-hók nehe' beneesései-[t].
"I must try to figure this out," said the oldest sister.

Séénook hé'ne'-hí'i-touku3eti-t toh-cen-bíh'iyóó-ni'.
She tied herself up with a rope when it was late at night.

Heï'-nókohu-ni3 hinoohowóho', séénook hi-tóu'cihíit.
Once her younger sister was sleeping, she used a rope on her [too].

He'=iis-í'-niisookú3eti-no'.
They were both tied to each other.

3ootéce', hinenítee he'ih-cih-no'okús.
At midnight a person crawled to the tent.

"Hiinóónonox,[6] heet-iitéíhi-t[7] cénoo-t?" nii-hók néhe' hiineehebéh'i-t.
"What could this possibly be, who will this one coming here turn out to be?" the one who had the younger sister said.

He'=iis-iihi' wóónitees, nii-wo'otééneihi-3i'.[8]
It was some kind of wolf, the ones that are black.

"Heeteh-éhk nó-otoowooh-éiit[9] noohowóh'-o'."
"This must be the one who has eaten up my younger sisters," [she thought].

3oxóo[10] hé'ih-cih . . . he'ih-'o'otoh[11] néhe' beneesései-t.
A meat pounder . . . the older sister had one attached to her belt.

Híhcebe' he'ih-cih-too'ús woonitéés.
The black wolf walked up close to them and stopped.

Cih-te'etínoo'oo, tih-'i3konóów-oot.
Its mouth was opening, since it was inhaling both of them.

He'ih-'iis-eh-niisóho'-wo'ówo'oo-no', toh-niisóokuhu-3i', hónoot
he'ih-'iisiitóh-u'.[12]
They had both gone farther along into its mouth, because they were both tied to each other, until he had caught them in his mouth.

Nehe', "Heetih-koh'úunóówo'oo-',"[13] heesí3ecoo-hók.
The older one, "When we have gone halfway down," she thought.

Néhe' hiinééhebeh'i-t, kookónoo' bééyoo hé'ih-koh'uus-otóób-ee,[14]
This one who had the younger sister, anyway just exactly when she had been halfway swallowed,

hiineehebéh'i-t he'ne'-'itén-oot 3oxóot.[15]
then the one who had the younger sister took the pounder.

Nii3ei'íinit[16] hinii3e'een-in he'ih-to'ób-ee.
She hit the wolf on his head with all her might.

Noxóbe3eih-ii.[17]
She killed it with the blow.

"Necíikou[18] cih-'e'inón-o' nii-níistoo-t," heeh-éhk.
"Now finally I have found out who is doing this," she said.

Hiineehebéh'i-t hi-wóoxe he'ih-'iis-í'-totís-ii-{n}[19] núhu' woonitéés.
The one who had the younger sister managed to cut open the wolf with her knife [down the throat].

"Cih-ce'-étis[ee], nih-neenii3i'oowóo'oo-n."[20]
"Come back out of there, you look like a captive," [she said to her younger sister].

Behis-íis-kó'e3ein-oot,[21] hinoohowóh'-o cih-noehi-nino nohkúuhu' hi-tonounóon-iníno.
When she had cut the wolf all the way open, her younger sisters came out with their belongings.

"Nei-neehebeh'íit!
"My younger sisters!

"Hohóu, nei-tous-eeyeih-{s}-ce'-noohów-oono'!"[22]
"Thanks be, how good it is to see them again!"

He'ih-beh-tousébi-no'.
They all bathed.

Tih-'ehíisébeti-3i', hísei-no' beh-'oon-ókoo[3]-cíi3ibii-no'.
After they washed themselves, the women all changed clothes.

He'ne'-cé3ei'oo-no'.
Then they set off again.

Ce'-hono'utonéíhi-no'.[23]
They were all back together again.

Part Eight: Looking for a Man

He'ih-no'úsee-no' biito'ówu-u' heenoo híni' [ho]nóuu=hii3etí-', woxú'-uno heet-í3eti-', néc héétoh-'ú3eti-', heet-ni'coo-', neeyéic-ii heet-í3eti-'.
They arrived in a country that seemed truly good, where the grass was good, the water was good and sweet, and the timber was good.

He'ih-'itét-owuu.
They reached this country.

He'ne'í-yoohu-3i' niisi-nóóyoti-' níiinon.
Then they put up their tipi just as it should look/be set up.

He'ih-néé'eesoo.
That's how it was.

"'inehóus, hono'út neh-beh-néyoo'uu-'.
"Well then, all of you should dress up nice.

"Hoot-notiih-óónee hinén," heeh-ehk beneesései-t.
"You will go look for a man," said the oldest sister.

"Toon=hee3{ée}-bii'iitii-néí'i, nihooni-yookox, toon=nii-xouubei-'i, toon=xonóuubee-', noh wo'éi3 howoh'uubíis; núhu' heh-niisei-'i, toon=hee3{ee}-niito'-bii'iitii-nei'i."

"[Bring back] whichever kind you find, yellow willow, straight ones, a straight one, or praying bush; of these two, whichever you find first."

He'ne'-notiitii-3i'.

Then they searched for the wood.

Cih-no'úxotii-no' howoh'uubíis.

They brought back praying bush.

"Heetee, nehe' honóh'oe nootiih-éiit, hit-óoo hoono'útoyoo-' noh hut-eixó'o-no."

"Before [he arrives], the young man who is looking for me, his bedding must be complete and his clothes," [said the older sister].

Núhu' bes he'ih-'íisibee-n[24] hóoob-e'.

This stick was laid down on the bed.

Teesíihi' bes, heixó'o-no he'ih'-teesi-ciinén-owuu, biikóó, toh-noo-nókohu-3i'.

On top of the stick, they put the clothes down on top of it,[25] at night, when they were sleeping.

Part Nine: Praying Young Man Comes to Life

Nohkúseic boh-'ówoto'óó-no' núhu' hísei-no'.

Early the next morning the women all woke up.

"Howoh'uunonoh'oe, neh-3ówo3ii, heti-bén," nii-hók beneesései-t.

"Praying Young Man, you better get up, you just drink," said the oldest sister.

He'íh-cii-noh'oowuní'iihi'.[26]

He did not move.

"Howoh'uunonóh'oe, neh-3ówo3ii, heti-hehíisi'ouh," nii3ee-téhk.
"Praying Young Man, you better get up, you must wash your face," he was told.

He'íh-cii-noh'oowús.
He did not move.

"Howoh'uunonóh'oe, neh-3ówo3ii, héti-bii3i."
"Praying Young Man, you better get up, you must eat something."

He'ih-noh'oowuní'ii.
He stretched a little.

"Howoh'uunonóh'oe, neh-3ówo3ii, heetih-notinóoxobei-[n]."
"Praying Young Man, you'd better get up, so you can look for horses."

He'ih-sii-siiciní'ii[27] honóh'oe.
The young man stretched as if ready to arise.

"Howoh'uunonóh'oe neh-3ówo3ii," [he]ti3ée-t honóh'oe.
"Praying Young Man, you better get up," the young man was told.

Hé'ih-3owó3-ceenók.
He sat down upright.[28]

Wootii hih-tousi-ni'éíh nohkuuhu' hi-tonounóo-no!
How good-looking he was with his clothes and possessions!

Bii3ih-éhk woohoníihi'.
He ate together with them.

Part Ten: Praying Young Man Searches for a Wife

Toh-'óote'éiniini howoh'uunonóh'oe he'né'-notíseinee-t neeyéic-i'.
Then afterward Praying Young Man went to look for women in the timber.

He'ih-cih-noo-no'uxóh-ee hísei-no.
He brought women back to the tipi.

"Hii-hoowu-néén.

"She is not the one.

"Ce'ixoh-ún," nii3-éihok hiteséi-wo.

"Take her back," his sisters kept saying to him.

Wot=howohuuhu' hísei-no nih-no'xoh-oohók.

He brought a whole lot of women to the lodge, [but the sisters always rejected them].

Part Eleven: Nih'oo3oo Usurps the Place of Praying Young Man

Nih'oo3oo he'ih-niitóbee, niitówoo3-ee.

Nih'oo3oo heard about this, he heard about Praying Young Man.

Howoh'uunonóh'oe hit-eixo'oniin-inoo he'ih-'ebíit.

Nih'oo3oo stole Praying Young Man's clothes.

Niisinóúhu-ni3, he'i=nee'eesinouhu-t.

The way Praying Young Man dressed, Nih'oo3oo dressed himself that way.

Heet-niitóbee-t hiséi-n hoot-niib-éini3 howoh'uunonóh'oe, he'ih-yíhkotii-n.[29]

Where he heard that there was a woman whom Praying Young Man was going to marry, Nih'oo3oo went there.

"Nenee-' wóów cénoo-t, howoh'uunonóh'oe," hee3éih-ehk.

"There he is coming now, Praying Young Man," people said.

Nih'oo3oo hé'=nee'ees-iniini-t.

It was in that way that Nih'oo3oo married her.

He'ih-nosoun-iinis[ee] howoh'uunonoh'oe neeyéic-i', biikóó, toh-noo-nókohu-3i'.

Meanwhile Praying Young Man was still wandering around in the timber, because he was still looking for the woman that he was going to marry.

Hiteséi-wo he'ih-3ooxuun-owuníno hi-tonounóo-no tih-'iiyohou'u-ní'i.
His sisters noticed that his clothing and possessions had disappeared.[30]

Niitóbee-nino Nih'oo3oo toh-niiw-oohók hini' hísei-n.
They heard that Nih'oo3oo had married that woman.

Notes

1. *Hoo3-* prefix, 'in s.o.'s interest, out of concern for s.o., looking out for s.o.'s benefit'. Cf. *hóó3eeneb-* 'think of s.o.'s needs and future, be considering their interests rather than one's own'.

2. AI *He-ih-née3-ooxúwu-* 2S-PAST/CONTRARY TO FACT-remain-determine/decide-. *He-ih-* forces nonaffirmative inflection, with the construction meaning 'you should have . . .'

3. *Nóno3=he-ih-cíín-iiseinééb-[i]:* earlier-2-PAST-NEG-advise (TA)-1S, 'didn't I advise you about this earlier?' With *hookóh* 'because' the sentence is literally 'because didn't I advise you about this earlier?', implying 'because didn't I advise you not to do this earlier?'

4. *Kookón beneet-nííhobéí-t,* literally 'she just wanted to come along for no particular reason'. *Kookon* strongly suggests a lack of a good reason and thus improper behavior.

5. Kroeber transcribes *nihi'niisee-* rather than the expected *níhi'néésee-* for AI 'walk rapidly'.

6. *Híinoonónox* 'to one's great surprise, astonishment'.

7. *Heet-iitéíhi-t* FUT-from there (AI)-3S 'where he will be from'.

8. The Arapaho form is not recognized today with the meaning in the story, but it seems to be related to Gros Ventre AI verbal noun *nóóniΘehíínotáasi-'*, meaning a coyote in rut, more specifically a coyote with quivering testicles. The final element- *taas* (Arapaho-*tees*) indicates testicles. The initial element in the word here is *woon-* 'new'. C'Hair did not recognize this meaning in the word but said that his grandmother often used the word *wóónotees* for a 'youngster, young man' and also *beh'éíhotees* for her husband, with a somewhat ironic sense similar to 'old geezer' in English (cf. *beh'éíh-ehi'* 'old man').

9. TA.DEPPART *no-otóówooh-éiit,* 1S-consume (TA)-3S.DEPPART, 'the one who has caused something of mine to be consumed'.

10. Arapahos today say that this is an older word for 'tomahawk'.

11. *Ho'otóhu-* II.PASS.IMPERF, 'attached by implement to s.t., as beads or teeth on a dress'.

12. Cf. *hiisííten-* TA 'catch, seize [by hand]'.

13. AI *heetíh-kóh'un-óówo'oo-',* so that/let it be-half-go down-OS.

14. *He'ih-koh'-úus-otóóbee-,* NPAST-half-PERF-consumed (AI.MID). The placement of the perfective morpheme is unusual here—normally it would be expected immediately after the NPAST prefix.

15. *3oxóo/3oxóót* is a common alternation: cf. *bexóo/bexóót* for 'decorative element'. The first form is a deverbal noun, while the second is a verbal participle used as a noun.

16. Kroeber transcribes *nii3ii'iinit.* He often misses /ei/ versus /ii/ contrasts.

17. Cf. *nóxow-* 'violently, intensely' and TA final *é3eih-* 'action by collision, blow' > TA *nóxobé3eih-*.

18. This word is not recognized by modern Arapahos. Kroeber glosses it as *necii kou* 'at last'.

19. Final <u>n</u> is unexplained here.

20. This form is unclear. *Neehii3-* means 'resemble, alike' and the noun *wowóo* means 'captive' (perhaps misheard as *woowóó'oo*). *Nih-neehii3-owóoni-n* would be 'you resembled a captive'.

21. As with note 14 above, the PERF morpheme occurs at an unusual place, after (rather than before) *behis-* 'all'.

22. *Hééyeih-* 'it is good that . . .' The /s/ is unexplained, unless the form is intended as *hééyeih-'iis-* 'it is good that [I] have managed to/gotten to . . .'

23. Literally 'they were complete/all present again'.

24. *Hiisíbee-n* 'it was put to bed'. The stick is being treated as animate (and obviative) here.

25. Kroeber's translation says specifically that the older sister does this, while the younger sisters are sleeping, but TI *téésciinén-owuu* is either 3PL or 4S, not 3S.

26. This form is not recognized today. *Nóh'oow'úsi-* means 'to move, to stir'. It is likely that the full form is *nóh'oowu-ní'iihi*. The final element means 'pull, exert force', so the sense here would be 'stretch out', as when waking.

27. The same remarks apply here as for *nóh'oowuní'iihi*. The first element *siisíic-* means 'stretch' (reduplicated), and the expected modern form would be *siisiicisi-*.

28. Kroeber's translation gives the more reasonable 'he sat upright'.

29. It is not clear why Nih'oo3oo would be treated as obviative here (*yíhkotii-n*, '4S walked over there').

30. Kroeber's translation adds 'and that he had become a stick again'. This is the standard ending of the story, though it is not included in the Arapaho here.

One-Eyed Sioux and His Mother-in-Law

Told by Cleaver Warden, August 9, 1899
Collected by Alfred Kroeber
NAA, MS 2560a, Notebook 6, pp. 38–41
English version published in Dorsey and
Kroeber [1903] 1997: 77–78

William C'Hair especially appreciated the following "old words" in this narrative: *yóhuh-* (similar to *yohóú-*) 'exemplary'; *3ooxúce'* 'right up next to'; *hooté'ein-* (modern *hootéin-*) 'soon after'; and *hoonónee* 'harder, stronger'.

This story has a rich set of terms describing being cold, as the central comic element of the story is the trickster's continual complaints about not being warm enough (at least in a certain spot). He is not just cold, but *hí3oowu-* 'truly, really' cold, *hééyeih-néeto3íne-* 'almost frozen to death'. It is *yóo'úh-* 'exemplarily, as in the old stories' cold. He *tóyot-etóuuhu-* 'makes cold-sounding cries'.

The rising exasperation of his mother-in-law is captured in phrases such as *'inehous, hiikóokónoo'* which could be glossed more fully as 'well good grief then, you might as well anyway' and *wo'úukóokónoo'* 'what in the heck is the problem anyway!?' or 'well just go ahead then anyway if you're going to make such a fuss!' or perhaps 'it's something that doesn't need to be brought up, but go ahead and say it anyway if you have to'.

The overall humor of the story relies on the fact that traditional Arapaho society observed strict avoidance between mothers-in-law and sons-in-law. Thus the entire situation of camping and going on the war path together (regardless of the sexual element) is completely incongruous and bizarre from a traditional Arapaho perspective, though Kroeber does record in a note with this narrative that "women sometimes chose to accompany husbands, doing cooking; they could return ornamented with the black war paint, thus distinguishing themselves. Also might get part of booty." Here, of course, the social custom is completely perverted, because the mother-in-law replaces the wife. More specifically, the story focuses on the combination of lack of hardiness, easy distractability (as when he looks at his mother-in-law's rear end), and general cowardice of the antihero One-Eyed Sioux—all elements antithetical to proper warrior behavior. In his notebook Kroeber recorded the following ethnographic note in the middle of his transcription of this story: "When no woman went on war-path, every man cooked for himself. If one was lazy, sponged on others, or slept too long, they made a sausage for him stuffed with hide + sinew, + when he woke, gave to him. This was great disgrace."

This information was provided by Kroeber's informants in the context of the story, which clearly shows that the antihero, anti–war path reading was central to their understanding of the story.

Kroeber also provides another bit of information from an informant: "called One-eyed Sioux on account of secret looking upon, etc. mother in law." Thus the name of the character refers not to the lack of an eye but rather to the one secretive, wandering eye, which looks at things not to be gazed upon openly by turning the head or looking with both eyes. Note that the only point in the story where One-Eyed Sioux shows avid interest is when watching his mother-in-law bend over. He uses the word *hoonónee* 'more! harder!' twice and is described using the verb *wo3óóhow-* 'look at someone avidly, with sexual desire' or more idiomatically 'look at someone hornily'. In relation to this Alonzo Moss says that the name of this Nih'oo3oo-like character, at least in modern Arapaho, is understood as 'pop-eyed Sioux.' Thus rather than *ko'-* 'remove a part from a whole' (as in removing an eye or tooth), the root is *ko'-* meaning 'pop, bang, explode', with the explicit sense of someone pop-eyed from looking at something exciting or enticing. Thus the meaning is similar to a Peeping Tom. Moss adds that the term is used today to tease brothers-in-law (especially, of course, if they actually happen to be Sioux). The relationship between both brothers-in-law and sisters-in-law is a teasing one, in which sexual allusions are especially enjoyed. This contemporary usage is likely very similar to that of 1900.

Sexuality and the warpath are also ironically linked when One-Eyed Sioux is feeling around in the dark and his mother-in-law asks, 'What are you looking for?' using the verb *notíí-tii-*. This same root occurs in the word used in the text for a war expedition (*notí-koní-*). Thus while he is supposed to be searching for one thing One-Eyed Sioux is busy searching for something else. The final verb *síiih-, síiiton-* also means specifically 'to seize by raid or plunder from an enemy' and is used virtually exclusively in connection with war expeditions; here, of course, it acquires a secondary comic sense of sexual seizure. One last example is the use of the verb *teesísee-* when the mother-in-law tells him to 'get on top'. That is the standard way of saying 'mount' (a horse, such as a war horse) but also 'mount' someone to engage in sexual intercourse, Moss notes. Thus the story on the one hand presents One-Eyed Sioux's sexual interests as antiwarrior but on the other hand suggests an intimate confusion of war and sex, at least in his mind.

Kó'ookunootinéi he'=notikonixoh-oohok hihéih-o.
One-Eyed Sioux took his mother-in-law on the war path.

He'=etéiniib-eehék híikoo'.
He camped for the night with her in the brush.

Wót=heh-'eeneisoo-' ce'esibesoowuu-yohkóni'.
They had two different brush shelters.

Hihéih-o hé'ih-'iisibí-n.
His mother-in-law went to bed.

Noh niixoo hi-besoowu-u' he'ih-cíi3iísib.
And he went to sleep too inside his brush shelter.

Toh-ceni-bíh'iyoo-ni', Ko'ookunootinéi wot=níh-toyotetouuh-ohk.
In the middle of the night One-Eyed Sioux was making shivering noises.

"Heeyeih-neeto3íne-noo.
"I am almost frozen to death.

"Cih-koho'uuhu' hot-óu-wo," nii-hok.
"Give me half of your blankets," he said.

Hei'í3ecoo-3i, "Úhuuhu, yohuh=tóyo3oo!,"[1] nii3etouuh-ehk Ko'ookunootinéi.
Whenever he would think this, then One-Eyed Sioux would call out, "Uuuuu, it is cold as hell!"

"Tousoo ne3é'ex? Koo-ho-tóe?"
"What's wrong, my son-in-law? Are you cold?"

"Héii, heeyeih-neeto3íne-noo.
"Yes! I'm almost frozen to death.

"Ceixótii ceese' hot-óu."
"Bring one of your blankets here."

"Híibeii, ne3e'ex he-ih-toe, níiyou céese'; hoyoos-in!"[2]
"Very well, my son-in-law, if you're cold, here's a blanket, cover that thing up!"

Ko'ookunootinéi he'=itén-o'ohk hiihóót[3] hóu.
One-Eyed Sioux took the blanket that she had lent him.

He'ih-'óote'ein,[4] kóóx=he'ih-toyotetouu.
Not long afterward he once again started making shivering sounds.

"Tóusoo, tóusoo, heeyóu ne3é'ex?"
"What's wrong? What's wrong? What is it, my son-in-law?"

"Híii,[5] noosóu-tóehi-noo.
"Brrrr, I am still cold.

"Nei-hóówooh-'óókuu'oo hoonó'."
"I'm not warmed up anymore."

"'inehóus, hiikookónoo', henei=cih-nóehi-n, heh-niisisíne-no'.[6]
"Well then, you might as well come out of your shelter and we could sleep together.

"Koo-ho-tóe?"
"Are you cold?"

"Hii3óówu-tóehi-noo, nehéihe."
"I really am cold, my mother-in-law."

"'inehóus, 3ooxúce'[7] cih-'íisibi, ne3é'ex."
"Well then, come to bed next to me, my son-in-law."

Híibeií, hé'ih-toyo3ís.
Then he slept warmly [for a while].

Kó'ookunootinéi, he'=iisib-ehk 3ooxúce'.
One-Eyed Sioux went to bed right up next to her.

"Hesow-hóoyó'owuu[8] ne3é'ex," hee3-éihok hihéih-o.
"Take this to cover yourself up, my son-in-law," said his mother-in-law
to him.

Toh-'óote'éin-iini koox=hé'ih-toyotétouu.
Not long afterward he once again started making shivering sounds.

"Tousóo ne3é'ex, heeyóu hei-notii3óó?"
"What's wrong, my son-in-law, what are you looking for?"

Noh "Héíhi-noo toh-tóehi-noo.
And "I told you that I'm cold.

"Nósouníihi', noosou-tóehi-noo.
"Still, I'm still cold.

"Neehéinoo'óó-noo, toh-tóehi-noo."
"I'm shivering because I'm cold."

"Toot=ho-tóe, ne3é'ex?
"Where are you cold, my son-in-law?

"Wo'úukookónoo' hini' tóehi-n!"
"Go ahead and say where you're cold, for goodness sake!"

"Híít, hiitíino, hii3oowu-tóehi-noo hiitíino ceeseyóón-e'."
"Here, right here, I'm truly cold here at this one place."

He'ih-tóutiibis héetoh-tóehi-t.
He was holding on tight to the place where he was cold.

Hihéih-o he'ih-'e'ín-owuu.[9]

His mother-in-law knew what he wanted.

"'inehóus, hooyo'ówuu, cih-teesís ne3é'ex, héetih-'ookúu'oo-n."

"Well then, cover yourself up, get on top, my son-in-law, so that you will warm up."

Tóh-'uus-íini, Ko'ookunootinéi noh hihéih-o, heh-niisóho' hini' nokoh-ehkóni'.

After he did this, One-Eyed Sioux and his mother-in-law, the two of them, they slept well.

Toh-nookéni-ni', kóox=he'ih-cé3ei'oo-no'.

When morning came they set off once again.

Wot=hih-tous-koutonéíhi-no' toh-notíkoniibéee-t![10]

How long they stayed out on the warpath!

Ko'ookunootinei héecis-iinísee-t, he'ih-'oo3isíne-n hihéih-o.

While One-Eyed Sioux was wandering around, his mother-in-law got pregnant.

Hihéih-o tih-'iini nóó'ootii-ní3, he'ih-nei'oohób-ee hisó'on-in.

When his mother-in-law was busy finishing up her work, he looked at her rear end.

"Hoonónee[11] híhcen-oo he-biixúut," nií3-oohok hihéih-o.

"Raise your dress up more," he said to his mother-in-law.

"Hoonónee hii-nonóu-nóó'ootii," nii3-oohok, toh'uu-wo3oohów-oot.

"You should bend over more as you're working," he said to her, when he was looking at her avidly.

Héecis-iinxóot-[o'] hihéih-o Ko'ookunootinéi, he'ih-ceníisib-é' honóh'oehíhi', hiníisoo-n.

While One-Eyed Sioux was wandering about with his mother-in-law, she gave birth to a boy, his child.

Heihii he'ih-béexookee-n hiníisoo-n.
Soon his son was big.

Wót=he'=nóhk-ce'-notiko[ni]-yóhk;
Finally he returned with her from the warpath;

hihéih-o, he'ih-'iníisooni-n, honóh'oehiho'.
his mother-in-law had a child, a little boy.

"Neixoo," nii3-éíhok.
"My father," the little boy said to him.

"Hehe', hííko, hííyoh=niiyoonib-é3en."
"Unh-unh, no, rather I'm your brother-in-law."

"Neixoo Ko'ookunootinéi," nii3-éíhok honóh'oehího',
"Father, One-Eyed Sioux," said the little boy,

"Ko'ookunootinei, nohowóh ho-wo'oto'éeet?"
"One-Eyed Sioux, what is the state of your black war/victory paint?"

"Hée, noh henei'towuun-e3énee nehe' honóh'oehíhi' nih-síiih-o'.
"Yes, I am about to tell you all, I captured this boy from the enemy.

"Nih-síiiton-o' nehéihe," heeh-éhk.
"I seized him for my mother-in-law," he said.

Notes

1. *Yóhuh=* 'as X as can be, an exemplary example of X'.
2. Cf. AI *hoyei-* 'shelter'. The verb here is TA *hoyoo3-* 'give it shelter, cover it'. The unstated thing to be covered is of course One-Eyed Sioux's penis.
3. *Hiihóót* NA.DEPPART 'thing loaned, lent to him/her' < *hiih-* TA 'loan, lend'.
4. *Hooté'ein-* 'not long afterward'. Cf. *hoo3i-* 'next [time]'. According to William C'Hair, the form has a secondary implication of letting people know about something ahead of time so that they can be included if they want, without necessarily requiring them to come to the happening. Thus the usage in this passage could be glossed more fully as 'as you would have expected, not long afterward' or 'just as you knew would happen, not long afterward'.
5. *Híii* also means 'snow'.
6. One would expect *heh-níisisíne-n* 'let's sleep together', with NONAFF inflections. The final *-no'*, however, suggests that *heh-* may simply be emphatic (thus the AFF inflections).

7. *3ooxúce'* PART.LOC 'right up next to'.

8. The initial element *he(e)sow-* is unclear, though it may contain *hees-* 'how',

9. Modern usage for 4S NONAFF is *-owun*, but the alternate form *-owuu* is recorded by Salzmann and has been recorded for one contemporary speaker in his eighties.

10. AI *notíkoní-* > AI.O *notíkoniibéee-* 'cause, facilitate s.o. to go on the warpath' or 'act as leader on the warpath'. Cf. AI *neyéi3éi-* 'learn', AI.O *neyéi3eibéee-* 'to teach'.

11. *Hoonónee* '[do it] hard, harder!'

Legends/Myths

Ho'éeetiinohóókee/Lime Crazy

Told by Cleaver Warden, on or after August 23, 1899
Collected by Alfred Kroeber
NAA, MS 2560a, Notebook 10, pp. 40–48, Notebook 12, pp. 1–2
English version published in Dorsey and
Kroeber [1903] 1997: 29–31

This text is associated with the Crazy Lodge of the Arapaho age-grade societies, the Hohóokóowu' (Kroeber [1902–1907] 1983: 188–96). The word *hohóok-óowu'* can be glossed as 'crazy-lodge'. The men of this lodge act in perverse and contrary ways in comparison to normal expectations of behavior. Lime Crazy's name can be glossed in modern spelling as *ho'óeetiin-ohóókee* 'clay/paint-crazy one'. Conversely, the "Fifth Lodge" men who are playing the drum in the story represent the Biíto-hóowu', sometimes glossed as the Spear Lodge. Both of these lodges had specific ceremonial roles within the Sun Dance. This story apparently suggests the relative roles and relationship of the two lodges, though the details are no longer clear. Certainly it is clear that the Crazy Lodge members traditionally would do the opposite of all expectations, just as Lime Crazy does in this story—in particular, by assaulting anyone they came upon outside their lodges during the Crazy Lodge ceremony. Alonzo Moss also notes that someone who fails to complete the Sun Dance is only allowed to go in on a later occasion and try again if he wears white paint rather than the usual red paint.

Despite the connections to craziness and ceremonial misbehavior, Lime Crazy, the younger brother in this story, can be compared to other Arapaho cultural heroes such as Se'esíwonóh'oe/Sleeping Young Man (see "The Beheaded Ones"), and Bii'óxuyoo/Found-in-the-Grass: he is socially marginal, without power or privilege and initially "pitiful," as Arapahos would say in English. Yet he turns out to be far more powerful and capable than anyone would have imagined, primarily by exercising his power in a patient and humble way rather than trying to impose on others. In the stories of Paul Moss (2005), the narrative of "The Arapaho Boy" contains many of these same themes, even though that story is set in historical times.

Structurally, the story offers a good example of the use of summational lines ('that's the way it was') to close out scenes, as well as many new scenes that begin with dialogue after preceding narration or via the proclitic *wot*= 'well, I guess' or a construction involving *tousi-* 'how . . . !' The story is segmented to highlight this rhythm.

Kroeber adds a note at the end of this story: White Owl "means blizzard killed him. Other version says he was killed by lightning."

> Hiiteen hih-tousi-woo3ee!
> What a large camp there was!

He'ih-niiséíh néécee.
There was one chief.

He'ih-'ineehebéh'ihih.[1]
He had a much younger brother.

Kookón wot=híni' kóuto'oowuuhúú-ho',[2]
The brother was just one of those late risers,

nii-cii3o'-cii-cih'ote'eihí-3i',
those who never comb their hair,

nii-cii-bebii3éneti-3i' hiitíxoniihi'.[3]
those who don't fix themselves up properly.

> "Yeheiyee[4] bé, hii-nohkúseic-3ówo3ii, hii-néyoo'úu, hii-cih'óte'eihi, hii-ni'íbouheti.
> "Gee, friend, wake up early in the morning, dress up nicely, comb your hair, perfume yourself.

"Honóh'o-ho' hii-noohow-ún;
"Look at the other young men;

"nii-beh-3ii-3í'oookúu-3i' no'eeteiniihi', coo-co'ótoyoo-ni'i híhcebe'.
"they all stand around at the river, on the hills nearby [where the paths lead down to the river].

"Noo-notín-ooni3i[5] hísei-no, niit-ookohóé-ni3i.
"They look for women, where the women fetch water.[6]

"Noh wo'éí3 niiniséé-3i', nii-noo-nó'usee-3i', hiisiiniihi' noh bíikóó.
"Or they walk around and arrive back here, day and night.

"Hii-hoowu-koo'ée-3i'óku-no' honóh'o-ho'," hee3-éíhok hiisóh'o.
"The young men don't sit around leisurely at home," said his elder brother to him.

   "Híh'óó,"[7] heeh-éhk.
   "All right," said the younger brother.

He'ih-'ehíísi'óúh, cih'ote'éíh, néyoo'óúh, koo-konikúutii hit-óu.
He washed his face, combed his hair, dressed himself up nicely, and shook out his blanket.

He'ih-ni'íbouhet.
He perfumed himself.

He'ne'-no'eehi-t heetoh-coo-co'ótoyoo-ní'i.
Then he went outside to the sand hills.

He'ih-3ii-3í'ookúu hiséí-no neeneit-ookohéí'i-ní3i.
He stood around at the places where the women went to fetch water.

Ci'=tótoos wonóó3ee-ni3i nookoheihíí-ho, niisíneet[8] cih-'itén-oohok tótoos hiisiihíí-ho.
And even though there were many fetching water, he would seize even the married ones.

   Wot=hih-tous-óuun-iiséíh!
   How feared he was [for his sexual aggressiveness]!

Hiisóh'o, hiniihéí'i, hiniito'éí-no—hitoníh'iin-ínoo, heeyóúhuu nih-'í3eti-nin[i-']—
His elder brother, his parents, his relatives—their horses, anything that was good—

nih-kocóó'o3tii-hók[oni'].

they lost them [in payment to the aggrieved women's families].

Tóh-noo3éíhi-t,[9] hiisóh'o he'ih-kohtowú3ecoo.

Because he was accused so much, his elder brother thought up a plan against him.

"Koo=wóów neisoh'óó, heebé3i-néécee?"

"Now, my older brother, are you a big chief?" [the younger brother asked him].[10]

"Hiikó, hóóno'," hee3-éíhok.

"No, not yet," the older brother said to him.

"Wohéí be, sooxe heet[n]-iinóó'ei-no'."

"Well, friend, let's go hunting" [the older brother said].

Niisóho'[11] ce3íkotii-no' hii3einóón-in.

They both went off together [to look for] buffalo.

Hités-eeno';

They came to some buffalo;

nehe' neecéé he'ih-neh'éhei.

the chief [older brother] killed one.

"Niscíbes, niiyou, bé.

"Here's a stinging wooden switch, friend.

"Hi'-kouuteso'on-ín nóubee-no'," hee3-oohók.

"Drive off the flies with it," the chief said to him.

"Hii-noo'éésee.

"Walk around [the carcass].

"Konowúuhu', hóót-won-ei'itóbee-noo," hee3-oohók hinoohowóho'.

"In the meantime I'll go inform everyone of the kill," he said to his younger brother.

He'ne'-nihi'[nee]-noo'éésee-t, toh-kóuutéso'ón-oot nóubee-no.

Then the younger one walked faster and faster around the carcass as he chased off the flies.

Hei'eenów-oot hinóóhowóho', cih-ce'-nehyonih-ee.

When he finally thought of his younger brother again, the chief came back to check on him.

He'ih-wonoh-noo'éesee-n.[12]

He was still walking around the carcass.

Nosou-kouutéso'ón-een nóubee-no.

He was still driving off the flies.

Wóówuh, woowuh he'ih-ceyooxohówoo.[13]

Now, now by this time he dug a deep hole for himself [with his walking].

"Nééhee,[14] cih-nó'eehi; sooxe woteeníihi'.

"My friend, come out of there; let's go back to the camp.

"Ni'ii-noo-no'o3íhee-noo.

"I'm being abused because of leaving you.

"Nei-hoowú-útonihi'.

"I don't have any horses.

"Nei-hoowú-úyeihi'.

"I don't have a lodge.

"Nei-hoowú-ubíí3hiin.

"I don't have any food.

"Heni'-hesoxuuhéíhi-noo.

"I'm whipped and beaten because of what I did.

"Ní'ii-koo-konó'ootii-noo,"[15] nehe' nii3-oohók hinóóhowoho'.

"I'm banished from camp due to my treatment of you," this one said to his younger brother.

"Koowót=héi3oohk?"[16]
"Will you do that?"

Nó3oon he'ih-nihi'inéés néhe' hinén.
But instead the man kept walking rapidly around the carcass.

He'ih-ce'ís.
The older brother went back.

"Nii-cii-ní'oow-o', nii-nóuheti-t," hee3-oohók hiníín.
"He won't agree, he refuses," he said to his wife.

Wót=nehe' honóh'e, tih'ini bixoo3-éíhok hinii3ébi-o.
Well, it seems this young man, his sister-in-law loved him.

"Hi3í=nonóónoko'[17] heenéti3-ot, toh-ciisib-étebínouhuuní-noo.
"Maybe you might as well talk to him, because I'm fed up with living pitifully like this.

"Het-níí-ni'iw-oo.
"Say good things to him.

"Het-bébiis-ei'itowúun-oo toh-ciiyeih'í-no', toh-ciitonih'í-no', ciisib-etebinouhuuní-no'," hee3-oohók hiníín.
"Explain clearly to him that we have no lodge, no horses, and are fed up with being pitiful," he said to his wife.

Nehe' hisei he'=nee'ees-cé3ei'oo-t.
Then this woman set off as he had asked.

No'usee-hék, béenihéhe' bés, niscíbes,
When she arrived, just a little bit of wood, the switch,

he'ih-bísi-noh'óówukúúh toh-nosou-kouuteso'ón-oot nóubee-no.
he was flicking it around and you could see it above the pit, because he was still chasing off the flies.

"Néi3eboo, ceh'é3ih-i hootn-ii3-é3en.
"Brother-in-law, listen to what I'm going to say to you.

"Hoonónee heni'-hetebínouhuuní-no' nenééni-n.
"Because of you we're really terribly pitiful.

"Kookuyón nii-hoon-o'ooxootíí-no'.
"We just camp at the very far edge of the camp.

"Wóótii hé3-ebii, nií3eenébee-no'.
"We're thought of like dogs.

"Heenee3eenébee-nou'u, ne'-neeneisihee-no'.
"Whatever they think of to do to us, that's how we are treated.

"Bééxo'-noo-no'o3ihéé-no'.
"We're just treated cruelly.

"Hóókoh nenééni-n tíh-niisíhee-no'."
"It's because of you that we're treated this way."[18]

"Héii, he3ebí-nee'eeseen-ínee néi3ebi."[19]
"Fine, show the way to my older brother over there, my sister-in-law."

Cih-bis-céno'oo-hók nohkúuhu' niscíbes.
He jumped up into view with his switch [still in his hand].

Ciitééx co'ookóó3-niisíkotii-no'.
Free from his task, the young man and his sister-in-law walked back home together.

Tih-'i3óu'oo-', heecisisee-3i', he'ih-bih'iyoo.
In the evening, while they were walking, it got dark.

Toh-nó'usee-3i' híitéén, nonoonééhei-3i' hé'ih-nosou-woteiho'yei-nó' níiinon-e'.
When they arrived at camp, the fifth-lodge soldiers were still playing the drum in a tipi.

"Noohow-unee woteiho'yeihii-ho'!
"Look at the drummers!

"Ceeneeniwotei'oo-3i'."
"They were playing Sun Dance songs."

Nee-nee-hohkóni' hiitéén nih-i'-ii-hí3eti-'.
It was thanks to them that the camp was in good order.

"Yihoo beeyoo heet-woteihó'oyooni-'.
"Go right where the sound of the drum is coming from," [the young man said].

"Het-ei'itowúun-oono', 'Ho'eeetiinohóókee noo'usee-t,' het-íí3-oono' ciitei-ninéhk."
"Tell them 'Lime Crazy has arrived,' you must say to them when you enter."

Hísei he'ih-yihoo, ciitei;
The woman went there and entered;

"Ho'éeetiinohóókee cee'i-no'úsee-t," hit-íí3-ooono.[20]
"Lime Crazy has come back" is what she said to them.

Téébe neehii3éí', nee'ei'i-nihii-hók.
She was just right in the middle of what she was going to say.

"Hii-hoowú-u3oobei.
"She is lying.

"Ce'i-nouukúu3-e', nóxowúh-u[n]," hee3-éíhok.
"Throw her back out! Kill her [if you feel like it!]," they said about her.

Tih-'ii3éíhi-t, he'ih-ce'i-nóuuhce.
When this was said to her, she hurried back outside.

"Teebe neehii3éí' neenei'i-nihii-noo 'óh cih-ce'-nouu[te]so'on-í3i'," hee3-oohók hinii3ébi-o.

"I was just right in the middle of what I was going to say, and they kicked me back out," she said to her brother-in-law.

"Hii-ce'i-yihóón-inee.

"Go back there to them.

"'Ho'éeetiinohóókee noo'úsee-t,' het-íí3-oono'."

"'Lime Crazy has arrived,' you must say to them."

Téébe benee3í-nihii-hok,[21] he'ih-'i3ikúu3oo.

When she got through speaking, she was seized.

Níinen hi'íihi' he'ih-sii'oonootoh-e'.[22]

They smeared her face with hot fat.

Xoo-xoxooyeineet.

She screamed for help.

"'ohéé," ho'éeetiinohóókee heeh-ehk, toh-cíitei-t.

"'ohee!" said Lime Crazy, when he entered.

"Hei-tóustoo-be?"

"What are you all doing?"

Koowot=héetii3ootiin.

No one said a word.

Beh-cééne'eicíítoon.[23]

Everyone sat humbly with bowed heads.

"Wohéí hiisóho' behií3oku-';[24]

"Well, you all sit like this;

"hííyoh=ko'eici-'," hee3-oohók nonooneehei-ní3i.

"sit in a perfectly round circle," he said to the fifth-lodge members.

Hé'i=beh-nee'ee3óku-ni3i.
They were all sitting as he told them to.

"Wohéí néi3eboo, hiiyóu kookó'oox.[25]
"Well, my sister-in-law, here is a round war club.

"Hono'út heetoxokú-3i' hixosoon-ínoo núhu', hí'ii-to'ootowúún-inee
nii3éí'init."[26]
"All of them who are sitting here, on their shins with this, hit their shins
with it with all your might."

Nehe' hísei kookó'oox he'ih-'iis-to'ób-ee noo'eeniihi', té3eiciihi'.
This woman hit each one of them, all around the circle, with the
war club.

Koowót=héetii3ei-níno.
No one said a word.

Tih-'iis-béh-to'ów-oot woxoson-e',
After she had hit all of them on the shin,

"Néi3eboo, nehe' nótiitii-n hónouu=huú3eti-n[i'] níiinon;
"My sister-in-law, you look for the very finest tipi;

"bee3iyóó-no hee3ei'-i3eti-n[i'i], noh ci'-bií3iwo, hiwoxuhóóx-ebii.
"and clothes as nice as you can find, and food too, and horses.

"Koo'ee-nótiih-ín hii3eihí-3i';
"Take your time and look for pretty ones;

"hono'út héi-ni'eenee3óó-no, ni'iine'ítii," hee3-oohók hinii3ébi-o
ho'eeetiinohóókee;
"everything that pleases you, live well," said Lime Crazy to his
sister-in-law;

"Héhnee=honouu=huú3eti-ni'[27] níiinon, bee3iyóó-no, kookon behííhi'
ciitoowúu' noh céee3i';
"The very best tipi, clothing, anything at all, inside and outside;

"niihéyoo hei-ni'éénee3oo-no."
"the things that you find pleasing to yourself."

Nehe' hísei hé'i=née'éestoo-t.
This woman did accordingly.

Ciitééx, nehe' néécee níiinon he'ih-3owoyookúu.
Without further ado, this chief's tipi stood upright again.

Hiiwoxuuhóóxebííni-t; he'ih-néén béhisiihi' hiitéén.
He had horses; he was the one who had the best of everything in
the camp.

Hiyeih'-ínoo he'=iis-iixowuh-niiseti-n, toh-cé'i-ni'iine'etíí-3i', néhe'
hiineehebéh'i-t.
Their lodge was acknowledged as the best in the camp, because they
were living well again, this one who had the younger brother.

He'i=néé'ees-iine'etíi-t.
That is how he lived.

"Koox=wóów béh'ee, heniinoo'éi-no' hóóxonó'oo hiisííhi'," heeh-éhk
néhe' hinén.
"Once again now, friend, we're going hunting across the river that
way," said the older man to Lime Crazy.

Toh-'okeéé-3i' niicíe, he'ih-ni'okéee-no', toh-cii-tébi-ni'.
When they crossed the river, they waded across safely, where it was
not deep.

He'=néé'ees-iinoo'éi-3i' neeyéic-i' hiisííhi'.
Then they hunted as the chief had proposed, for a day.

Néhe' benéexookee-t he'ih-ce'-noníikoo.
Then Lime Crazy's older brother again ran away from him.

Ho'eeetiinohóókee he'íh-néés-woo-wó'oten-ee biíí-no, hé'=iisííhi'[28]
nii-nookó3oni-3i', tih-'ii3íw-oot hiisóh'o.

Lime Crazy stayed behind gathering eagle plumes, those white tail feathers of the young golden eagle, since he missed his brother.

Hei'íiseeniit, cése'ehí-o he'ih-cih-'iiseinééb-e'.
After getting enough, an animal came and advised him.

Wot=hééyei-n, "Het-eenetí3-oo niicíe neniihenéíh-t.
A swift hawk [said to him], "You must speak to the owner of the river.

"'Cih-'okéeexoh-u,' het-íí3-oo," hee3-oohók.
"'Carry me across,' you must say to him," said the swift hawk to him.

"'Nuhu' nooko3ónii-no bé, heti-inookúun,' het-íí3-oo hiincebíít.
"'These eagle tail feathers, friend, you will use them for a warbonnet,' you must say to the Water Monster.

"Hoot-cih-bíxousee-t niiton-éíninéhk," heeh-éhk hééyei ho'éeetiinohóókee.
"It will appear above the water when it hears you," said the swift hawk to Lime Crazy.

"Hiiyóu-no hó-nookuú-no," tih-'íí3-oot.
"Here are your feathers," he said [to the Water Monster when he appeared].

Ses3óówu-u' bixo'oe-too'úsee-n.[29]
Water Monster came up out of the water at the edge of the stream and stopped.

Too-toukutón-ee biii-no hinii3e'één-in, hiniiní3-in.
Lime Crazy tied the plumes on to his head, his horns.[30]

"Tonóó'usee-3i, cih-'ii-néén-íí3-ot héesííhi'."
"Whenever he stops, say the same things again just like that."

He'ne'=nih-'íístoo-t.
And that's what he did.

"Hooton-oxonih-éín neehii3éí' 3oonó'oo'.

"He will [try to] harm you in the middle of the river channel.

"Hihcébe' kokúy.

"Above is a whistle.

"Niitowoo3ee-téhk, honóóyoo het-íisitoo núhu' hee3-e3en.

"When you hear it, make very sure to do what I am telling you.

"Hoton-iíni . . . ,[31] xoo-xonóu hihcébe' niitóbee-ninéhk, hóonónee heti-noho'úhce," heeh-éhk hééyei.

"You must . . . , right away when you hear the whistle above, jump as hard as you can," said the swift hawk.

Hiitouúk, néhe' ho'éeetiinohóókee he'ih-noh'úhce.

Sure enough [when he reached the middle and heard the whistle], Lime Crazy jumped.

Nohkuúhu' nec, ceecii3ów biito'owú-u' he'ih-'iis-éh-ko'ús.

With the water, he reached the land, but at the wrong place due to inattention/distraction.

Ne'=nih-'iis-iixokooo-hók.[32]

That is how he crossed the river.

Toh-ce'-no'úsee-t hiitéén, hiisóh'o he'ih-'iinooxuwúh-e'.

When he got back to camp, his elder brother determined that he should wander about again.

Koowot=íi3-oohk nehe' ho'eeetiinohóókee.

But Lime Crazy absolutely refused to consent this time.

Tih-'iinísee-t, nooku-béé3ei-n he'ih-neh'-e'.

Later, when Lime Crazy was wandering around, white owl killed him.[33]

Notes

1. *Nééhebéhe'* means younger same-sex sibling. Thus AI 'to have a younger same-sex sibling' is *hineehebéh'i-*. AI.DIM is *hineehebéh'ihih-*.

2. Exactly the same word is used to describe Sleeping Young Man, the hero of the myth of "The Beheaded Ones."

3. Kroeber glosses this form as 'do not care'. Alonzo Moss recognized the word and agreed that the overall translation of the sentence is correct but could not recall the exact meaning and usage of the word.

4. *Yehéí* means 'gosh, gee whiz, golly'. The form *yeheiyee* is not recognized today.

5. The manuscript has *notón-ooni3i*. This could be *notton-* 'ask s.o. s.t.', although Kroeber glosses 'look for'.

6. This was in fact a common practice of young men in the old days. In the "Life of Mrs. White Bear" (see appendix A) she describes how men would wait for the young girls fetching water in this way, hoping to talk to them (at least).

7. Kroeber actually transcribes *íhih'oohóó*. This seems to be simply an overly phonetic hearing of the particle.

8. The form is not recognized today. Kroeber glosses it 'at once'.

9. The verb is not recognized today.

10. C'Hair says that this phrase is used commonly in Arapaho when someone is perceived as taking too much authority, trying to dictate, and so forth. The line suggests that certain details have been left out immediately prior in the story and/or that the younger brother clearly perceives the ill intentions of his older brother and does not accept the following invitation to go hunting naively.

11. The modern form is *nííso'úúhu'*.

12. The preverb *wonóh-* means the same thing as *nosou-* 'still' but is much less common and is perhaps more emphatic.

13. *Cey-ooxoh-ówoo-* 'deep-dig hole by instrument' (TI)-SELFB(AI)-.

14. According to William C'Hair, the vocative *nééhee* is a woman's word meaning 'friend' and in particular 'dear friend', in reference to a lifelong female (nonsexual) companion of another female. This is or was an Arapaho institution. A more common word is *notóu* (which is not vocative, however). It is unclear why the woman's word would be used between men in this story—but remember that the narrative was collected in Oklahoma not Wyoming, where C'Hair is from.

15. *Kono'óótii-* AI.T 'to be spatially separated from a place, at a remove'.

16. *Hei-3oo-hok* 2S-thing done-SUBJ. Cf. *niisí3oó* 'thing made/done' < *niisi-too-* 'do/make'.

17. *Hi3í=* is used here in the sense 'if' or 'possibly later'.

18. Because they left him behind, violating duties to help out the family.

19. One would expect the vocative form *nei3oboo* here.

20. The form *hitii3óoóno* is an NA.DEPPART, from ii3- TA 'say to s.o.': *hit-ii3-óoó-no* = 3S-say to(AI)-3/4.DEPPART-4PL. The form could be glossed either as 'the ones she said it to' or 'the thing she said to those ones'.

21. The initial change is aberrant with a subjunctive inflection.

22. *Síí'oonóóton-* TA 'rub someone's face' is the more usual form of this verb. The form here appears to be *síí'oonóótoh-* TA 'rub someone's face by means of a tool'.

23. *Ceene'éici-* AI 'sit with one's head down'. The final *–[e]ci-* is a variant of *oku-* 'sit'.

24. Is the intended meaning *bebíi3óku-'* AI 'sit properly'?

25. *Kó'oox* is apparently an alternate form of *cé'eex* 'tomahawk'. The vowels *e* and *o* alternate in vowel harmony in Arapaho, and *k* mutates to *c* before *e*. Compare the common word *henéécee* 'buffalo bull' with an older form *bo'onóókee* 'red bull'.

26. The form *ni'ii3íí'init* appears to be an alternate form of the modern AI verb *ni'ii3íí'óo3e-* 'to do something with all one's might'.

27. The archaic form *héhnee=* corresponds to the modern emphatic proclitic *héh=*. The earlier form is also found in texts of John Goggles collected by Salzmann.

28. The form *he'íisíihi'* is unclear. The most obvious meaning is 'DUBIT-like this', producing an overall literal meaning of 'the way they have white rump [feathers]'.

29. *Bix-o'óet-too'úsee-n* = 'appear-at river-stop-walk' (AI)-4S. Cf. *no'óetei'* 'to/at the river'.

30. This act echoes a ritual gesture performed in the Sun Dance ceremony.

31. The manuscript actually has *hotniihi*.

32. One would expect *-íix-okéee-hók* here. The form may be *-íix-okóoo'oo-hók* (inchoative).

33. White owl is a figurative expression for frost, cold, and snow. Thus he died in a blizzard.

The White Crow

Told by Cleaver Warden, Oklahoma, August 22 or 23, 1899
Collected by Alfred Kroeber
NAA, MS 2560a, Notebook 10, pp. 15–22
English version published in Dorsey and Kroeber
[1903] 1997: 275–77

This story has a number of important etiological themes, tied both to various Arapaho ceremonies and to traditional cultural practices. The story is one of several that begin in the time before present-day (traditional) Arapaho culture, in that the central relationship between the Arapahos and the buffalo is not yet established. (Another example of such a story is the race between the buffalo and the horse, to determine which will be eaten and which will be ridden.)

The Wheel Game being played at the beginning of the story is more significant than first appears. The Wheel in question is a secular variant of the Sacred Wheel, which is the second most important religious object held by the tribe, after the Sacred Flat Pipe. Moreover, the Sacred Wheel itself replicates the overhead design of the Sun Dance lodge. Finally, ceremonial fasting sites in the mountains sometimes had Wheels of rock (the most famous being in the Bighorn Mountains of Wyoming). Indeed, that site is known as *hííɜeinóónotíí* 'buffalo wheel' in Arapaho. (See that story and the introduction to it in Moss 2005, as well as the story "The Forks" in the same volume for more on these connections.) Thus the Wheel is linked symbolically to the buffalo in Arapaho culture. In the beginning of the story the text says that the young men were often losing at the Wheel Game. Cowell suggests that this refers to the lack of buffalo in these "precultural" days, because they did not yet control the buffalo. More generally, it invokes the incompleteness or insufficiency of ceremonial and symbolic relationships with the natural world at that time. More specifically, the obstacle toward which the Wheel rolls presages the door or obstacle encountered later in the story, which keeps the buffalo corralled inside White Crow's hollow mountain.

Another important point that might escape those reading quickly is the behavior of the young boy toward White Crow at the beginning of the story.

He is described as someone who 'bothers' people (AI *cóó'u3éi-* or *cóú'u3éi-*). The word has clear negative implications and can also be glossed as 'molest' (including sexually). The boy also uses an emphatic imperative marker *neh-* 'you'd better', which is inappropriate for addressing a visiting stranger and suggests effrontery. Yet his excessive curiosity and even effrontery turn out to be highly useful. Arapaho stories include many such young boys who, while violating traditional norms, end up bringing benefits to their families or the tribe (see "The Beheaded Ones," for example, or the story "The Arapaho Boy" in Moss 2005). The young boy thus brings up the more general theme of the proper balance between manners and curiosity and (Cowell suggests) the need for the culture to have a few curious "outliers."

It is also important to recognize that the Arapaho word *hóuu* can mean both 'crow' and 'creator'. The story (as Kroeber's notes at the end of this introduction emphasize) clearly plays on the two meanings of this word. Moreover, the crow was often seen symbolically as a messenger to and from the Creator (see especially Kroeber [1902–1907] 1983: 319ff. on the Ghost Dance and 363ff. on the Crow Dance). The need to watch where the crow flies and follow it in this story clearly ties into this idea of the messenger. The initial white color of the crow is a further link to the Creator and the power of creation: Cowell notes that white buffalo cows were an important symbol in Plains Indian culture, and the Arapahos saw white animals as having special powers. See, for example, the story "The Enemy Trail" in Moss 2005, where a specifically white horse must be procured to accomplish the mission in question.

Other seemingly passing details in the story are very important: it is finally the buffalo cow (*bíí*), and most specifically the young buffalo cow (*nónooni*), that "seduces" the crow. The cow was the preferred target of Arapaho hunters, with the young cow being the most prized prey of all. That high status in a sense makes her worthy to capture the White Crow. Note also that the design pattern described on the arrow with which she is associated is a specifically Arapaho pattern (see "The Life of Medicine Grass").

Why the "short-legged dog"? As Kroeber's notes make clear, the theme of eating dogs is an underlying part of this story. Dogs—and in particular puppies—were eaten ceremonially. The puppy is the required choice in the Kingfisher Ceremony (also called Dog Ceremony), which is performed around Christmas time in association with the Crow/God Dance. As in the case of the young buffalo cow, the high status of the small, cute dog, which can be understood as a puppy, makes it worthy to "seduce" the crow (and his son) a second time. William C'Hair said that after hearing this story (which he had not known before) he finally understood why the puppy is so important in the Crow Dance.

Why specifically "two young men [*honóh'oho'*]" who follow the crow both times? While we cannot say with certainty, Cowell notes that it is interesting to look at "The Forks" in Moss 2005, which is a somewhat similar tale of tribal hunger and need resolved through medicine power. In that story as well, two young men are sent out by the elders to ride a particular path that will bring in game for the tribe. The "two young men" seem to be part of the theme of medicine power. As noted, "The Forks" is itself very closely associated with the image of the Sacred Wheel, whose power is used to procure game.

As Kroeber's notes show, the theme of "forced reciprocity" is central to the story. Once the crow accepts the implicitly proffered gift of the short-legged dog, he must reciprocate, but he has nothing to give in return except the buffalo. More generally, much of Arapaho traditional religion could be understood as an attempt to force reciprocity from the Creator, especially through suffering and sacrifice. Specifically, the annual sacrifice of the puppy during the Kingfisher Ceremony, as part of the Crow/God Dance, is symbolically replicated in this story. Indeed, the concluding word of the story (*hóóxohoeníihi'*) is the most important Arapaho word expressing the ideas of exchange, trade, and reciprocity. In addition, according to William C'Hair, older people used to say *wohéí híiwo' hoséíno' heetbii3íno'óhk* 'well what do you know, we're going to eat some meat!' when they heard a crow calling. This was a formulaic expression that evoked the connection of the crow to the buffalo. Additionally, crows and/or ravens (both can be referred to as *hóuu*) were used in former times to find herds of buffalo, by following the movement of the birds.

Kroeber's notes say:

> Because [Crow] took the present of the dog, he could not refuse to show and give the buffalo. [Crow] looks on because he can do nothing, and all he gets is the eyes. Just so, he now watches during the butchering, helpless and can get only what is left. The dog stuck to buffalo and was part of him, being rump + tail. The dog could not have been Nih'oo3oo as with Blackfeet, for then he would not be eaten (as dogs are, especially at dawn and feasts), but would be called our father. Spider web = noyootino, fish lines (c.f. rainbow); whites called spider because hairy body. The crow is our father, but the dog is part of buffalo, is food.
>
> This is why dog is used in dog dance. The white crow is the nokuwuhesi of buffalo dance: for both are the owners, the boss of the herd. The sun was a dog [c.f. English sun dogs], as story shows. Nih'oo3oo had power or privilege of imitating all animals he wanted to; thus he learned their ways.

These notes link the story implicitly to "The White Dog and the Woman," where the dog is also identified as the sun. The dog (sun) clings to the tail of the buffalo, which is echoed in the Arapaho Sun Dance ceremony, where the *nookohóe* is a ceremonial buffalo tail, without which the Sun Dance cannot begin.

Note finally the four-part structure, as well as the four animals (rabbit, antelope, elk, buffalo) that the crow visits before being seduced by the choicest of them, the buffalo.

Part One: Visit from White Crow

Wot=hii3einóón-no' tih'ini néseih-ehk.[1]

In the beginning the buffalo were wild.

He'ih-nookéíh houu, noononíh-oot, nii-3eiiso'ón-oot híí3einoon-in.

There was white crow, who kept the herd, and corralled it.

Wot=neene-hék nih-niihenéíhi-t hííteen.

He was the one who owned the [buffalo] tribe.

Béteenó3-ii, betéénotííb-e' he'ih-cebiihetiitoon.

With the medicine arrows and the medicine wheel people were playing a game.[2]

Hokóusíwoo[3] héetoo-t, he'né'-nih'ikúúhu-t hótii.

Where the obstacle was, then the wheel was tossed that direction.

Heh-niisí-3i' honóh'o-ho' wootii tih-nonouhtíítooni-', nii3ei'ikooh-ehkóni',

Two young men, as when people are running a race as fast as they can,

hééyeih-nó'únoo'oo-3i hotii hokóusiwóón-e', núhu' heh-niisí-3i' honóh'o-ho' he'ih-cébii-n[o'].

whenever the wheel was about to get to the obstacle, these two young men shot at it.

Wot=hih-tous-no'o3iikóhutii-no'.[4]

Well, I guess they were having the wheel get away from them a lot [without their hitting it].

Nóko3ee[5] honóh'e hé'ih-noocóúbee, ciitó3oo he'ih-3éí'iikóhee.

Off on one side was a young man who had a white robe and was carrying a quiver on his back.

Cih-no'úsee-t, xoxoo'oot-iisíb[6] híhcebe' tih-'ésooku'óó-t.

He came over and lay down flat on his stomach to watch on.

Kónow-eebiiheti-',[7] céése' honóh'e, heenoo híni' nii-có'on-coo'ú3ei-3i', he'ih-nééni-n:

While they were playing, one boy, one of those who always have to bother people, it was him [who went over to the stranger]:

"Béh'ee, hi3í=neh-noohóót héík-o," hee3ee-tehk nehe' noo'u-céítee-t.

"Say, old fellow, you'd better let me look at your arrows," he said to the one who had come to visit.

He'ih-bii'iní-no hi-ciito3óón-e' besíísei, toon=he'ih-niiwookús.

Eyes were found in his quiver, ones that he had brought along as food for the journey.

"Héii, nookóuu, nenééni-t.
"Look, it's White Crow.

"Hoonoyoohób-e' toon=heesíh'ohu-[t]."
"Watch him, wherever he flies."

He'i=nee'ees-oonoyoohobéíhi-t.
He was watched as the boy had said.

Part Two: Ensnaring White Crow

[At this point White Crow wanders off, watched by the people, who hope to find his secrets. He comes upon a series of animals, who are pretending to be dead and seek to entrap him. The transition is not made clear in the Arapaho text.]

Nóóku he'ih-'éix[8] ho3.
A rabbit had an arrow on him.[9]

"Tóusoo híni' ho3?" heeh-éhk houu.
"What kind of arrow is that?" said Crow.

Ceeti3-éíhok.
The rabbit did not answer him.

Ce'íkoyih'o.
He flew away again.

Koox=heet-ko'ósi-' nookóuu:
The same thing happened once again where White Crow landed:

nisíce híni' nii-koxcei'í-3i', neene-hék hé'ih-se'is.
a pronghorn antelope, the ones that are fat, he was the one lying there.

Ho3 he'ih-'éix.
There was an arrow on/in him.

"Tousoo híni' ho3?" nii-hók.
"What kind of arrow is that?" said Crow.

Noh "Wóó'oteeyoo-';
And "It's black," [said the antelope];

"Cei hení'i-wohonó3oo-'."[10]
"It's painted with tar."

Noh "Hoow-úu-néén," heeh-ehk houu.
And "That's not it," said Crow.

Ce'i-cesíh'o.
He flew away again.

Koox=hiwóxuu, híni' nii-koxcei'í-3i', he'ih-nééni-no' henéíx-o' ho3.
Then next there was an elk, the ones that are fat, he is the one wearing/bearing an arrow.

"Tou3ohonó3oo?"
"What kind of paint does it have?"

Noh "Nee'eesoo-'," hee3-éíhok.
And "It's like this," said the elk to him.

Noh, "Hoow-úu-néén," heeh-ehk.
And "That's not it," he said.

Ce'ikoyih'oh-éhk nookóuu.
White Crow flew away again.

Wot=hini' neic nookunéyeihi-3i'[11] hiwóxuu, hé'ih-neen henéix-o' ho3.
I guess next there was an arrow in one of those elk that have white fat on the meat, he was the one with an arrow in/on him.

"Tou3ohonó3oo?"
"What kind of paint does it have?"

"Nee'ee3ohonó3oo-'," hee3-éíhok.
"It has that kind of paint," it said to him.

"Hoowúuni," heeh-éhk nookóuu.
"That's not it," said White Crow.

Koox=he'ih-ce'íkoyih'o.
Then once again he flew away again.

Bíiti' nónooni[12] nii-koxcéi'i-3i' he'ih-se'ís.
Now it was the turn of a young buffalo cow—the ones that are fat—to be lying down.

Ho3 he'ih-'éix.
It had an arrow on/in it.

Nookóuu he'ih-nottóbee, "Tou3ohonó3oo?"
White Crow asked about it, "What kind of paint does it have?"

"Xonóuuwúcihi-'[13] nóko3ee.
"It has a straight mark on one side.

"Céése' ceeceiwucíhi-'," hee3-éíhok bíi.
"On the other side it has a crooked snakelike mark," said the buffalo cow to him.

"Necííkou[14] cih-xouuwoo'óó-noo," hee3éé-tehk.
"Finally I have got just what I was aiming for," Crow was told [by the one who captured him].

Hiisiiténoo nookouu.
White Crow was seized.

Níiinón-e' hihcébe' he'=iis-iisiiténoo, níiinon tih-nouutootesítoo'oo-'.[15]
He was kept at the top of the tipi, the place in the tipi where the smoke comes out.

Heihii nookóuu he'ih-wo'otééheih.
Soon White Crow was turned black.

Howóh nih-'iisi-nookéíh-t!
He was no longer white![16]

Part Three: Ensnaring Crow Again

Cesíh'o.
He flew away [after they released him].

"Hoonoyoohób-e' hees-noononoo'óó-t, heesíh'ohu-t," hee3-éíhok.
"You all watch where he's circling, where he's flying," [the young boy] said about him.

Heh-niisí-3i' honóh'o-hó' he'ih-3ookúh-eeno'.
Two young men followed him.

Bíí'iitii-no' níiinon he'ih-'óotee.
They found a tipi set up.

Wot=hih-tóusí-hi3eih nehe' hinén!
How good this man had it [with meat]!

Honóh'o-ho' he'ih-ce'ísee-no' toh-won-ei'tóbee-3i'.
The young men returned to report what they had observed.

He'ih-béhisi-yihkon.
The whole band moved over there [to where Crow's tipi was].

He'ih-niii-n[o'] híhcebe'.
They camped close by.

Ciiyitó'e3oon[17] hóuu.
They cleaned Crow out of meat.

Toh-ceikóni-', to'óóneehíhi' hé'ih-wóotii-nóo3oo.
When the band moved back this way, a short-legged dog was left behind [on purpose].

Wootíi hínee, "Neixoo, to'óóneehihi'!
Apparently at that place Crow's son said, "Father! a little short-legged one!

"Wootii heh-nees-iinisééhih-t![18]
"It looks like the poor thing has been left behind just wandering around!

"Heetíh-'itonih'i-noo neixóó!
"I want it for my pet, father!

"Yóhou=hoxóoteihih!"
"Look how cute it is!"

"Nei, cíinih-ín."
"Son, leave it there."

"Hííko neixóó!
"No, father!

"Hootni-itonih'i-noo, howóh?"
"It will be my pet, okay?"

He'ih-cih-ce'-beh-'óónoyoohobéíh.
The dog was watched by everyone in the tribe, looking back as they departed.

"Wohéí heet[n]i-itoníh'i-n neí," heeh-éhk hóuu.
"Well then, it will be your pet, son," said Crow.

Ciiteex, he'ih-cih-ce'kón nehe' hi'iihí' to'ooneehíhi'.
Without anyone giving an order, the whole band came back because of the short-legged dog.[19]

Part Four: The Gift of the Buffalo

"Wohéí hóuu, toot=hii3éínoon hénitoo?"
"Well, Crow, where are the buffalo?" [they asked, once they had turned around and come back].

"Hínee siiyóni' nee'éetoo-t," heeh-éhk houu.
"The herd is there at that sandstone area," said Crow.

"Wohéí sooxé héetoo-t híí3einoon," heeh-éhk hóuu.
"Well, let's go to where the buffalo are," said Crow.

No'uxóótiini-'éhk, heebe3ííhi' hoh'onóókee he'ih-tecenooniin.
When everyone arrived there, there was a big rock and there was a door.

Hóuu xonou he'ih-kooniiteen-ee tecenoo-[n] hoh'onookee-n.
Right away Crow opened the door in the rock.

Hikoob-e' to'ooneehíhi' he'ih-'éneebínet.[20]
At his back the short-legged dog was darting about anxiously.

Tih-'iis-koonén-oot tecénoo-n, he'i=béhisi-níiciséisé-'.[21]
After he opened the door, it was all hollow inside the mountain.

Téébe ceensei'-[o']éhk[22] hóuu, 'oh woowuh he3 ciitoowú-ú'
he'ih-béebee.
Crow had just taken one step in, and now the dog was barking inside
the mountain.

Wot=heebeté3.
Somehow it was a large dog now.

Henii3éínooniini-t he'ih-noh'oowús.
The mass of buffalo stirred.

Hetóuu ciitééx hii3éínoon.
The buffalo began bellowing all on their own.

He'ih-nouu3íito'oo.[23]
They came out here in a long row.

Hóuu he'ih-bi'i-hésooku'oo.
Crow just watched the spectacle.

Howóh neniihenéíhi-t híí3einoon-in!
The buffalo that were once his were all gone now!

"Hóó3o' heet[n]-iisííten-o' he3," nii-hók hóuu.
"I bet I'll catch the dog [at least]," said Crow.

Toh-bée3i-nó'ehi-t hii3einoon, he3 he'ih-kohyeibikoo hitihíín-e'.
When the herd finished going out, the dog clung tight to the tail [of one
of the buffalo].

Heeneeteese-'[24] heet[n]ii-woo3ee-t hii3éínoon, hee3ooxúwu-'ehk.
From now on there will be plenty of buffalo, that is how it has been
determined.

"Heniis-nee-neh'ehootiini-'i, hóuu, heet[n]ii-noo-no'úxohu-n.
"After people kill [the buffalo], Crow, you can come over.

"Koun besíísei heet[n]i-itét-ow," hee3ee-téhk hóuu.

"You will only get the eyes," Crow was told.

Ciitééx hii3einoon noowuúúhu' noh nenebííhi', he'ih-behínouh.

On their own the buffalo spread, to the south and the north, they spread to cover the whole earth.

Ne'=níí'-tonóuni-t he3; toh-nééni-t ceneesíh-oot hii3éínoon-in.

That is why the dog is used; because he is the one who provides the buffalo for them.

Hóuu heisonóón-in hooxoheenííhi'.

The Crow is our father in return.

Notes

1. The manuscript actually has *tih-nih-*, although these two tense/aspect prefixes never co-occur. But detached prefix forms (*tih'ini, nih'ini, he'ih'ini*) are very rare in Kroeber's texts, so the exact reading here remains in question.

2. In particular the Wheel Game (*béexotíí* 'big wheel'). The wheel was rolled and then shot at with arrows.

3. *Hokousi-* AI 'lie blocked' > TA *hokousiw-* 'position s.t. to block s.t. else' > AI.MID *hokousibee-* > deverbal *hokousiwoo* 'thing that lies blocking s.t.'

4. *Nó'o3íikoh-* TA 'many escape from s.o.' > AI.T *nó'o3íikoh-utii-* 'have many of s.t. escape from one'.

5. This term is archaic in modern Arapaho. See Gros Ventre *nokoθaah* 'on the side, off to the side'.

6. The element *xoxoo'oot-* is unclear. Kroeber glosses it 'on his stomach'.

7. One would expect *cebííhetí-* here.

8. The verb used here literally means 'to wear'. Thus it is not clear whether the arrow is actually in the animal or just lying on top of it.

9. Various animals will be used as bait in order to capture the crow and discover his power.

10. The form *wohono3oo-* is not recognized by modern speakers but is documented in Kroeber's field notes, meaning 'painted, decorated'.

11. The AI final *-neyeihi* refers to fat on meat, as in *no'o3neyeihi-* 'have a lot of fat on the meat'; and *wo'teen(i)neyeihi-* 'have black/dark fat on the meat'.

12. *Nónooní* is a young buffalo cow, while *bii* is a mature buffalo cow.

13. *Xouuwucihi-* and the verb *ceceiwucihi-* in the next sentence are both used specifically to talk about patterns on arrows: a straight line and a crooked/snaking line.

14. The word *neciikou* is not recognized today but occurs in two other of Kroeber's texts, both times glossed 'finally, at last'.

15. *Nóuutóótesítoo'óó-* II 'smoke comes outside'. William C'Hair appreciated this old word.

16. *Howoh* plus the verb is an idiomatic expression, with *howoh* indicating roughly surprise that something that used to be the case is no longer the case, as in 'What the . . !? It used to be white!'

17. This word not recognized today—the exact transcription and translation are uncertain, and based on Kroeber's gloss.

18. AI *hiinísee-* 'wander around' > AI.DIM *hiinisééhih-*.

19. The dog was another trap; once Crow accepted it, he had to reveal where he got all his meat.

20. *Héneebetí-* AI.REFL 'restless, anxious, cannot restrain oneself'. Cf. *héneebínoo'oo-* AI 'restless, anxious'.

21. *Niiciseise-* VII 'hollow in[side] s.t.' Cf. *ce'eise-* II 'liquid is present in(side) s.t.'

22. *Ceensei'-* TI 'take one step on/to s.t.'

23. Note the close resemblance of this verb to the one used to describe the smoke hole in the tipi, where the smoke comes out and where the White Crow was turned black.

24. Literally 'wherever [events] transpire' or more loosely 'whatever may happen', with *heeneet-* 'where.REDUP' being used in a temporal sense, as often occurs in Arapaho.

The White Dog and the Woman

Told by Cleaver Warden, Oklahoma, August 11, 1899

Collected by Alfred Kroeber

NAA, MS 2560a, Notebook 6, pp. 81–90

English version published in Dorsey and

Kroeber [1903] 1997: 207–209

This story was not known by William C'Hair, in contrast to most of the others included here. The transcription is somewhat difficult in that at two points the narrator seems to make false starts of several lines and then go back and retell the same events in more detail. Kroeber rearranged or deleted lines before publishing. At several other spots a single word or phrase seems repeated, again offering alternative ways of saying the same thing. A number of obviously misglossed forms occur in the text as well, giving the impression that Kroeber was shaky in his overall understanding of this narrative. This is probably a result of the transcription process, with the teller perhaps correcting himself or improving things as he went.

The story turns out to be about a visit from the Sun to an overly prideful woman. This is not explicitly stated in the narrative, but Kroeber's notes at the end from the consultant say: "Halfway on her journey dog tracks changed to men's. Followed sun; near sunset came to this tepee, that is why red. He also wore red painted robe."

At the end of the story he adds "doubt as to end of story," as well as "old people particularly pray to sun." Connections between dogs and the sun also occur in the story of "The White Crow" in this volume. The dog/man is said to be the Sun, probably making it more significant that the robe he is wearing toward the end of the narrative is described as being pink. This is an unusual and notable color and is quite likely linked to the Arapaho Sun Dance: among the different ceremonial paint patterns worn by the Sun Dance participants is a Pink Paint and a Pink Calf Paint (Dorsey 1903: 163). Modern consultants do not make this connection, but this entire narrative was unknown to them. Similarly, the red paint on the face and hands in one ceremonial Sun Dance paint represents the Sun (Dorsey 1903: 169–70).

That echoes the very precise detail given in this story about the woman putting red paint on her hand and then on the back of the young man who comes to her as she embraces him. Most generally, though neither Dorsey's consultants nor modern ones explicitly make the connection, Cowell suggests that the entire episode of the woman's copulation with the symbolic Sun in this story should be compared to the symbolism of the Lodge-Maker's Wife and her symbolic copulation with the Transferrer during the Sun Dance ceremony (Dorsey 1903: 172–78). Whether or not this narrative can be connected directly to the Sun Dance, the overall symbolism employed in it at least strongly echoes themes of mythical relationships between the human/Arapaho world and the sacred.

Linguistically, the story provides a virtual dictionary of terms for surprise and consternation, as seen in the woman's remarks when she discovers that she has slept with a dog. Many of the forms used are archaic or becoming obsolete in contemporary Arapaho. Equally rich are the terms describing pride, stubbornness, and egotism. More broadly, this story is one of several in the collection that focus on the tenuous boundary between the human and animal worlds. The theme occurs in two forms: someone can actually transform into another species, as in "The Man Who Turned into a Spring" and "The Girl Who Became a Bear," or a sexual or amorous encounter can occur across such lines, as in "Big Belly's Adventure" and "The Woman and the Horse." In virtually all cases, Cowell suggests, the character who crosses the boundary is depicted as excessively egocentric, stubborn, individualistic, or otherwise isolated from the surrounding human community, unwilling fully to socialize with its demands.

Finally, note the close attention and rich vocabulary concerning tracks in this story, as in "The Man Who Turned into a Spring."

Wot=hísei hih-tousí-ni'eih.
A certain woman was extremely good looking.

He'ih-cíis: hini' nii-béeseenébeti-3i'.
She was not married; she was one of those who think too highly of themselves.

Wot=hini' ni'iine'etii-3i'.
She was one of those who live well.

Nih'íi-boh'ó'oo3ootiini-';[1] ni'i3ecooton-eihok.[2]
All the men were after her; they all thought eagerly about her.

Wot=hini' nouuneehí-3i';
[But she was one of] those who are stubborn and difficult;

nii-cii-beetoh-'úusi-3i'.
one of those who do not want to marry.

Wot=nehe' hísei, tih'ii-ní'iine'etii-hók.
This woman was living well.

Niihéyoo he'ih-'íyeihi'.
She had her own lodge.

Cíitoowuu', he'ih-'ono'útoyoo héetoh-niihenéíh-t néhe' hísei.
Inside the lodge every possible thing anyone could need was owned by
this woman.

He'íh-behíi3etí-n.
It was all good.

He'ih-nokúneih.[3]
She was fine/attractive.

Hiikoot toh-wohowúutoni-t.[4]
Moreover, she was charming/desired by all.

He'ih-boh-'oo3oníhoo, tóh-'oo3oni-ni'i3ecootonéíhi-t.[5]
Everyone failed to get her, for she failed to be impressed by any of
them.

Tótoos nih-'oo3on-ko'owuheih-éhk.[6]
She even failed to accept offerings of gifts.

Hehnee=houuneeh-éhk.
She was extremely stubborn.

Hiiwo' tootouti'[7] heetn-íito'óó-t hootn-iisehton[ih]-oot hónouunéíhi-ni3,
nii-beeseenebeti-ní3.

Who knows the place that he will come from, the one who will outwit this stubborn one, who thinks so highly of herself.

Kookonoh'óó[8] he'ih-bíh'iyoo.
Finally, one evening it was entirely dark.[9]

Howóh heenees-benéih'ikotii-t[10] honóh'oe.
She was startled to discover that a young man had come unbeknownst to her.

Howoh heetoh-teyeihi-t.
She was shocked to discover how she had been shamed.[11]

Honóh'oe tih'ii-nii-ni'í3ecoo-t.
The young man was feeling quite happy.

Toh-cen-bih'iyóó-ni', nehe' hísei he'ih-'owo3ínoo'oo.
During the middle of the night, this woman suddenly woke up.

Hiinóónonox, honóh'oe he'ih-niicóób-e'.
To her astonishment, a young man was lying with her.

He'ih-bisi-noocoubee.
He had on an all-white robe.

He'ih-bisi-nookeihi-n hit-óu-w.
His robe was entirely white.[12]

"Heet-iitéíhi-t néhe' ne-niicoob-éiit?
"Who is this person who is lying with me?

"Wo'úunoononóho',[13] howóh tih-béeseenébeti-noo.
"What in the world will people say, especially since I thought so much of myself.

"Heet-iitéíh-t ne-niicoob-éiit," nih-'íí3et-éhk, nii-hók.
"Who is this one who is lying with me," she said to herself, she was saying.

Tih-kokoh'ú3ecoo-[t], he'ne'=nii'-ceiwohoe-[t], hinów-un
toh-notín-oot.
While she was thinking, then she moved her hand off to the side,
because she was looking for red paint.

"Hi3í=heetih-'e'ínon-o' he'iiteihi3i nehe' nonoocóubee-t," nii-hók.
"This way I will know later who this one with the white blanket is," she
was saying.

He'ne'i-behisí-inowóhee-t hinowo'oeetínooo.
Then she put her whole hand inside the paint container with the red
paint.

Noh núhu' tih-'eene'iitén-oot, hikóów-un he'ne'-ii3én-oot[14] hiicét,
tih-nóóhoot-[o'];
And while she was holding him in her embrace, she held her hand on
his back, so that she would see the mark;

"hi3í=heetíh-'e'ínon-o' he'iitehí3i."
"so that later I will know who this is," [she said to herself].

"Howóh tih-beeseenébeti-noo," nii-hók.
"And to think that I used to think so highly of myself!" she was
saying.

"Hiiwó' he'iitehí3i.
"I wonder who it is.

"Hiiwó' he'=iis-iitehí-3i ne-e'inon-éiit."
"I wonder who in the world this is who knows me."

Noononóx, hóhkonee . . . "Heetn-e'ínon-o' ne-bii'ó'oo.
To her surprise, finally . . . "I will know who my lover is.

"Hiiwo' he'iitehí3i."
"I wonder who he is."

Toh-cih-noh'ookéni-ni', nehe' honóh'oe he'ih-nó'ee.
When dawn broke, this young man went outside.

Koowót=wootii cih-'iicéhe'ee[15] hisei.

This woman quickly became pregnant.[16]

Hei'-kóu3-hoo3is, hei'-kou3-itéhe'ei, nehe' hísei he'ih-cii-nonihi'
hih-cíitei'on-éiiton.

When she had been pregnant for a long time, when she had been long
pregnant, this woman did not forget the one who had come into her
tent.

Xonóu toh-nookéni-ni', tih-'iis-bii3ihi-t, he'ih-beséee.

As soon as it was light, after she had eaten, she went to gather wood.

"He'íneyoo heet[n]i-ites-éinoo," nii-hók.

"Certainly he will come to meet me," she was saying.

He'ih-noonoo'éin, tih-not-noohow-oot.

She looked all around, since she was trying to find/catch sight of him.

Hiinoononóx, heebeté3 he'ih-cih-bíxoo'ukóó.

To her astonishment, a large dog came into view running out of the
timber.

Cih-nee'ee-neeneekooni[nee].[17]

It was wagging its tail at her.

Wóotii honóh'oe he'ih-cih-'oxóu'ei'oo.

It was smiling at her like a young man.

Wot=he'=nookeih-ehk nehe' hé3.

This dog was white.

Toh-cih-no'kóóhu-t nehe' hé3, hikóób-e' beecét he'ih-nooxéis
hinowún-e'.

When this dog came running to her, there was the mark of a hand on its
back, in red paint.

"Wo'uu3óó3onoon!

"Of all the low-down things!

"Howóh tih-béeseenéet-owoo neténeyooo!
"And to think I used to think so highly of my body!

"Wooxeihi-t het-bii'o'oo3-éinoo.
"This ugly one must be my lover.

"Neih-'oow-úusi3ecoo, tih-cii-ko'eeneet-owoo neténeyooo."
"I would never have been able to imagine this, when I would not think of sharing my body."

Hoh'onóo3-e' núhu' he3-ebii hinii3e'één-in he'ih-í'-noxowúh-uu.
She struck this dog on its head with a hatchet and killed it.

He'ne'-co'ookootoxúuutii-[t].[18]
Then she brought wood back to her home.

He'ih-hoote'éin nehe' hiséi tih-'esówobeih-t.
Soon afterward this woman got sick.

Koowót=hinenítee-n he'=e'inón-e' tih-'esówobeih-t.
No one knew that she was sick.

Heet-íikoo′wootii he3, he'ih-ceniiséi.
In the brush like a dog, she gave birth.

Heh-niiseihí-3i' honoh'oehih'-ó', heh-niiseihí-3i' hiseihíh'-o'.
There were two males and two females.

"Wot=hiinoononox, howóh tih-béeseenebeti-noo," nii-hók nehe' hísei, toh-ceníisei-t.
"I'm astounded at this, and to think I used to esteem myself so highly," this woman was saying, after she gave birth.

Héíhii núhu' he3-ebii he'ih-beesei3é-no'.
Soon the dogs grew large.

He'ih-'iinikotíí-no' ciitoowúu'.
They played inside the tipi.

Wot=néhe' hísei hiiniisooni-t hih-tousi-bixoo3-ee.
This woman who had the children loved them enormously.

He'ih-'oxób-ee.
She fed them.

Wot=hih-tousi-noxúhu-no'.
She couldn't believe how fast they grew.

Nuhu' cih-noo-noh'oe-' ceee3i' nehe' hísei;
When morning came this woman would be outside her tipi;

heenei'i-noo-nookéni-'i, 3ii-3i'ok-éhk.
every day as soon as morning came she would sit around.

He3 he'=cih-nooxéih-éhk hiso'ootééb-e'.
The tracks of a dog led up to the entrance of the tipi.

Ce'i-ko'einooxéih-éhk.
Then the tracks turned back around.

Nuhu' wottowusóo-no', nóónonox he'ih-3ook-cih'ooxéihi-no'.
These mongrel little puppies, to her surprise, small tracks followed [the
big ones] up to the tipi.

"Wo'úunónonox, neniisoonóh'-o', he'=iisi-ihoo-nóó3i,[19]
toh-nihi'-bixoo3-óú'u.
"What in the world is going on, I wonder where my little children are
going, because I love them to pieces.

"He'=iisi-ihoo-nóó3i."
"I wonder where they are going."

Nehe' hiséi he'ne'-ce'-cii3ihcehi-t hiyeih'-é'.
Then this woman ran back inside her tipi.

Wo'oh-no hee3ei'-hi3eti-ní'i he'ih-een-etén.
She took out all of her good moccasins.

He'-nouutóóx-ehk.[20]
She carried them out on her back as a bundle.[21]

Béébeet hee3ooxeihi-ni3i hiniisóó-no, hiit hiisiihi' he'ne'=e3eb-iicisee-hék;[22]
Just where the tracks of her children were, she followed them there in that direction as she walked;

noh húnee he'ih-nosounooxeihi-níno.
and those tracks were still going on.

Ceese' he'ih-beexooxéih, 3ookuuhu' cih'ooxeihi-nó'.
There was one set of large tracks, and behind were small sets of tracks.

Tei'yoonóh'-o' núhu' he3ebiisoo-no', biixoo3eihí-3i'.
The children, these dog children that were all so loved by the woman.

Kookonoh'óó nehe' hísei hiiníinooxu-t.
This woman ended up carrying her bundle along on her back.

Hé'ih-ce'exowó'oo{t} nooxeihiit-onó.
Then the tracks changed.

3owo3inenítee nooxéihiit-ono, tei'yoon-ooxeihiit-ono,
They were human tracks, children's tracks.

"Neniisoonóh'-o', toh'uni bixoo3-ou'u!
"My little children, whom I love!

"Noononóx he'=iisi-ihoo-noo3i.
"I can not imagine where they are going.

"Noononóx heetíh-noohow-óú'u tóót=heetí-ihoo-3i'[23] neniisoonóh'-o'."
"I just hope that somehow I'll see them, wherever my little children must be going."

Ceecíis níiinon he'ih-béisi-bé'ee.
Suddenly there was a tipi before her, all red-colored.

Beeyoo he'ih-ceite'eitee nehe' hisei heesísee-t.
It was set up facing exactly where the woman was going.

Heetii3o', nei-hók.[24]
???

'oh beeyoo he'ih-yii3ooxeihi-níno hi-3ookuhóoo-no.
And the tracks of the ones that she was following led straight over there.

Híhcebe' he'ih-seh-noohób-ee hinén-in.
Near [the tepee] she saw a man.

He'ih-'e'eite'éicihí-n.
His head was bound up/wrapped with a rag.

He'ih-beis-bihceyéíhi-n hit-óu-w, hini' hooyoo'uu-t[25] nehe' hinén.
His robe was all pink, the one the man was wearing.

"Hi3í=hiiwookú'oo," hee3-oohók hiníisoo-no nehe' hinén.
"Come peek out," said this man to his children.

Céése' tei'yoonehe', he'ih-'iiwookuhcehihíh.[26]
One of the little children peeked out quickly.

Hinen, "Neixóó, neinoo heh-neeni-t cénoo-t," nii-hok.
[The child said to the] man, "Father, that's my mother who is coming," the child said.

Ci'=céése' he'ih-'iiwookuhcehíhih.
Another little child peeked out quickly.

"Hií3oowu-neeni-t neinoon-ínoo," nii-hók, heeh-éhk, hee3-oohok hiniisónoo-n.
"That truly is our mother," the child said, it said to its father.

Beeyoo hee3e'éitee-' he'ih-tóó'usee nehe' hísei.
The woman came to a stop right smack in front of the tipi.

"Tousóó, heeyóu he-notii3óó?" hee3-éihok núhu' hinen-in ciitoowúu'.
"What is it, what are you looking for?" said the man inside the tipi to her.

Noh "Nii-notiih-ou'u neníisoo-no'," heeh-ehk néhe' hísei.
And "I'm looking for my children," said the woman.

"Hiikó, ce'isee," hee3-eihok nuhu' hinén-in.
"No, go back," said the man to her.

"Neixoo, ciitéí-hee[27] néinoo," céese' tei'yoonéhe' heeh-ehk.
"Father, have my mother enter the tipi," said one of the children.

"Híiko, hei'towúun-e' ce'iséé-hee," heeh-ehk néhe' hinén.
"No, tell her that she must go back," said the man.

"Neinoo, ciitéi-hee, néénowo'!
"My mother, let her enter, hurry!

"Neixóó, néinoo ciitei-hee, neixóó."
"Father, have my mother enter, father."

"Hih'óo, ciitecinéíh-in nehe' hísei."
"All right, call for this woman to enter."

Hé'ih-ciitéi.
She entered.

Hiinoononóx wot=hih-tousi-ni'éíh honóh'oe nee'éeteeb-e' he'=3i'ok-éhk.
To her amazement, the handsomest young man she had ever seen was sitting at the back of the tipi.

Hit-óu-w hooyoo'uut-o'ehk koowót=hiisiini.[28]
The robe he had on was charming.

"Heeyóu he-notii3óó, tih'ini wosóo-' nih-'íisih-in?
"What are you looking for, since you did a bad thing to me?

"Neh-ce'i-nó'oehi," hee3-eihok nehe' hísei.

"You'd better go back outside," he said to the woman.

Noh "Nóno3=núhu' heesi-ni'éíhi-n, heih=nee'eesi-ni'éíhi-n,

And "If earlier you had been so handsome, had you been as handsome as you are now,

"Heih=nee'ee3éíhi-n, tih-'ites-in níito',
see=heih=nee'ee-niisí-woxuh-e3en."[29]

"Had you looked like you do now, when you first met me, then I certainly would not have been bad to you like that."

Nehe' hiisíis he'ih-néén.

He was the sun.

Nehe' hiisíis, hé'ih-neen nih-nooku-he3.

The sun, he was the one who was the white dog.

Nehe' ce'isee-hék, nehe' hísei.

She went back, this woman.

Wó'oo[30] he'ih-ce'í-nii3oon-e' hiníisoo-n noh wo'éi3 cése' he'ih-ce'ís.

It's not known whether her children went back with her or whether she returned alone.

Notes

1. *Boh'ó'oo3éi-* AI.O 'all court/date/be lover of a person' (cf. *bii'ó'oo3éi-* AI.O 'court/date/be lover of a person') > II.IMPERS *boh'ó'oo3óótiini-*.

2. Literally 'they were happy with regard to her'.

3. The verb is not recognized today.

4. The verb is not recognized today.

5. Literally 'she failed to be made happy by them'.

6. *Ko'owuh-* TA 'to part with things for s.o.' > AI.PASS *ko'owuheihi-* 'to receive things that s.o. has parted with'. Cf. *beexowuh-* TA 'to bestow s.t. on s.o.'

7. *Tootóu* II.INTERR 'where?' The form *tootóúti'* is archaic and apparently specific to Oklahoma. Cf. modern *heeyóu* 'what?': archaic Oklahoma form *heeyóúti'.*

8. Cf. *kónoh-* 'all, every single one'.

9. The next three lines are absent from Kroeber's published translation. They also seem to have been misunderstood by Kroeber when he was working with his consultant, as he glosses them 'all those who came and went back disappointed, man, too many to mention

who were disappointed, young man who wanted to marry'. As the following lines suggest, the consultant seems to have stopped after the three lines and gone back to retell the same situation slightly differently.

10. *Howóh* 'discovery of surprising, unexpected circumstances, changed from normal or previous situation'. *Beih'-* 'treacherously', so *beih'íkotíi-* AI 'come/go treacherously'. The initial changed form *beneih'ikotii-* is unexplained.

11. Literally 'where she was ashamed'.

12. Here *hou* refers not to a blanket but to a buffalo robe, which is animate.

13. *Wo'uunóononóho'* 'What will people say!?' 'This is so embarrassing!?' Used especially when expectations, promises, or plans have fallen through catastrophically, and someone is facing a major loss of face due to this.

14. One would expect *íiten-* TA 'hold' here.

15. The form *-'iicehe'ee* for 'pregnant' is not recognized today. Note that in the following line the form *-'itehe'ehei* is used, with the same meaning. One of these forms must be a mistranscription. The second form appears to contain the medial and final *-teh'ei-* for 'belly' (cf. *cei'teh'ei-* 'little round belly').

16. This line and the following two lines seem out of place in the narrative, as if the narrator told too much too quickly and then decided to go back and retell what follows in much more detail (as happened earlier in the narrative as well).

17. The initial root of this verb is *neeneek-* 'swing, sway' (see 'swing' in modern Arapaho). Tail wagging is expressed in modern Arapaho with *nóo-noh'oow-óónee-kóóhu-* using *noh'oow-* 'wavy motion, as flag in the wind'.

18. This form has the medial *óxuuú-* 'wood gathering'. Cf. AI.O *beséee-* 'gather wood', deverbal *cih'óxuuú* 'wood chips'.

19. *He'=íísi-ihoo-nóó3i* DUBIT-in which direction-go-3PL.ITER or DUBIT-how-go-3PL.ITER.

20. *Nóuut-óoxú-* AI 'carry outside on one's back, as in packing s.t.' Cf. *nóoxú-* AI 'pack on one's back'.

21. This action suggests that the woman believes that she may be going on a long enough journey to wear out several pairs of moccasins.

22. *Hiicisee-* seems to be a variant of *heecisísee-* 'while walking'.

23. *Toot=* 'where?' requires nonaffirmative inflection; *heti-ihóó-3i'* would be 'where they must be going'. The two elements do not fit together, however.

24. This line is completely obscure. It is possible that the narrator was trying to say something like *ceetii3ei-hok*, 'she didn't say a word, she didn't know what to say'. Alternately, *het-ii3-oo* means 'you must say it to him/her'.

25. Cf. *nééyoo'úú-* 'dress up fancy'.

26. AI *híiwookúhcehí-* 'peek quickly' > AI.DIM *híiwookúhcehí-hih-*.

27. This is an indirect imperative form (AI.3S). Additional forms occur following this line.

28. Kroeber glosses this word as 'charming'. It may be that the word is simply *hiisííni-* II 'how it is', so that the overall construction means something like 'you've never seen one like that before'.

29. *See=* is a variant of *sii=*, indicating intensive or emphatic meaning.

30. This form is glossed 'whether or not' in the manuscript. It is likely a version of modern *wohoe'-* 'maybe' or 'I don't know whether'.

The Alligators

Teller unknown, Wyoming, July 1927
Collected by Truman Michelson
NAA, MS 2988, pp. 64–66

The Hííncebiit 'Alligator' (more commonly 'Water Monster', with the old word extended in modern times to refer to alligators as well) is a common mythological being in Arapaho tradition (see Dorsey and Kroeber narratives 72–76). This text is not really a narrative but rather a description of the basic characteristics of the Water Monster. The text does not explicitly include details such as the fact that lightning striking the water represents an attempt by the Thunderbird to kill the Water Monster and the fact that the rainbow is the Thunderbird's fishing line, as he tries to catch the Water Monster (*noyóót* means both 'fishing line/pole' and 'rainbow' in Arapaho). Drownings are often attributed to the Water Monster.

The detail about the Water Monster having metal horns may seem surprising, but metal appears thematically in other traditional narratives as well, notably in "The Beheaded Ones," where the young adventurer encounters an old woman living in a metal house. Note that the monster that arises from the water in the story of the "Breaking of the Ice and the Splitting of the Tribes" ("The Arapaho Migration across the Missouri River to the . . ." in this volume) is also often identified as a Water Monster.

Linguistically, note that many verbs have subjunctive endings, meaning 'they say that'. This ending indicates reported rather than directly seen evidence in Arapaho. Other verbs have the dubitative proclitic *he'=* followed by nonaffirmative inflections. This form in everyday Arapaho is normally translated as 'probably'. Thus even though the account is ethnographic, it uses the linguistic features characteristic of traditional narrative.

Most generally, stories of snakelike water monsters are a feature of many Native American traditions, including those far-removed from the Arapahos, such as the Cherokee tradition (Walker 2004).

[English only]: If a Thunderer [Thunderbird] is caught under this, the thunderer is a goner. "The Alligators" had horns. Often horns would be of a golden color.

238

Hiincebíít-owuu neníísoonee-', cé'eseih-ehkóni'.
There are two different kinds of Water Monsters.

Hoo3oo'o' he'ih-biiséíhi-no', nóh hoo3oo'o' he'ih-cii-bííseihi-no'.
Some were furry, and others were not furry.

Hi3óóbeciihi' nee'eet-iine'itíí-hohkóni'.
Under the water is where they live.

Nóh hoo3oo'o' hi3oowo'wu-u' hóóxebecéí-'i he'=nee'eet-ííne'itii-3i'.
And under the ground in spring water is where others live.

He'=eenéíniinisi-no'.
They have horns.

He'i=neniiskósei-no'.
They have cloven hooves/claws.

Towú'éí-hohkoni'.
They have short, flat faces.

Nii-beesei3e-'éhkoni'.
They have large bodies.

Neeyooceih-ehkoni'.
They have long, snakelike bodies.

Heenéétoo-noo3i, boh'óoo né'-cih-cou'utii-hok.
Wherever they are found, then the Thunderbird comes and strikes.[1]

Híni' noyóót, nee-néé-hehkoni' neniihéneihí-3i' núhu' noyóót.
That rainbow, the Thunderbirds are the ones who own it.

3eneinih'ohú-3i bóh'ooo,[2] niisiitenéí-hok néhe' boh'óoo.
Whenever the Thunderbird flies under the rainbow, the Thunderbird catches things.

Héétoh-'iisííten-óó3i hiincebíít-owuu, hini' hóóxébi-no
niiyohóú-'éhkoni'.

Wherever he catches a Water Monster, those springs dry up and
disappear.

Nuh'úúno ní'ec-íí ci'=niiyohóú-'ehkoni'.

These lakes disappear too.

Boh'óoo nii-biin-oohók núhu' hiincebíít-owuu.

The Thunderbird eats these Water Monsters.[3]

Nehe' hiincebíít nii-bee-bei'cí3eiyeiní3ee-hek.

The Water Monster has metal horns.

Noh hisíísei nii-cee-ce'ese3oo'oo-yehkoni'.

And its eyes have a glimmering, variegated color.[4]

Hinenítee-no nih-woxuh-oohók hihii3ííhi' nuhu' hóóxebin-e' noh néc-ii
hihíí3iihi',

The Water Monster harms people from within springs and lakes,

nóh 3owo3nenitee-no' ne'=nii'-ííx-oo3i'.

and that's why the Indians fear it.

Notes

1. Literally 'bothers, molests [that place]'.

2. The manuscript gives *3eniin-ih'ohu-,* but one would expect *3enein-ih'ohú-.* Cf. *heet-3ein-óotee-'* 'underpass' ('where the road/path goes under').

3. *Hiincebíít-owuu* is both plural and obviative in Arapaho, so the translation could be singular or plural.

4. Alonzo Moss explains that the verb here can also be used to describe the effect of the sun shining on an oil slick—the color varies with the perspective and from any angle tends to be multiple.

Tooteeceet or Hiinohootéinit/Open Brain or Tangled Hair

Told by Caspar Edson, Oklahoma, July 19 and earlier, 1899

Collected by Alfred Kroeber

NAA, MS 2560a, Notebook 3, pp. 48–79, Notebook 5,

pp. 1–26 (dated July 19)

English version published as "Found-in-the-Grass" in

Dorsey and Kroeber [1903] 1997: 378–87

First part published in Arapaho as "Tangled Hair"

in Kroeber 1916: 127–30

This story is intricately tied to a number of other Arapaho narratives as well as to Arapaho ceremony. For example, compare "The White Crow" to the conclusion of this story: both offer explanations for why the Crow always trails behind the Arapahos after a buffalo kill and eats the eyes of the buffalo. In "The White Crow," the Crow is tricked into accepting a gift and forced to reciprocate by giving away the secret of the buffalo to the Arapahos. Here the Crow itself tricks some of the Arapahos and gets a gift. But the gift (the older sister in the story, whom the Crow marries) turns out to be of little value. Meanwhile, some of the Arapahos benefit indirectly from the Crow's trick by having Spring Child marry into the family and tribe and thus receive the benefit of the buffalo as well. Thus in both stories a series of exchanges between Crow and the Arapahos leads to Crow's being ultimately deceived or disappointed by his gift and the Arapahos receiving the gift of the buffalo in return. Crow must in a sense be "sacrificed" for the Arapahos to receive the buffalo.

A second example of the links to other stories is the way in which Spring Child is found by an old woman while lying in the grass. This episode closely parallels one found in "The Porcupine and the Woman Who Climbed to the Sky." In that story the boy who is found turns out to be Found-in-the-Grass, a great mythical hero and provider for his relatives and the tribe, much as occurs in this story. One of Kroeber's consultants said that the boy in this story in fact is Found-in-the-Grass. The same consultant noted that the bow and arrows made by the father in this story are the "first" bow and arrows.[1] In addition, the lesson not to peek out of holes in the lodge is a key part of the Crazy Lodge Age-Grade Society ceremony: the crazy dancers move through the camp and will shoot into the lodge of anyone who peeks at them in this way.[2] Also, the ceremonial double-sided knife used in the Arapaho Rabbit Lodge and Sun Dance ceremonies is the knife used by Tangled Hair to cut open the wife in this story (Dorsey 1903: 123).

The episode involving the killing of the Thunderbirds is closely tied to Arapaho ceremony as well: see the introduction to "Found-in-the-Grass." The young boy being blown away at the end of the narrative is explained by the fact that the highest, greatest Thunderbird, who is believed to control the winds, is angry at the loss of its children (Dorsey 1903:14). The nest structure placed on the Center Pole of the Arapaho Sun Dance Lodge is symbolically the nest of the Thunderbird (Dorsey 1903: 114).

The episode of the killing of Tangled Hair is linked to the origins of the sweat lodge. Heating the rocks and placing them inside his head become the first instance of the heating of rocks and placing them inside a location, which is a key part of the sweat lodge ceremony (note how the rocks are specifically described as smooth and round [*cetey-*], just like the river rocks used in sweat lodges at present). The hole dug at the center of sweat lodges, where the hot rocks are placed, is known as "Open Brains" in Arapaho (Dorsey 1903: 49–50). As a side note, the verb describing how Tangled Hair stuffs (*3eiikuu3-*) the twins away after killing their mother is exactly the same one used to describe how they put the heated river rocks into his brains. The earlier episode of the revival of the mother celebrates the healing and re-creative power of the sweat lodge.

To give one more example, the singers and drummers in the Sun Dance lodge are known as "grouse" and the Sun Dance ceremony overall is often linked metaphorically in Arapaho thought to a grouse lek, with singing and dancing. Thus the grouse are extremely powerful birds, which should be respected. This explains in part why the twins get in trouble for their abuse of the grouse.

Other parts of the story require a good knowledge of Arapaho society for full understanding. For example, it was not uncommon for a man to marry sisters in the days when men had multiple wives. Thus when the older sister begins making overtures to Spring Child at the end of the story, this must be understood as her attempt to "join in" on the marriage now that it is clear that Spring Child is both good looking and a good hunter/provider of meat. This desire is greeted with displeasure by her younger sister, who enjoys the privilege of being the "favorite" (and only) wife. The intervention of

Spring Child's grandmother illustrates another typical social relationship in Arapaho society: while parents are expected to provide for and discipline children, grandparents typically become advocates for them in the larger society and sources of emotional support. The ceremonial role of "grandfather" that an older man maintains with a young Sun Dancer is the ritual version of this common social role.

Finally, from a strictly linguistic standpoint, this text has more archaic features than any other in the collection. It features a distinction between 3S.SUBJ inflection –(*y*)*ohk* and 4S.SUBJ –(*y*)*ohkon*. The latter is absent in modern Arapaho and in virtually all of the texts in this collection as well, having been replaced by the 3S form. Similarly, it offers examples of a distinction between singular and plural objects for fourth person/obviative possessors: the respective endings are –*in* and –*ino*. The latter has virtually disappeared from modern Arapaho (with even the former now becoming obsolete) and is rare in this collection as well. As a third example, AI verb stems meaning 'to possess an X' are converted to participles in this text. The base meaning of such participles is 'the act/state of possessing an X'; but the actual meaning here is more specifically 'the X that I possess thanks to your offer/gift'. Such a usage is undocumented elsewhere in this collection and even in this text occurs only at moments of key possession (the dish used to serve Tangled Hair, the bow and arrows of the Twins), suggesting retention of an archaic grammatical feature at significant moments.

Additionally, Arapaho transitive verbs with animate objects (TA verbs) can take inflections indicating two fourth person/obviatives acting on each other (4/4 inflections). While in theory relative clause verbs (called dependent participles in Arapaho grammar) can also occur in this form, this text is the only place where an actual instance of this form is documented, when the Twins are talking about 'that (OBV) one, Tangled Hair, who killed their (OBV) mother'. Finally, this text is the only one that contains examples of the imperative-only verb *sóóxe* 'let's go!' used in a transitive form as *sóóxeen-ínee* 'let's go to him/her/them!' Thus this text is not only the most heavily freighted with sociocultural and ceremonial connections among all the texts in this collection but is also the most grammatically archaic. Note, however, that this is among the first texts that Kroeber recorded, and he marked very few pitch accents—only one every five to ten words in many cases. These are minimal and largely meaningless (given that virtually every Arapaho word has at least one pitch accent and often more), so the accents have not been marked here.

William C'Hair gives the first name in the title (Tooteeceet) as *toontééceenéét*. He notes that an alternate version of the name Tangled Hair is *neniikóte'eit*.

Part One: The Visit from Tangled Hair

Hinen he'=niixootii-hek.
A man was camped alone.

Ne'-he'=iinoo'ei-hok.
Then he went off hunting.

He'=ei'towuun-oohok hiniin hoton-iinoo'ei-t.[3]
He told his wife that he was going hunting.

"Honooyoo ciibeh-tokoohow-unee hooton-ites-ein.
"Don't you dare pay any attention to the one who will come to you.

"Nono'oteihi-t.
"He's powerful.

"Hiinohooteini-t.
"He's a person with tangled hair.

"Hiihoow-uuxowooteih ci'.
"He cannot be satisfied either.

"He'ineyoo hooton-ites-e'.[4]
"There's no way you can miss him when he comes.

"Noh ciibeh-yíí3e'eini.
"But don't look over there.

"Hites-eininehk, he'ineyoo.
"When he comes to you, you can't miss it.

"Hoton-niitouuhu-[t] cenoo-3i.
"He'll holler whenever he comes.

"Honooyoo ciibeh-nei'oohow-unee.
"Don't you dare look at him.

"Nono'oteih-[t] he-ebeh-cih-ciitei heyeih'-e'," hee3-oohok hiniin-in toh-ce3ei'oo-t.

"[If you do], this powerful one might come inside your lodge," he said to his wife when he set off.

Noh nee'ee-cesis-iinoo'ei-hok, tih-'iisi-nihii3-oot.

And then he started off to hunt, after he had said this to her.

Hiniin noh ne'-noo3-oohok, toh-'uunoo'ei-t.

Then he left his wife behind, because he was going hunting.

Noh he'ne'-ites-eini3 hiniin hiinohooteini-ni3.

Then Tangled Hair came to his wife.

Noh he'=cii-tokoohow-oohok.

But she did not pay any attention to him.

Noh ne'-ce'isee-yohkon[5] toh-cii-nei'oohow-oot.

Then he left again because she did not look at him.

He'=ce'isee-yohkon{i'} heetisee-ni3 nuhu' hiinohooteini-ni3, tih-'oo3onih-eit[6] nuhu', teebe tih-'ites-eit, nuhu' hoohookeeni-ni3.

This Tangled Hair went back where he had come from, since he failed to trick her, the first time he came to her, this crazy one.

Heeyow-utes-ei3i, nih-cii-tokoohow-oohok.

Every time he came to her, she would pay him no attention.

Noh yeneini'owoo-ni-', he'=tonoo'oh-o'ohk hecesi-beih-e' hoxuut niiinon-e'.[7]

But the fourth time she made a hole with a small awl right up against the side of the tipi.

Toh-'iin-ce3ei'oo-ni3, hi'iihi' beih-e' tohuu-hii3i-hiiwoohow-oot; "3i'=he'ii3eihi3i?" heeh-ehk.

When he wandered off, she peeked out here at him [through the hole she had made] with the small awl; "I wonder where he is from/what kind of a person he is?" she said.

He'ne'-iiwoohow-oot hihii3iihi' nuhu' heet-tonotihi-ni',[8] hoxuut[9] hihii3iihi'.
Then she peeked at him from the small hole, on the side of the tipi.

"Hoheis," hee3-eihok.
"Crazy woman!" he said to her,

Ne'-iineesee-yohkon{i'}.[10]
Then he turned back around.

Toh-ciitei'on-eit, hee3-eihok, "Toh-nihi'esinee-noo."
When he came inside, he said to her, "I am really hungry."

Noh "Cih-'oxow-u," hee3-oohok nuhu' hisei-n.
And "Feed me," he said to the woman.

He'ne'-hotiiciih-eit[11] ho'oeenooo.
Then she offered him food on a clay dish.

"Hiihoow-neeniisou'u[12] no-otiiciit-ono."
"That's not the kind of tray I use," he said.

He'ne'-hotiiciih-oet besinooo.
Then she offered him food on a wooden dish.

"Hiihoow-neeniisou'u no-otiiciit-ono," heeh-ehk.
"That's not the kind of tray I use," he said.

He'ne'-hotiiciih-eit kokoohowoot.
Then she offered him food on a warbonnet.

Koox=he'i=nee'eihi-t.
Once again he said the same thing.

He'ne'-hotiiciih-oet hi-biixuuton-in.
Then she offered him food on her dress.

"Tonoo-nee-'," hee3-oohok.
"That's almost it," he said to her.

Noh he'ne'-hotiiciih-eit hi-wo'ohn-ino.[13]
Then she offered him food on her moccasins.

"Tonoo-nee-'," hee3-oohok koox.
"That's almost it," he said to her once again.

He'ne'-hiisibi-ni3 hoo3i3iniihi'.
Then she lay down on her back.

"Nenee-'," hee3-oohok.
"That's it," he said to her.

Noh toh-'otoowu-ni3 . . .
And when he finished eating, [he wiped his knife on her].[14]

Heenoo nii-cee-ceetesi-'i.
"It will happen that things are accidentally cut," [he said to her].

He'ne'i-koe'3ein-eit.
Then he cut her open.

Noh he'ih-niiseih, niiso'uuhu' honoh'oehih'-o niisoo-no'.
And she was pregnant with twins, both of them little boys, twins.

He'ne'i-hiten-oot.
Then he took them.

Ceexoon nuhu' honoh'oehiho' he'ne'i-won-sii'iheiw-oot hooxebin-e'.
Then he went and put one of the little boys into the water of a
spring.

Noh ceexoon he'ih-3eiikuu3-ee 3eeyokooxuu-niiinon-e'.[15]
And he threw the other one into the hole at the base of a tipi pole.

He'ne'-noo3i-ce3ei'oo-t, tih-'iis-3eiikuu3-oot tei'yoonoh'-o.
Then he went off and left them behind, after he had thrown the children
into those places.

He'ih-no'ookei nehe' hinen.

The man brought back meat from hunting.

He'ih-niisih'-ee hiniin.

He called his wife's name.

He'ih-ceetii3ei-n toh-niisih'-oot hiniin.

But there was not a sound when he called her name.

Noh xoo-xonou he'ih-'e'in toh-neh'-eini3, toh-ceetii3ei-ni3.[16]

And right away he knew that Tangled Hair had killed her, because she did not respond to anything.

He'ne'-cii3i-noohow-oot.

Then he saw her inside.

'oh he'ih-koe'3eineih.

And she had been cut open.

"Ne-ih-cii-nihii3oo-no{'ou},"[17] hee3-oohok.

"Didn't I tell her about these things?!" he said about her.

He'ne'i-biiwoohu-t.

Then he cried.

He'ne'-noo3i-no'oehit, toh-woni-biiwoohu-t heetoh-co'otoyoo-ni'i, tih-'iisi-noohow-oot hiniin.

Then left her behind and went outside, because he was going out to the hills to cry, after having seen his wife.

Part Two: The Discovery and Capture of the Twins

Noh kou3iihi', hei'-cih-'eecikoohu-t, he'ih-nih'eiyeisise-nino huneik-o noh hi-beete'.

And after a long time once he came home, his arrows and his bow were lying scattered all over.

He'ne'-oo'ein-o' hineik-o,

Then he gathered up his arrows,

noh he'ih-3eiin hi-ciito3oon-e' hineik-o noh hi-beete'.
and he put his arrows and his bow into his quiver.

He'ne'-ce'-no'usee-t, tih-3eiin-o'.
Then he went [to the hills] again, after he had put them inside the quiver.

Noh koox=hei'-ce'-no'usee-t, he'ih-nih'eiyeisise-nino hineik-o.
And yet again when he arrived back his arrows were lying scattered all over.

Noh nuhu', noh neneesiihi' he'ne'-3i'en-oot hit-ou-w.
And this man, then he arranged his buffalo robe upright on a stick, pretending [that it was really him].

He'ih-nihii3-ee, "Heti-biiwoo," hee3-oohok hit-ou-w.
He said to it, "You must cry," he said to his buffalo robe.

He'ne'-cih-'otino3-oot[18] hiniisoo-no.
Then he snuck up here to his children.

He'ih-bisiikohei'i[19] nehe' 3eeyokooxuuhu' nehe' honoh'ehihi'.
He got to where he could spy on them, this under-the-tipi-pole little boy.

Noh ceese' he'-cih-'iitisee hooxebin-e'.
And the other one had come here from the spring.

Toh-cih-won-iinikotii-t, "cihnee hooxebine'," heeh-ehk ceese'.
When he came here to play, "Over here, Spring Child," the other one said.

"Heetih-'iinikotii-no'," hee3-eihok 3eeyokooxuusoo-n hooxebine'.
"Let's play," said Under-the-Tipi-Pole Child to Spring Child.

"Heetih-{ne}'iinikotii-no'," heeh-ehk 3eeyokooxuusoo.
"Let's play," said Under-the-Tipi-Pole Child.

He'ne'-iinikotii-3i'.
Then they played.

"Heisonoon-in noosou-biiwoohu-t," hee3-oohok.

"Our father is still crying," Under-the-Tipi-Pole Child said to Spring Child.

'oh he'ih-kotousine-n[20] hihcebe' hiyeih'-inoo.

But he was waiting hidden near their lodge.

Noh he'ne'-cesis-iinikotii-3i',

And then they started playing,

'oh he'ih-kotousine-n hiniisonoon-inoo woowuh kookootooyei' niiinon-e'.[21]

but their father was waiting hidden now right by the lodge ready to pounce.

Noh beexoo3iihi' tih-'iinikotii-3i', he'ne'-ii'isee-ni3 hiso'ooteeb-e', toh-niisiiten-ei3i'[22] ceese' nuhu' honoh'oehih'-o hiniisoo-no nehe' hinen.

And a little later while they were playing then he walked up close to the doorway, because this man planned to catch one of his little boys.

Noh hiixoo3iihi' hiinikotii-3i', noh ceese' heeh-ehk,

After they played some more, then one of them said,

"Noohoot-oo, teneenise-' neic," hee3-oohok hiisoh'o hooxebine' 3eeyokooxuusoo.

"Look! my arrow is lying touching it," Under-the-Tipi-Pole Child said to his older brother Spring Child.

"Hee,[23] hiihoow-teenis," heeh-ehk hooxebine'.

"No, it is not lying touching it," said Spring Child.

Noh "Noohoot-oo hihii3iihi' no'koowuuhu'," hee3-oohok hiisoh'o 3oeyokooxuune'.

And "Look at it from right on the ground level," said his older brother to Under-the-Tipi-Pole Child.

Noh hooxebine' he'ne'-noohoot-o'.

And then Spring Child looked at it.

Noh toh-'iisibe'eini-t, he'ne'-cii3ihcehi-ni3 hiniisonoon-inoo.
And when he had his head down on the ground, then their father rushed inside the tipi.

Noh he'ih-'iisiiten-ee 3eeyokooxuu.
And he grabbed Under-the-Tipi-Pole Child.

Hooxebine' he'ih-nouuhce, toh-ce'-yihkoohu-t nih'ii-cih-'iitisee-t hooxebine'.
Spring Child ran outside, because he was running back over there to the spring where he had come here from.

"Teiitoonoku nei," hee3-oohok nehe' hinen hiih'o 3oeyokooxuusoo-n.
"Sit still, son," said this man to his son Under-the-Tipi-Pole Child.

Toh-'iisiiten-oot, he'ih-koo-kou'uci3-e' noh he'ih-too-toyob-e',
After he had caught him, he scratched his father and he bit him,

'oh he'ih-nei'en-ee.
but his father kept him firmly in his grasp.

"Hooton-niisitii-noo he-beete' noh heik-o," hee3-oohok nuhu' hiih'o 3oeyokooxuu.
"I will make your bow and your arrows," he said to his son Under-the-Tipi-Pole Child.

Hoonii he'ih-ciinoteibi-n.
After a long time he quit crying.

"Nei, het-eti3-oo heeseh'e.
"Son, you must call to your older brother.

"Hootoni-ce'-woni-biiwoohu-noo.
"I am going to go cry again.

"Noh hootoni-cih-ce'-no'usee-noo hiibinee noh heet[n]-iisiiten-o' hooxebine'.
"And I will secretly come back here and I will catch Spring Child.

"'Ne-ih-'oow-uusiiten-e' nehe' heisonoon-in,' het-ii3-oo ciitei-hok.
"'Our father didn't catch me,' you will say to him when he enters.

"Noh beex-kou3iihi' cenih-'i3ikuu3-ot, noh he[t]-nei'en-oo.
"And after a while then you come seize him, and you must hold on to him firmly.

"Ciibeh-ciinikuus-in[24] hiisiiten-otehk.
"Don't let go of him when you have caught him.

"Noh hoot-cih-cii3ihcehi-noo.
"And I will rush inside here.

"'Noxuhu!' het-cih-'iis.
"'Hurry!' You will say to me.

"Cii-cii-ni'oow-otehk, 'Ne-ih-'oow-uusiiten-e',' het-ii3-oo, 'heisonoon-in.'
"If he won't agree to come in, 'He didn't catch me,' you will say to him, 'our father.'

"'Cih-neesii,'[25] het-ii3-oo.
"'Come over here,' you will say to him.

"Cii-ni'oow-otehk, 'Neene'ee-[hek] heisonoon-in heetoh-co'otoyoo-ni',
"If he won't agree, 'There is our father out in the hills,

"'Noosou-3i'ookuu-t, nii-biiwoohu-t,' het-ii3-oo.
"'He is still standing there, he is crying,' you will say to him.

"'Wonoo3ei-'i heic-in noh he-beetein-in nohkuuhu'.' "
"'We have many arrows and [many] bows along with them.' "

Noh he'ne'=ii'-iisiiten-oot ceexoon, nuhu' hooxebine'.
And then he caught the other one, this Spring Child.

Koox=he'i=nee'ee-koo-kou'ci3-eit, toh-'i3ikuu3-oot.
Once again he scratched the father as before, when he seized him.

Noh kou3iihi' he'ih-ciinoteibi-n.

And after a long time he quit crying.

"Nei, hooton-iinikotii-nee heeseh'e," hee3-oohok.

"Son, you and your older brother are going to play," said the man to them.

"Noh hooton-niistii-noo heik-o noh he-beete'.

"And I will make your arrows and your bow.

"Hooton-i'-cee-coboo-nee heehebehe' 3eeyokooxuusoo."

"You and your younger brother Under-the-Tipi-Pole Child will shoot with them."

Noh hei'-iisi-itowuh-oot, he'ne'-nii-niisitii-t hineiciin-inoo, nuhu' hiih'o-ho hineiciin-inoo noh hi-beetein-inoo.

And once he had calmed them down, then he made their arrows, his sons' arrows and their bows.

Part Three: The Twins Bring Their Mother Back to Life

Ceesey hiisi' he'ih-nihii3-e',

One day they said to him,

"Neixoo neh-cih-nii-niistii he-beeteiniit-ono[26] ho'ooxuucoo-no, noh cih-yee-yeinee-no[27] ho3-ii nohkuuhu'.

"Father, you better do your bow-making with the short/end rib of a buffalo, and there should be four arrows with them.

"Noh heetih-niisitii-t hi-beeteiniit-ono ho'ooxuucoo-no."

"And let the bows that he makes be made with the short ribs of the buffalo."

Noh heh-yee-yeinenei-'i hiniiciit-ono hiih'o-ho.

And his sons each had four arrows.

"Wohei neixoo," hee3-eihok, tih-'iiston-oot hi-beetein-inoo,

"Now, father," they said to him, after he had finished making their bows for them,

"neh-ciibeetei'i neixoo.
"you better make a sweat house, father.

"Noh het-ciiten-oo.
"And you will take her inside.

"Hiis-niisen-owuninehk ciibeet, neinoo het-ciiten-oo noh het-iisiben-oo
nee'eeteeb-e', hoo3i3iniiihi'," hee3-eihok, hiih'o-ho hooxebinoho'[28] noh
3oeyokooxuusoo-n.
"After you have covered up the sweat lodge, take my mother inside and
lay her down at the back, on her back," they said to him, his sons Spring
Child and Under-the-Tipi-Pole Child.

He'ne'-ciiten-oot hiniin, tih-'iis-ciibeetoe'i-t.
Then he took his wife inside, after he had finished making the sweat
lodge.

He'ne'-iisiben-ee nee'eeteeb-e' hiniin.
Then he laid his wife down in the back of the lodge.

Hee3ei'towuun-eit hiih'o-ho, he'i=nee'eesitoo-t.
As his sons had told him, that's what he did.

Noh tih-'iis-ciiten-oot hiinoon-inoo, "Nei'okoh-oo," hee3-eihok.
And after he had taken their mother inside, "Shut it up tight," they said
to him.

He'ne'-okoh-o' behiihi' hi'iihi' hou-wo', hei'-iis-beh-niiseni-'[29] ciibeet.
Then he shut up the whole thing with robes, after the sweat lodge was
entirely covered.

"Neixoo," hee3-eihok hooxebine', "hiit 3i'ookuu."
"Father," said Spring Child to him, "stand here."

He'ne'-3i'ookuu-[t] heetoh-nihii3-eit.
Then he stood where Spring Child told him to.

"Hoonoyoohoot-oo ciibeet.
"Watch the sweat house.

"Heet-noo-noh'oowunoo'oo-' nuhu' ciibeet; hooton-ihci3owoo-ni'."
"This sweat lodge will shake; we are going to shoot upward."

"Wohei," hee3-oohok hinoohowoho' hooxebine', "niito' coboo."[30]
"Now," said Spring Child to his younger brother, "you shoot first."

He'ne'-coboo-[t] hihciihi'.
Then Under-the-Tipi-Pole Child shot upward.

"Wootoo no'oo!" heeh-ehk.
"Get out of the way, mother!" he said.

He'ih-noo-noh'oowuhcehi-n[31] hiinoo-n.
His mother was moving around jerkily.

"Wohei biiti' neh-coboo hooxebine'," hee3-oohok hiisoh'o
3oeyokooxuusoo.
"Now it's your turn, you'd better shoot, Spring Child," said Under-the-
Tipi-Pole Child to his elder brother.

He'ne'-coboo-t.
Then he shot.

Toh-'uus-coboo-t, he'ih-noo-noh'oowunoo'oo ciibeet.
After he had shot, the sweat lodge was shaking.

"Wohei," hee3-oohok hinoohowoho', "neh-'ihci-coboo
3eeyokooxuusoo."
"Now," he said to his younger brother, "you'd better shoot upward,
Under-the-Tipi-Pole Child."

He'ne'-ihci3obee-t ceese'.
Then the other one shot upward.

He'ih-noo-no'o3-noh'oowunoo'[oo] nuhu' ciibeet.
The sweat lodge was really shaking a lot.

"Wohei neixoo neh-niisitii hiisoho'.
"Now, father, you'd better do it one more time like this.

"Het-ihcikuutii ciibeet.
"You must throw up the cover of the sweat lodge.

"Neinoo hoton-ii-cih-no'oehi-t."
"My mother will come out here."

He'ne'i=nih-'ii3-eit 3eeyokooxuusoo-n.
That is what Under-the-Tipi-Pole Child said to him.

"Wohei," hee3-oohok hiisoh'o hooxebinoho', "neeco'oo neh-coboo!
"Okay," he said to his older brother Spring Child, "go ahead, you'd better shoot!

"Heinoon-in heet-ne'-cih-noehi-t."
"Then our mother will come out here."

"Hih'oo," heeh-ehk.
"All right," said Spring Child.

He'=nee'ee-coboo-t hihciihi'.
Then he shot upward just like that.

Toh-'uus-coboo-t, hiinoo-n, "Wootoo no'oo!" hee3-oohok.
After he had shot, his mother, "Get out of the way, mother!" he said to her.

"Wootoo no'oo!" hee3-oohok.
"Get out of the way, mother!" he said to her.

"Wootoo no'oo!" hee3-oohok.
"Get out of the way, mother!" he said to her.

Noh tih-'iis-ii3-oot hiinoo-n, he'ne'-ei'towuun-oot hiniisonoo-n:
And after he had spoken to his mother, then he told his father:

"Koonen-oo, neinoo hotnii-cih-no'oehi-t," hee3-oohok.
"Open it, so my mother can come out here," he said to him.

He'ne'-koonen-owuni3, 'oh hiinoon-inoo he'ih-cih-no'oehi-n.
Then he opened the sweat lodge, and their mother came outside.

Nuhu' heetoh-kooneni-ni' ciibeet, he'=ce'-iiyei-yohkon{i'}.[32]
At the place where the sweat lodge was opened, she was alive again.

Hini' nih-'ii3eihi-ni3 heniine'e3eihi-ni3.[33]
She was the way she had been when she had been alive.

Part Four: Killing Tangled Hair

He'ne'=nii'-cee-coboo-ni3i hiih'o-ho.
Then his sons went shooting.

He'ne'-ei'towuun-oot, "Ciibeh-yihoo-' hinee heetoh-no'otoo'oe-' koh'owu-u'."
Then he told them, "Don't go there where the timber is thick, at the stream."

He'ne'i-niisee-ni3i hiih'o-ho.
Then his sons were scared.

"Niiton-i'.
"Hear me.

"Ciibeh-neeheyei'oowu-'.
"Don't go near the water/streams.

"Nono'oteih-t heenitoo-t.
"A powerful one lives there for sure.

"Neneeni-t hih-neh'-eiiton heinoon-inoo.
"He's the one who killed your mother.

"Hiinohooteini-t ni'ii3ee-t, noh wo'ei3 hiitoniteecee-t.
"He's called Tangled Hair or Open Brain.

"Nee'ee-niisooneenih'i-t."
"Those are the two different ways that he's named."

Tih-'iisi-nihii3-oot hiih'o-ho, he'ne'-cee-coboo-ni3i.
After he had said this to his sons, then they went off shooting.

"Wohei," heeh-ehk ceese' nuhu' honoh'oehih'-o', "sooxe heetih-yihoo-no'
heisonoon-in niitoh-nihii-t;
"Okay," said one of the boys, "let's go to where our father talked about;

"3i'=he'ii3ou'u heeneine'etii-no', hinee niitoh-nihii-[t] heisonoon-in.
"I wonder what kind of things live over there, where our father was
talking about.

"Wohei sooxeen-inee," heeh-ehk hooxebine'.
"Well, let's go over to him," said Spring Child.

He'ne'i-yihoo-3i' nuhu' hiniisonoon-inoo nih-'iitoh-'ei'towuun-ei3i'
hot-cii-yihoo-3i'.
Then they went over to where their father had told them not to go.

"Hiikookonoo' sooxeen-inee heetih-noohow-oono' 3i'=he'=eesii3eihi-3i,
nehe' hinen nih-noh'-oot heinoon-in."
"Anyway, let's go over to him, so we can see what he's like, this man
who killed our mother."

He'ne'i-yihoo-3i'.
Then they went over there.

Noh toh-'e3ebi-nou'usee-3i', "Hiiwo' he'=nee-hek neisii hooxebine' noh
3eeyokooxuu.
And when they arrived over there, "Well, what do you know, you must
be my grandsons Spring Child and Under-the-Tipi-Pole Child.

"Toot=(h)ei-ihoo-be neisiiho-ho'?"
"Where are you going, my grandsons?"

"Nii-cih-ceitoon-een," hee3-eihok nuhu' 3eeyokooxuu.
"We have come here to visit you," Under-the-Tipi-Pole Child said to him.

"Neisiiho-ho', neh-cih-'i3ooxuh-u'!"
"My grandsons, you better delouse me!"

"Wohei," hee3-eihok.
"Okay," they said to him.

He'ne'-i3ooxuhee-t niiso'uuhu'.
Then he was deloused by both of them.

'oh he'ih-'iteib nooxobei'i.
And he had lice that were frogs.

"Hii-xo'ow-u' nehe' netei-wo'," hee3-eihok nuhu' hiniisiiho-ho.
"Put my lice in your mouths," he said to his grandsons.

He'ih-bii'inee-nino heebe3-nooxobei'i hinii3e'een-e'.
Large frogs were found in his hair.

Noh beex-kou3iihi' he'ne'i-nokohu-t.
And then a while later he went to sleep.

'oh "3eeyokooxuu, cih-notiih-in ceteyoh'onookee-no'.[34]
And "Under-the-Tipi-Pole Child, look for those round river rocks.

"Noh bii'in-otehkoni', het-cih-woti3-oono' {hi}hisitee.
"And when you find them, you must put them in the fire.

"Kookon konowuuhu' hii3ooxuh-o'.
"In the meantime I'll just continue delousing him.

"Woowuh nookohu-t."
"Now he's sleeping."

He'ne'-woti3-oo3i' nuhu' hoh'onookee-no hisitee ciitoowuu' hiyeih'-in.
Then they put these rocks into the fire inside his lodge.

Tih-'iis-iini hesixoh'-oe3i' hoh'onookee-no, he'ne'i-touku3-oo3i' hi-nohootein-ino hokooxun-e'.
After they had finished heating up the rocks, then they tied his tangles of hair to the tipi poles.

He'ne'-ihcoo'oh-oe3i' hoh'onookee-no.

Then they picked up the rocks with pronged sticks.

Noh nuhu' heetoh-tooteecee-ni3, 3eiikuu3-eeno' hoh'onookee-no
bei'ci3ei-ni3i.

And at the spot where his brains were open, they threw the red hot
rocks in there.

He'ne'-nouuhcehi-3i', tih-'iis-3eiikuu3-oo3i' hoh'onookee-no.

Then they rushed outside, after they had thrown the rocks inside
there.

He'ne'i-noh'-oo3i' nuhu' tooteecee-ni3, hih-neh'-eiiton-in[35]
hiinoon-inoo.

That's when/how they killed Open Brain, the one who had killed their
mother.

"Wohei hooxebine'," hee3-oohok hiisoh'o, "heet-neh-ciitei-no'.

"Well, Spring Child," Under-the-Tipi-Pole Child said to his older
brother, "let's go back inside there.

"Woowuh neece-' hiinohooteini-t."

"Tangled Hair is dead now."

He'ne'-ciitei-3i', tih-'iis-noh'-oo3i' hi'iihi' hoh'onookee-no.

Then they went inside, after they had killed him with the rocks.

"Heetih-koo-ko'un-oono' hi-nohootei, heisonoon-in noh heinoon-in
heetih-biin-oono' nuhu' hinii3e'ee,

"Let's pluck off all his tangles and give his hair to our father and our
mother,

"heetih-'eeneiseenookuuwu-3i'."

"so that they can use them for ropes."

"Hee, hii3oobei-n," heeh-ehk ceese'.

"Yes, you're right," said the other.

He'ne'-eecikoohu-3i', toh-'uus-koo-kou's-oo3i' hi-nohootein-ino.
Then they went home, after they had cut off his tangles of hair.

Noh toh-no'eecikoohu-3i', "Neixoo," hee3-oohok hiniisonoo-n hooxebine',
And when they arrived home, "Father," said Spring Child to his father,

"hiiyou he'=iseenookuuw," hee3-oohok hiniisonoo-n, "nuhu'
wo-nohootei."[36]
"here are your ropes," he said to his father, "these tangles of hair."

"Hohou nei!
"Thanks, son!

"Toot=he-ih-'iten?"
"Where did you get them?"

Noh "Hii3e' hinee nih-'iitoh-nihii-n, 'Ciibeh-yihoo-','
And "Over there where you said, 'Don't go there,'

"Nih-yihoo-no' 3eeyokooxuu.
"We went over there, Under-the-Tipi-Pole Child and I.

"Nih-'i3ooxuh-oono'.
"We deloused Tangled Hair.

"Tih-'iis-iini hi3ooxuh-oono', nih-nei'-nokohu-t.
"When we finished delousing him, he went soundly to sleep.

"Ne'-woti3-oono' hoh'onookee-no' ceeteyouhu-3i', tih-'iis-bei'cixuh'u-3i',
nuhu' hoh'onookee-no'.
"Then we put the spherical rocks in the fire, after they were heated red
hot, these rocks.

"3eeyokooxuu, ne'=ii'-touku3-oono' nehe' hinen hi-nohootei hokooxun-e'
hiyeih'-e'.
"Under-the-Tipi-Pole Child and I, then we tied this man's tangles of hair
to the tipi poles of his lodge.

"Tih-'iis-touku3-oono', ne'-3eiikuu3-oono' hoh'onookee-no' hi-toteeceen-e'.[37]

"After we had tied it up, then we threw the rocks into his open brains.

"Hoh'onookee-no', noh nee'ee-noh'-oono'."
"With rocks, that's how we killed him."

"Wohei biiti' noh hiiyou he-seenookuuw," hee3-oohok hiinoo-n 3eeyokooxuusoo.
"Now it's your turn, and here's your rope," said Under-the-Tipi-Pole Child to his mother.

"Ceiten-oo."
"Bring it here."

"Hohou," hee3-eihok hiinoo-n 3eeyokooxuu.
"Thank you," his mother said to Under-the-Tipi-Pole Child.

Part Five: Killing the Water Monster

Kooxuuhu'[38] hoot-cee-coboo-ni3i hiih'o-ho.
Once again his sons are going out shooting.

He'ih-'ei'towuun-ee, "Ciibeh-'e3ebi-yihoo-' hinee koh'owu-u'.
He told them, "Don't go over there to that stream.

"Nono'oteihi-t cese'eihii heenitoo-t, heebe3iihi' hiincebiit.
"A powerful being is there, a big Water Monster.

"Nii-toun-oot hinenitee-no."
"He captures people."

Noh toh-ce3ei'oo-3i' honoh'o-ho', hooxebine' heeh-ehk, "Sooxe heiso-noon-in 'ciibeh-yihoo-',' niitoh-huhuut.[39]
And when the young men set off, Spring Child said, "Let's go where our father said 'don't go.'

"Wohei sooxeen-inee," hee3-eihok hinoohowoho' 3eeyokooxuuxoho'.

"Well, let's go over to him," said his younger brother Under-the-Tipi-Pole Child to him.

He'ne'i-yihoo-3i'.

Then they went there.

He'=iis-eh-no'usee-no'.

They arrived over there.

He'ih-noohob-eeno' nuhu' cese'eihio, heeteihi-yohkon, "Hih-nihii3-ooon heisonoon-in,

They saw the being, what he was like, "The one our father mentioned to us,

"Heet-teexokuuton-oono'," heeh-ehkoni' niiso'uuhu', toh-noohow-oo3i' nec-i'.

"We will ride on him," they both said, when they saw him in the water.

"Neeto'ohnii," hee3-eihok hiisoh'o 3eeyokooxuu.

"Take off your moccasins," his older brother said to Under-the-Tipi-Pole Child.

He'ne'-neeto'ohnii-t.

Then he took off his moccasins.

"Noh niixoo neeto'ohnii," hee3-eihok hinoohowoho' 3eeyokooxuu.

"And you take off your moccasins too," said younger brother Under-the-Tipi-Pole Child to him.

"Hiiwo' he'=nee-hek hebesiibeih'-in hiincebiit."

"So, you must be our grandfather Water Monster."

"Hee," hee3-eihohkoni'.

"Yes," he said to them.

"Koot-cii-ni'-teexokuuton-ee?"

"Can we ride on you?"

"Hih'oo," hee3-eihohkoni'.
"All right," he said to them.

"Neh-cih-sii'iheisee-' neisiiho-ho'," heeh-ehk nuhu' cese'eihii.
"You'd better come into the water, my grandsons," said this being.

He'ne'-niiso'-sii'iheisee-3i'.
Then both of them went into the water.

He'ih-teexoku-no' hikoow-un.
They sat on his back.

He'ne'=nii'-inowousee-ni3 nohkuuhu'.
Then he dove under the water with them.

He'ih-cii-ni'iiniih-oei'i.[40]
But he could not harm them.

Hei'-neetoxuuh-oo3i', he'=iis-iinikotii-no'.
Once they had tired him out, they finished playing with him.

He'ne'-noh'-oo3i'.
Then they killed him.

"Wohei," hee3et-ehkoni', toh-'uus-noh'-oo3i' nuhu' hiincebiit, 'oh heeti-koo-ko'oh-oe3i' hiniini3-o;
"Well," they said to each other, after they had killed this Water Monster, then they will break off its horns;

"Heinoon-in heeti-biin-oono' nuhu' hiniini3-o, hotn-eeneiteebiyooni-t."
"We'll give the horns to our mother, so that she'll have spoons."

He'ne'-ce'-eecikoohu-3i' toh-noh'-oo3i' nuhu' hiincebiit hii3oon-inoo hihii3inenitee-no'.[41]
Then they went back home, after they had killed this one that the old-time people called *hiincebiit* ['Water Monster'].

Toh-no'eecikoohu-3i', noh hee3-oohohkoni', "Hiine'ee-no hiniini3-o.
When they arrived back home, they said to their mother, "Here are its horns.

"Nih-cih-too-towowuun-een, hoton-eeneiteebiyooni-n.
"We broke them off for you, so you can have spoons.

"Noh noh'-oono' hiincebiit hini' neisonoon-inoo hi'iihi' nih-'ii3ooon.[42]
"And we killed that Water Monster our father told us about.

"Nih'ii-tee-teexoku-no'," heeh-ehkoni'.
"We rode on it," they said.

"Neih'o-ho', hoh-tous-noh'-oobe?
"My sons, how did you kill him?

"Nono'oteihi-t.
"He is powerful.

"Nii-bi'-i3konoo3ei-t.
"He just sucks people in.

"Nii-noh'-oot hinenitee-no."
"He kills people."

"Nih-bi'-coboo-no', hei'-neetoxuuh-oono';
"We just shot him, once we had worn him out;

"noh nee'ees-noh'-oono' nehe' nono'oteihi-t he-ii3-ooo."
"and that's how we killed this one that you call powerful."

Part Six: Killing the Thunderbird

Kooxuuhu' hoot-cee-coboo-ni3i hiih'o-ho.
Once again his sons are going to go out shooting.

He'[ih]-'ei'towuun-ee, "Ciibeh-'e3ebi-yihoo-' hinee heetoh-co'otoyoo-'.
He told them, "Don't go over there to where the mountain is.

"Nono'oteihi-3i' heenitoo-3i'."
"Powerful ones live there."

"Hih'oo," hee3-eihok niiso'uuhu', koox=heeh-ehkoni'.
"All right," they both said to him, they said once again.

"Wohei," heeh-ehk 3eeyokooxuu, "neisoh'oo, sooxeen-inee, heisonoon-
in 'ciibeh-yihoo-',' niitoh-'ii3-eino'."
"Well," said Under-the-Tipi-Pole Child, "brother, let's go over to him,
where our father said 'don't go there.'"

"Wohei," heeh-ehk hooxebine', "heetih-yihoo-no'."
"Okay," said Spring Child, "let's go there."

Noh ne'i-yihoo-hohkoni'.
And then they went there.

Toh-yihoo-3i' heetoh-co'otoyoo-ni', he'ih-noohob-eeno'
nii'ehiisoo-no.
When they went to where the mountain was, they saw some eaglets.

Hihcebe' hoh'en-i' he'ih-'eeneinohuuxoni-no' hoh'onookei'i.
[The parents] had a nest in the rocks up on the mountain.

Boh'ooonii'ehiisoo-no nii3-oohohkoni'.
They call them Thunderbird eaglets.

Noh toh-'itox-oo3i', he'ih-noo-notton-eeno':
And when they reached them, they asked them questions:

"Wohei cih-'ei'towuun-ei'ee'," hee3-oohohkoni', "hii-tousoo heinoon-
inoo noo'uh'ohu-3i?"
"Well, tell us," they said to them, "how is your mother when she comes
flying?"

"Nii-wo'oteeyoo-' hiinoono'et."
"It's a black cloud."

"Hih'oo," hee3-oohohkoni' ceese'.
"All right," they said to one of the eaglets.

He'ne'i-tebe'eikuu3-oohohkoni'.
Then they broke/twisted its head off.

Tih-'iis-ei'towuun-ei3i', "Wohei biiti' neh-cih-'ei'towuun-ei'ee," hee3-oohohkoni' ceese' nuhu' nii'ehiisoo.
After the first one had told them this, "Well, your turn, you better tell us," they said to another of the eaglets.

"Hii-tousoo heinoo heesinonee-3i?"
"How is your mother when she is angry?"

"Nii-wo'oteeno'eti-', nii-be'ei-'i ceheekuut-ono."
"There's a black cloud, and the bolts of lightning are red."

"Hih'oo niisoo-yohkoni'," hee3-oohohkoni',
"All right, so that's how they are," they said to it.

He'ne'i-tebe'eikuu3-oo3i'.
Then they broke/twisted off its head.

Noh ceexoon he'ne'-notton-oo3i':
And then they asked another one:

"Hii-tousoo heinoon-inoo[43] nono'otisee-3i?"
"How is your mother when she arrives powerfully?"

"Noh nii-no'oteese-' noo'usee-3i neinoo."
"There's a lot of wind when my mother arrives."

"Hih'oo, niisoo-yohk," hee3-oohohkoni'.
"All right, so that's how it is," they said to them.

Koox=he'ih-tebe'eikuu3-eeno', tih-'iis-ei'towuun-ei3i'.
Once again they twisted/broke off their heads, after the eaglets had told this to them.

Yeneini'owoo-ni3 he'ne'i-yihoo-3i', heetoh-3i'oku-ni3.
Then they went over to the fourth one, where it was sitting.

"Hii-tousoo heinoo cee'-nii-won-noohob-einoni?"[44]
"What's your mother like when she returns to come see you?"

"Nii-no'oteese-', noh nii-no'otoosoo-', nii-koo-koxoo'ei'i-t[45] boh'ooo noo'u-noohob-einooni neinoo," hee3-eihohkoni'.
"There's a lot of wind and a lot of rain, and the thunder resounds all around when my mother comes to see me," it said to them.

"Hih'oo niisoo-yohk."
"All right, so that's how it is."

Nonoohob-ei3i' heinoo.
Their mother saw [the twins].[46]

He'ne'i-tebe'eikuu3-oo3i'.
Then they broke/twisted its head off.

He'ne'-eecikoohu-3i' hiyeih'-inoo.
Then they went home to their lodge.

Toh-nosousee-3i', he'ih-cih-bixo'uxoo.
When they were still walking, clouds began to build up in their direction.

Hoono' he'ih-cii-neeheyei'oo-no' hiyeih'-inoo.
They had not yet gotten close to their lodge.

He'ne'-no'oosooti-ni'.
Then a rainstorm arrived.

He'ih-cee-ceheekuun.

Lightning was striking.

He'ne'=nih-'ii'-koxoo'ei'i-ni3 hihcebe', toh-'esinih-oo3i' boh'ooo.

Then a bolt of lightning struck nearby, because they had made the Thunderbird mad.[47]

"Wohei," hee3-oohohkoni', "nuhu' hiis-koyein-owuninehk, heetni-i3oow-no'oteihi-n."

"Okay," they said to the Thunderbird, "if you manage to pull this out, you'll be truly powerful."

He'ne'-coboo-3i' heh-niiseti-ni' hiniic-inoo hoh'onookei'i.

Then they shot one of their arrows into a rock.[48]

He'ih-'inowunoo'oo hoh'onookeen-i' heetoh-beesei3e-ni3, hee3e'eisee-3i'.

It disappeared into the rock where it was big, the direction they were facing.

Toh-'uus-iini coboo-ni3i hoh'onookei'i, "Wohei neh-cih-koyein-oo," hee3-oohohkoni' nuhu' boh'ooo-n.

After they had shot into the rock, "Well, you'd better pull them out," they said to the Thunderbird.

He'ne'-cih-cenih'ohu-t hot-koyein-o' hiniiciin-inoo niiso'uuhu' hooxe-bine' noh 3eeyokooxuu.

Then she flew down to take both their arrows out of the rock, Spring Child's and Under-the-Tipi-Pole Child's.

He'ne'-niitouuhu-t boh'ooo, toh-neenou'u-t hi'iihi' hiniiciin-inoo hot-koyein-o'.

Then the Thunderbird screamed, because she was preparing to pull out their arrows.

Tih-'iis-neenou'u-t, he'ne'-cih-'oowuh'ohu-t.

After she was prepared, then she flew down here.

He'ne'-i3ikuutii-t nuhu' ho3-ii, 3ii'ookuu-ni'i hoh'onookei'i.

Then she seized the arrows, which were standing embedded in the rock.

Tih'iis-i3ikuutii-t, he'ne'-ihcih'ohu-t nohkuuhu' hiniiciin-inoo.

After the Thunderbird had seized them, then she flew upward with their arrows.

He'ih-siikooceikuutii.

She stretched them out [as they remained embedded in the rock].[49]

He'ne'i-cih-teenisi-' hi'iihi' nuhu' ho3-ii; hitiitoono3.[50]

Then she was jerked back down onto the rock by the arrows; it was a tendon-arrow.

He'=iisi-noxowus hoh'onookei'i, teesiihi' heetoh-so'oku-ni3 hoh'onookee-n.

She smashed into the rock [and was killed], on top of the area where it was flat.

"Wohei sooxeen-inee," hee3et-ehkoni'.

"Okay, let's go to her," they said to each other.

"Nooxowusibeti-t teesiihi' hoh'onookei'i hi'iihi' heic-in.

"She has smashed herself onto the top of the rock with our arrows.

"Heetih-koo-kou'uniiinee-no' heisonoon-in, heetih-'eeneibiiini-t."

"Let's pluck feathers for our father, so that he will have feathers to use."

"Wohei hih'oo, hii3oobei-n."

"Okay, all right, you're right."

He'ne'-koo-kou'uniiinee-3i'.

Then they plucked out the feathers.

Toh-'uus-noh'-oo3i', noh toh-no'eecikoohu-3i',

After they had killed her, and when they got home,

"Neixoo," hee3-oohohkoni', "niine'ee-no' he-biii-no' nuhu'."
"Father," they said to him, "here are your feathers."

"Hohou!
"Thank you!

"Ho-tous-noh'-oobe nono'o3ii'eihii?" hee3-eihohkoni' hiniisonoon-inoo.
"How did you kill the powerful bird?" their father said to them.

"Noh nih-bi'-ceniikuu3-oono'," hee3-oohohkoni'.
"We just jerked her down," they said to him.

[p. 80 of MS missing: the twins likely repeat the preceding episode to their father]

Part Seven: Shooting Grouse

Kooxuuhu' hoot-cee-coboo-ni3i hiih'o-ho.
Once again his sons are going out shooting.

He'ih-'ei'towuun-e', "Ciibeh-'e3ebi-yihoo-'," hee3-oohok.
Their father told them, "Don't go over there," he said to them.

Koox=hoot-cee-coboo-ni3i.
Yet again they are going shooting.

"Hinee heetoh-nookhoosei'iini-'," 3eeyokooxuu hee3-oohok hiisoh'o hooxebine':
"That place where the sagebrush is," said Under-the-Tipi-Pole Child to his older brother Spring Child:

"Heet-yihoo-no' niitoh-nihii-t 'Ciibeh-yihoo-' hinee heetoh-noo-no'otoo'oe-' nookhoosei.'
"We will go there where he said 'Don't go to that place where the sagebrush grows really thick.'

" 'Nono'oteihi-3i' heniine'etii-3i' nii'ehii-ho', ni'iihi-3i' cenee-no'.' "
" 'Powerful birds live there, called sage grouse.' "

"Hiiko, ho-otn-ii-beexu-yihoo-n," toh-'ei'towuun-ei3i'
hiniisonoon-inoo.

"No, we shouldn't go there," [he said], because their father had told
them.

"Wohei sooxe, heetih-neh-cee-coboo-no'."

"Well, let's go, let's go shooting over there."

Ci'=he'ih-'ei'towuun-ei'i hot-ce3ei'oo-3i' hiniisonoon-inoo.

Their father told them again that they must set off somewhere else.

"Hii3oobei-n, ho-otn-eihoow-uu-yihoo-n," hee3-oohohkoni'
hiniihein-inoo.

"You're right, we won't go there," they said to their parents.

He'=nee'ee-ce3ei'oo-3i'.

Then they set off just as they had said [they wouldn't].

Noh toh-'uus-ce3ei'oo-3i', he'ne'-e3ebisee-3i'[51] heetoh'uni
nookhoosei.

And after they had set off, then they went to the place where the
sagebrush was.

Noh toh-'e3ebi-nou'see-3i', he'ih-bii'iih-eeno' cenee-no.

And when they got there, they found the sage grouse.

"Heetih-cee-coboo-no'," hee3et-ehkoni'.

"Let's shoot them," they said to each other.

He'ne'i-yihoo-3i' hihcebe' toh-noohow-oo3i'.

Then they went over close by where they saw them.

"Wonoo3ee-3i'," hee3et-ehkoni'.

"There are a lot of them," they said to each other.

"Heh-noo-noh'-oono'," hee3et-ehkoni' "hoo3oo'o', heetih-'eeneibiiini-t
heisonoon-in."

"Let's kill some of them," they said to each other, "so that our father
will have feathers from some of them."

"Wohei cenee heetih-coboo-no'," hee3et-ehkoni'.
"Okay, let's shoot some sage grouse," they said to each other.

Hooxebine', "Hih'oo," heeh-ehk.
Spring Child said, "All right.

"Heet-niito'-cob-ou'u nuhu' cenee-no'," heeh-ehk hooxebine'.
"I'll shoot these grouse first," said Spring Child.

He'ne'-iten-o' ceesey hineic.
Then he took one of his arrows.

"Wohei," hee3-oohok hinoohowoho' 3eeyokooxuu, "neh-neenou'u.
"Okay," he said to his younger brother Under-the-Tipi-Pole Child,
"you'd better get ready.

"Heet-cob-oono' niiso'uuhu'."
"We'll both shoot them."

"Hih'oo," heeh-ehk 3eeyokooxuu.
"All right," said Under-the-Tipi-Pole Child.

He'ne'-iten-o' ceesey hineic hot-cob-oot hi'iihi'.
Then he took one of his arrows to shoot them with.

He'ne'=ii'i-yihoo-3i' yiisiihi' hihcebe'.
Then they went over there closer.

He'i=neh-cee-cob-oo3i'.
They shot them over there.

Toh-noohow-oo3i' no'koowuuhu' nookhoosei, he'ih-nee-neh'-eeno'.
When they saw them right on with the ground under the sagebrush,
they killed some of them.

Tih-'iisi-noo-noh'-oo3i', "Sooxe, heet[n]-eeneiten-oono' biii-no', hot-biin-
oono' heisonoon-in."
After they had killed them, "Let's go, we'll get some feathers, to give to
our father."

He'ne'i-yihoo-3i' heetoh-noo-noh'-oo3i' nuhu' cenee-no.
Then they went to where they had killed the grouse.

Noh tih-'iis-eeneiten-oo3i' biii-no, "Sooxe, heetih-'eecikoohu-no'," hee3et-ehkoni'.
And after they had gotten the feathers, "Let's go, let's go home," they said to each other.

He'ne'-eecikoohu-3i'.
Then they went home.

Heecisisee-3i', he'ih-no'oeseni-ni'.
While they were walking, the wind blew up.

Noh beexoo3iihi' he'ih-beex-uu3iton-eeseni-ni'.
And a while later it got a little more windy.

He'ne'i-neinoo'oo-t hooxebine'.
Then Spring Child got scared.

"Heh=wohei heetih-nihi'koohu-no'," hee3-oohok hinoohowoho'.
"Okay now, let's run," he said to his younger brother.

He'ne'-nihi'koohu-3i' yiisiihi' hiyeih'-inoo.
Then they ran toward their lodge.

Hei'-ouu-no'oteeseni-ni',[52] he'ih-to'usibeti-no' biito'owu-u'.
When the wind became extremely strong, they threw themselves down on the ground.

Heecisikoohu-3i' he'ih-'eyeih-no'o'eesi-no'.
While they were running, they were almost blown away.

Hei'-eyeih-no'ukoohu-3i' hiyeih'-inoo, hooxebine' he'ne'i-noh'ukuu3-eit heseisen.
When they had almost arrived at their lodge, then Spring Child was suddenly lifted up by the wind.

He'ih-noni3ees.
He was lost to the wind.[53]

He'ih-niiseih no'eecikoohu-t.
Just one child arrived home.

"Toot=hooxebine'?" hee3-eihok 3eeyokooxuu, toh-no'eecikoohu-t niisiihi'.
"Where's Spring Child?" they said to Under-the-Tipi-Pole Child,
because he had arrived home alone.

Hee3-oohok hiniihei'i: "Hooxebine', heseisen, cee3i3eesib-eit heseisen."
He said to his parents: "Spring Child was carried off by the wind."

"Nih-cih-nihii3-eenee nuhu' nono'oteihi-3i' nii'ehii-ho', ni'iihi-3i'
cenee-no'?"
"I told you that these birds are powerful, the ones called grouse."

He'ne'-biiwoohu-ni3i hiinoo-n noh hiniisonoo-n, toh-noni3eesi-'
hooxebine'.
Then his mother and father cried, because Spring Child had been lost to
the wind.

He'ih-cii-bii'iih-eeno', toh-notiih-oo3i'.
They did not find him when they looked for him.

Noh ne'=nih-'iisi-noni3o'oo-hok nehe' 3eeyokooxuu hiisoh'o.
And that's how Under-the-Tipi-Pole Child's older brother got lost.[54]

Part Eight: Spring Child Is Found in the Grass

Noh huu3e' nih-'iitoh-'e3eb-ciineesi-', he'=nee'eet-bii'inee-t
betebihehiho'.
And over there where he had been set down by the wind, that was
where he was found by an old woman.

Nih-bii'ineihi-hok heetoh-'eyosoo-ni'i woxu'-uno.
He was found where the grass was high.

Toh-koo-ko'oh-owuni3, he'ih-noohob-e' hi'oot-o nuhu' betebihehiho'.
When she was gathering the grass, the old woman saw his feet.

"Neiwoo," hee3-eihok, "ciibeh-cih-cetoh-u.[55]
"Grandmother," he said to her, "please don't put me to death.

"Neneeni-noo hooxebine'."
"I am Spring Child."

"Ho-tous-ceito'oo nuhu' heetoh-'eyosoo-'?" hee3-eihok nuhu' betebihehiho'.
"How did you get here in this high grass?" said the old woman to him.

"Heseisen nih-noh'ukuu3-einoo.
"The wind suddenly lifted me up.

"Noh nee'ees-ceito'oo-noo hiit."
"And that's how I got here."

He'ne'-hookoo3-eit hiniiiwoho'.
Then his grandmother took him to her home.

"Benii'in-o' hooxebine' woxu'un-e'.
"I have found Spring Child in the grass.

"He'ih-cih-ce3i3eesibee-n[56] neyooxet-ii."
"A whirlwind carried him away."

He'ih-beh-ben-nei'oohowoo toh-bii'inee-t.
They all clustered around to look at this one who had been found.

He'ih-'oxuu3ee noh he'ih-'oono'uunookuuhuu[n].[57]
He had a dirty nose and was dirty-eyed.

Part Nine: Spring Child/Found-in-the-Grass Tries to Trap the Porcupine

Noh hei'-beex-kou3e-enitoo-t he'ih-niitobee ceese' hinen heeh-ehk:
And once he had been living there quite a while, he heard a certain man say:

"Hono'ut hinenteeniit, toon=heniisiiten-oot nouu,[58] heet[n]-iini niiw-oot notoone."
"Among all the people of the tribe, whoever catches a porcupine will marry my daughter."

He'ih-beh-ciineni-no noyoot-ino, toh-beh-neyei3-hiisiiten-ei3i' nouu-ho'.
All the traps were set, because they were all trying to catch porcupines.

Hooxebine', "Neiwoo," hee3-oohok, "heet-neyei3-hiisiiten-o' nehe' nouu."
Spring Child, "Grandmother," he said to her, "I will try to catch this porcupine."

"Hih'oo," hee3-eihok hiniiiwoho'.
"All right," said his grandmother to him.

He'ne'-niiteheib-eit nuhu' betebihehiho', hiniiiwoho'.
Then this old woman helped him, his grandmother.

Noh toh-'uus-ciinen-o' hi-noyoot, he'ih-cih-noot.
And after he had set his trap, he left it behind [and came home].

Toh-nookeni-ni', he'ih-ce'i-yihoo nih-'iitoh-ciinen-o' hi-noyoot.
When it was light, he went back to where he had set his trap.

Toh-nehyonitii-t, 'oh he'ih-'iisiiten-ee nouuhu'!
When he checked on it, he had caught a little porcupine!

He'ih-noohob-ee houu-n toh-3i'ookuu-ni3 nih'iitoh-ciinen-o' hi-noyoot.
He saw Crow standing there where he had set his trap.

Noh toh-noohow-oot houu-n he'ih-'eten-een[59] nouuhu' hi-noyootin-e'.
And when he saw Crow, he was taking the little porcupine out of Spring Child's trap.

Noh toh-'itox-oot, hee3-oohok, "Be, toot=hini' nouu?
And when he reached him, he said to him, "Friend, where is that porcupine?

"Neneeni-noo toh-'uusiiten-o'," Hooxebine' hee3-oohok houu-n.
"I am the one who caught it," said Spring Child to Crow.

"Hiiko," heeh-ehk nehe' houu.
"No," said Crow.

"Neneeni-noo toh-niito'-hiisiiten-o' nehe' nouu."
"I am the one who caught the first porcupine."

"Heihoowu-u3oobei," Hooxebine' hee3-oohok ci'.
"You do not speak the truth," said Spring Child to him again.

"Nih-noohob-e3en toh-'eten-oot no-noyootin-e'."
"I saw you take it out of my trap."

"Heihoowu-ni'-biin-e3," heeh-ehk nehe' houu.
"I cannot give it to you," said Crow.

"Hee, hootn-ei'towuun-o' nei'eibehe' toh-'ebiiteb-in no-nouuheb."
"Okay, I will tell my grandmother that you stole my porcupine."

He'ne'-eecikoohu-3i' niiso'uuhu'.
Then they both went home.

Noh toh-no'eecikoohu-t, nehe' houu, "Heniisiiten-o' nouu," heeh-ehk.
And when he arrived back home, Crow, "I caught a porcupine," he said.

He'ne'-won-biin-oot nuhu' hinen-in hiitoonehi-ni3.
Then he went to give it to the man who had the daughter.

Noh xoo-xonou he'ih-biinoo[60] hot-niiw-oot hitooneh-in beneesesei-ni3.
And right away he was given the man's oldest daughter to marry.

He'=iis-niib-ee nuhu' hiseihiitei'yoo-n, he'ne'-ei'towuun-oot hiniiiiwoho' Hooxebine':
After Crow had married this girl, then Spring Child told his grandmother:

"Neneeni-noo toh-'uusiiten-o' hini' nouu.
"I'm the one who caught that porcupine.

"Houu nih-noohow-o' tih-'iten-oot hihii3iihi'[61] no-noyootin-e'.
"I saw Crow when he took it from my trap.

"Nih-siiin-einoo.
"He robbed me.

"Neiwoo, hih'oo, yihoon-inee hini' hinen.
"Grandmother, all right, go to that man.

"Noh het-ei'towuun-oo neneeni-noo toh-'uusiiten-o' hini' nouu.
"And you must tell him that I'm the one who caught that porcupine.

"No3=nih-siiin-einoo[62] beh'ei-houu."
"It's obvious that Old Crow has robbed me."

"Hih'oo, heet-yihoo-noo neisii," hee3-eihok hiniiiwoho' Hooxebine'.
"All right, I'll go, grandson," said Spring Child's grandmother to him.

He'ne'i-yihoo-ni3 toh-won-ei'tobee-ni3 tih-'iisiiten-oot[63] hini' nouuhu' hiniisio.
Then she went to go tell the man that her grandson had caught that porcupine.

Noh toh-'e3eb-no'usee-t hiyeih'-in nuhu' hinen-in hiitoonehi-ni3, he'ih-'ei'towuun-ee:
And when she arrived over at the tent of this man who had the daughter, she told him:

"Hooxebine' nih-nihii3-einoo, nee'ee-coo-noo.
"Spring Child said this to me, that's why I have come.

"Hoton-ei'towuun-e3en nehe' heetebinouhuuni-t honoh'oehi' nih-'ii-t.
"I'm going to tell you what this pitiful boy said.

"'Nih-'iisiiten-o' hini' nouu-n[64] hih-biin-eiitooninoo,'"
"'I caught that porcupine that [Crow] gave to them,'"

noh nuhu' hiniiiwoho' hooxebine' hee3-ooyohkoni'[65] nuhu' hinen-in.
said Spring Child's grandmother to the man.

"Neisii, 'Neneeni-noo tih-'i3oow-uusiiten-o' hini' nouu.'
"My grandson [said], 'I'm the one who truly caught that porcupine.'

"Niistii-[t] neisie," heeh-ehk betebihehiho', tih-'ei'towuun-oot
hinen-in.
"My grandson did it," said the old woman when she told the man.

Noh tih-'iis-ei'towuun-oot, "Hih'oo, hii3eti-'," heeh-ehk nehe' hinen.
And after she had told him, "All right, good," said the man.

"Heet-niiw-oot nuhu' heecesesei-ni3 heisie," hee3-oohok hooxebinoho'
hiniiibeih'-in.[66]
"Your grandson will marry the younger girl," he said to Spring Child's
grandmother.

"Hohou," hee3-oohok nuhu' hinen-in.
"Thank you," she said to the man.

Noh xoo-xonou toh-cih-ce'no'usee-ni3 hiniiiwoho', "Hooxebine' neisie,"
hee3-eihok, "hootni-iniini-n.
And right away when his grandmother arrived back here, "Spring
Child, my grandson," she said to him, "you'll have a wife.

"Beniin-einoni hitooneh-inoo hini' heecesesei-ni3.
"They are giving you their youngest girl.

"'Het-ei'towuun-oo cih-coo hiiwoonhehe' nuhu' tih-'iisiini-'.
"'You must tell him to come right now, this very day.

"'Xoo-xonou hoot-niiw-oot, cih-no'usee-hek,' heeh-ehk nehe'
hinen."
"'When he gets here, right away he will marry her,' said this man."

"Hohou.
"Thank you.

"Hii3eti-'.
"It is good.

"Heet-yihoo-noo," hee3-oohok hiniiiwoho' Hooxebine'.
"I'll go," said Spring Child to his grandmother.

He'=nee'ee-yihoo-t.
Then he went just as the man had asked.

Noh toh-'uus-eh-no'usee-t, xoo-xonou he'ih-niib-ee ceesey
hitooneh-in.
And after he arrived there, he immediately married his other daughter.

Nuhu' ne'=nih-'isiin-ohk.
That's how he got a wife.

Part Ten: The Two Sisters Get Into a Quarrel

Noh toh-kou3iiniini-t, beexu-kou3iihi', benih'iyoo-ni'i he'ih-'enee3eih.
And when he had been married a long time, a while later, at nighttime,
he would change.

He'ih-ni'eih honoh'oe.
He was a good-looking young man.

Noh hiniin he'ih-'ei'towuun-een hibih-in,
And his wife told her older sister,

"Nebihoo," hee3-ooyohkon, "Hooxebine' nih-'enee3eih-t benih'iyoo-
ni'i," hee3-ooyohkon hibih-in.
"Older sister," she said to her, "Spring Child is different at night," she
said to her older sister.

"Hii3oobei-noo, tih'ii-nii-ni'eihi-t hi3oowuuhu',
"I'm telling the truth, that he really is very good looking,

"hiihoowuuni hoxuuniin hi'is noh hisiisei,
"[that] his nose and eyes really are not filthy,

"tih'ini hiiyooteih-t hei'-iisibiitooni-ni'."
"that he's clean at bedtime."

"Heneih'is=iis-iini[67] hiiyooteihi-3i!?" heeh-ehk, nehe' beneesesei-t heeh-ehk.
"How could he possibly be clean!?" said the older sister.

"Ni'ii-hesowobeihi-noo nenei'oohow-ou'u.
"Whenever I look at him, it makes me sick.

"Heneih'i(i)s=iiyooteihi-3i!?
"How could he be clean!?

"Heihoowu-u3oowoton-e3 nuhu' heihi-n hi'iihi' hees."
"I don't believe what you're saying about your husband."

"Hi3=hoot-noohow-ot.
"Later you'll see him.

"No'uxoo-yehk, hootnii-beh-nei'oohobeih-t," hee3-oohok hibi-o toh-cii3oowoton-eit.
"When the appropriate time comes, he'll be admired[68] by everyone," she said to her older sister, who did not believe her.

Noh toh-'uu3-oot hibi-o, he'ih-'oxoob-e'.
And when she said it to her older sister, the older sister mocked her.

"Neenih-'oxooteenow-ot[69] nees," heeh-ehk heh=nehe' heecesesei-t, hooxebine' hiniin.
"Just keep on misjudging and underestimating my husband," said the younger girl, Spring Child's wife.

"Heih=cih-'oto3ih-e'[70] heix, nii-hoxuu3ee-ni3," heeh-ehk nehe' beneesesei-t.
"You should be ashamed of your husband, he has a filthy nose," the older girl said.

Part Eleven: Spring Child Makes Buffalo

"Wohei betebi, nooke-'ehk nohkuseic het-noxuhu noh
het-cih-nookohoeyei.

"Well, old woman,[71] early tomorrow morning you must hurry and fetch
me water.

"Hootnii-hehiisi'ohu-noo.

"I'll clean my face.

"Hee'inon-e3en toh-'esinee-[n].

"I know that you're hungry.

"Heet-neyei-niisih-o' hii3einoon beexu-ciisiihi'," heeh-ehk.

"I'll try to make buffalo a little distance off," said Spring Child to his
wife one day.

He'ne'-iisibi-t, tih-'iis-ei'towuun-oot hiniin.

Then he went to sleep, after he had told his wife this.

Toh-nookeni-ni', hiniin he'ih-3owo3ii-n.

When morning came, his wife got up.

Toh-nei'oohob-eit, he'ih-'enee3eih.

When she looked at him, he was different/changed.

"Wohei," hee3-oohok hiniin,

"Well," he said to his wife,

"Heisonoo het-ei'towuun-oo hoot-no'o'usee-noo, hot-niisih-o'
hii3einoon."

"You must tell your father that I'm going out away from camp to make
buffalo."

"Hih'oo, he-e[t]-won-ei'towuun-ee neisonoo,"[72] hee3-eihok hiniin.

"All right, I suppose I'll go tell my father," his wife said to him.

He'ne'-no'oehi-ni3 toh-'ei'towuun-oot hiniisonoo-n.

Then she went out of the tipi to go tell this to her father.

"Nehe' hooxebine', hinen . . . ," noh tih-'iis-ei'towuun-oot, hiniisonoo-n he'ne'-beh-ei'tobee-ni3 hinenteeniit,

"This Spring Child, this man . . . ," after she had told him, then her father told all the tribe,

nehe' hot-won-niisih-oot hii3einoon hooxebine'.

that this Spring Child was going to go make buffalo.

He'ne'-ce3ei'oo-t no'o'uuhu'.

Then he set off out away from camp.

"Hiihoowu-ciisiihi'," heeh-ehk; "hoot-niisih-o' hihcebe'," hee3-oohok hiniin.

"Not too far away," he said; "I'll make [buffalo] nearby," he said to his wife.

"Neh-neenou'u-hee[73] nesi3e hiiwoonihehe'."

"My father-in-law better be prepared right now."

Noh toh-ce'no'usee-t, "Woowuh heniisih-o' hii3einoon," heeh-ehk.

And when he returned, "Now I've finished making buffalo," he said.

"Neh-won-ei'towuun-in heisonoo," hee3-oohok hiniin.

"You'd better go and tell your father," he said to his wife.

'oh he'ih-'enee3eih.

And he had changed.

Hono'ut hinenteeniit he'ih-cee'inonoo toh-neeni-t Hooxebine', toh-ni'eihi-t honoh'oe.

He was not recognized by any of the people as Spring Child, because he was now a good-looking young man.

He'ne'-ei'tobee-ni3 hono'ut hinenteeniit toh-niisih-oot hii3einoon-in.

Then his father-in-law informed the entire tribe that Spring Child had made buffalo.

Hinii3ebi-o he'ih-cii-nehtiih-e'.

His sister-in-law did not recognize him.

Noh beexoo3iihi' he'ne'-e'inon-oot toh-neeni-t Hooxebine'.
But later, then she knew that he was Spring Child.

He'ne'-o3ii'oohu-[t] toh-'uus-ei'tobee-t toh-'iisih-oot hii3einoon.
Then he went out after game, after he had informed them that he had made buffalo.

He'ih-'i3oow-uusih-ee.
He had really made them.

Hono'ut hineni-no' he'ih-yih'oowoo-no',
Every single one of the men went out on the chase,

noh he'ih-neh'ehootiin hinenteeniit.
and everyone killed some.

Hineniteeniit noh tih-'iis-nee-neh'ehootiini-', he'ne'-cee-ceniihootiini-'.
And all the people, after everyone had made a kill, then the people butchered the meat.

He'ne'i-cih-'ites-eit hinii3ebi-o heetoh-ceniihei'i-t.
Then his sister-in-law came to where he was butchering.

'oh he'ih-cii-tokoohob-ee hinii3ebi-o.
But he did not look at/pay any attention to his sister-in-law.

He'ih-'e'in tih'ii-woxeeneb-eit teebe tih-'iniini-t hinii3ebi-o.
He knew that his sister-in-law had despised him when he was first married.

"Hooxebine', nei3eboo," hee3-oohok, "heh-tounowuun-e3."
"Spring Child, brother-in-law," she said to him, "let me hold it for you."

"Hih'oo."
"All right," [he said].

He'ne'-tounowuun-oot[74] hinii3ebi-o hi'oo3-in nuhu' heneecee-n.
Then his sister-in-law held the leg of a buffalo bull for him.

"Wootoo!
"Get out of the way!

"Heebeh-[be]'iinisine," hee3-eihok hinii3ebi-o.
"You'll get blood on yourself," he said to his sister-in-law.[75]

Nehe' hisei, "Neenih-'eesiini," hee3-oohok hinii3ebi-o hooxebine'.
This woman, "Don't worry about that," she said to her brother-in-law Spring Child.

He'ne'-neneesiini tees-cesin-o' be' hi-biixuuton-in noh hiwo'ohn-in.
Then he pretended accidentally to drop blood on her dress and her moccasins.

He'ih-cii-nii3eyou[76] nehe' hiseihiitei'yoo toh-be'iiniih-oet hinii3ebi-o.
This girl just ignored the fact that her brother-in-law got her all bloody.

Noh hinoohowoho' hee3-eihok, "Wooce' he-ih-woxeenow-oo[77] hei3ebi.
And her younger sister said to her, "Remember, you supposedly have contempt for your brother-in-law.

"Neh-cesisisee. Yihoo hees, houu," hee3-eihok hinoohowoho'.
"You should go away. Go to your husband, Crow," her younger sister said to her.

He'ih-cii-nii3eyou tih-'ii3-eit.[78]
She ignored what the younger sister said to her.

"Ne-et-tousih-oo wooxeih-t?" hee3-oohok hiix houu-n.
"What am I going to do with that ugly one?" she said about her husband, Crow.

'oh he'ih-bee-benee3ihce[79] toh-biino3ee-ni3 nuhu' hinii3ebi-o.
And she kept clumsily trying to jump in and help when her brother-in-law was loading the horses.

'oh he'ih-cii-tokoohob-ee.
But he did not pay any attention to her.

"Howoh'oe, wootoo, hiit 3i'ookuu, he-e[beh]-be'iinisine," hee3-eihok hinii3ebi-o.

"Wait, get out of the way, stand here, you might get blood on you," her brother-in-law said to her.

"Neenih-'eesiini; hoot-niiteheib-e3en nei3eboo," hee3-oohok.

"Don't worry about that; I'll help you, brother-in-law," she said to him.

"Hiiko, hoot-niihen-biino3ei-noo," heeh-ehk hooxebine'.

"No, I'll load on the meat by myself," said Spring Child.

Toh-'uus-ii3-eit, he'ne'-noo-noh'en-o' hoseinou.

After he said this to her, then she lifted up the pieces of meat.

'oh he'ih-be'iinis[80] hi-biixuuton-e'.

And there was blood all over her dress.

Hi-biixuut nih-'i3eti-yehk, niscehinoni-biixuut.

Her dress had been very pretty, a buckskin dress.

He'ih-noxow-nonihi' hiix houu-n.

She completely forgot about her husband, Crow.

He'ih-cii-noxow-3ooxu3ecooton-ee hiix nuhu' beh'eihouu-n hi'iihi' hinii3ebi-o.

She didn't give her husband, Old Crow, a thought, on account of her brother-in-law.

Noh huux, houu-n, nehe' hiseihiitei'yoo he'ih-beh'ini ko'osine-n hookuhu'een-e', tih'ii-woo-wo'ten-owuni3 hisiiseyook hot-no'ookei-ni3.

And this girl's husband, Crow, was landing on all the heads [of the dead buffalo], picking fat from the eyes to take home as meat/food [for his family].

He'ih-noo3-eeno' houu-n heetoh-'einootee-ni'i hookuhu'ee-no.

They left Crow behind where the buffalo heads were lying about.

He'ne'-nee3o'oo-t nehe' houu.

Then Crow remained behind.

Noh toh-3ooku-no'usee-t, he'ih-no'uxotii hisiiseyook.

And when he arrived in their wake, he brought the fat from the eyes with him.

He'ih-cii-nohkoohob-e' hiniin.

His wife did not look at him when he had that with him.

Noh toh-no'eecikoohu-3i', nehe' houu hiniin he'ih-bii-biin-e' hi-biixuut-ono hiniiibeih'-in Hooxebine' heetih-'eenehiisetoo-n.

And when they arrived home, Crow's wife gave her dresses to Spring Child's grandmother for her to wash [and keep] for herself.

"[Missing]," hee3-oohok nuhu' betebihehiho'.

"I give you this because I want you to have a dress,"[81] she said to the old woman.

Noh ne'=nih-'iis-iine'etii-hok, nehe' nih-noni3eesib-eit neyooxet-ii.

And that's how he lived, this one who was blown off by the whirlwind.

Notes

1. Tall Bear, Kroeber MS 2560a, Notebook 12, p. 15.

2. Kroeber, MS 2560a, Notebook 12, p. 10, Cleaver Warden, consultant.

3. Here, as well as in the next line and elsewhere in the text, future and future obligation are indicated by *hoton-/heton-*, which seems to be a shortened form of *hotwon-/hetwon-* but may be simply an allomorph of *hot-/het-*. Gros Ventre regularly uses *ʔoton-* in this role, corresponding to Arapaho *hoton-*.

4. *He'ineeyoo* 'it is obvious, clear to all, can't be missed'. Note that the following verb is inflected with nonaffirmative affixes, so that the entire construction means 'should he come to you, it will be obvious'.

5. Kroeber gives *-ohkóni'*, which would be 3PL.SUBJ, but the subject here is 4S, so the form should be *-ohkon*.

6. The use of *tih-* here is anomalous. One would expect *hé'ih-* or *nih-*, because otherwise the clause has no main verb, but the usage is not unprecedented.

7. Kroeber provides a gloss of 'on the left side of the tipi'; however, in modern Arapaho at least, *hoxuut(on)-* means 'right up against, right next to'.

8. II *tónotini-* 'there is a hole' > II.DIM *tónotihi(h)ni-* 'there is a small hole'.

9. Again Kroeber glosses *hoxuut* as 'left side' rather than the modern 'right next to, right up against'. But in MS 2560a, Notebook 5, p. 55, and Notebook 9, p. 10, he gives this word for 'sides of the tipi'.

10. The manuscript has *ne'iineesoo-yohkoni'*.

11. *Hotiiciih-* 'offer s.o. food on some kind of serving implement—traditionally a piece of rawhide serving as a dish'.

12. *Neeníisóu'u* is II affirmative, but *hiihoow-* requires nonaffirmative inflection. This inconsistency is unexplained.

13. *Wo'óhn-ino*=moccasin-4.POSS.P. This is a rare occurrence of plural marking on a noun possessed by a fourth/obviative person.

14. Kroeber gives this bracketed clause in his translation, but it is not in the Arapaho.

15. Kroeber provides the gloss 'the right/south' of the door, but all modern Arapahos agree that the word here means 'right up underneath something'. Moreover, the tipi always faced to the east, so the right side as one entered would be the north side not the south side.

16. The use of *céétii3-* 'say nothing' twice consecutively might be meant to create a subtle echo of *céetes-* 'accidentally cut' a few lines earlier.

17. Kroeber gives the gloss of 'didn't I tell you', but the transcription does not support this, although the final syllable here is unclear. *Neih-cíí-nihíí3oo* would be 'didn't I tell her!?'

18. *Hotino3-* TA 'to stalk, as a predator stalking game and getting ready to pounce'. The word can be used for a cat stalking a mouse, for example. The children are presented as being not quite human but rather like little animals in a sense.

19. *Bisíikoh-* TA 'appear/show up on s.o.' (cf. *nonííkoh-* 'escape from, disappear on s.o.') > AI.O *bisíikohéí'i-*.

20. More specifically, 'waiting under cover, in ambush'. This word continues the imagery of a hunt, as with *hotino3-* (see note 18 above).

21. *Kóókootóóyei-* PREFIX 'nearby, within range to grab' and more specifically 'present ahead of time, ready to grab' (cf. *wootóóyei-* 'ahead of time, early'). The hunting imagery continues.

22. One would expect *toh-'unsíiten-éí3i'*. The use of IMPERF /n/, *niisíiten-* is unusual. Alternately, this could be *toon-iisíiten-éí3i'* 'he has almost caught them'.

23. *Hee* 'yes' is used here in the sense of 'yes, I see what you are saying, but . . .'

24. The manuscript has final *-inin* rather than just final *-in* on this verb.

25. Imperative particle *cíhnee* 'over here, this way'. Apparently used as an AI verb *cih-néési-* 'lie down over here', with standard imperative form *cihnéésii.*

26. *Beeteini-* AI 'have a bow' or 'make(?) a bow'. Here a participle appears to have been formed, *bééteiníít* 'act of making a bow' and by extension 'the bow that is made'. Thus *he-bééteiníít-ono* is literally 'your bows that you make'.

27. This is a relatively common use of what is essentially an II imperative construction, with prefix *cih-* (EMPH.IMPER) and nonaffirmative inflection on the verb. It is best glossed as 'it should be . . .'

28. The obviative form of *hooxebíne'* is *hooxebínoho'.*

29. Literally 'wrapped'.

30. The manuscript has *cobohoo,* which is likely just *cobóo.*

31. The manuscript has final /nin/ rather than final /n/ on this verb.

32. See note 5 above on the subjunctive inflection.

33. *Hiine'e3éíhi-* 'alive'. This is a rare form, apparently a diminutive. Cf. the very common *hiine'étii-* 'live'.

34. Round and smooth river stones are the best stones for use in sweat lodge ceremonies.

35. This is an NA.DEPPART with fourth-person possession marking suffix /-in/. Both Open Brain and 'their mother' are obviative in this sentence: in other words, this is a 4/4 DEPPART, equivalent to such forms as TA 4/4 *neh'-éíni3* 'he killed her' (versus TA 4/3 *neh'-éít* and TA 4/3 DEPPART *neh'-éiiton*).

36. *Wo-* indefinite possession prefix, because the previous possessor is now dead.

37. The manuscript has *hihi-* rather than *hi-*.

38. *Kooxuuhu'* is a rare variant of *koox=* 'yet again, once more'.

39. The element *huhuut* is unclear.

40. *Ni'iiniih-* TA 'able to harm'. Cf. *hesiiniih-* TA 'injure'.

41. The prefix *hihii3-* means 'from', but its function here with the word 'person' is unclear.

42. More properly *hih-'ii3-óoon* (NA.DEPPART, 3/4).

43. 'Your (PL) mother', though everything else suggests that there is only one addressee.

44. Again, the form *-einoni* indicates 2PL addressee, though in the preceding line 'fourth' has 4S inflection *-ni3*.

45. This verb is actually used to indicate the striking of lightning and the associated pealing of thunder with the bolt, so it could be translated 'the lightning strikes and the thunder sounds'.

46. Kroeber glosses this line as 'that is how your mother looks when she comes'. The verb actually means 'she sees them', so instead of *heinoo* 'your mother' perhaps *híinoon[inoo]* 'his [their] mother' was intended, since the mother appears a few lines later.

47. The Thunderbird is the mother of the eaglets they have killed.

48. Kroeber's manuscript has an explanatory note: "They both pretended to shoot, but shot only one arrow, to make it stronger, they both put their minds and their powers in the one arrow, because she might have pulled off."

49. These are special arrows made of tendon.

50. *Hitiitoo* is the large tendon on the back of a buffalo. These are very strong and are used to attach axe heads to handles and for similar purposes (Kroeber, MS 2560a, Notebook 12, p. 16). Here the word *hitiitoon-o3* 'tendon-arrow' has been created.

51. The manuscript has *ti'* rather than *3i'*.

52. The manuscript has *-inini'* rather than *-ini'*.

53. Literally 'lost due to action of the wind'.

54. The verb does not refer to wind action in this case and could be used for people who simply wandered around and lost their way. This concluding verb thus diminishes the role of the wind, while suggesting that more blame should be placed on the child (as the story implies more generally as well).

55. *Cetoh-* TA means 'cause someone to be dying, cause extreme, near-death pain' in modern Arapaho (cf. *ceto'oo-* AI 'dying, in agony, near death').

56. This verb is 4/4 TA: *he'ih-ce3eesíb-ee-n*, 'a whirlwind (OBV) carried him (OBV) away'.

57. *Hoono'uunookú-* AI 'have dirty eyes' > *Hoono'uunookúúhuu* NA 'one who has dirty eyes' > AI *hoono'uunookuuhúúni-* 'be a dirty-eyed person'.

58. Kroeber consistently glosses *nouu* as 'porcupine', but it actually means 'swift fox'.

59. This is another TA verb with 4/4 inflection /-ee-n/, as both Crow and the little porcupine are OBV.

60. *Biinoo-* AI middle voice, more normally *biinee-*.

61. The manuscript has *hihii3iihi3i'* rather than *hihii3ííhi'*.

62. *No3=*, 'you should know that, it's obvious that, it's clearly evident that, everyone can see that . . .'

63. Both 'porcupine' and 'her grandson' are obviative, so this verb should have 4/4 inflection *-ooni3* rather than *-oot*.

64. The manuscript has *houun* 'crow' rather than *nouun* 'swift fox'.

65. This is 4S.SUBJ/4 rather than 3PL.SUBJ/4, because 'his grandmother' and 'this man' are both OBV.

66. This is a 4.POSS form.

67. *Henéi'isíisííni* 'I wonder how that can be?' 'How could that possibly be?'

68. Literally 'looked at'.

69. *Nenih-* 'let it be as it is/continue on as things are'. *Hoxó'oteenew-* TA 'think of s.o. as laughable, to be laughed at'.

70. TA nonaffirmative *he-ih-cih-'oto3ih-e'* = 2S-PAST/CONTR-to here-be ashamed of-3S, 'he should make you ashamed of him'.

71. *Betébi* 'old woman' and *ne-betébihéb* 'my old woman' are common forms used for 'wife' and 'my wife'.

72. Kroeber actually transcribes *heisonoo* 'your father'.

73. *Neh-néenou'ú-hee* = EMPH.IMPER-get ready (AI)-3S.INDIR.IMPER 'make sure and have him prepared'.

74. The verb apparently should be inflected as /-eit/ rather than /-oot/.

75. The passage actually says 'his sister-in-law said to him'; based on the following line, however, this must be an error.

76. *Nii3eyóúhu-* AI 'pay attention to/be concerned with s.t.' > *Cii-nii3eyou[hu]-* AI 'ignore s.t.' Cf. TA *he-ihoow-nii3eyoohúúton-é3* 'I am ignoring you'.

77. TA.NONAFF *he-ih-woxeenów-oo* = 2S-PAST/CONTR-despise/scorn-3S 'you are supposed to despise him'.

78. Kroeber transcribes /s/ for /3/ in the last verb.

79. *Bée-benee3íhcehí-* = REDUP- obstruct s.o. rapidly (TA)-.

80. *Be'ííni-* 'bloody' > *be'iin-isi-* AI.RESULT 'end up all bloody, covered with blood'.

81. This is Kroeber's gloss. The Arapaho is illegible in his transcription.

Bii'oxuyoo/Found-in-the-Grass

Told by John Goggles, Wyoming, September 26–27, 1910
Collected by Truman Michelson
NAA, MS 2708, 54 pp.

This version of Tangled Hair/Found-in-the-Grass is shorter and less detailed than the one recorded by Kroeber from Caspar Edson, Nevertheless it is still an interesting and effective version of the story, especially notable for the series of closely parallel repetitions at key moments in the narrative. Among these moments are the visit of the stranger (who is actually Tangled Hair, even though he is not identified as such at that point in the narrative) to the woman in the tipi and the series of offers of a plate made by the woman; the repeated encounters between the father and his two wild sons; the shooting of the arrows to revive the dead mother; and the father's repeated warning not to engage with various challenges (Tangled Hair, the broken-topped tree, the young Thunderbirds, and the sage chickens). We have tried to translate the text to preserve these repetitions as closely as possible.

In combination with the repetitions, the narrative uses a very spare style: the repeated words are quite common, and gain their effect from the repetition itself rather than from any particular unusual "color" or descriptiveness that they have on their own. This allows certain thematic motifs to appear clearly across several sections of the story. These include, for example, a contrast between the lexical roots 'going/coming in' (*ciit-/cii3-*) and 'going/coming out' (*nouu[t]-*, *noehi-*), which we have italicized as they occur in the text. This theme is echoed by the many instances of going out away from camp, involving the roots *(he)3eb-* and *yih-*, both meaning 'over there' or 'toward over there', as well as the form *no'o'* 'away from the camp, out in the hills, in the wilds', followed by returns to the tipi or the camp (especially forms of the verb *heeckoohu-* 'go/come home' and the root *hookoot-/hookoo3-* 'homeward'). Thus on both a very local and a very global level, the text is dominated by comings and goings, movements from and to central spaces. See Anderson 2001: 91–118 for a discussion of such complementary movements more generally in Arapaho life and mythology.

The text is also dominated by repeated prohibitions (*ciibéh-* 'don't') and repeated breaking of those prohibitions, which follow hortative forms that encourage the transgressions (*3i'*= 'maybe I'll . . . , why don't I . . .'; *sóóxe* 'let's go [and . . .]'; *cih-* = emphatic imperative; *neh-* 'let me . . .'). More specifically, the theme of prohibition almost always involves not going to locations 'outside,' or 'over there', while the emphatic forms and imperatives almost always suggest movement to those very same locations.

William C'Hair knows this story very well. Indeed for him it seems to be perhaps the richest and most important of all Arapaho stories. Many of its meanings are not at all apparent from the literal contents of the story but rather are embedded in the interpretive traditions that surround it. Of course these traditions also change over time and vary from person to person within the tribe. One example, concerning section five, gives a sense of his view of the material. The Northern Arapahos currently have one particularly sacred ceremonial drum, used at all official tribal functions, known as the Eagle Drum, with an eagle image on its surface. The singers and drummers are themselves known as Eagles. As C'Hair explains, when the eagle in this story tries to fly away with the arrow and then is pulled back onto the rock and killed, as if attached to a rubber band, that symbolizes the way in which the eagle ends up depicted flat on the Eagle Drum, with wings and tail feathers spread, as when it was flattened against the rock. Originally the eagle was not dead when it hit the rock, so people got sticks and started beating it. When they hit it, thunder would sound; and when the eyes flashed, lightning would strike. This was the first drumming. So when the drummers play the drum now, the pounding of the drum is equivalent to the calls of the eagle, literally in/on the drum, which are linked to thunder and ultimately to the Thunderbird. Whether this exact interpretation would have been offered by anyone in 1900 is unknown, but the mode of thought represented by C'Hair's connection of the story to the Eagle Drum is typical of traditional Arapaho uses of narratives.

Finally, although the particular exploits of the twins at the end of the story differ from the version told by Caspar Edson, this story also contains three successful exploits followed by a fourth, the encounter with the grouse, that leads to trouble. Recall (see "When Nih'oo3oo Witnessed the Sun Dance") that sage grouse are closely associated with the Sun Dance ceremony. Their calling at the lek can be compared to the singing at the Eagle Drum for that ceremony.

Part One: The Visitor to the Camp

Hinen he'ih-'ootii.

A man was camped.

He'ih-teco'on-iinoo'ei.
He was always hunting.

Noh hiniin he'ih-'ii3-ee, "He-ebeh-niiton-oo biikoo.
And he said to his wife, "You might hear him at night.

"He-ebeh-cih-no'usee; *ciibeh-nouu*-noohow-un!" hee3-oohok hiniin.
"He might come here; don't go outside to see him!" he said to his wife.

Noh ci'=he'ih-'iinoo'ei.
And again he went hunting.

Noh biikoo he'ih-cih-no'usee.
And that night someone came here to the tipi.

Noh nehe' hisei he'ih-niitobee hinenitee-n.
And the woman heard a person.

He'ih-niitouuhu-n biikoo too3iihi' hiyeih'-inoo.
He hollered during the night near their lodge.

Noh he'ih-'e'in niisi-nihii3-eit hiix: "*Ciibeh*-noohow-un!"
And she remembered what her husband had said to her: "Don't look at him!"

"*3i'=neh*-noohow-oo," heesi3ecoo-hok.
"Just let me go take a peek," she thought.

He'ih-kohei'i.
She got up.

He'ih-'iiwooku'oo.
She peeked out.

He'ih-cih-???
She . . .[1]

He'ih-*ciitei* hinen.
A man entered.

He'ih-ceenok nee'eeteeb-e'.
He sat down at the back of the lodge.

Noh nehe' hisei he'ih-'oxob-ee.
And the woman fed him dinner.

"Hii-hoowu-neeneisou'u[2] no-otiiciit-ono," heeh-ehk nehe' hinen.
"These aren't the kind of plates I use," said this man.

Noh he'ne'i-ce'esoo-ni'i.
And then she brought different ones.

He'ih-'iten nooko3oni'.
She got a white eagle tail feather.

He'ih-neeni-nino; "Ho-otiiciihooo?"[3]
Those were what [she used as plates]; "Is this your plate?"

"Hii-hoow-neeneisoo-no," heeh-ehk.
"They aren't like that," he said.

Noh ci'=he'ih-'okoo3oo-nino:
And once again there were different ones:

He'ih-'iten hinotoo-ho; he'ih-koto'ohu-nino.
She got her leggings; they were beaded.

He'ih-neeni-nino: "Ho-otiiciihooo?"
Those were what [she used]): "Is this your plate?"

"Wuho'woohu'!" heeh-ehk.[4]
"Almost right on!" he said.

Noh ci'=he'ne'i-ce'esoo-ni'.
And then again she brought a different one.

Hi-biixuut he'ih-neeni-n; "Ho-otiiciihooo?"
It was her dress; "Is this your plate?"

"Wuho'woohu'!" heeh-ehk.
"Almost right on!" he said.

Noh he'ne'i-kokoh'u3ecoo-t.
And then she thought some.

He'ne'i-beis-iisibi-t.
Then she lay completely down as if going to sleep.

He'ne'-teesi-ciinen-o' bii3iwo.
Then she put the food down on top of her.

"Ho'eii!" heeh-ehk.[5]
"Thank you!" he said.

He'ne'i-cesisi-bii3ihi-t.
Then he set to eating.

Noh heeh-ehk, "Heenoo nii-ceetesi-'i se'nooo-no," heeh-ehk.
And he said, "It often happens that plates are accidentally cut," he said.

He'ih-ko'e3eikuu3-ee.
He cut her open at the belly.

Tei'yoonoh'-o he'ih-'e3kuu3-ee.
He tore children out of her belly.

Ceexoon hiso'ooteeb-e' he'ih-ko'usib-ee noh ceexoon nee'eeteeb-e'.
One of them he threw down at the entrance and the other at the back of the lodge.

He'ne'i-*noehi*-t.
Then he went out.

Part Two: The Father Catches the Wild Sons

Noh kou3iihi' biikoo hiix he'ne'i-no'usee-ni3.
And later that night then her husband arrived.

He'ih-bih'inootee-n.
The camp was all dark.

Noh he'ih-'eenet: "Nohowoh?" heeh-ehk.[6]
And he spoke: "Is everything okay?" he said.

He'ih-ceetii3ootiini-n,[7] noh he'ih-'e'in xonou;
There was not a sound to be heard,[8] and he knew right away [what had happened];

Noh heeh-ehk, "See=ne-ih-cii-nihii3-oono'?" heeh-ehk.
And he said, "I'll be damned if I didn't tell her about these things!" he said.[9]

He'ih-*ciitei.*
He went inside.

He'ih-noohob-ee hiniin.
He saw his wife.

He'ih-ko'e3ei-n.
She was cut open.

He'ne'i-bebii3en-oot hiniin.
Then he fixed up his wife as best he could.

He'ih-'iisiben-ee.
He put her in bed.

He'ne'i-ce'-*nouusee*-t co'otenii honoot toh-nookeni-ni'.
Then he went back out into the hills until morning came.

He'ne'i'-*ce'eecikoohu*-t.
Then he came back home.

He'ih-*ciitei* hiyeih'-e'.
He went inside his lodge.

He'ih-noohoot niitoh-'iinikotii-ni3i tei'yoonoh'-o hi-beete' noh hineik-o.
He saw where children had been playing with his bow and arrows.

He'ih-3oo-3o'eekuu-nino hineik-o, noh he'ih-kohtowu3ecoo.
His arrows were all stuck into the ground, and he thought that this was very strange.

He'ne'i-bii3ihi-t.
Then he ate.

Noh tih-'iisi-bii3ihi-t, he'ne'i-ce'-*nouusee*-t.
And when he had finished eating, then he went back out [to the hills].

Noh koox=hi3ou'uuni-' he'ne'i-*ce'eecikoohu*-t.
And then once again in the evening he came back home.

Noh koox=he'ih-noohoot hineik-o he'ih-3oo-3o'eekuu-nino.
And once again he saw his arrows all stuck in the ground.

Noh he'=nee'ei'-e'in-o'.
And that's when he understood what was going on.

He'ne'i-'eteini-t hiyeih'-e'.
Then he spent the night in his lodge.

Noh toh-nookeni-ni' he'ne'i-ce'-*nouusee*-t.
And when morning came then he went back out [to the hills].

Neneesiihi' he'ih-noh'ohusee co'oteni'.
He pretended to walk up into the hills.

Noh he'ih-cih-ce'koo noxohoeniihi'.
And he came running back quickly.

Ne'ih-cih-nihi'koo koh'owu-u' too3iihi' hiyeih'-e'.
He ran back to a gulch near his lodge.

He'ih-cowouute-n.
There was a ridge there.

Hiibineeniihi' he'ih-no'usee; he'ih-kotous.
He arrived there in secret; he hid.

He'ih-ceh'e3tii.
He listened.

He'ih-niiton-ee ceese' hiih'o.
He heard one of his sons.

Heihi-yohkon,[10] "Cihneecis be!" heeh-ehk ceese'. "Heetih-niinikotii-no'!"
heeh-ehk.
He said, "Come on and let's go, friend!" said one son. "Let's play!" he said.

"Wohei tous!" heeh-ehk.
"Okay then!" said the other one.

He'=nee'ei'-eeneiten-ou'u ho3-ii, he'ne'i-3i'eyei-3i'.
Then they gathered up the arrows, then they stuck one in the ground.

He'=nee'ei'-cesis-cebiiheti-3i' ho3-ii.
Then they started playing a game with the arrows.

Nehe' hinen he'ih-seh-koxo'-no'usee.
The man slowly crawled over there to the lodge.

He'ih-seh-'iiwooku'oo.
He peeked in on them from outside.

He'ih-noohob-ee honoh'ehih'-o he'ih-'iinikotii-nino ho3-ii.
He saw the young boys playing with the arrows.

He'ih-koxuuten-*cii3ihce*.
The father suddenly jumped in there.

He'ih-'iisiiten-ee ceexoon.
He caught one of them.

He'ih-too-toyob-e'.
The child bit him all over.

He'ih-koo-kou'u'ein-e'.
It scratched him all over the face.

Hoonii he'ne'-iis-teteesih-oot.
After quite a while then he managed to calm [the child] down.[11]

Noh hee3-oohok hiibineeniihi', "Ci'=heet-nenees-*nouusee*-noo.
And his father whispered to him, "I'll pretend to go outside again.

"Heeti-nenees-iinikotiiw-o' hi'iihi' neik-o," hee3-oohok;[12]
"I'll pretend to play with my arrows," he said to his son;

noh "Het-i3kuu3-oo,"
and "You must seize [your brother]," [his father said],

noh "Neixoo het-ii."
and "Father, you must say."

Noh "Heet-cih-*cii3ihcehi*-noo noh heetn-iisiiten-o'," hee3-oohok.
And ["once you say 'Father'] I'll jump in here and I'll catch him," he said to his son.

"[Hih'oo]," heeh-ehk nehe' honoh'ehihi'.
"All right," said the young boy.

Noh he'ne'i-ce3ei'oo-t.
And then his father left.

No'o' beebei'on he'ih-seh-koxtisee.
Way far out in the hills he walked, out of view on the other side of the ridge.

Noh noxohoeniihi' he'ih'-cih-ce'koo niihiihi' koh'owu'.
And he came running quickly back here along the gulch.

He'ih-cih-ce'-no'koo too3iihi' hiyeih'-e'.
He arrived back here near his lodge.

He'ih-kotous; he'ih-ceh'e3tii.
He hid; he listened.

Noh kou3iihi' he'ih-niiton-ee.
And after a while he heard them.

"Heetih-'iinikotii-no'!" heeh-ehk nehe' honoh'ehihi' nih-'iisiiteneih-t
hiniisonoon-inoo.
"Let's play!" said the young boy who had been caught by their father.

Nehe' ceese' honoh'ehihi' he'ih-neseih.
The other young boy was wild.

"Hiiko," heeh-ehk, "toh-'uusiiten-ein heisonoon-in," hee3-oohok.
"No," he said, "because our father caught you," he said to the first
boy.

Noh ci', "Heetih-'iinikotii-no'!"
And again, "Let's play!"

"Hiiko, heisonoon-in toh-'uusiiten-ein," hee3-oohok.
"No, because our father caught you," he said to him.

"Hiiko, ne-ih-'oow-uusiiten-e'; nih'ii-too-toyow-o'," heeh-ehk.
"No, he didn't catch me; I was biting him over and over," he said.

"Wohei tous, *cih*-neecis!"
"Well then, come on and let's go!"

He'=nee'ei'-cesis-iinikotii-3i'.
Then they started playing.

He'ih-'iten-owuu beete' noh ho3-ii.
They got the bow and arrows.

He'ne'i-nii-niihootii-3i'.
Then they gambled for fun.

Noh beexoo3iihi' he'ih-'i3ikuu3-ee, noh heeh-ehk,
And later the young boy grabbed his brother, and he said,

"Neixoo, ceikoohu! nih-'iisiiten-o'!" heeh-ehk.
"Father, run in here! I have caught him!" he said.

Noh hiniisonoon-inoo he'ih-*cii3ihcehi*-n.
And their father leaped inside.

Noh he'ih-'iisiiten-ee;
And he seized the child;

noh nih-'ii3-oohok, "Ciini-biiwoohu!" hee3-oohok.
and he said to him, "Stop crying!" he said to him.

"Heetnii-niiston-e3enee beetei noh ho3-ii heetih-i'-'iinikotii-nee,"
hee3-oohok.
"I'll make a bow and arrows for you, so you can play," he said to them.

Part Three: They Revive the Mother

"Hih'oo," hee3-eihok.
"All right," they said to him.

"Wohei neh-niistii beete' noh ho3-ii.
"Well, you'd better make a bow and arrows.

"Cih-niiseenoo ho3-ii:
"There should be two types of arrows:

"ceese' cih-be'ee-ni noh ceese' cih-wo'teeni-ni."
"one should be red and the other should be black."

Noh nehe' ceese' honoh'ehihi': "Cih-nee'eesiini," heeh-ehk.
And the other young boy: "It should be like that," he said.

Noh nehe' hinen he'i=nee'eesitoo-t heesi-nihii3-eit.
And the man did just what the boys had told him to.

Noh tih-'iistii-t beete' noh ho3-ii, noh hee3-eihok, "Niistii ciibeet!
And when he had made the bow and arrows, then they said to him,
"Make a sweat lodge!

"Ciiben-ono cih-be'ee-nino noh cih-beteetosoo'eti-[ni]no," hee3-eihok.
"The frame pieces should be red and there should be one hundred of
them," they told him.[13]

Noh "Neinoo het-*ciiten*-oo," hee3-eihok.
And "You must take my mother inside," said one of them to their father.

Noh he'=nee'eesitoo-t.
And their father did that.

Noh tih-'iisitii-t ciibeet, he'ne'-*ciiten*-oot hiniin ciibeet.
And when he had finished making the sweat lodge, then he took his
wife inside the sweat lodge.

Noh nuhu' honoh'ehih'-o', ceese' he'ne'-ihci3obee-t.
And these young boys, then one of them shot up into the air.

Noh heeh-ehk, "Wootoo[14] no'oo*! nouuhcehi*!" heeh-ehk.
And he said, "Get out of the way, mother! Run outside!" he said.

Noh neniisi'owoo-', he'ne'-ihci3obee-t;
Then a second time he shot up into the air;

"Wootoo no'oo! *Nouuhcehi!*" heeh-ehk.
"Get out of the way, mother! Run outside!" he said.

Noh nuhu' ciibeet he'ih-noh'oowunoo'oo.
And the sweat lodge was shaking back and forth.

Noh nehe' ceese' honoh'ehihi' ci'=he'=nee'eesitoo-t.
And the other young boy did the same thing.

Noh hei'-bee3-ihci3obee-t, "Wootoo no'oo! *Nouuhcehi!*" heeh-ehk.

And once he had finished shooting up into the air, "Get out of the way, mother! Run outside!" he said.

Noh hiinoon-inoo he'ih-*nouuhcehi*-n.

And their mother came running outside.

Noh hiniisonoon-inoo he'ih-ni'i3ecoo-n.

And their father was happy.

Part Four: They Kill Tangled Hair and Bring Ropes

Noh he'=nee'ee-ce'-iine'etii-3i'.

And thus they were reunited as a family.

Noh kou3iihi' nuhu' honoh'ehih'-o' he'ih-beexookee-no'.

And later the two young men were grown up.

Noh he'ih'ii-teco'on-hiinisee-no'.

And they were always wandering around.

He'ih'ii-cee-coboo-no'.

They would shoot at things.

Noh hiniisonoon-inoo nih-'ii3-eihohkoni', "Hinee heetoh-no'otoo'ee-' *ciibeh-3ebisee-'.*

And their father told them, "That place where the brush is thick, don't go over there.

"Hinenitee heenitoo-t noo-no'oteih-t," hee3-oohok.

"There is a person there who is very powerful," he told them.

"Hih'oo," hee-hee3-eihok.

"All right," they assured him.

Noh hoo3iihi',[15] "*3i'=sooxe* hinee heetoh-no'otoo'ee-', heisonoon-in niitoh-nihii-t," heeh-ehkoni'.

And later, "Why don't we go over there where the brush is thick, the place our father spoke of," they said.

Noh he'ne'-*yihoo*-3i', noh he'ih-'itet-owuu.
And then they went there and reached that place.

Niiinon he'ih-'ootee-n.
A tipi was set up.

He'ih-*ciitei*-no'.
They went inside.

Beh'eihehi' he'ih-'entoo.
An old man lived there.

Noh hee3-eihohkoni', "Hiiwo' he'=nee-hehkoni' neisiiho-ho'!" heeh-ehk.
And he said to them, "Well, you must be my grandsons!" he said.

"Het-ii-cih-'i3ooxuh-ube," hee3-oohok.
"You must come delouse me," he said to them.

"Hih'oo," heeh-ehkoni'.
"All right," they said.

He'ne'i-i3ooxuh-oo3i'.
Then they deloused him.

Noh he'ih-nei'oohoot-owuu he'ih-tonoti-n 3ooniteec.
And they looked and saw that there was a hole in the top of his head.

Noh nehe' he'ih-'eni'ei; wootii seenook-uu he'ih-nee'eeesoo-n hinii3e'ee.
And this old man had long hair; his hair looked like ropes.

Noh hoo3iihi' he'ih-nokohunoo'oo.
And later he fell asleep.

Noh ceese' nuhu' honoh'ehihi' he'ih-wotikuu3-ee hoh'onookee-n hisitee;
And this one young boy threw a rock into the fire;

'oh hei'-bei'ci3ei-ni3, he'ne'-*cii3ikuu3*-oot hinii3e'een-in.
And once it was red hot, then he threw it inside the old man's head.

Noh nuhu' hinii3e'ee-no he'ih-toukuhu-nino hokooxun-e'.
And the boys tied the strands of his hair to a tipi pole.

He'ih-neh'-eeno', noh he'ih-koo-ko'un-owuu hinii3e'een-in.
They killed him, and they pulled out all his hair.

Noh he'ne'-*ce'eecikoohu*-3i'.
And then they went back home.

He'ih-*no'eeckoohu*-no'.
They arrived home.

He'ih-biin-eeno' hiniisonoon-inoo.
They gave the hair to their father.

"Heetih-seenookuu," hee3-oohohkoni'.
"Use it for ropes," they said to him.

"Nih-noh'-oono' hini' hinen hei-nihii3-ooo," heeh-ehkoni'.
"We killed that man you spoke about," they said.

"He-ih-tous-noh'-oobe?" hee3-eihohkoni' hiniisonoon-inoo.
"How did you kill him?" said their father to them.

Noh "Nih-'i3ooxuh-oono', noh nih-nokohu-t;
And "We deloused him, and he went to sleep;

"noh nih-*ciitoo'e3eih*-oono'[16] hoh'onookee-n hinii3e'een-e';
"and we plunged a hot rock into his head using a forked stick;

"noh nee'ees-noh'-oono'," heeh-ehkoni'.
"and that's how we killed him," they said.

"Hih'oo, hii3oobei-nee," hee3-eihohkoni'.
"All right, you were right to do it," he said to them.

Part Five: They Kill Young Eagles and Bring Plumes

Noh cih-kou3iihi' hee3-eihohkoni':
And a little while later he said to them:

"Hinee hohoot hoowuniihiihi', neniisookuu-t hohoot, nohuux heinootee-'.
"That tree downstream, that tree that stands alone, there's a nest in it.

"Nii'eihiisoo-no' heenitoo-3i'," hee3-eihohkoni' hiniisonoon-inoo.
"There are eaglets in it," said their father to them.

"*Ciibeh*-cou'uh-e'!" hee3-eihohkoni'.
"Don't bother them!" he said to them.

Noh kou3iihi', "*Sooxe yihoo*-no'," heeh-ehkoni'.
And later, "Let's go over there," they said.

"Wohei tous," heeh-ehk ceese'.
"Well okay then," said the other one.

He'ne'i-*yihoo*-3i'.
Then they went there.

He'ih-'ites-eeno' nuhu' nii'eihii-ho.
They came to the eagles.

He'ih-noh'ouuhuuton-eeno', noh he'ih-'iten-ee;
They climbed up to them, and one young man got one.

Noh hee3-oohok "Hii-tou3o'et heisonoo noo'usee-3i?"
And he said to the eaglet, "How are the clouds when your father comes?"

Noh "Nii-wo'teeno'eti-' noo'usee-3i neisonoo," heeh-ehk nii'eihihi'.
And "The clouds are black when my father comes," answered the little eagle.

Noh ceexoon he'ne'-iten-oot, noh hee3-oohok, "Hii-tou3o'et heinoo noo'usee-3i?"

And he grabbed the other eaglet and said to it, "How are the clouds when your mother comes?"

He'ih-ce'-ceceibii3oon-ee.
He twisted the eagle's beak backward.

Noh heeh-ehk nii'eihihi', "Nii-no'oteese-' neinoo noo'usee-3i," hee3-eihok.
And the little eagle said, "There's a lot of wind when my mother arrives," he answered him.

Cih-'oo3iihi' he'ih-noono'et; he'ih-tes-wo'oteeyoo; he'ih-no'ees.
A little later clouds built up; it was extremely dark; the wind came up.

Noh ne'-ceese' honoh'ehihi' heeh-ehk . . . he'ih-coboo hoh'onookei'i.
And then one boy said . . . he shot into some rocks.

Noh heeh-ehk, "Hih-koyikuutii-ninehk nuhu' neic, heet-neh'-ei'een," hee3-oohok heebe3ii'eihio.
And he said, "If you can remove the arrow from the rock, you'll kill us," he said to the golden eagle.

He'ih-no'otoosoot, noh nehe' heebe3ii'eihii he'ih-cih-'oowuh'o[huu]koo.
There was pouring rain, and the golden eagle plunged downward.

He'ih-'i3kuutii beic.
It grabbed the arrow.

He'ih-nohkuhcih'o.
It flew up with it.

Noh nuhu' beic he'ih-cih-ce'-noo-no'unoo'oo;
And the arrow came rushing back down to the rock;

noh heebe3ii'eihii he'ih-noxowus hoh'onookee3-i'.
and the golden eagle was smashed dead against the rock.

Noh ceese' nii'eihii he'ih-cih-'oowuh'o;
And the other eagle dove down;

noh beebeet heestoo-ni3 niito' nii'eihio, he'=nee'eesitoo-t, noh he'ih-noxowus.

and just as the first eagle had done, he did the same thing, and was smashed dead.

Noh nuhu' honoh'ehih'-o' he'ih-ko'ookuuneen-eeno'.

And the boys plucked out their feathers.

He'ih-*nohkeeckoohu*-no' nuhu' biii-no.

They went home with the feathers.

He'ih-biin-eeno' hiniisonoon-inoo.

They gave them to their father.

"Heeyou?" hee3-eihohkoni'.

"What's this?" he said to them.

Noh "Hini'iit hohoot heetoh-niisookuu-t, nih-*'e3eb*-no'usee-no';

And "That tree that stands alone, we went over there;

"noh nih-noo-noh'-oono' heebe3ii'eihii-ho," heeh-ehkoni'.

"and we killed golden eagles," they said.

"Hih'oo, hii3oobei-nee," hee3-oohok.

"All right, you were right to do it," said their father to them.

Part Six: They Destroy the Deadly Tree and Bring Firewood

Noh ci'=he'ne'i-nihii3-oot: "Nehe' hohoot teebe'ei-t, *ciibeh*-tootisee-';

And then again he said to them: "That tree that is broken off at the top, don't walk near it;

"nii-noxowo'on-oot hinenitee-no," hee3-oohok.

"it crushes people," he said to them.

"[Hih'oo]," hee-hee3-eihok.

"All right," they assured him.

Noh kou3iihi' he'ih-*yihoo*-no'.
And later they went there.

He'ih-'ites-eeno' hohoot-in.
They came to the tree.

Too3iihi' he'ih-3i'ookuu-no'.
They were standing near it.

Noh nehe' hohoot he'ih-*yih*-3ooninoo'oo heetoo-ni3i.
And the tree came crashing down toward where they were.

He'ih-'iiyohootinoo'oo-nino.
They disappeared in the wink of an eye [just before it hit them].

He'ih-3o'us nehe' hohoot.
The tree shattered to pieces.

He'ih-'eeneiten-owuu.
They gathered up the pieces.

Bex-o he'ih-*'ookootii*-no'.
They took home pieces of firewood.

He'ih-*ciiten*-owuu.
They took it inside.

"Het-ibeseb," hee3-oohohkoni' hiinoon-inoo.
"Your firewood," they said to their mother.[17]

"Toot=hei-hiitixotii-be?" hee3-eihohkoni'.
"Where did you bring it here from?" she said to them.

Noh hee3-oohohkoni', "Hini'iit neniisookuu-t hohoot, nih-'oninoo'oo-t, noh nih-3o'usi-';
And they said to her, "That tree that stands all alone, it fell over and shattered against the ground;

"noh nih-cih-'eeneiten-owuno'."
"and we gathered up the pieces and brought them."

"Ke-i3oobei-be?" hee3-eihohkoni'.
"Are you sure?" she said to them.

"Hii3oobei-no'," heeh-ehkoni'.
"We're sure," they said.

Part Seven: They Pursue Sage Grouse and Found-in-the-Grass Is Blown Away

Noh hee3-eihohkoni' hiniisonoon-inoo: "Hinee hii3e', *ciibeh-'e3ebisee-'*.
And their father said to them, "That place over there, don't go over there.

"Heentoo-3i' cenee-no'.
"There are sage grouse over there.

"Ciibeh-cebii-'.
"Don't shoot them.

"Hii-hoowu-cebii-no'," hee3-eihohkoni'.
"They're not shot," he said to them.

Noh hoo3iihi' he'ih-*yihoo*-no'.
And later they went over there.

He'ih-noohob-eeno' cenee-no, noh he'ih-cee-cebii-no'.
They saw sage grouse, and they shot at them.

He'ih-cii-bes-eeno'.
They didn't hit them.

He'ih-koyih'ohuukoohu-nino.
The sage grouse flushed and flew off, escaping.

Noh xonou he'ih-noohoot-owuu heseis.
And right away they saw the wind [coming up in the distance].

He'ih-*'ookoo3*-ce3ikoohu-no'.
They ran off toward home.

Ceese' he'ih'iis-*cii3ihce*, noh ceese' he'ih-*no'o'*ees beebei'on.
One managed to get inside, but the other one was blown far out away from camp.

He'ih-nous hiikoo', noh kou3iihi' he'ih-bii'in-e' betebihehiho'.
He got stuck in the brush, and later a little old lady found him.

Noh hee3-eihok, "Hiiwo' he'=nee-hek!? Neisie Bii'oxuyoo!"[18]
And she said to him, "Well, who are you!? My grandchild Found-in-the-Grass!"

Part Eight: Found-in-the-Grass Seeks a Wife

He'ne'-*ookoo3*-eit heetoh-'ootee-ni'.
Then she took him home to the camp.

He'=nee'ee-nii3in-oot.
Thus she came to have a grandson.

Noh kou3iihi' neecee he'ih-noooxunee, noh heeh-ehk,
And later the chief made an announcement and said,

"Toon=cee3-oot beexouu hoot-niiw-oot notoone," heeh-ehk.
"Whoever catches a red fox will marry my daughter," he said.

Noh nehe' Bii'oxuyoo hee3-oohok hiniiiwoho',
And Found-in-the-Grass said to his grandmother,

"Heet-nii3-noyei-noo," hee3-oohok hiniiiwoho'.
"I'm going to take part in the trapping too," he said to his grandmother.

Noh hee3-eihok, "Hei-hoowu-ni'-nii3-noyei, toh-woxeihi-n," hee3-oohok.
And she said to him, "You can't take part in the trapping, because you're ugly," she told him.

Noh Bii'oxuyoo he'ih-nihi'nei.
And Found-in-the-Grass wanted to try.

Noh he'ne'-nii3-noyei-t, noh toh-nooke-' he'ih-ce3-ee beexouu.
And then he took part in the trapping too, and in the morning he found that he had caught a red fox.

He'ih-'i3eihi-n, ceebe'ei-ni3.
It was a nice-looking one, the best of everyone's.

Noh houu ci'=he'i=neh-ce3ei-t.
And Crow caught something out there too.

He'i=nee'ee-niisi-3i' cee3eihi-3i'.
Thus there were two of them that were caught.

Noh Bii'oxuyoo he'=neen hii3eihi-ni3 hi-ce3-ooon;
But the one Found-in-the-Grass caught was the best-looking one;

noh nehe' houu hi-ce3-ooon he'ih-cii3eihi-n.
and the one Crow caught was not very nice looking.

Noh Bii'oxuyoo he'ih-cih-'eti3-e' noh houu hinen-[in] hiitoone-ni3.
And Found-in-the-Grass was called over by the man who had the daughter, and Crow as well.

Noh hiseihih'-o' hee3ee-tohkoni',[19] "Henee'=he-et-niib-eiit?" hee3-eihok.
And the daughters were told, "Who will marry you?" he said to the oldest.

Nehe' beneesisei-t noh heeh-ehk, "Houu heet-neeni-t ne-niib-eiit, toh-woxeihi-t Bii'oxuyoo.
And the older one said, "Crow is the one who will marry me, because Found-in-the-Grass is ugly.

"Nehe' heet-neeni-t neniib-eit Bii'oxuyoo-n," heeh-ehk nehe' beneesisei-t.
"This [younger] one is the one Found-in-the-Grass will marry," said the older one.[20]

Noh Bii'oxuyoo he'ne'-niiw-oot nuh'uuno hecesisei-ni3.
And then Found-in-the-Grass married this younger girl.

Part Nine: Found-in-the-Grass Triumphs and in the End Gets Buffalo

He'ne'-beneesisei-t houu he'ih-neeni-n hi-niib-eiiton.
So then the older girl, Crow was the one who married her.

Noh hoo3iihi' Bii'oxuyoo he'ih-ce'eseih.
And later Found-in-the-Grass looked different.

He'ih-tes-'i3eih, noh he'ih-beexookee.
He was very good looking, and he was a full-grown adult.

Noh beexoo3iihi' he'ne'i-nihii-t Bii'oxuyoo, noh heeh-ehk . . .
And sometime later then Found-in-the-Grass spoke, and he said . . .

noh hee3-oohok neecee-n, "Het-noooxunee," hee3-oohok.
and he said to the chief, "You must make an announcement," he said to
him.

"Nooke-'ehk heet-biskoohu-noo; hii3einoon heet-notiih-o'," heeh-ehk.
"Tomorrow I'll run out onto the plains; I'll look for buffalo," he said.

Noh nehe' neecee he'ne'-noooxunee-t, noh heeh-ehk,
And then the chief announced this, and he said,

"Bii'oxuyoo heet-biskoohu-t nohkuseic; hii3einoon-in heet-notiih-oot,"
heeh-ehk neecee.
"Found-in-the-Grass will run out onto the plains in the morning; he'll
search for buffalo," said the chief.

Noh toh-nookeni-ni', he'=nee'ei'-biskoohu-t,
And when morning came, then he ran out onto the plains,

noh he'ih-bii'iih-ee hii3einoon-in.
and he found buffalo.

Noh he'ne'i-konohxootiini-',[21] noh he'ih-noh'-eeno'.

And then the whole camp went out on the plains, and they killed the buffalo.

Noh ne'=nih'ii-teco'on-niisitoo-hok.

And that's what he would always do, they say.

Noh ne'=nih-'ii'-ciin-esinootiini-'ehk.

And then hunger came to an end, they say.

Noh Bii'oxuyoo he'ih-neeceen.

And Found-in-the-Grass became a chief.

Noh nehe' houu he'ih-3onou.

And Crow was lazy.

He'ih-woxeeneb-e' hiniin.

His wife was scornful of him.

Nee'ei'ise-'.

That's how the story ends.

Notes

1. The original manuscript is damaged here.

2. The final *-ou'u* (II, 0PL) is ungrammatical with the negative prefix.

3. This is an archaic word that refers to a piece of rawhide used as a dish or table laid out on the ground in traditional times. All the items proposed as a plate are made of buckskin, the same material that would be used for rawhide.

4. *Wúho'kúúhu'* is the modern Arapaho form of this word. Alonzo Moss and William C'Hair had not heard *wuho'woohu'*. The word is used in situations such as barely missing the bull's-eye by the tiniest bit when throwing or shooting at a target—in English one might say 'ALLLLLLLLLLMOST!'

5. At least in modern Arapaho, this word for 'thank you' is used only in ceremonial or ritual contexts, in recognition of someone fulfilling an obligation in the proper manner or some similar type of event. The word suggests that the woman is feeding the visitor—or sacrificing herself to him ritually.

6. The particle *nohowóh* is or was normally used as a greeting, especially by men, and is considered archaic by contemporary Arapaho speakers. It means 'are things okay?' It is perhaps related to the tag question word *howóh*, used by men and women, meaning 'right?'

7. Modern Arapaho II impersonal verbs end with *-iini* or *-ooni*. This verb as 0.OBV inflection. There are many examples of the ending *–iini-ni* or *–ooni-ni* in the Gospel of Luke from 1903.

8. *Ceetíí3ei-* means literally 'no one said a word', as when someone asks a question and no one has an answer.

9. *Neihcíínihíí3oono'* is 'didn't I tell them!?' The initial form *see=* is a variant of the intensifier *sii=*.

10. The use of *héihi-* 'said' is uncommon in narratives. The final subjunctive form is either *-yohkóni* (3PL) or *-yóhkon* (4S). Subjunctive inflections with *-yóhk* following vowels, rather than modern *-hók*, occur commonly in the Gospel of Luke from the early 1900s but are almost unattested in modern Arapaho. A distinction between 3S.SUBJ and 4S.SUBJ is found both here and in the Gospel of Luke but not in modern Arapaho.

11. *Tetéésih-* means 'to treat in a friendly manner' or 'to act cooperatively toward someone'. Here it is really the child who is made to act in a 'civilized' way toward the father.

12. The verb *hiiníkotiiw-* is TA, but arrows are inanimate, so the agreement appears to be ungrammatical, unless these arrows are being treated as animate due to their saliency in the story, as can occur in Arapaho.

13. Red is the most sacred Arapaho color. The detail of one hundred arrows recalls the one hundred pieces of sinew needed to get down from the sky to the earth in "The Woman and the Porcupine." As one more example of a potential resonance, the most prestigious of all Arapaho quilled robes supposedly had one hundred lines of quills (Anderson 2013: 60–61).

14. The particle *wóótoo* is used only as an imperative and means 'watch out, be careful, get out of the way!'

15. Michelson records this form as *xoo3iihi'*, but this is unrecognized in modern Arapaho (whereas *hoo3ííhi'* means 'next time') and often records initial /x/ for /h/ in cases where the form unambiguously has /h/.

16. TA *cíit-oo'-e3ei-h-* = enter/into-by long implement-collision-CAUS-.

17. Arapaho women were responsible for gathering firewood.

18. *Hííwo' hénee'eehék* 'well, who is this?!' also occurs (in more rapid speech) as *hííwo'óéhnee'eehék,* which is very difficult to distinguish in Michelson's orthography from *hííwo' he-nee-hék* 'well, who are you?!'

19. This is AI middle voice *hee3ee-*. The final *-t* is apparently epenthetic. The same form occurs several times in the Gospel of Luke from the early 1900s.

20. In traditional age-graded Arapaho society, the older sibling would always have the first choice in situations such as this.

21. This is a II impersonal verb, derived from AI *konohúsee-* 'every single one/all of them walk'.

The Cannibal Boy

Told by Little Shield, John Goggles interpreter,
Wyoming, October 5, 1910
Collected by Truman Michelson
NAA, MS 2708, 8 pp.

This text is untitled in the original manuscript. The title was supplied by C'Hair and Moss. This text can be compared to "The Cannibal Babe" in Dorsey and Kroeber [1903] 1997, narrative 71. More generally, cannibalistic dwarves are a common motif in Arapaho narratives (see Dorsey and Kroeber narratives 62, 64–68). The text was recorded in English only. The original Michelson version is presented here, with added (bracketed) editorial guides. Cowell suggests that the story seems to be about the triumph of summer over winter, day over night, and heat over cold, but also of humans, aided by fire, over the danger of the raw elements of nature. The Morning Star was an object of veneration in Arapaho religion, while the White Owls symbolize night, winter, and cold.

[Part One: Four People Are Eaten]

There were Indians camped in a big bunch. There was a woman that had a baby. While they were in camp, the baby was born. After four days they heard of a big chief that had been eaten up by somebody. There was nothing but bones. Someone shouted out: "A big chief has been eaten up by someone," he said. They did not know how that happened. Again the same way another man was eaten up. Again in the morning "Somebody has eaten a chief up," someone shouted. And again the next morning a man shouted out, "Somebody [has been] eaten up by somebody."

[Part Two: Identifying the Culprit]

In the daytime the baby was sound asleep. He had teeth. There was meat on his teeth. They thought he must be the person who killed the people. They were going to watch him that night, his father and mother, to see what he was going to do. When they went to bed with the baby they kept watching him until midnight. He was sleeping between them. He moved around and cried. They paid no attention. Then he rolled out and started to go out. They were watching him. About daylight he came back. He came where he was. His parents knew what he had been doing. These parents said nothing to him. That morning a man shouted out: "Someone has been eaten up." His parents knew he had been out that night; and they also saw flesh in his teeth. They said they had better move away and let him stay.

[Part Three: The Baby Abandoned; The Four Elements of Storm (Cold Wind, Rain, Hail, Snow)]

That morning the baby went sound asleep. While he slept they began to move away. They put him against a wood pile. They let him stay. They were gone a long distance. When the baby woke up there was nobody where he was. Then he had a buffalo calf robe. He put it around himself and began running about where the camp had been. While he was alone it was cold and the wind blew. He got up, shook his robe, and sat down again. Somebody said that there should be thick rain on him. He got up, shook his robe, and sat down again. He was still alone. Somebody said—"Let there be hail thick on him"—and there was hail thick on him. He got up and shook his robe. He was still alone. Somebody said, "Let there be a big snow storm, freeze hard so that he will freeze to death." There was a storm. He got up, shook his robe, and sat down again.

[Part Four: Gambling; Magical Production of Fat, a Tongue, Pemmican, and Fire]

Then four men said, "Let us go to him," and they got around him. They sat around him and told him to gamble. "Wherever that stick falls I shall get fat." He let it fall and let it drop towards the boy. They said the boy was beat—so he went to get fat. He ran a distance towards a tree. He rubbed off some bark. He came back with it turned to fat. They gambled again. The stick fell over towards the boy again. He had to get some tongue. There was still a storm. Where the camps were he got an old moccasin. It turned to a cooked tongue. He brought it to the four men. They gambled again. The stick fell towards the boy. He had to get pemmican. He picked up a buffalo chip. He brought it to the men. It turned into pemmican. They gambled again. The stick fell towards the boy. He had to get fire. He started some distance. He came back with fire.

[Part Five: The Fire of Morning Star Chases Away the Storm of White Owls]

It was part of the Morning Star. They saw a great big light, when he came back. All the snow was melted. When he got close to the four they could not stand the heat. They ran but turned into White Owls. The boy said—"You shall be this way always during hot weather." This is why the White Owls can't stand hot weather.

Heetitee'ei3i'/The Beheaded Ones

Told by Cleaver Warden, Oklahoma, August 18, 1899

Collected by Alfred Kroeber

NAA, MS 2560a, Notebook 9, pp. 65–76

English version published in Dorsey and

Kroeber [1903] 1997: 133–35

This is one of two versions of this story known in Arapaho. The other was recorded by Zdeněk Salzmann around 1950 but never published. It is a classic example of a highly sequenced, highly repetitive story that builds gradually to its climax. We have divided the narrative into sections. Note the use of the proclitics *wot=* ('I guess, apparently') and especially *koox=* ('yet again, once again') in the opening lines of virtually all of the sections. These elements formally divide up the narrative into units.

The exact meaning of the Arapaho title is unclear. It resembles the word *heetesé'ei-t*, 's/he is bald'. An alternate title used by Arapahos for this story is *Se'esíwonóh'oe* "Sleeping Young Man." This is the title that John Goggles gave to Zdeněk Salzmann for his version of the story recorded around 1950 in Salzmann's field notes.

This story can be compared the story of ear-piercing recorded by Dorsey (1903: 180–82). That story also begins with dirty young men who are "too lazy to wash themselves or to comb their hair" (180), phrases explicitly echoed in this story. Those men, like this one here, are criticized by their fathers. In response the young men "started out voluntarily in search of 'distant wonders'" (180) and eventually become valuable to the tribe. The narrator of Dorsey's narrative states at the beginning that "Indian children are brought up 'easily,' and are therefore very soft. Young men . . . have all the time they wish to sleep, and they get up whenever they wish. Their parents do not disturb their rest" (180). Thus the narrative here can be understood as an account of why the Arapaho style of child-raising is practiced and more specifically as a defense of that practice. In that regard note the role of the grandmother, who acts protectively toward the child, while the parents are harshly critical. This closely echoes the expected role of grandparents in Arapaho culture to this day.

Introduction: Leaving the Camp

Wot=honóh'e tousi-nókohuuhúun!

There was once a young man who was quite a sleeper!

Nonóo-nookéni-'i, he'íh-niis-wonoh-sée-se'is;

Every morning he was the only one still lying around in bed;

'oh wóów he'ih-ceciinitéisee.[1]

And it seemed as if he slept right through the turn of the seasons!

Teetéibin, nehe' hé'ih-ciini 3ówo3ii.

Too late, this young man would not get up.

"Hoonó' tih-'itóx-ot heetitee'ei-ní3i," hiniisónoo-n nii3-éihok nonóo-nookéni-'i.

"You haven't yet come upon the beheaded ones," his father would say to him every morning.

Hiniisónoo-n he'ih-koo-konikúu3-e'[2] hit-óu-w.

His father tugged his robe back and forth.

Hóóyo'usii-t[3] hiso'ootééb-e' hiniisónoo-n he'ih-koo-ko'úsetii-n.

Then his father threw his sleeping covers down by the tipi entrance.

"3ówo3ii!

"Get up!

"Hóóno' heetitee'ei-ní3i tih-'itéx-ot."

"You haven't yet met up with the Pinheads."

"Hé'=ii-koo'oe-se'ísin?" nii3-eihok hiniisónoo-n.

"Why is he lazing around in bed?" his father would say about him.

Néhe' honóh'e, "He-ih-ce'isí3ei!

This young man [would say], "Why don't you go do something else!

"He-ih-kóónee{nee}.[4]

"I suppose you're going to plead with me.

"Ne-íh-kónowu-noo-nókohu.

"Let me stay asleep while [others are awake].

"He-ih-'iisih-é3!" hiniisónoo-n nii3-oohók, hoowoten-éi3i heeyowúuhu'.

"I haven't done anything to you!" he said to his father every time his father woke him up.

Sleeping Young Man Departs

Wot=nehe' honóh'e koutó'oowúuhuu téécixo' he'ih-beh-'eeneis-bíi3ihiitoon, 'oh he'ih-nósou-níi'eis.

Well, one day this sleepy head still had his head covered up while everyone else had long ago finished eating breakfast.

Hiniisónoo-n he'ih-noxú3ecooh-e', tih'ii-kóuto'oobe-'; he'ih-3óxon-sii-siiín-e' hit-óu-w.

His father was worried that he was sleeping so long; he cruelly seized his robe from him.

Kóókonoh'óó nehe' honóh'e he'ih-ciisibíhoo toh-'owóteneihi-t nohkúseic.

The young man had finally had enough and was fed up with being awakened every morning.

Ciisibíwoo hi'ííhi' heetitéé'ei-ni3i.

He was tired of hearing about the Pinheads.

Nehe' honóh'e he'ne'-o3i'eebi-t:

Then the young man asked his parents to do this for him:

"Wo'óh-no woo3ee-nóóhee[5] he-niisi3oon-ínoo;

"Your work is to arrange for me to have many moccasins;

"téi'oo-noohee,"[6] hee3-oohok hiníihei'i.

"you must arrange for them to be strong/durable," he said to his parents.

He'ih-'iisihi-níno hi-wo'óh-no, nehe' honóh'e he'ne'-cé3ei'oo-t;

When his moccasins were made he started out;

kookuyón hi-wo'óh-no he'ih-'iníinoox toh-cé3ei'oo-t.
he just threw his moccasins on his back when he set off.

Camp 1

Hei'-iis-ii3íkotii-t, noh húnee hiitéén he'ih-'itét.
After traveling this way for some time, he reached a camp.

Wo3éinokós[7] he'ih-'o'óoxootee heetoh-no'úsee-t.
There was a worn-out old tipi standing at the edge of the camp where he arrived.

Wot=betebihokós.
It was the tipi of an old woman.

"Hiiwo' neisííhoo, he'=nééni-yohkón se'isíwonóh'e.
"Well, my grandson, he must be Sleeping Young Man.

"Toot=(h)éi-ihoo?" hiniiiwóho' hee3-éihok.
"Where are you going?" his grandmother asked him.

"Heetitee'éi-3i' neiwoo, nii-nótiih-ou'u."
"The Pinheads, grandmother, I'm looking for them."

"Nei-hoowe-e'inón-oono'," hee3-éihok hiniiiwóho'.
"I don't know about them," his grandmother said to him.

He'ne'-cé3ei'oo-[t] noh húnee hees-íitisee-hék.
Then he set off again, traveling as before.

Camp 2

Koox=hé'ih-'itét hiitéén.
Once again he reached a camp.

He'ih-'óotee-n, he'ih-'o'óoxootee wo3éinokóy.
There was a camp, and at the edge of the camp was a worn-out old tipi.

"Hiiwo' neisíe! He'=nee-hék, se'isíwonóh'e!
"Well, it's my grandson! It must be him, Sleeping Young Man!"

"Toot=(h)éi-ihoo?"
"Where are you going?"

"Nii-nótiih-ou'u neiwóó héétitee'éi-3i'."
"I'm looking for the Pinheads, grandmother."

"Nei-hoowu-niitówoo3-oono'," hee3-éihok.
"I haven't heard of them," she said to him.

Camp 3

Koox=he'ih-cebís hees-iitisee-hék.
So he went on and continued traveling this way.

Noh húnee hiisíi tecé'-ii he'ih-'itét hiitéén.
And after several days and nights he reached a camp.

Wo3éinokós ho'ooxootéé.
There was an old worn-out tipi at the edge of the camp.

He'ih-yihóó.
He went to it.

"Neisíe, híiwo' he'=nee-hék, se'isíwonóh'e!"
"Oh, why it's my grandson, Sleeping Young Man!"

Xonóu he'ih-nehtíih-e'.
She recognized him immediately.

"Neiwóó, heetitee'éi-3i' nii-nótiih-ou'u," hee3-oohók.
"My grandmother, I'm looking for the Pinheads," he said to her.

"Néisie ceniixokú-3i'," hee3-éihok.
"They live a long way off, grandson," she said to him.

Camp 4

Koox=he'ih-cebís.
Once again he set off.

Hees-íitisee-hek noh húnee, koox híisii noh téce'-ii.
He continued traveling on this way for several more days and nights.

He'ih-'itét hiitéen; ceneito'ooxóótee-ni' wo3éinokós.
He reached a camp; here toward this end of the camp was an old worn-out tipi.

He'ih-yíhkotii; cih-bisi-nó'ehi betebíhehi'.
He went over there; an old woman came out.

"Neisíe, hiiwo' he'=nee-hék, se'isiwonóh'e!
"Oh, why it's my grandson, Sleeping Young Man!

"Toot=(h)éi-ihoo neisíe?"
"Where are you going, my grandson?"

"Nii-nótiih-ou'u heetitee'éi-3i' neiwóó."
"I'm looking for the Pinheads, grandmother."

"Tih-'ii3ei'eséi-noo, nih'ii-niitówoo3-ou'u," hee3-éihok.
"When I was a girl of your age, I would hear about them," she said to him.

Tih-'iisi-bii3íhi-t, he'ne'-cebísee-t.
After he had eaten, then he walked on.

Hees-iitisee-hék.
He walked on this way some more.

Camp 5

Noh húnee koox=he'ih-'itét híitéén.
And there once again he reached a camp.

He'ih-cih-'ooxo'óotee wo3einokóy.
There was an old worn-out tipi over here at the far end of the camp.

He'ih-yíhkotii{n}.
He walked over to it.

Cih-nó'e betebí.
An old lady came out.

"Hiiwo' neisíe! He'=nee-hék se'isiwonóh'e!
"Oh my grandson! It's him, Sleeping Young Man!

"Toot=(h)éi-ihoo?" hee3-éihok hiníiiwóho'.
"Where are you going?" his grandmother said to him.

"Nii-nótiih-ou'u héétitee'éi-3i'neiwóó."
"I'm looking for the Pinheads, grandmother."

"Neisíe, hehnee=nonó'oteihí-3i'.
"Grandson, they are surely very powerful.

"Neisíe, het-óónoyoohóótowoo."
"Grandson, you must watch out for yourself."

Camp 6

He'ne'-cebísee-t koox.
Then once again he walked on.

Hees-iitisee-hék, noh húnee heecisísee-t, he'ne'-nih'inéésee-t;
He walked on this way some more and as he walked he picked up his pace;

hee3e'éisee-t hihcébe' nii'ehii-hó' he'ih-'iino'óo-no'.
up in the air ahead of him, birds were circling about.

Wootii niiwohéé-no he'ih-'eteinóo-n.
There was a sound like a signal coming from them.

Wot=hih-tou3einóo-n, hitét-o'ohk hiitéén.

They made the most unusual sound, if [a person] arrived at the camp.

Níisootox honóh'e boh'oo'óubetí-no'.

Seven young men [brothers] lived together there in one tipi.

Nehe' honóh'e, heecis-cii-wotéésee-t híiteen, híseinibiixúut-ono
he'ih-3eeyóo-cíi3ibii, hotni-iseibéee-t.

This young man, before he went into the camp, wriggled his way into
long women's clothing, so that he would be like a woman.

The Young Man Disguises Himself as a Woman

Wot=núhu' honóh'o-ho' hih-tousi-ni'éíhi-no'!

You wouldn't believe how nice the young men looked!

Hé'ih-koo-kou'óneti-no'[8] nuhu' húsei-n.

The young men were all competing to outdo each other to win this
woman.

He'ih-'iiyohóot nii-níiw-oot núhu' húsei-n.

There was not one who did not want to marry this woman.

"Néhe', noh wo'éi3 hínee, noh wo'ei3 nenééni-noo, noh wo'ei3 nenééni-n,
henéi=niiw-ot," neenei3et-ehkóni' niisootox honóh'o-ho'.

"This one or that one or me or you could marry her," the seven young
men kept saying to each other.

Hóónii céése' he'ih-níib-ee nuhu' húsei-n.

After a long while, one of them married this woman.

He'íh-'eeneyei3ecootón-eeno' hi'óó3-in hi'íihi'.

They were all suspicious of her due to her legs.

"Nooxéihi' hii-hoowuuhu' húsei," níi3et-ehkóni', tih-noo-nóxoo3itoo-t
nehe' hísei.

"Maybe she's not a woman," they said to each other, since they saw that
her legs looked different [from those of most women].

Hooníi he'ih-xouuwoo3í-iniini-no'.[9]
Nevertheless, after a long while, they decided to allow the marriage.

He'=néé'ees-iniiní-t céése'.
Then one of them married her.

Cii-kóhtowuh-ee biikóó.
That night he did not bother her [sexually].

Núhu' honóh'o-ho', nohkuuhu' híiniiní-t, he'ih-'iinóó'ei-no'.
The young men, along with the one who married her, went hunting.

Nenée-neh'ehei-nóó3i núhu' honóh'o-ho', hinii3ebih-ínoo
he'ih-cee-céé'in-eeno'.
Whenever the young men killed something, they all distributed some to
their sister-in-law.

Wot=néhe' hísei hih-tóu{s}3e'éi-cee'iní3ecoo,[10] níisiheihi-t.
This woman was as grateful as could be for the way she was treated.

Climactic Moment: The Escape

Koox=núhu' honóh'o-ho' he'ih-'o3ii'oohu-no';[11]
Yet again these young men ventured out looking for game;

céése' he'ih-nées-toyoohób-ee hinii3ébi-o.
but one of them stayed behind to watch over his sister-in-law.

"Hi3í=héh-'i3ooxuh-é3?"
[When the rest had all gone, she said to him], "Why don't you let me
delouse you?"

He'=nee'eesi-i3óóxuh-oot.
Then she deloused him just as she had proposed.

Nowone'éici3-oohók.
He got drowsy from her working her fingers around his head.

Toh-nókohu-ni3 hi-i3óoxuh-ooo, wóoxe hitén-o'ohk,
tebe'eikuutes-oohók.
When the one whom she was delousing was sound asleep, she got a
knife and sliced off his head.

Xonóu he'ih-nohku-ce3ikóó nii3éí'iinit.
She immediately ran off as fast as she could go.

Xoo-xonóu toh-ce3ikóóhu-t, nii'ehii-ho' koox=he'ih-'étei'oo-no'.
As soon as she started running away, the birds made their noise
again.

Xonou he'ih-'e'ín-owuu nuhu' honóh'o-ho'.
Immediately the other young men knew what had happened.

He'ne'í-yeihon-óó3i'.
They pursued her.

No3=hesii{3}kúhnee-hék nehe' bei'íis-hísei.[12]
Of course this pretend woman escaped with all due speed.

Nohó'owoh[13] ce'e'ei3i-'éhk.
He looked back every now and then, as if expecting something.

Hoo'oonókoo'oo3i[14] he'ih-ce'e'einíhce.
He repeatedly took brief looks back behind him.

Camp 7

No'ukóo betebihokós.
He arrived at an old lady's tipi.

Bei'ci3einokós.
It was an iron tipi.

"Nonó'oteihi-3i' neiwóó, ne-yeihon-eiitóno'."
"They're powerful, grandmother, the ones who are chasing me."

"Yéin cih-noo'eekoohú-n."
"You run around the tipi four times," [she said].

Yein he'ih-noo'eekóó, hee3éihi-t.
He ran around four times, as he was told.

Kooniiteenowúúnoo tecénoo.
The door was opened for him.

"Ciitei!" hee3-éihok.
"Come in!" she said to him.

He'=nee'ees-cíitei-t.
He went in just as she told him to.

Tíh-'iis-ciitei-t, tecénoo he'ih-'o'owúnoo'oo.
Once he had gotten inside, the door slammed shut.

Hó'ooto' nuhu' honóh'o-ho' he'ih-no'ukóóhu-no'.
Just at that moment the young men came running up.

"Cih-nouuten-ín hi-bii3hiiniit,"[15] nii3-éihok nehe' betebí.
"Bring out our food," they said to the old woman.

"Hiinéénowo'!"[16]
"Hurry up!

"Neh-cih-nouutén-in!
"You'd better send him outside!

"He-ebéh-nóhkúh-ee."
"We might include you [in the meal, if you don't]."

"'inehous, heet-[n]eh-'ii'-wo'óben-o'.[17]
"Well then, I will push him close to the door.

"Cih-'ii'ísee-'," nii3-oohók nehe' betebí.[18]
"Come up close," the old lady said to them.

He'ih-cih-wo'wusee-níno; noxowuuhu' híhcebe'; héhnee=too3íihi'!

Then they came up closer; they were very near now; they surely were close!

"'inehóus, het-cih-beh-ciite'einí-be;

"Well, okay now, you all stick your heads inside;

"hoot-neh-'ii'-wo'owucí3-o'."

"I'll shove him closer to you."

He'ne'-beh-ciite'einí-3i'.

Then they all stuck their heads in.

"Cih-wo'wúuhu'," nii-hok nehe' betebi, hiibei'ci3einokóyoni-t.

"Farther in here," said the old woman who owned the iron tent.

Toh-cih-beh-ciite'eixoo'oo-3i', he'ih-cenís néhe' tecénoo; béhis-tébe'ei3éíh.

When all their heads were inside, the door came down; all their heads were cut off.

Conclusion: The Return Home

"'inehóus, neh-cee-cenííhei'i," hee3ee-téhk nehe' honóh'e.

"Now, you better go and butcher them all," the young man was told.

He'=nee'ees-cenííhei'i-t.

Then he butchered them just as she told him.

Céee3i', hix-óno he'ih-nih'eisíse-no.

Outside bones were lying scattered about [from times when she had done this before].

Tou3óóko3,[19] toh-no'otéíhi-t betebí, nohkúuhu' híyeihi'.

In the end the old woman was too powerful to be resisted, with her lodge.

Nehe' honóh'e he'ne'-ce'eecikóóhu-t.

Then the young man went back home.

Hees-iitisee-hék noh húnee, no'úsee-hek hiitéén bíikoo.
He walked on this way for a while and arrived at the camp at night.

Xonóu híyeih'-inoo he'ih-nótiitii.
Right away he looked for the family's lodge.

Bíí'iitii.
He found it.

He'ih-cíitei.
He went inside.

Hiisíb.
He went to bed.

Toh-nookéni-ni', hiniihéí'i, "Hiixowuh-nééni-t," nii3-éihok.
When morning came, his parents, "It sure looks like him," they said about him.

"Hiixowuh-nééni-t heih'éh-in," níi-yohkóni'.
"It sure looks like our son," they said.[20]

Hiniihéí'i he'ih-3ii-3iiyoohu-níno.
His parents had cut their hair.[21]

Hetebinouhuuni-níno.
They were pitiful.[22]

Wóówuh niihéyoo he'ih-'owóto'oo.
Now he woke up on his own.

"Néixoo, núhu' het-i'-iseenookúúw," hee3-oohók hiniisónoo-n.
"Father, you must use this for your rope," he said to his father.[23]

Yihkúuton-oohok bei3e'ée-no.
He threw the heads over there [to his father].[24]

Notes

1. *Hééyeih-céciinitéísee-t* 'it is almost a winter sun now' is an Arapaho idiomatic expression meaning that someone has slept so long that the season has changed from summer to winter.

2. Kroeber glosses this verb as 'pulled the covers off him', but that would be *kóónooyookúú3-ee*.

3. *Hooyo'úsi-* AI 'lay covered up'. *Hooyo'usíít* is a deverbal participle, meaning roughly 'sleeping under the covers'; by extension it is used as a noun meaning 'sleeping covers'.

4. *Kóónee-* AI 'beg, plead' (cf. TA *kóóneeb-* 'beg s.o. for s.t.'). The form given is possibly *kóóneenée-* AI.MID 'to be begged for s.t.'

5. This is a 0P indirect imperative.

6. This is another 0P indirect imperative.

7. The modern form of this word is *wo3éínokóy.*

8. *Kookóú'on-* TA 'push aside, elbow out of the way, shove away, in trying to obtain s.t.'

9. *Hinííni-* AI 'have a wife, be married'.

10. We interpret the preverb here as *tou3e'ei-* 'give a gift', though the transcription in the manuscript is closer to *tous3ehe'ii-*.

11. *Ho3ii'óóhu-* TA 'venture out looking for something, attempt to locate something'; used most often in relation to hunting.

12. *Bei'-* means 'pretend', as in the word for a doll, *béí'-iisóó* 'pretend young one'. The element *-iis-* following *bei'-* is unexplained here (and seems unlikely to derive from *béí'-iis-* unless based on a reanalysis of that form).

13. This word is not recognized today. We use Kroeber's gloss 'every now and then'.

14. This word is unrecognized today. We use Kroeber's gloss 'repeatedly'.

15. *Hibíi3ihííni-* AI 'have food to eat' > *hibíi3ihiiníít* 'thing one has to eat, one's food'.

16. *Hiineenowo'* is used specifically in situations of urgency, where danger may be involved.

17. *Neh-'ii'-wó'oben-* = from here-close-push/shove/move (TA). Cf. *hii'óotéé-* II 'located close to, nearby'.

18. *Hii'ísee-* 'walk up near, close' (cf. *hii'óotéé-* 'located near, close by').

19. *Tou3óóko3* 'when all is said and done', 'in the end, X is the best', 'you really can't argue with X'. Cf., for example, *tou3óóko3, nenééninoo niinóno'éítinoo,* 'after all, I'm the one who speaks Arapaho' (i.e., 'you have to admit, I know best, and you can't argue with me about the language').

20. *Híixowúh-* 'it looks like, but I'm not sure yet', 'it could be, but I can't quite tell'.

21. I.e., they were in mourning, thinking that their son was dead.

22. I.e., in mourning.

23. Compare this line to the scene in Found-in-the-Grass where the twins return from killing Tangled Hair and toss his hair to their father to use as rope. In both cases a tone of 'I/we knew better than you did' is implied, although here the sense is more of a rebuke, whereas the father in Found-in-the-Grass ends up approving of his sons' action.

24. It is considered very impolite to throw something to a person in Arapaho culture, especially a gift.

The Man Who Turned into a Spring

Told by Cleaver Warden, Oklahoma, August 23, 1899
Collected by Alfred Kroeber
NAA, MS 2560a, Notebook 10, pp. 23–25, 35–39
English version published as
"The Man Who Became a Water Monster"
in Dorsey and Kroeber [1903] 1997: 145–46

The title above is given in Kroeber's notes. He also recorded: "This is the origin of going on warpath, + also of presents given to springs as worship. Hiincebiit also means youngest child. Also tie offerings of cloth to fork of sun-dance pole, or below. After sun dance, all the dirtiest child clothing is hung all around the lodge, a sort of worship for the y. children. It is a gift, is left there." Cloth offerings are indeed a central part of the Sun Dance ceremony, tied to the rafters of the lodge, and gift items were likewise left at springs by warriors. The Water Monster is traditionally believed to reside in springs among the Arapahos. The Thunderbird constantly seeks to kill the Water Monster via lightning strikes, which especially seem to strike water. An echo of this belief shows up in this story, when the Water Monster disappears into the water amid flashes of lighting (*céheekú-* literally 'blink the eyes', the word used for both lightning and the eye-blinking of the Thunderbird that causes this lightning). See Dorsey and Kroeber [1903] 1997: 143 for another narrative where the Water Monster is described as having eyes flashing like lightning. In relation to the detail that it is the youngest brother who becomes the Water Monster, see Dorsey and Kroeber [1903] 1997: 139, 143, where narratives relate that the Water Monster was also called *hítooxúúsoo* 'last child' (i.e., 'youngest child') by the Arapahos. More generally, Susan Preston (2005: 231), writing about East Crees, notes that in the conceptual geography of Algonquians water is linked to increased tension, to special powers, and to transformation, while mountains are also often the site of exceptional creatures and activities. Although this narrative occurs far from the world of the East Crees, that geography seems to retain its resonance.

This story features many fine examples of narrative detail. A number of the words here have not been documented in any other Arapaho texts (though they are known to native speakers), so quite a number of detailed notes and glosses have been added. The tracking of the buffalo and the journeys through the tunnel in the mountain receive especially close attention. To give just one set of examples, the verb for 'leave tracks' *(-óoxéíhi-)* is used in many different descriptive combinations, including:

cow-óoxéíhi- 'leave tracks [traveling along]'
hee3-óoxéíhi- 'how the tracks go/are'
woon-óoxéíhi- 'fresh, new tracks'
néé'ee3-óoxéíhi- 'that is how the tracks go/where they lead'
cíit-óoxéíhi- 'tracks go inside a place'
ko3ik-óoxéíhi- 'tracks go through mud/are in a muddy place'.

In fact we could argue that pathways and journeying are the central theme of this text. Jeffrey Anderson's study of Arapaho quillwork (2013: 78–79) also notes the importance of this motif. In this story virtually every single line contains at least one verb related to traveling, walking, following, entering, exiting, or some other detail concerning a path or trajectory. Susan Preston (2005: 231–32) provides an interesting discussion of the symbolic importance of tracks for the East Crees that could easily be extended to the Arapahos and to this story in particular; tracks indicate everything from cultural activity on the landscape to a language of movement and events, a link to dreams, or an expression of cultural values and competence. In contemporary Arapaho and Arapaho English, expressions such as 'when he saw me, he made tracks' (i.e., left), 'he thought that's where his tracks would end' (where he would die), and many others with this image are pervasive.

Honóh'o-ho' he'ih-cé3ei'oo-no'.
Some young men set off.

Heecísisee-3i', hiit hiisiihi' cenih-'iit-eeséni-ni', hii3einoon
he'ih-cowooxeih.
As they were walking, here in the direction from which the wind is blowing, there was the trail of a buffalo herd.

Béébeet nuhu' honóh'o-ho' he'ih-nowúh-eeno' hee3ooxéihi-ní3.
The young men just followed the trail where it led.

Noh húnee hees-íít-3ookuh-óóhohkoni'[1] hiisíi; bííkoo he'ih-'etéíni-no'.
And they followed the trail this way during the day; they made camp during the night.

Kookonoh'óó hííɜeinoon he'ih-woonóoxeih.
Finally they saw that the tracks of the herd were fresh.

Núhu' honóh'o-ho' honouu=niihí'neesee-3i', noh húnee hiisíi noh huusíi.
The young men walked as fast as they could, for days and days.

Bééyoo heeɜé'eisee-t he'ih-co'ótoyoo.
Right straight in front of them where they were headed was a round mountain.

He'=iis-eh-tónot.
There was some kind of hole/cave in it up there [ahead of them].

Bééyoo hiiɜéínoon he'i=nee'eeɜooxéíhi-t.
The tracks of the herd led straight up to the hole.

Tesi-woonóoxéíh.
The tracks were very fresh.

Núhu' honóh'o-ho' he'ih-ceneeyohwúsee-no'.
The young men kept following the trail on and on.

He'=iis-iitét-owuu nuhu' tóónotí-ni'.
They finally got to the cave entrance.

hiiɜéínoo[n] he'ih-ciitooxéíh.
The tracks of the herd led inside it.

"Wohéí heetíh-ɜookuh-óóno'; heetíh-'e'in-owúno' he'=iisóú-'u[2] niitóó-t hiiɜéínoon," heeh-éhk céése'.
"Okay, let's follow them, so that we'll know what kind of place the buffalo live at," said one of the men.

"Wohéí," heeh-ehkóni'.
"Okay," they said.

He'=nee'ees-ciiteí-3i'.
Then they went inside as they had agreed.

He'i=néé'ees-niiteisee-3i'.
They went one by one in a line, as they had agreed.

Neehii3éí' núhu' heet-tónoti-', néc he'ih-cebínoo'oo.
In the middle of the cave, there was flowing water.

Wot=hih-tousí-í3et!
It was really sweet!

Bee-béne-no'.
They all drank some.

Cee-cé3ei'oo-no'.
They all set off again.

Hees-hiitiséé-hehkoni', ko3ikooxéíh-ehk hii3éínoon;
As they were walking through the cave, the tracks of the herd went through mud;

he'=iis-eh-ce'-konóh'ee[3] heecísisee-3i'.
Then finally they dried out again as they were walking.

Toh-nosou-cébisee-3i', beenihéhe' he'ih-nóh'oé heecísisee-3i', wootíí tih-nooké-'.
As they continued to walk, a little bit of light became visible as they were going, as when dawn is breaking.

Hee3é'eisee-3i', he'ih-néé'eesoo.
Up in front of them, that's what it looked like.

"Hííwo' he'=xóóku-tónot," nii-hók neniitobéet.
"Hey, the cave must go through to the other side!" said the one going first.

Hé'ih-'í3oowu-xooku-tónot.

It truly was a tunnel through the mountain.

Toh-nó'eehí-3i', toh-nonóó'eini-3i', heenee3é'eini-3i' henii3éínoonííni-t.

When they came out, when they looked around, everywhere they turned there were buffalo.

Hé'ih-behínou,[4] bée-beyookuu hi3o'owú-u', nii-niihííhi' koh'owú-u niicíího-ho.

The herd covered the ground; they were standing all over the prairie, along all the streams and rivers.

He'ih-nii-nííheekuu, kóó-koo'ouutís nó'eeteiniihi' noh ce'i-nó'o'uuhu'.

They were standing alongside the waters, raising dust as they walked to the river and back out of the water.

"Hi3oowúuhu' hii3einoon benii'iih-óóno'.

"We have truly found the buffalo.

"He-bii3híín-in, hot-óúw-un, ho-wo'óhn-in, he-seenookúúw-un, kookón behííhi',"[5] heeh-ehkóni'.

"We'll have our food, our robes, our moccasins, our ropes, just everything we need," they said.

He'né'i-ce'iisee-3i' hotn-ei'tóbee-3i' híí3einoon-in toh-wóó3ee-ni3.

Then they turned around to report back that they [had found] many buffalo.

Nih-cih-'íít-nó'ehi-3i'[6] heet-tónotí-ni', ce'i-cíitei-no' toh-ce'eecikóóhu-3i'.

The hole they had come out of, they went back into it so that they could go back home.

Nih-'iitoh-necííni-ni', hinenítee he'='iis-eebé3-tókooxuus.

Where the stream was, some kind of large body of a person was lying across the path.

Beh-'ihcí-teecis[7] hihcébe'.

The body filled the passageway all the way to the top.

Noh "Heet-ííteih-t nehe' heecísi-'?"[8] níí-hohkoni'.
And "Who is this who is lying blocking the way?" they said.

"Ho-ot-tóustoo-n?" neenei3et-ehkóni'.
"What will we do?" they said to each other.

He'ne'-wotitonóóton-oo3i'.
Then they built a fire up against the body.

Noh húnee hees-ii3-wotitonee-hohkóni', 3ii-3iixuh'u-n.[9]
And once they had the fire burning this way, [fat from the body] began
running down.

Ceneeyóhowu-wotitonooton-eeno'.
They kept the fire going against the body.

Cebítee he'ih-'oon-óówuu'oo.[10]
Fat was flowing down off the body everywhere.

Hohkónee núhu' honóh'o-ho' he'ih-koh'oxúh'-uuno'.
Finally the young men managed to burn the person in two.

"Yeh, neiteh'éího-ho', yóhou=ni'oxúhu'!
"Look, my friends, it cooked just perfectly!

"Hóó3o' he'=ni'icéíh," nii-hohk céése'.
"I bet it tastes good," said one of them.

"Yeh, be ciinih-ín, toh-nó'oteih-t," nii3-éíhok hiniiteh'éího-ho.
"Gee, friend, leave it alone, because it's powerful," his friends said to
him.

"Hoo3ó' he'i=ni'céíh: nookóseineehi-t.
"I bet it tastes good: it has white meat.

"Nooxéíhi' nee-ni'icéíhiihii," nii-hók néhe' nii-beetoh-bíín-oot.
"Maybe these ones are real tasty," said the one who wanted to eat it.

He'=íís-oo3i-totóuwoo, 'oh he'ih-nihi'néí.[11]

He was warned not to do this, because they were concerned for him, but he insisted.

Noh "Neníihenéíhi-n," hee3-eihohk hiniiteh'éího-ho.

And "It's up to you then," his friends told him.

He'=néé'eesi-bíín-oot.

And so he ate it as he wanted.

Ni'céíh.

It tasted good.

Tei'céíh.

It tasted fatty/greasy.

"Biín-e' neiteh'éího-ho'," nii-hók.

"Eat it, my friends," he said.

He'ih-cii-ni'óótowoo.[12]

But he could not get them to agree to his suggestion.

Tih-'iisi-bíín-oot, he'ne'-cé3ei'oo-3i'.

After he had eaten it, then they set off.

Kohkuséé-3i' céébi3síne-ni3;[13] nee'eecísisee-3i'.

They passed through the body lying across the path; as far as they had come, they walked back.

Kóox=ce'-iis-no'eehí-no', nih-'ii3-cíitei-[3i'].

Finally they got back outside, by the way where they had originally entered.

He'=iis-eh-'etéíni-no' biikoo.

That night they camped over there.

Toh-nookeni-ni', nehe' honóh'e nih-bíín-oot[14] hiinecíbi-ni3,[15] hi'oot-ó neenowó' he'ih-behisí-noocoo-níno.

When morning came, the legs of the young man who had eaten "the owner of the waters" were all white.

"Ne-ih-cíí-nihii3-óóno'!" nii3-éíhok hiisóh'o-ho.
"Just as we told him!" his older brothers said about him.

Kóóx=he'ih-ce3íkotii-no'.
Once again they set off.

Hookoo3íihi' cí'=hé'ih-'eteiní-no'[16] biikóó.
On the way home they spent the night in a camp again.

Nehe' honóh'e he'ih-beh-'oonibéíh tih-biin-oot hini'.
The young man was criticized by everyone for having eaten that thing.

Koowót=heetii3ei.
He had nothing to say for himself.

Toh-nookeni-ni', hiténeyóoo biiti' he'ne'í-noocooni-ni'.
When the next morning arrived, his whole body in turn was white.

"Kóokon nih-'óo3i-totóubee-n, 'oh niihéyoo nih'íi-no'oonoxúubeti-n.[17]
"You were warned for your own good, but you talked yourself into doing it anyway.

"Noh ne'=nih-'iisi-biin-ot," hee3-eihohk hiniiteh'éího-ho.
"And you went ahead and ate it," said his friends to him.

Cé3ei'oo-no'.
They set off.

Cí'=he'=iis-eh-'etéíni-no'.
Again they spent the night farther on.

Nehe' honóh'e he'íh-ce'-oon-ooníbet nih-'íistoo-t.
The young man was blaming himself over and over for what he had done.

Koox=toh-nookéni-n[i'], he'ne'-behisi-nookéíh-t.

The next morning, he was completely white.

Kookónoh'[oo] hih-biin-óoo[n] hé'i=néé'ee3éíh-t: tih-'ííncebiitowúúni-t.

Just like the one that he had eaten, that's how he was now: like the one who is the Water Monster.

Cé3ei'óó-no', no3=hee3eitisee-hehkóni'.[18]

They set off again and had already traveled a good way.

Hooxeb he'ih-'etebísee-no'.

They made it to a spring.

"Wohéí bé, hiit cih-sii'ihkuus-i.

"Okay, friend, throw me in the water here.

"Heneen-etebísee-noni, nootikónini-nóni, het-ii-toukutii nih'óó3eeyou-wo núhu' híhcebe' hooxebín-e'.

"Whenever you reach this place, when you're on the warpath, you must tie pieces of cloth above this spring.

"Híí3eti-' wo'ótoeet hootnii-nohk-no'úsee-n," heeh-éhk néhe' heníínicebíítowúúni-t.

"You'll arrive home with the good black warpaint," said the one who was now a Water Monster.[19]

He'ne'-sii'ihkúú3-oot hinóóhowoho'.

Then the older brother threw his younger brother into the spring.

Sii'ihiihoo3inoo'oo-n[20] bis-cee-céheekuu-n.

He disappeared into the water accompanied by flashes of lighting.

Hiitouúk nehe' honóh'e heneen-étebisee-3i notikoníit, he'ih-tóúkuton-e' heeyouhúú-ho.

Sure enough, whenever the brother reached/came upon this spring while on the warpath, he tied things there for the Water Monster.

Noh he'ne'=nih-'iis-tounínee-t.

And that's how he was able to make conquests in battle.

Notes

1. One would expect *hees-ii3-*.
2. *He'=iisóú-'u* = DUBIT-what sort/type(II)-0.ITER.
3. *Koníh'ee-* AI 'dried up' is the modern Arapaho form, but Gros Ventre has *konóh'oo-*.
4. *Behínouhu-* AI literally 'clothe everything'.
5. The manuscript has *beheihin*.
6. *Nih-cih-'iit-nóehí-3i'* = AI, PAST-to here-where-come outside (AI)-3P.
7. *Beh-'íhci-teec-íse-* II all-upward-fit-lie-.
8. *Hecísi-* AI 'lie blocking/shutting off an area'.
9. *3ii-xuh'ú-* AI 'running body fluid due to heat' (cf. the root *3ii-* in 'diarrhea', 'runny nose').
10. *Hoow-úú'oo-* II 'liquid seeps/oozes down a surface' (cf. *cen-íí'oo-* 'liquid leaks/drops down'; *bis-íí'oo-* 'liquid seeps out/appears').
11. The prefix *hoo3i-* means 'looking out for someone's best interests, out of concern for s.o. else'. It implies that the person doing so is older, wiser, or more mature than the other person, as parents in relation to a child.
12. *Ni'óótowoo-* AI.SELFB, 'get agreement for what one wants' (cf. *ní'oow-* TA 'agree [verbally] to a request or proposition').
13. *Cebi3i-síne-* AI 'crossways-lay' (cf. *ceb(i)tokóy* NI 'a square tent, with cross-poles').
14. One would expect *hih-biin-óót* TA.DEPPART 'the one who had eaten it'.
15. The verb *hinecíbi-* AI 'own water' is proposed as the basis of the noun *híincebiit* 'Water Monster'. This is a folk etymology. In reality the verb would give *hincibiit* not *hiincebiit*; furthermore, the plural of Water Monster is *híincebíit-owuu*, whereas plurals of verbal participles take the form *-ono*.
16. The manuscript has *henih'eteino'*.
17. *Nó'oon-oxúub-etí-* AI.REFL 'talk oneself into s.t. with effort' (cf. Gros Ventre *nyóʔoob-* TA 'talk s.o. into s.t., convince s.o. to change his/her mind' and Arapaho forms such as AI.REFL *nó'-oxúúh-etí-* 'get oneself to a place with great effort or difficulty').
18. This form likely should be *hee3é'eiséé-3i'* AI 'in the direction they were headed, toward where they were going'.
19. Black war paint is symbolic of victory.
20. *Síí'ih-iihoo3-inoo'oo-* = into water-disappear-INCHOAT(AI)- (ff. *hiihóóte-* 'gone, dead').

Hisei noh Houu/The Woman and the Porcupine

Told by John Goggles, Wyoming, September 22, 1910
Collected by Truman Michelson
NAA, MS 2708, 18 pp.

This narrative is widespread in Native America, particularly on the northern plains. Other Arapaho versions occur in Dorsey and Kroeber, narratives 134–38. This version is told in a fairly plain style and is a good deal shorter than the versions recorded by Kroeber. It seems to assume a fair amount of knowledge of the plot already: a reasonable assumption within the Arapaho community but problematic for outsiders reading the story. For example, when the woman descends the rope of sinew, she comes to a stop before reaching the ground. As explained in other versions of the story, this is because she made a mistake and did not gather all of the one hundred required pieces, getting only ninety-nine instead. When something central to the narrative goes wrong in virtually all Arapaho stories, some violation of a social norm accounts for that: rarely is random chance invoked. Beyond not counting correctly, the woman's mistake is not listening carefully enough to the old woman who tries to help her: she consistently comes up just short (the prefix *noxow-* used to describe how she almost reaches the porcupine is often used to indicate 'just right there a fingernail-width away from getting it' or 'right on the verge of succeeding'). Finally, she seems to allow emotion to get the best of her: her failure to listen to the old woman in her eagerness to get back down home echoes her failure to listen to her friend as she eagerly climbs up the tree after the porcupine earlier in the story.

The story makes notably careful use of perspective as well: the particle *ceno'úuhu'*, for example, means 'down at the bottom, from the perspective of above', while *no'koowúúhu'* means 'down at the bottom, from the perspective of the bottom'.

Star Child is one name given to Venus, the Morning/Evening Star, in Arapaho culture. Some Arapaho prayer songs are directed to Ho3o'úúsoo, the Star Child, who watches over the Arapaho tribe. In a sense the Star Child's caring for the old woman at the end of the story, invoked so briefly, can be

344

understood as a figurative caring for the entire tribe into the future. The Morning Star is also understood as a messenger from Above to the Arapaho ceremonial Four Old Men (Dorsey 1903: 14). The story contains other profound connections to Arapaho ceremony and myth: the digging stick that is used in the Arapaho Sun Dance is the stick used by the woman in this story to dig for roots (Dorsey 1903: 55–56, 114). The sinew used in the Sun Dance ceremony is likewise the sinew used by the woman in this story to try to escape from the heavens (Dorsey 1903: 54–55, 59, 114). Finally, the Center Pole of the Sun Dance lodge is the tree that the woman climbed in pursuit of the porcupine (Dorsey 1903: 112)—the pole carries people's prayers up to the heavens, just as it lifted up the woman. The porcupine itself is generally understood as being a star, according to William C'Hair.

3owo3nenitee-no' he'ih-'ootii-no' too3iihi' niicii.[1]
Some Indians were camped near a river.

He'ih-ko'einootii-no', noh hiseihih'-o' he'ih-'iinikotii-no'.
They were camped in a circle, and some girls were playing.

Biikoo he'ih-noh'oesei'oo-n, noh he'ih-see-se'isine-no'.
The moon was out, and they were lying down.

He'ih'ii-nee-nei'oohob-eeno' ho3o'-uu.
They were looking at the stars.

Noh ceese' ho3o' he'ih-tes-noh'oeseih.
And one star was extremely bright/brighter than all the others.

Noh ceese' hiseihihi' nii-hok, "'oh hinee ho3o' yoh=tes-noh'oeseih!
And one girl was saying, "How wonderfully bright that star is!

"Ne-ih-niib-e'," heeh-ehk.[2]
"I wish he were my husband," she said.

Noh ceese' hiseihihi' heeh-ehk, "Wono'oh hexoohu',"[3] hee3-oohok.
And another girl said, "You shouldn't say that!" she said to her.

Noh he'ih-ciin-iinikotii-no'.
And they quit playing.

Noh toh-nooke-' nuhu' hiseihih'-o' nih'ii-nihii-3i',
And when morning came the two girls who had been talking,

he'ih-neeni-no' beseee-3i' hiikoo'.
they were gathering firewood in the timber.

Noh he'ih-noohob-eeno' houu.
And they saw a porcupine.

Hohoot-i' he'ih-'ouu3ine-n.
It was up in a tree.

Noh ceese' heeh-ehk, "Heet-noh'ohouuhuuton-o' nehe' houu," heeh-ehk
ceese'.
And the one said, "I'm going to climb up to this porcupine," said the
one girl.

Noh he'ih-neyei-noh'ohouuhuut het-cenen-oot nuhu'.
And she tried to climb up to that spot to bring down this porcupine.

He'ih-noxow-no'ouuhuuton-ee.
She was just about to get up to it.

He'ih-ciinowo'on-coon-iteton-ee.[4]
But it kept moving out of her reach.

Noh ceese' hiseihihi' tokoo3 he'ih-3i'ookuu.
And the other girl was standing down below.

He'ih-cih-'eenet: "Cih-ce'-oowus!" hee3-oohok.
She called up to her: "Come back down here!" she said to her.

Hinee noo-noh'ohouuhu-ni3.
That porcupine kept on climbing up and up.

"Nee'ee, heeyeih-'iisiiten-o'," heeh-ehk.
"Wait, I've almost got him," said the girl in the tree.

Heihii he'ih-cii-niiton-ee heecisi-ce'eti3-eit.
Pretty soon the girl in the tree couldn't hear her friend as she was calling back to her.[5]

"Wohei sooxe," hee3-oohok nuhu' hiseihihi'.
"Well, let's go!" said the porcupine to the girl.

"Neneeni-noo hini' tohuu-tes-noh'oeseihi-noo.
"I'm that one who shines the brightest.

"Heet-neeni-noo toh-niib-e3en," heeh-ehk nehe' hoo.
"I'm the one who's to marry you," said the porcupine.

Wohei he'ih-'ihco'oo-no' hihcebe'.
Well, they kept on going upward into the sky.

He'ih-seh-no'usee-no' hihcebe'.
They arrived up there in the heavens.

Noh he'i=nee'ee-nii3iine'etiibeti-3i'.
And that's how they came to live with each other.

He'i=ne'eh'entoo-3i'.
They stayed up there.

Noh he'i=nee'ei'i-hitei'yooniibi-3i', honoh'ehihi' wot.
And that's when they had a child, a little boy I guess.

Noh nehe' hinen he'ih-'iinoo'ei teco'oniihi'.
And this man [the porcupine] was always going hunting.

Noh nehe' hisei he'ih'ii-teco'on-iinisee.
And this woman would always be wandering around.

He'ih-koo-koxoh-uu xoucen-ii, hiih'ehiho' toh-uu-biin-ooni3.
She dug for wild onions, because her little son ate them.

Noh hiix he'ih-'ii3-e', "Ciibeh-koxoh-un xoucen-ii!"
And her husband told her, "Don't dig up those onions!"

Noh ci'=he'i=koxohei-t.
And again she dug for them.

He'i=seh-xook-tone3eih-o' biito'owu'.
She stuck a hole down right down from the surface through the ground.

He'ih-seh-ce'-noo-noohoot biito'owu' niit-cih-'iitisee-t.
From up in the sky she could once again see down to the earth, all of where she had come from.

He'ih'ii-noohoot heeteih-t.
She was looking longingly at her home.

Noh xonou he'ih-biiwoo toh-noohoot-o' heeteihi-t.
And right away she cried because she saw her home.

Kookuyon he'ih-'iinisee.
She just wandered around aimlessly after that.

He'ih-neetou3ecoo.
She was homesick.

Hoonii he'i=cii-no'eecikoohu-t.
She did not go back to the lodge for a long time.

Hiix he'ih-noohob-e'.
Her husband saw her.

He'ih-'e'inon-e'.
He knew something was wrong.

"He-ih-tousitoo?" hee3-oohok hiniin.
"What did you do?" he said to his wife.

"Kookon," hee3-oohok hiix.

"Oh nothing," she said to her husband.

Koox=toh-nooke-' he'ih-seh-3ebisee nuhu' nih-'iit-tonooxohei'i-t.

Once again, when morning came, she walked over there where she had dug the hole.

Koox=he'ih-'iinoteibisee.

Once again she wandered around crying.

Kou3iihi' he'ih-biiwoo, tih-kokoh'eeneet-o' heet-niis-oowusee-t.

She cried for a long time, because she was considering how she could get back down.

Noh kou3iihi' he'ih-niiton-ee hinenitee-n.

And after a long time she heard a person.

"3iwoo, neheic, tousoo hei-biiwoohu-n?" hee3-eihok.

"Well now, come here, why is it that you're crying?" said the person to her.

Noh "Nih'ii-koxohei-noo," heeh-ehk nehe' hisei.

And "I was digging," said the woman.

"Noh noo-noohoot-owoo nih-'iitisee-noo, heeteihi-noo.

"And I could see all of where I came here from, my home.

"Ne'=nii'-biiwoohu-noo.

"That's when I started crying.

"Ceno'uuhu', nee'eeteihi-noo," hee3-oohok betebihehiho'.

"Down below there is where I'm from," she said to the old woman.

Noh "Het-bee3-ko'ox hooto-ho," hee3-eihok nuhu' betebihehiho'.

And "You must cut off many pieces of sinew," responded the old woman.

"Cih-beteetosoo'eti-no," heeh-ehk betebi, heeh-ehk nehe' hisei.

"There must be one hundred of them,"[6] said the old woman, she said to the young woman.

Noh toh-'oo3-iisiini-ni' he'ih-ceixotii hooto-ho.
And the next day she brought the pieces of sinew.

He'ih-biin-ee betebih[oh]o'.
She gave them to the old lady.

Noh he'i=nee'ei'-niisitii-ni3 beeteyook.
And then the old lady made something like a bowstring.

He'ih-noxuhu, he'ih-'iisitii.
She hurried and finished it up.

Noh he'i=nee'ei'i-yihoo-t nuhu' nih-'iit-tonooxohei'i-t.
And then the young woman went over to where she had dug the hole.

Noh he'ih-'iten bes.
And she took a stick.

He'ih-toukutii beeteyook.
She tied it to the long string of sinew [to hold the string in place when she jumped down].

He'=nee'ei'i-no'uuwoonouh-t.
Then she put her child on her back.

He'ih-touku3et.
She got everything tied on her.

He'ine'i-hoowuhcehi-t.
Then she jumped down.

He'ih-seh-'oowo'oo koxo'uuhu'.
She was descending slowly along the rope.

Noh heecet he'ih-tou'uhce.
And before she got to the ground, she jerked to a stop.

Noh hiix hei'-no'usee-ni3, he'ih-'iiyohoot.
And when her husband got home, she had disappeared.

Noh he'ih-notiih-e'.
And he looked for her.

He'ih-bii'iitii-n heet-oowusee-t.[7]
He found where she had gone down.

He'ih-noohob-e' no'koowuuhu'.
He saw her down near the earth.

"Wohei!" heeh-ehk, "Ceese' neih'e heetih-'ine[n]teeni-t neih'e," heeh-ehk nehe' hinen.
"Well!" he said. "At least my son will be saved," said the man.[8]

Hoh'onookee-n he'ih-'iten-ee.
He grabbed a rock.

He'ih-'oowkuu3-ee.
He threw it down.

Noh hiniin he'ih-3o'ei3eih-ii.
And he hit his wife right on top of the head.

He'ih-koxunoo'oo.
The rope of sinew suddenly broke.

He'ih-ko'us biito'owu-u'.
She fell to the ground.

He'ih-nece-n hiniin.
His wife was dead.

Noh nehe' honoh'ehihi' he'ih-niise-entoo.
And the little boy was left all by himself.

Noh wo'ooto' he'ih-noko,
And just when he happened to be sleeping,

noh betebihehihi' he'ih-cih-no'oeteisee.
then an old woman came walking down to the river.

He'ih-nowuh-ee tei'yoonoho'.
She was following the tracks of a child.

He'ih-nowuh-ee.
She was tracking him.

He'ih-seh-'iikooxeihi-n.
The tracks led over into the brush.

He'ih-seh-3ookuh-ee.
She followed them over there.

He'ih-bii'in-ee tei'yoonoho'.
She found a child.

"Nonii! neisiihoo!"
"How cute! my grandson![9]

"Hiiwo' he'=nee-hek ho3o'uusoo!"
"This must be Star Child!"

He'ih-'iten-ee.
She took him.

He'ih-'ookoo3-ee het-niii'oh'-oot.
She took him home to raise him.

He'ih-noxohoeniii'oo-n.
He grew up quickly.

Ceece3o'oh he'ih-beexookee-n.
Before you knew it he was fully grown.

Noh he'ih-'iine'etiih-ee hiniiiwoho'.

And he provided for his grandmother from then on.

Notes

1. One would expect locative *niiciihéhe'* here.

2. Normally 'I wish' is expressed by the proclitic *kookóós-* along with nonaffirmative inflections. Here, unusually, only nonaffirmative inflections are used, with no procltiic.

3. *Hexoohu-* is not recognized today. We use Michelson's gloss.

4. The element *ciinowo'on-* is not understood today.

5. This sentence is ambiguous for two reasons. First, the narrator may have switched the proximate focus at this point. Second, the ending on the first verb could be either *-ee* (3/4) or *-e'* (4/3) because Michelson's orthography is ambiguous. So it is not clear which girl can't hear the other and which one is calling back to the other, but the general meaning is apparent—the girls are now far apart and out of hearing range.

6. It is worth noting that in terms of women's work the "one hundredth robe," which supposedly consisted of one hundred lines of quillwork, was the most prestigious accomplishment for a woman (Anderson 2013: 60–61). Thus the requirement of one hundred pieces of sinew should likely be read as symbolic of extreme effort and very high achievement.

7. The manuscript has *hee3oowuseet,* which we consider an error, but which could be read 'how she had gone down'.

8. The verb *hinenitééni-* means 'to recover, get well'. Here it is used ironically, suggesting that the wife will not recover from the injury that she is about to receive.

9. *Nonii* could be translated 'why look here!' 'why look at this!' It is often used by women when seeing a cute new baby.

The Porcupine and the Woman Who Climbed to the Sky

Told by Philip Rapid/Rabbit, Oklahoma, August(?) 1899
Collected by Alfred Kroeber
NAA, MS 2560a, Notebook 6, pp. 33–37
English version published as note 3, pp. 339–40 in Dorsey
and Kroeber [1903] 1997

Although this is a very short version of the so-called Star Husband tale, it contains many linguistic and thematic features found in other versions as well. Note that the boy (Found-in-the-Grass) is precocious, like all mythical children in Arapaho narratives. (Note also that the origin of Found-in-the-Grass is obviously difficult to pin down, as he appears both here and in the "Tangled Hair or Open Brain" story.) He is repeatedly described using diminutives: *nókohuhúh-t* AI.DIM 'sleep'; *neisííhehi'* 'my little grandson'; *honóh'oehíhi'* 'small boy'. The woman who finds him is likewise a *betebíhehíhe'* 'little old woman'. This theme of the young and precocious child found by an old person, usually a woman, who becomes a culture hero is a common Algonquian motif (see Buszard-Welcher 2005). The story contains a number of key words that underline the intensity of the central moment when the woman is trying to escape: she acts *híibinee* 'secretly'; she lowers the string quickly (*hoowooceikuutii*); she acts 'anyway' (*kóokónoo'*), suggesting going ahead despite hesitation or the consequences; she literally causes herself to drop or fall (-*ko'ús-etí-t, -etí-* indicating reflexive); the word *néénowo'* 'hurry, it is urgent, there is danger' is used; her husband finds her *céecíís* 'suddenly'.

Hiséino' he'ih-nookohóe-no'.
Some women were fetching water.

He'ne'i-noohow-óó3i' hoonínouhó'.[1]
Then they saw a little porcupine.

354

'oh ceese' hísei he'ih-ni'eenéb-ee.
One of the women liked the porcupine.

"3i'=heetih-'iisíiten-o'!" heeh-éhk ceese' hisei.
"Maybe I'll try to catch it!" this one woman said.

He'ne'-ihkóuuhu-t.
Then she climbed up a tree.

He'ih-noxowu-no'óuu.
She had nearly climbed to where the porcupine was.

Teebe hetn-ii-hiten-oohok, he'ne'i-ce3óuuhu-ni3.
Just when she was going to get it, then it started climbing away from her.

He'ih-ko3én-ee.
She missed getting it.

He'ne'i-ce'-3ookóuuhu-t.
Then she climbed after it again.

Koox=he'ih-noxowu-no'ouu.
Yet again she had nearly climbed to where the porcupine was.

Teebe hotni-itén-ee, he'ih-wo'owouuhúhcehi-n.
Just as she was going to get it, it scurried up a little farther.

Koox=he'ih-ko3én-ee.
Yet again she missed getting it.

Núhu' nih'iis-ko3én-oo[t], noh núhu' tih-wo'owóuuhuhcehi-ní3.
Each time after she missed it, then it would quickly climb farther.

Woowuh hé'ih-ceneibíh-e';
Now it had lured her here;

he'ih-cií-ni'-cih-co'oowús honoót.[2]
until she could no longer come back down here.

"Heet[n]-iisíiten-o'!" héési3ecoo-hók nehe' hísei.
"I'll catch him!" this woman thought.

'oh he'ih-cee'in toh-nehtonih-éít nuhu' hoonínouho'.
But she didn't know that this little porcupine was tricking her.

'oh he'ih-no'éibih-e' hinee hihcebe'.
It lured her all the way up to the sky.

Ceeciís he'=iis-éh-no'ú-noo3-e'.
Before you know it, it had managed to fetch her up there to the sky.

Tih-'e3ebi-no'úsee-t, he'i=cih-céitoon-éihok biikousíís-ii.
When she arrived there, the Moon came to visit her.

He'=hoxóo3-éihok.
He laughed at her.

"Ne-ih-cíí-nihii3-oonó'{ho}," hee3-éihok.
"Didn't I say all this [would happen]?" he said to her.

He'ne'i-niib-éit nehe' hiisíís-ii.
Then the Moon [i.e., the porcupine] married her.

Wot=hínee hihcébe' heeyóuhuu híh-'ii-hoowóóyoo[3] nehe' hiisíís,[4]
tih-no'ookéi-t.
Well, up there in the sky the Moon had everything that he needed, since
he brought in lots of meat.

He'ih-bee3-wo'3ítii.
He hoarded it all up.

"Hóotohówoono[5] hiiwo' cih-'iis-íís-noniikuhnee-nóóni,"[6]
heesi3ecoo-hók.
"I wonder if I could escape from here using sinews," she thought.

Hííbinee[7] nehe' hísei he'ih-beé3-nii3óotee núhu' hóoto-ho.
The woman secretly braided all the sinews into a single strand.

Hoonii wóotii he'i=neetooteeyei-hók.
After a long time I guess she was tired from braiding.

He'ne'i-tóukutii-t núhu' beeteyóók.[8]
Then she tied this string to something.

Toh-'uus-toukú3et-ehk, he'i=hoowooceikuutii-t nuhu' beetéyook.
Once she finished tying herself, she quickly lowered the string down.

Hé'ne'=nii'-beestonoti-'éhk hihcébe', núhu' hoot-niit-hoowoocéinet-ehk.
Then there was a large hole in the sky, where she would lower herself down by the string.

Kookonóo'=he'i=hoowu-3o3óh-ko'usíbeti-t[9] núhu' beeteyóók.
So she just lowered herself quickly down the string, bit by bit.

He'ih-kónowu-néi'iitiib.
All the time she was holding on tight as she descended.

Hoonii, wóotii he'-íitox-úuus, toh-'oowooceínet-ehk, hohkoyóó!
After a long time, a number of days, after she had lowered herself down on the string, it fell short!

Nehe' séénook he'ih-'óówoh-cooníte3ís[10] biito'owú-u'.
The rope didn't quite reach the ground.

"Neenowó'!"; he'íh-'oúú3.
"Hurry!"; [but] she was suspended there.

He'íh-coon-ookúnet.
She could not release herself [because she was too high above the ground].

Ceecíis, hiix he'=cih-bii'iih-éihok.
Suddenly her husband came and found her.

He'ih-notiih-e'.
He had searched for her.

Nuhu' heet-tonoti-' hihcébe', he'ih-cen-noohób-e' hiniin.

At the spot where the hole in the sky was, he saw his wife down below.

Toh-'óuu3íne-ni3,[11] he'ne'-hésinónee-t.

When [he saw her] hanging, then he got mad.

Heebetoh'onóókee-n he'ih-cen-hoowu-to'ób-ee.

He hit her down below with a large rock that he dropped.

Wo'éi3ow he'=tone'eihee-hok hiníín.

It hit his wife right smack on the head and busted it open.

Xonóu he'ih-nec nehe' hísei.

The woman was killed instantly.

Heetee wot=nehe' hisei nih-'oo3isi-'éhk.

This woman had been pregnant before [she was killed].

Woowuh he'=iitox-úuus toh-se'ísi-', he'ne'i-ceníisei-t.

Now after she had lay there dead some days, then she gave birth.

Nehe' téi'yoonehe' toh-cenisi-', he'ih-cesis-iiníkotii.

After this child was born, he started playing right away.

He'ih-cesiicís[12] woxu'ún-e'.

He walked off into the grass.

Kookon hé'i-nokohuhuh-t woxu'ún-e'.

The little one just slept there in the grass.

Hi3=betebíhehiho' nih-'iis-ciino'oniséé-[ni]3 he'ih-bii'ín-e'.

Later a little old lady who was walking about found him.

Núhu' betebíhihiho', "Wo'úunoonononox neisiihehi'-hók," heeh-éhk néhe' betebéhehihi'.

This little old lady, "Well, my stars, this must be my little grandson!" said the little old lady.

He'ne'-ookóó3-oot núhu' tei'yoonóho'.

Then she took the child to her home.

Nee'ee-nii3in-éihok nehe' téi'yoonehe'.

That was how she came to have this child.

He'ih-yoóhu-no' heebetokóy.

They set up a large tipi.

He'ne'=nii'-behí-ni'eenebee-téhk nehe' honoh'oehíhi'.

Then this little boy was liked by all.

Wot=he'i=hííxon[on]oh'ehííni-t.

I guess he became a very capable and helpful young man.

He'ih-nó'oteih yeihowóot noh boo3etíit.

He was very good at hunting/chasing buffalo and at fighting.

Notes

1. *Hoonino'* (OBV *hooninoú*) means 'porcupine quill' in modern Arapaho. Formerly it was used at least by some speakers for 'porcupine'. The form here is diminutive.

2. The placement of *hónoot* 'until' at the end of the sentence is syntactically anomalous.

3. The verb II *hóów-ooyóó* is a lexicalized negative form meaning 'not rare, not uncommon' or 'there is no need of anything' (misglossed in Salzmann's dictionary as 'rare, uncommon'). William C'Hair gives II *hoow-óówooyóó* as the modern form for 'it is scarce, rare', with negative *hoow-* added to the now-lexicalized original negative form.

4. The word *hiisíís* is normally used for 'sun' but can also be used for the moon.

5. The word *hóotóhowóoo* means 'a thing used as a sinew' or 'by process of using sinew'. The form here is NI.PL.

6. *Cih-* is used in place of *he'=* as a DUBIT marker. *Cih'iis-* 'somehow' *hiis-noníikúhnee-* '-that direction-escape from place/person'.

7. More usual would be *híibineeníihi'*.

8. The word used here actually means 'bowstring' specifically.

9. *3o3óh-* (also *3o3óú-*) means 'bit by bit' or 'in parts, piece by piece' (cf. *heet-3óo-3o3óú-biin-é3en* 'I will give them to you in separate bunches/bundles').

10. *Hoowoh-coon-íte3-ísi-* = AI barely-not able-reach (cf. *hitet-* TI)-RESULT/POSITION.

11. Transcribed by Kroeber as *hoowu3ine-*. There is no obvious reading for such a transcription, but *hoowóu3íne-* would be 'hanging down'.

12. William C'Hair gives *cesíicis(ee),* with the same meaning as what Kroeber transcribes as *ce3iicis.*

The Man Who Sharpened His Foot

Told by Philip Rapid/Rabbit, Oklahoma, August 16, 1899
Collected by Alfred Kroeber,
NAA, MS 2560a, Notebook 9, pp. 46–49
English version published in Dorsey and
Kroeber [1903] 1997: 257

Although this story shares with a trickster story the motif of the sharpened foot or leg, it has little else in common with it. It does have many common motifs of Arapaho narratives more generally, however. The trick gone wrong is one example. The lone individual who becomes a crazy, nonhuman being is another. A third is the impoverished, precocious child, virtually always living with a grandparent, who has the power to save the camp when no one else can. And fourth are the seemingly magical weapons and powers used by the child. Finally, the burning up of every trace of the monster is a common theme.

In terms of the social factors behind the story, the war context is important. When men went on a war party, they were of course held to the highest standards in terms of both helping each other out and being tough. The young man who is the victim of the trick eats his own calf muscle, which indirectly suggests that he was unable to endure the hardships of the war party. In such cases it was not uncommon for the other warriors to play a trick on the one who was seen as not living up to expectations. See the story "One-Eyed Sioux and His Mother-in-Law" in this volume and in particular Kroeber's notes, cited in the introduction to the story. To be the victim of such a trick was an extremely shameful fate for a warrior. Thus the young man's reaction in this story symbolically captures the extreme shame and rage that could result from such a fate.

Structurally, note the way in which the narrative can be segmented based on the narrator's use of time markers. The particle *wóówuh* 'now' and variants is central to the structure of the smaller segments, as is the perfective marker *-iis/-uus*. These forms are italicized in the text.

Honóh'o-ho' he'ih-'iinoo'ei-no'.
Some young men went hunting.

360

Toh-bih'iyóó-ni', he'ne'-ootii-ní3i.
When it got dark they set up camp.

He'ih-yóohu-no'.
They erected their lodges.

Toh-nóóke-', ceese' hinén he'ih-'ésinee.
When daylight came one of the men was hungry.

Hei'-coonéihi-t,[1] he'ih-ko'ús-ii hi-ci'í3-in.
When he could not stand it any longer, he cut off his calf [muscle].

He'ne'i-hóókouhu-t.
Then he cooked it for himself.

Hei'-*iis*-ookouhú-t, he'ne'-toxu'óh-o' hí'oo3.
After he had cooked it for himself, then he sharpened his leg.

Toh-nosou-toxu'oh-o', he'ih-'ihco'ootón-e' hiniiteh'éiho-ho.
When he was still sharpening it, his friends caught sight of him.

He'ne'i-néhtonih-eit.
Then they played a trick on him.

Tebe'éibes he'ih-ciinén-owuu teesiihi' hóób-e'.
They put a stump of wood on top of his bed.

Níisiyoohu-no,[2]
His bedding was all sewn together,

Noh hóoko[y]ooo[3] he'ih-kotoyóh-owuu nuhu' tebe'éibes.
They covered up the stump of wood with thick blankets.

Hiibinee he'né'i-cih-ce'-tokohú-3i'.
Then they secretly ran off again over this way.

Woowuh he'ih-'oxón-ceníikóóhu-no'.
Now they ran way the heck away from there.

Hei'-*iis*-tóxu'oh-o' hí'oo3 nehe' honóh'oe, he'ne'i-kóheisihcéhi-t.
After this young man had finished sharpening his leg, then he jumped up.

He'ih-cii3íhce niiinón-e'.
He ran into the tipi.

Xonou he'íh-tó'oxon-ee núhu' tebe'eibes-í'.[4]
He immediately kicked the wood stump.

Xonou he'ih-'e'ín toh-néhtonihee-t.
He knew immediately that a trick had been played on him.

He'ih-nouúhce.
He ran outside.

Toh-'*uusi*-nouuhcehí-t, he'ih-yihoon-ee hohóot-in.
After he had run outside, he went over to a tree.

Koxkoh'e3ei'on-oohók.[5]
He stabbed it and split it apart with a blow from his foot.

Xonou he'ne'-3ookúkoohú-t.
Then right away he ran after [the others].

'oh *woowuh* hé'ih-'éyeih-noo-nó'eso'ei-nó'[6] nuhu' hiiniiteh'éiheh'í-3i'.
And now the ones who were his friends had almost arrived where they were fleeing to.

Ho'ooto'[7] he'íh-no'eso'éi-no' . . .
Just as they were about to reach [the camp] where they were running to . . .

Ceese' he'ih-'eso'ooníisebei.
One of them had a very fast horse.

Woowuh niiinón-e' he'ih-no'ukóohuuh-e'.
Now he arrived at [his] tipi on horseback.

Xonou he'ne'-oo3ítee-t: "Neiteh'eiheh-inoo nonó'o3íheti-t.

Then right away he told the story: "Our friend has done something terrible to himself.

"Tóóxu'oh-o' hi'óó3, noh cenih-yeihon-einó'."

"He has sharpened his leg, and he is pursuing us back here."

Xonou he'né'i-eeneitoo'éetiiní-'.[8]

Immediately they all grabbed their weapons.

Xonou he'ih-cesisi-boo3-óó,[9] beetéi noh kokuy-óno.[10]

Right away they started fighting against him, [with] bows and guns.

Wot=nih-ciihínee-hek.[11]

[But] he could not be overcome.

Woowuh hées-éyeih-noo'oohée-[3i'], honóh'ehihi'.[12]

Now almost everyone had been slaughtered except a little boy.

He'ih-cei'teh'éi; he'ih-niise'etii-no'[13] hiniiiwohó' he3owokoyón-e'.

He was a little kid; he and his grandmother lived together in a dog hut.

"Wo'úu-wóówuh, he'ih-'oo3oníhoo[14] néhe' hohóókee," heeh-éhk nehe' honóh'ehihi'.

"It can't go on, this crazy one that can't be stopped," said this boy.

He'ne'i-itoo'éi-t.

Then he got his weapons.

Hiicóó he'ih-'ibéetein noh béihooo he'ih-'íniic.

A rib was his bow and a collarbone was his arrow.

He'ne'-cih-nóehi-t, toh-'úus-woxusin-éit hiniiiwóho'.

Then he came outside, after his grandmother had finished painting him.

Woowuh hé'ih-'éyeih-noo'ooh-ee[15] nehe' nóónox[on]ouhu-t[16] hinén.

Now this man who acted terribly toward himself had slaughtered almost everyone.

Xonou he'=née'éé-hihcen-o' hi-nesiiyouhú-no.

Right away then [the little boy] pulled up his sleeves.

Teebe hé'ih-cebikóohu-n, he'ne'i-siikoo'éi-t yein.

Just as [the crazy man] was running by, then he drew his bowstring four times.

Yeneiní'owoo-ni', he'ne'-cób-oot.

On the fourth time, then he shot him.

He'ih-cebitoo'oo3-ee.[17]

He hit him in the side.

Beebeet he'ih-siíco'oo nehe' nóónox[on]ouhu-t[18] hinén.

The man who did these terrible things to himself was just stretched out flat on the ground [dead].

Toh-'*uus*-neh'ée-t, hé'ih-tebe'eis-óó.

After he was killed, he [the boy] cut off his head.

Kookon hé'ih-cih'es-oo.

He just cut him to pieces/dismembered him.

Hei'-*íis*-cíh'es-iit, he'ih-wotí3-oo honoot he'ih-beetoxóhu'.

After he cut him to pieces, then he put him in the fire until he was burned up.

Hit-íxonów-o he'ih-nohku-beetetee-nino ceeceece'oh.[19]

His bones were quickly burned up with the rest of him.

Notes

1. *Coonéíhi-* 'unable to do something, incapable'.

2. *Niisi-yóóhu-* = together-sewn (II.PASS.IMPERF)- (cf. *hoxyóót-* TI 'sew', II.PASS. IMPERF *hoxyóóhu-* 'sewn').

3. This word appears to be *hookoy-* 'thick' + -*óoó* 'flat container/receptacle' (cf. *hóoó* 'bed').

4. Note that *tebe'éíbes* is treated as animate here.

5. TA *kóxuk-koh'-e3éí-'on-* = stab-split-by collision-by foot (TA)-.

6. *No'éso'ei-* AI 'arrive while being herded or chased', 'arrive while running as a herd'.

7. *Ho'óóto'* 'just then, right then'.

8. *Heenéitoo'éí-* 'grab weapons' should produce II.IMPERS *heenéitoo'óótiini-'*.

9. Here and below the normal 3S/4 NONAFF ending *-ee* seems to be consistently replaced with *-oo*.

10. Kroeber transcribes *kokiyone'*, which is a locative form and seems incorrect here.

11. The verb *ciihinee-* is not recognized today. We use Kroeber's gloss.

12. This is an idiomatic expression: literally 'this young boy has almost been slaughtered [like the rest of them]'.

13. *Céi'teh'éí* is a vocative term used with younger siblings, particularly males. It means 'little round-bellied one'. The use of the term here implies that the boy in question is relatively small and inconsequential. AI *niis-íine'étii-* 'live as two'.

14. *Hoo3onih-* TA 'fail to do s.t. to s.o.' > AI middle voice *hoo3oníhoo-* 'fail to be stopped from doing s.t.'

15. The manuscript actually has *noo'ootee.*

16. *Nóon-óxon-óúhu-* = REDUP-hard-SELFB(AI).

17. William C'Hair says that this would be *he'ih-cebitoo'óh-ee* in modern Arapaho.

18. Kroeber transcribes this as *noonokouhut*. Given that he twice "missed" the extra syllable in the our proposed reading *nóonóx[on]óúhut* (see note 16 above) and gives a different consonant here, this is perhaps a different word; but what that word would be is unclear.

19. This form likely corresponds to modern *céeco'óh*, 'all of a sudden'.

The Midgets

Teller unknown, July 1927
Collected by Truman Michelson
NAA, MS 2988, pp. 28–30

Stories of Little People are widespread among Algonquian groups (see Costa 2005 on Miami-Illinois, LeSourd 2005 on Maliseets). Other versions of this story appear in Dorsey and Kroeber [1903] 1997, narratives 64 and 65. Additional details about Little People documented in contemporary Arapaho narratives are that they live near springs and are very difficult to see, though the remains of their campsites are sometimes seen (see Moss 2006, "Stories about Little People"). They sometimes visit a lone camper at night: that person must take care not to invite them into the camp or offer them anything to eat, because the camper himself/herself is on the menu (Underwood 2010). They typically live in the mountains, according to some consultants, and people should especially avoid going out alone there. But they are also sometimes reported to help people home who have gotten lost in the mountains. Arapahos often tease short people about being "Little People" in a good-humored way, with no implication of criticism or negative judgment. Some Arapaho people today still report seeing actual Little People, more often of the harmless or helpful variety than of the evil variety.

There is a linguistic peculiarity in this story. The normal Arapaho word for 'my heart' is *nétee*, 'your heart' is *hétee*, and so on. In this story, however, the Little People child uses *necítee*, *hicítee*, and so forth. This is not an Arapaho diminutive form. Rather it seems to be a speech form unique to either Little People generally or the Little People child specifically. Cowell suggests that this may partially be a pun on the verb *néce-* 'die': when the child is forced to say *neciítee* rather than *nétee* for 'my heart' at the end of the story, he includes the verb *néc(e)-* in his statement. Moss and C'Hair were unsure of this.

Another connection between tipis and hearts can be found in Anderson (2013: 44, 56–57) in relation to women's quillwork. He notes that some symbolic elements could represent either hearts or tipis and also notes connections between tipis and bodies (33). Thus the fact that the Little People in this narrative leave their hearts in their tipi when they depart at least resonates with those symbolic images.

Hinéé tih-'ííne'etíítooni-', hé'ih-níí3iine'ítii-no' hinenitéé-no'.
Back in the old days, some people used to live around regular humans.

He'ih-'okeciihíh-no'
They were little.

Hecesííteihíí-ho' he'ih-'íí3oo-no'.[1]
They were called Little People.

Nóh 3owo3nenitéé-no he'ih'ii-bíín-eeno'.
And the Little People would eat Indians.

Wót=hii-hoowu-nóh'oo-no'.
I guess they couldn't be killed.

Hiteeh-ínoo he'ih'ii-noot-owuu hiyeih'-ínoo.
The Little People would leave their hearts at home in their lodges when they went out.

He'ih'ii-nees-tóúkuhú-no hokóóxun-e'.
They would leave their hearts behind tied to the tipi poles.

Hinén he'ih-'itét níiinón.
One day a man came to one of their tipis.

He'ih-ciitei.
He went in.

Téi'yóónéhe' he'ih-nosoun-[oo]kóhowoo[2] hókok hí'iihi' betíít.
A child was busy dipping up soup for himself with his heel.

Nehe' hinén he'ih-noohoot betóó-ho.
The man saw the hearts.

He'ih-noo'ee-toukuhu-níno hokóóxun-e'.
They were tied all around the tipi on the lodgepoles.

"Henee' nuhu' hítee?"
"Whose heart is that?" he asked.

"Neisónoo hicítee," heeh-éhk néhe' hecesííteihii-soo.
"My father's heart," said the Little People child.

Néhe' hinén he'ne'-koxkóh-o'.
Then the man stabbed it.

"'óh núhu' hénee' hítee?"
"And whose heart is this?"

"Néínoo hicítee," heeh-éhk néhe' hinén.
"My mother's heart," he said to the man.

He'ne'-koxkoh-o'.
Then he stabbed it.

"Noh núhu' hénee' hitee?"
"And whose heart is this?"

"Neeséh'e hicítee," heeh-éhk.
"My older brother's heart," he said.

Nehe' hinén he'ne'-kóxkoh-o'.
Then the man stabbed it.

"'oh nuhu' hénee' hítee?" hee3-oohók.
"And whose heart is this?" he said to him.

"Nébi hicítee," hee3-éíhok.
"My older sister's heart," the child responded to him.

Kóóx=he'ih-koxkoh.
Once again he stabbed it.

Noo'eeníihi' hokóóxun-e' he'ih-tóúkuhú-no betóó-ho,
All around the tipi on the lodgepoles hearts were tied,

Nuhu' hecesiiteihii-ho' hitééh-inoo nuhu' behííhi'
neenei3o'óúbetiitooni-'.
The hearts of the whole clan of Little People.[3]

'óh he'ih-'i[t]óóx-outé{i}-n tei'yoon-bétee.
And one last heart—a child's heart—was hanging there.

"'óh núhu' hénee' hitee," héé3-oohok núhu' hecesííteihiisoo-n.
"And whose heart is this?" he said to the Little People child.

Nóh "Nétee," níí-hok.
And "My heart," he says.

He'ih-cii-bee3í-nihii.
He didn't say it completely.

Nehe' hinén he'ih-nihi'neetón-ee.
The man insisted that he do it.

"Henee' hítee?" níí3-oohok.
"Whose heart?" he says to him.

Nóh "Necítee," hee3-eihok.
And "My heart," he responded to him.

Hé'ne'-kóxkoh'-o'.
Then he stabbed it.

He'ih-síícoo'ouhu-n.
The child stiffened out dead on the ground.

Noh ne'=nih-'í(i)s-noo'oohéé-tohkóni'[4] núhu' hecesííteihii-ho'.
And that's how they these Little People were killed off.

Tih'íi-noxownoo-', tih-biin-oohohkoni'.

It used to be really dangerous, because the Little People ate Indians.

Notes

1. The noun contains the root *hécex-* 'little' and the suffix *-éíhii* meaning 'one who is/ does X' and thus means basically 'little one'.

2. The manuscript has *nosoukóóxowoo* here.

3. The final verb literally means 'all the ones who were related to each other'.

4. AI middle voice *noo'oohee-* 'massacred', with epenthetic /t/ prior to subjunctive inflection.

The Little People

Told by (Alexander?) Yellow Man, Oklahoma, 1899
Collected by Alfred Kroeber
NAA, MS 2560a, Notebook 13, pp. 26–27

This is a story about the Little People (*hecesíiteihiiho'*), mythological dwarves known in particular for being cannibalistic. The title was supplied by the editors. The detail about being picked up and then beating the person about the face occurs in a modern Arapaho story on the same topic told by Mary Kate Underwood (Underwood 2010), showing that the Little People theme and details are widely known. In NAA, MS 2560a, Notebook 24, Kroeber recorded additional notes on the Little People, including that they were "little men, short people, cannibals and very strong. Can carry buffalo. Could not be killed, for left their hearts and blood in trees when they went out."

This exact version of the story does not appear in Dorsey and Kroeber [1903] 1997, but a similar, slightly more detailed variant does appear (narrative 62). In that one the trickster (Nih'oo3oo) carries the Little Person. That version makes clear that the one carrying the Little Person thinks that the Little Person is dead and that the hand is simply getting snagged in a bush and then coming loose, thus whipping the branch into the face of the carrier, rather than actively hitting him.

In his manuscript Kroeber glosses several of the verbs with 'I' even though they have narrative past tense marking, which is normally only usable with third person, and have 3S/4 person inflections in all cases except the first line. We have glossed these as third person verbs, referring to 'a man'. We have divided the story into smaller sections. Note that each section leads up to a final direct citation, providing an overall rhythm of description followed by reaction.

Alonzo Moss points out that a common pun probably known to all Arapaho speakers is the word *ci(h)'ohwoot*, which means either 'dancing lame' (*ci'-ohwoot* 'lame-dancing') or 'marrow' (*cih'ohwoot*). That same pun seems to be partially echoed here, where first the man in the story says that his family should have a feasting dance (*not-ohowoot*), and then one of his children talks about having marrow from the dwarf to eat (*hicih'ohowootiini-*).

The joke is finally on the family, as the supposedly dead dwarf escapes, but Moss's larger point is that stories can contain language lessons in the form of jokes and puns, which serve to heighten speakers' awareness of their own language and its intricacies.

He'ih-ce3ikoh-éínoo.
A Little Person escaped from me.

He'ih-'onínoo'oo.
He fell over.

He'ih-neciwóo-n.[1]
He was pretending to be dead.

He'ih-nehyo'oo-besen-ee.[2]
[A man/I?] touched him to check to see if this was so.

He'ih-coowu3óówu-n.
He was not breathing.

Koh'ooxób-e'[3] he'ih-besén-ee.
He touched him in the sternum area.

He'ih-coowu3óówu-n.
He was not breathing.

He'ih-beetoh-tonés-ii.
[The man] wanted to cut a hole open in him.

"Henéi=bee'eini-t, tones-ó'."
"He would produce [too much] blood if I cut him open," [the man thought to himself].

Ne'-noh'ouukóh-oot.
Then the man loaded the Little Person up onto his back.

He'ne'-cesíseiikoh-óot.
Then he set off carrying him on his back.

Nenei'itiibíhcehi-[t].
The Little Person seizes tightly onto [a limb of a bush].

Hení'-tébe'eih-iit.
The Little Person hits him in the face with the limb [by suddenly letting go of it].

Henei=koxóx-o'.
He could cut off [the Little Person's hand].

Henéi=bee'éini-t.
But then there would be lots of blood.

Hetin . . . "Ne-et-cii-koxóx."
"I might . . . I guess I won't cut it off," [he said to himself].

Konóu'eino3-éit.
The Little Person is making his face swell from blows.

"Yoh=ne-ciisíbe'einó3-e'!"
"I'm really getting sick and tired of him hitting me on the face!" [he thought to himself].

"Tih-'ei'-nóusi-' bes-e', ne-eti-hóu3-oo.
"Once he gets stuck in a bush, I think I'll hang him there.

"Ne-eti-hi'ooxuh-e'."
"I'll hide him there for future use."[4]

Toh-no'úsee-t hiyeih'-é', hiníisoo-no, "Hee[t]n-eteini'óokú-n.[5]
When he got back to his lodge he said to his children, "Grease up your eyes for tomorrow.[6]

"Heniiyeih-e3énee.
"I am providing you with quite a feast.

"Heetih-'íísi-nótohowóó-no'."
"Let's have a feasting dance."

"Heet[n]i-itisinébi-noo."[7]

"I will have the liver," [one child said].

"Heet[n]i-icih'ohowóotiiní-noo."[8]

"I will have marrow," [another child said].

Toh-nóóke-', yihóó-noo.

The next morning I went over there [where the Little Person had been left hanging].

Kouun hix-óno.

There were only bones lying there.

Kouun he'ih-cée-cenoxús.[9]

They had all fallen to the ground, rotted apart.

Néé'ei'íse-'.

That's the end of the story.

Notes

1. *Néce-* AI 'to be dead' + *bee-* 'act in the capacity of . . .' > *nécibée-* AI 'act as a dead one'. This form produces *neciwóót-* TI 'act dead in relation to s.t.' and TA *néciwoon-* 'act dead in relation to s.o.' Here the form *nécibée-* seems to occur as *neciwoo-*, with the final /n/ being a 4S marker.

2. Cf. TA *néhyonih-* 'to check on s.o.' (as when guarding horses, for example).

3. This word is not recognized today but derives from *koh'-* 'half' or 'split' and *-ooxobe',* an archaic form for 'chest' documented in NAA, Kroeber MS 2560a, Notebook 1, p. 8, and NAA, Gatschet MS 231, p. 88. Thus 'the middle/split area of the chest'.

4. More literally 'he could be useful to me sometime later'.

5. *Heetn-eteini'-ooku-n-* = FUT-???-eye(AI)-2S. *Heteini-* is an AI verb meaning 'to spend the night', which may have something to do with the gloss 'for tomorrow'.

6. The meaning of this expression is unknown.

7. *His* 'liver' > *hit-isineb* 'his/her liver' (a food object, not one's own body part) > *hítisinébi-* 'to have a liver'.

8. *Cíh'oh(o)wóót* 'marrow' > *hi-cíh'ohowóót-ino* 'his marrow' (for food) > *hicíh'ohowootiiní-* 'have marrow for food'. Kroeber glosses the full form 'have a shin bone for marrow'.

9. *Cen-ox-úse-* = II down-rotten-fall-.

The Girl Who Became a Bear

Told by Philip Rapid/Rabbit, Oklahoma, August 15, 1899
Collected by Alfred Kroeber
NAA, MS 2560s, Notebook 9, pp. 34–39
English version published in Dorsey and
Kroeber [1903] 1997: 238–39

A similar version of this story explains the origin of the Pleiades, though that story involves six brothers and a sister. That story is documented in Arapaho in Salzmann 1956b: 267–70. It also includes playing at being a bear, with the bear becoming real and pursuing brothers and sisters, and a ball thrown up into the air and taking the children with it. The detail about the bear's claws and feet is perhaps important. The motif of the bear claws is prominent in Arapaho artwork as well as in place-names. The motif is linked specifically to Whirlwind Woman, who herself was involved in the creation of the world (see Cowell and Moss 2003; Anderson 2013: 34, 61, 113, 140). Thus this story may indirectly be invoking the transformative powers of the time of creation and of Whirlwind Woman, Cowell suggests, and perhaps the dangers of treating them cavalierly.

It is not known which stars are referred to in this story. Note also that specifically 'scabby' dogs, like small and seemingly insignificant young children, often play heroic roles in Arapaho stories.

Structurally, the key transition points in this story seem to be marked primarily by *koox*= 'yet again, once again', *wot*= 'I guess, apparently', and *'oh* 'but, and then'; the story is divided into sections based on the use of these forms. The introduction of the ball and then the moment when the ball speaks also seem to be central. The markers of new sections, as interpreted here, are italicized.

Lexically, the story is extremely intense: the root -*koohu*- 'run' occurs over and over, with a number of other roots: no one ever just walks or goes in this story. *Tokohu*- 'flee in fear' also occurs several times: the narrative is dominated by frenetic motion, interspersed with 'every single' dog in camp barking, the bear 'ripp[ing] open' the flesh of the younger brother, the bear 'charg[ing] furiously at' the other children, folks getting on 'the fastest horses available,' and similar moments. In all these cases a more precise and intense lexical item is used in place of more general ones that could have been used, or an extra prefix is added to produce the same effect. Heightening the tension is the contrast of a very high number of uses of the root/prefix *nee3-/nees(i)-* 'left behind, remain behind' and the parallel uses of forms of *-ookut-* 'tie' to describe both the claws tied to the older sister's hands and the two younger siblings tied helplessly to a cottonwood tree. The many uses of *neesi-* are interesting as well due to their similarity in sound (though the forms are unrelated) to the word *neeso* 'three times', which becomes a key aspect of the children's escape at the end of the story. The related form *nees-ou3i-* 'three hanging', which concludes the story, subtly echoes the morpheme for 'left behind' as well.

Finally, note that the Big Dipper (part of the larger Great Bear of many astronomical traditions) is known as 'broken back' or 'broken shoulder' in Arapaho. Whether the story here might in part refer to that constellation and in particular to the three stars of the handle is unknown, but the image of the bear falling backward and breaking its back is at least suggestive. It is also interesting to consider the difference between the rather bumbling bears of other Arapaho stories and the very ferocious human-turned-bear in this story.

He'ih-'óotee heebe3ineniteeníit.
A large tribe had set up camp.

Tei'yoonóh'-o' he'ih'ii-woo-woxuuwoohu-nó' noobéi'i.
The children were pretending to be a bear in the sand.

Heh-níiseihi-t hiseihihi' he'ih-béesesei.
There was one who was an older girl.

Núhu' heniiníkotii-nóó3i, "Heti-cei3-óóbe hit-eíhtoo-no!"[1] heeh-éhk nehe' hiséíhihi'.
When they were playing, "Bring its claws!" said this girl.

He'ne'i-oon-oyóokutoo-t[2] hiicetín-e' núhu' hit-eíhtoo-no.
Then she tied its claws to her hands.

He'ih-coo-co'óóbe'iini heet-íyeih'i-t nehe' wox.
She [pretended] to be a bear with its lodge in sandy hills.[3]

'oh bíino he'ih-woo3ee-níno híyeih'-e'.
There were a lot of berries at her lodge/den.

Nuhu' téi'yoonoh'-o' he'ih'ii-cih-won-ko'úyei-no'.
The children would come and pick berries.

Noosou-ko'úyei-noo3i, he'ih'ii-cíh-kouso'ooton-e' nuhu'
nii-woxuubéee-ní3.
While they were picking the berries, the one who played bear would
come out and [pretend to] charge furiously at them in attack.

Hé'ih-co'óo'eeniin nih-'íit-nókohu-t.
There was a willow area where she would sleep.[4]

Nehe' nih-woxúunoo'oo-t, he'ih-koe'kúutii hinoohowóho' hi-cii'ón-in.[5]
This one who [actually did] turn into a bear, she ripped open her
younger brother's back.

Wot=nih-nó'o3ih-oohók.
I guess she hurt him badly.

Hii3óu'oo-ni'i, he'ih'ii-beheeckoohu-no' núhu' tei'yoonóh'-o'.
In the evenings all the children went home.

"Ceebeh-'ei'tóbee toh-woxúunoo'óó-noo," nii-hók nehe' hiseihihí'.
"Don't tell that I have turned into a bear," this girl said.

"Noottob-éinooni néinoo, heti-yooton-óóbe," heeh-éhk.
"When my mother asks about me, you must hide this from her," she said.

"Tooto'óe, héi'tobee-nééhek, hoot-ne'-woteekóohu-noo," nih-'ii-hók
nehe' woxúunoo'oo-t.
"And anyway, if you tell, I'll come storming into camp," the one who
had turned into a bear said.

Hinoohowóho' toh-'eecikoohu-ní3, *wot*=hih-'oow-éi'itóbee nehe'
heesiiniihée-t.
When her younger brother went home, well, I guess he didn't tell that
he had been injured.

Koox=hé'ih-bíh'iyoo, tih-'eeneisibiitooní-', he'ne'=nih-'ii'-hihco'óotonée-t néhe' honóh'ehihi'.

Once it was night again, when everyone went to sleep, then this boy's injuries were noticed.

Toh-nótitonée-t, he'ne'i-hei'itóbee-t heesi-woxúunoo'oo-ní3 híbi-o.

When he was asked about it, then he told how his older sister had turned into a bear.

He'ih-nosoun-oo3ítee, kookonoh'óó he3-ebíi he'ih-beebéé-no'.

He was still in the process of telling the story, when every single dog in the camp started barking.

He'ne'-cih-woteekóóhu-t néhe' nih-woxuunóó'oo-t.

Then the one who had turned into a bear came storming into the camp.

Xonóu he'né'-heen-éso'oo-teesisée-3i' tei'yoonóh'-o' noh húsei-no'.

Right away the women and children got on the fastest horses available.

He'ih-beh-tokohúutoon.

Everyone fled in fear.

Honóh'o-ho' he'ih-neesi-boo3-eeno' nuhu' wóx-uu.

The young men remained behind to fight the bear.

'oh wóów he'ih-cenii-tokohúutoon,

And now everyone had fled far away,

nehe' honóh'ehi' noh hútesei-w he'ih-nees-niisooku3óo-no' hohóót-i', tih-'ei'tóbee-hék.

but the boy and his other sister were left tied together to a tree, since he had told on his older sister.

He'ih-nosou-boo3óó néhe' wox,

The bear was still being fought.

Kokuyé3-ebii[6] he'ih-neesi-niiseih woti'iíín-e'.[7]
A scabby dog had been left behind alone where the camp had been.

He'ih-'ówouunón-e' núhu' neniisookuhu-ní3i.
It took pity on these two who were tied together.

He'ne'-oon-ooków-oot nuhu' séénook-uu.
Then it worked to loosen the rope with its teeth.

He'ih-koo-koxób-ee.
It tore the rope asunder with its teeth.

Toh-'uus-oon-ookúneti-3i', he'né'i-cesis-tókohu-3i'.
Once the children had freed themselves from the remaining strands, they began to flee in fear.

Kookuyón 3ookúh-uu.
They just followed [whatever people were still in sight].

'oh wo'óóto' he'ih-noo'óóh-ee hih-nees-eco'on-éiitono[8] néhe' wox.
But right at that time this bear had slaughtered all those left behind to block her pursuit.

He'ne'-3ookukoohu-t níh'iis-tokohúutooni-'.
Then she went running after everyone who was fleeing.

He'ih-ce'e'éikoo nehe' honóh'ehihi'.
The boy turned back to look as he was running.

Nóónonox he'ih-ceikoo néhe' wox.
To his consternation, [he saw that] the bear was running this way.

He'ih-'ikoh'owoooní-no' núhu' tei'yoonóh'-o'.
These two children had a ball with them.

Too'oxon-oonóó3i, he'ih-'ihcino'oo-nó'.
Whenever they kicked it, they rose up in the air with it.

He'ne'=nih-'iistoo-3í' heeyeih-'eteb-einoo3i, hónoot
he'ih-niisóho'-neeteihcehí-no'.
That's what they did whenever the bear got close to overtaking them,
until they both got tired out from running.

He'ih-'eenet *nehe' koh'owóoo.*
The ball spoke.

"Neeso het-cih-'ihcikuus-íbe.
"You must throw me up three times.

"Noh yeiní'owoo-', het-cih-'ihce3ei'on-íbe.
"And the fourth time you must kick me upward.

"Noh hóotni-ihcíno'oo-nee hínee hihcébe'.
"And you will rise up to the sky.

"Hootnó-owoh-'enitóó-nee," hee3-eihohkóni' nuhu' koh'owóoo-n.
"You will enjoy being there," said this ball to them.

Koox=hé'ih-noxow-eyeih-etéb-ei'i.
Once again the bear had very nearly caught up to them.

Neeso he'ih-'íhcikúu3-ee nehe' honóh'ehihi' núhu' koh'owóoo-n.
The boy threw the ball up three times.

Toh-yeini'owoo-ní', he'ih-'ihcikuu3-ee.
When the fourth time came, he threw it up.

Toh-cih-ce'-óówo'oo-ní3, he'ih-cíitonihce3ei'ón-ee.[9]
When it was coming back down, he kicked it up into the air from
underneath.

Beebeet hé'ih-nohku-uhcíno'oo-no' nuhu' koh'owóoo-n.
They just rose upward with the ball.

Núhu' nenéé-3i' neneesouu3i-'i ho3o'-uu núhu' huhcébe'.
They are three stars hanging in the sky.

'oh nehe' wox, toh-'oo3ónitoo-t, he'ih-noxowu-néetéteehee.[10]
And after the bear failed to catch them, she became mad with rage.

Beebéet he'ih-'oo3í3in-niitouu.
She fell backward, hollering.

He'ih-cii-noh'oowus.
She didn't stir.

Nee'ei'ísi-' hiii.
That's how far the snow goes.[11]

Notes

1. More normal is *se'-éíhtoo* 'flat-foot, claw'. Here the form is *hit-éíhtoo*, 3S possessed form. The manuscript has *hitiitoo-no*.

2. *Hoyookútoo-* = AI.REFL/SELFB 'tie s.t. [next] to a part of oneself' (cf. *hoyóku-* 'sit next to/in contact with s.o.').

3. The Sand Hills are a mythological location where the dead are said to live.

4. The manuscript has *he'ih-co'oo'óenin*, which Kroeber glosses 'willow hut'.

5. Kroeber glosses this term as 'flesh on the back', but the actual meaning is more specifically 'tenderloin'. The word *hicii'o*, locative *hicii'one'*, is documented in Truman Michelson, NAA, MS 2988, with this meaning. Interestingly, the tenderloin was subject to various eating taboos within Arapaho culture (see Hilger 1952: 12–14), so the use of the word here evokes the broader issue of taboo-breaking (likely by the older sister) and the unexpected negative consequences, though the exact nature of the moral lesson here is unclear.

6. *Kokuyé3* 'scabby dog' is not recognized by modern speakers.

7. *Woti'-* 'remove and get rid of, discard and leave behind' + *íii-* 'camp'.

8. This is a dependent participle based on the TA verb *hecó'on-* 'to block s.o.'s path, impede; quarantine'.

9. *Ciiton-* '(from) underneath'.

10. The AI verb *néet-éteeh-ee-* means literally 'die from [an angry] heart'.

11. When listening to traditional narratives, people said 'snow' to show that they were still awake and listening. Thus the end of 'snow' is the end of the story.

Blue Bird, Elk Woman,
and Buffalo Woman

Told by Wolf Bear, John Goggles interpreter,
Wyoming, September 1910
Collected by Truman Michelson
NAA, MS 2708, 17 pp.

This text was taken down only in English; the original Michelson version is used. Other English versions of this text are Dorsey and Kroeber [1903] 1997, narratives 144 and 145. The title above is supplied in the manuscript, in English only. The story is rich in allusions to the various Arapaho ceremonial lodges and other practices. One of its primary purposes is as an etiological narrative, explaining the origin of various objects and practices. The versions in Dorsey and Kroeber are richer in detail than this one and make the etiological function clearer.

There was a bunch of camps. Blue Bird's father was a chief. Blue Bird was a lazy boy. He slept all the time.[1] He used to go around the camps. He met a boy with a friend. He called the boy Yellow Bird. After they went around the camps they went home. He told Yellow Bird to go home for a while. He told him that he, Blue Bird, was going to get married. He got married to Elk Woman. After he was married he told his father to wake him in the morning. His father told him to get up. His father said he had no red-headed eagles with yellow wings.[2] "All right." He went right away. He got his bow that was outside and started off. His father began to look for him a little later when he had not come back. He asked other persons if they had seen him. They said they had seen him going off.

While he was going on he got into a spring. There were buffalo in the water. The buffalo began to come out when they saw him coming to the spring.[3] As he walked towards the spring he saw a buffalo sitting down in the mud. He stood close to him and punched him with his bow. He turned around and started home. He got home. His father heard when he got home. He stayed at home for a little while.

Someone told him that a buffalo had a child. The baby said, "Blue Bird is my father." The buffalo was coming towards the camp where Blue Bird was. He sent out and saw her coming with a boy. The boy said "Here's my father." He ran towards Blue Bird. Blue Bird said "This is my boy."

His wife came out. When she saw Buffalo Woman standing there she commenced to say some words—that Buffalo Woman had the funniest looking hair on her head. Buffalo Woman said the Elk Woman had the funniest looking eyes. They were jealous of each other. Buffalo Woman felt sorry how she had talked with Elk Woman. She then started off with the boy.

While she was going towards the hills the first ridge she got on top of she saw quite a man sitting down. She went by on his left side. She got on the second ridge. When she got over it there were two old men sitting down. She went by on their left side. She reached the third ridge. When they went over she saw three old men sitting down; she went by on their left side. The fourth ridge as they went down they saw four very old men sitting down.[4] She went by on the left side. These old men told her to go over where yon tipi was in the center of a bunch of buffalo. She went over. She went in this tipi. This was her father's tipi. So she stayed at her father's tipi.

Then Blue Bird had commenced to look for his boy. He asked other people if they had seen them. When he was looking for his boy when he got back to his camp he called his friend Yellow Bird. He told him that he was going out and look for his boy; he also told his friend that he might look out for dust that went up to the sky and that would tell his friend that he was in trouble.

So he started out and at the last tipi he asked the old woman if she [had seen] them. She said she saw them going towards the hill. He followed her tracks. He got on the first ridge, went down to the foot of the ridge. He saw a man sitting down and he told him that she had passed by on the left side. He got on the second ridge; at the foot he saw two old men sitting down. They told him she had passed by on the left side. When he got on the third ridge as he was going down he saw three very old men. They told him she had passed by. When he got to the fourth ridge as he was coming down he saw four old men. They told him she had passed by and was going to that tipi around which were the buffalo. They told him his boy looked almost like the yellow color of a buffalo calf.[5]

So he walked towards the tipi. His boy was told that he was coming. His boy ran towards him as he was coming. He then walked over and entered the tipi. When he got in his boy told him that the first thing to do they were going to run a foot race with the buffalo. His boy was going to run for him.

He said he could run as well; that his boy might be beaten. He didn't want his boy to run. He preferred [wanted] his son to beat the buffalo. He would take his boy back home.

They got ready for the races. There were four buffalo calves and Blue Bird. The buffalo stood in a string the way they were going to run. They started, two buffalo on each side of him. Before they started his boy told him to beat [the buffalo] so they could go home at once. He won.

When the race was over the boy told his father that they were going to make Blue Bird dance with the buffalo for all night, and if he didn't get sleepy or fall down while dancing he would save his boy. The dance was started. He didn't go to sleep.

After the dance was over the boy told his father that they were going to sing all night; if he did not sleep until morning he could take his boy with him. They sang until morning; Blue Bird was awake. The third time they had him sing all night. That is how the Indians got the buffalo dance.[6]

The boy told his father they were going to tell stories for four nights, and if he didn't sleep he could have his boy again. So they told him a story the first night. An old man told the story. He didn't sleep.[7] He was all right until the second morning. The second day all day until night, until the third night towards morning he was just about to fall asleep when his boy kept waking him up. The fourth day until night, until towards morning Blue Bird was very [sleepy]. His boy kept trying to wake him, but could not. He shook him hard and cried.

Then the boy quit. He stepped aside and said to the old people who were telling stories that they had beat him. They then got up and turned into old buffalo. They began to go around in a circle till he [Blue Bird] was crushed to pieces, till there was nothing left but dirt. The dirt went way up in the sky. Yellow Bird knew that he was gone by that sign. The dirt looked blue. One little feather, very small, of Blue Bird, was not destroyed.

Yellow Bird said he was going to look for his friend. He started out. For a long while he was looking around for him. He came back. The second time he started out. Then he found the place where they had destroyed him. While looking close to the ground he heard the voice of his friend. He could not see where he was till he saw that little piece of feather. That was the way he found him [and revived him, returning him to life].

When he got him he began to turn towards the camp. Yellow Bird was flying. They came in by the top of a tipi. The people cried out that Blue Bird was back home. Yellow Bird said "The buffalo are going to come." The buffalo started towards the camp. While going (when they started for the camp) they played wheel games.[8] Yellow Bird said he would go back to see how far back they were.

When he got to where the buffalo were, while they were playing the wheel game, he flew towards where the arrows were.[9] He got one of those arrows. He went back home with it. He showed the people the arrow. He said the buffalo were very close.

Then Blue Bird went to see how far the buffalo were. When they were camped they danced a spear dance.[10] He flew down and got one of the spears. He flew back and showed the spear and said the buffalo were very close.

Next Yellow Bird started out to see how far the buffalo were. He had a piece of fat with him. When he got where they were camped they were dancing the spear dance again. He flew down and got one of the spears and started back with it. There were magpies after him. They flew very fast. He flew up, down, every way but they were after him. He could not get away from them. He flew down a small mud hole. While close to the mud he dropped the fat. The magpies stuck in the mud. He went home with the spear, showed it to the people, and said the buffalo were very close.

Blue Bird started out to see how far the buffalo were. He got to where they were. They were dancing the Crazy dance.[11] He flew and got the crazy spear—(the white spear,[12] we call it). He started back home. They were after him. They nearly caught him. He shouted out to his friend Yellow Bird to throw (shout) out fat for him—Yellow Bird did and he got away. He got to the camp. He said to the people, sticking the spear to the ground, "This spear tells the story right."

The buffalo got to the camp. They camped all together. After this, white spear, being the last spear, said, "It shall never more be such kind of troubles, but all straightened out again. That the Indians come to be good, that they might not touch the animals as they got the boy from them." After this was over they danced four kinds of dances as the buffalo had danced while coming. When these dances were over, it settled everything—all their trouble was over.

Notes

1. Compare this to "The Beheaded Ones," which also features a sleepy young boy.

2. The meaning of these eagles is unclear.

3. Compare "The Man Who Turned into a Spring" for another example of the special power associated with springs.

4. Four is the Arapaho sacred number; in addition, life is often conceived of in terms of the "four hills/ridges of life," so the image here is rich in resonance.

5. The Arapaho word for a young buffalo calf is *nihoon-óú'*, 'yellow calf'.

6. This is apparently a reference to the Arapaho women's ceremonial lodge, the *ben-ouhtóowu'*, a word whose meaning is unclear other than that *–oowu'* means 'lodge'.

7. It was a common practice for elders to tell stories at night, with the listeners saying *hííí* 'snow' to show that they were still awake. When the last person quit answering, the storyteller would stop.

8. This is the game played at the beginning of "The White Crow," closely associated with the buffalo. See the notes there.

9. See "The White Crow" for another example of the importance of powerful arrows.

10. The 'spear lodge' (*bíítohóowu'*) was one of the seven Arapaho age-grade lodges and ceremonies.

11. The 'crazy lodge' (*hohóokóowu'*) was another of the seven Arapaho age-grade lodges and ceremonies.

12. The Crazy Lodge was associated with Lime Crazy (see the story in this volume) and with white ceremonial lime/paint.

Animal Stories

The Turtle and the Rabbit

Teller unknown, Oklahoma, August(?) 1899
Collected by Alfred Kroeber
NAA, MS 2560a, Notebook 6, pp. 13–14

There are similar stories of this type among the Arapaho—in particular a race between a fox and a wood tick (which is won by the wood tick) as well as stories of how a bear underestimates a skunk (to his chagrin) and how a golden eagle underestimates a peregrine falcon (again to his chagrin). Of course, this is a common folktale motif generally. It is important to remember, however, that in Arapaho and Algonquian creation stories the turtle is the heroic figure who succeeds in bringing up the first earth from the bottom of the sea, so the resonance of this story is more than just slow versus fast.

The title here was supplied by the editors. Despite its brevity, this story has a good deal of zest at certain moments. For example, the turtle uses *heh=* 'surely, certainly' when he proposes the race, underlining his confidence and bravado. The rabbit, conversely, uses the colorful expression *he-néí'ei3ehéhk* 'who do you think you are?' or 'you don't know what you're talking about!' in response to the proposal. The expression is used most generally to suggest that someone is greatly overestimating his/her own status, ability, or position and is typically used confrontationally or scornfully.

Later the turtle is described during the race as *ceneeyóhwo'oo-* 'plugging along slowly and steadily'. The relatively uncommon prefix *ceneeyóhw-* means 'keep right on going, keep at it, follow through to the end, continue with persistence' and virtually always has positive connotations in Arapaho. In contrast, the rabbit is described with a less common word, *teebe-híhcehí-*, which combines *téébe* 'just now' (as in 'just now got started') with the AI final *-íhcehí-* 'rapid motion, run, jump'. The overall meaning is waiting until the very last moment and then trying to leap into action or (as in this case) leaping into action just after the deadline has already passed.

Despite its brevity, the narrative has an internal structure formed by the use of *wohéí* 'well, then, so' to conclude each short segment. This particle is common in spoken Arapaho and also used as a formal discourse marker of narrative segments by Paul Moss (2005) in his historical narratives. It is not commonly used as a formal narrative structuring device in the texts in

389

this collection, however, and its use in this text provides a less formal, more colloquial feel to the narrative.

Be'énoo he'=itex-oohok nóóku[o].[1]
Turtle met up with Rabbit.

"Toot=(h)éí-ihoo?" hee3-oohok nóóku[o].
"Where are you going?" he said to Rabbit.

"Wohéi, heh=nonouhti-no'," be'énoo heeh-éhk.
"Well, surely we're going to race," said Turtle.

"'ee'ee, he-nei'ei3eh-ehk [no]-nonouhtiib-eiit?!"
"Gee, who in the heck do you think you are to race with me?!"

"Wohéi, sooxe, neneeco'oo-'!"[2]
"Well, let's go, we're on our way!"

Ne'i-yihoo-hohkoni' heetoh-3i'óku-ní3 koo'oh-wuu.
Then they went to where Coyote was sitting.

"Tóusoo?" hee3-éihohkoni'.
"What's up?" he said to them.

"Néhe' nii-beet-nonouhtiib-einoo, be'énoo," heeh-ehk nooku.
"This guy wants to race with me, Turtle," said Rabbit.

"Henéi=3ii'eyóóni-n."
"You could be the end-marker."

"Wohéi," heeh-ehk koo'oh.
"Okay," said Coyote.

Ne'-yihkooh-éhk heet-niit-too'úhcehi-ni3i.
Then Coyote ran over there to where they would stop running.

Wohéi, ce3kooh-ehkóni'.
Well, they set off running.

Neehii3éi' nóóku too'uhceh-ehk hot-nokohú-t.

In the middle, Rabbit stopped running so he could take a nap.

He'=ceneeyóhwo'oo-hok be'énoo.

But sure as can be Turtle kept plugging along slow and steady.

Cebixoo3-oohok nooku[o] be'énoo.

Turtle passed Rabbit by.

No'kóoh-ehk be'enoo koo'óh-wuu.

Turtle arrived at Coyote.

He'=teebehihceh-ehk nóóku.

Rabbit waited until it was too late to get going.

Notes

1. Note that 'rabbit' never has OBV marking in this story though it would otherwise be expected.

2. Kroeber transcribes *neneeko'oo-*. The expected modern form is *nenééco'oo-*.

The Skunk and the Rabbit

Told by Cleaver Warden, Oklahoma, August 17, 1899
Collected by Alfred Kroeber
NAA, MS 2560a, Notebook 9, pp. 50–53
English version published in Dorsey and
Kroeber [1903] 1997: 236–37

This story, like several others in the collection, is highlighted by a series of highly complex and highly comical polysynthetic expressions that come at the key moment. Even at the beginning the two adversaries are described as *nííso'u-too'uxóóton-etí-* (both-stop walking at the location of someone-REFL) 'they both came to a stop right in front of the other one'. As Skunk prepares to loose his scent on Rabbit, he is described as *híinee-too'-úhcehí* (turn back around-stop-quickly) 'he stopped and spun back around quick as can be'. He tells the rabbit *cih-bebíis-néí'oohóót-oo* (to here-carefully-look at-it) 'look right in here real carefully'. Rather than the more usual *níh'iw-* 'spray someone with something' the narrator uses *nonookóónitíí-* 'let a liquid substance/scent loose on something' or more idiomatically 'let loose with all of it' to describe the skunk spraying the rabbit—or more literally 'dousing' or dumping water on him. The rabbit is then described as *bée-bé'e3inii-no'úusí'oo* (REDUPLICATION–butt first–close eyes) 'his eyes closed and his butt sticking up wriggling around in the air' after having gotten sprayed.

The other element of the story that stands out is Skunk's repeated uses of warnings and imperatives to the rabbit, such as *ceibís'* 'step aside!'; *nii3é3en* 'I'm telling you!'; *nííhi'néíhinoo* 'I insist on it!'; *koxúús* 'walk somewhere else!'; *hiinéénowó'* 'this is urgent!'; *heetnóóxonixóóni'* 'I must really hit the road!'; *héhmi'óóxuwúheé* 'let me explain the rules here for you!'; *hiinó3oon* 'I insist'; and *neh-* 'you'd better . . .' Of course, despite this virtual language lesson in command and request forms, the rabbit is not smart enough to obey and gets another sort of lesson. This makes it all the funnier when the skunk casually walks away like a modern action-movie hero, saying, 'I'm tough . . . I told you . . . I insist . . . I can't be stopped . . . I leave them all in my wake'.

The term *béh'ee* 'old man' is the special vocative/address form of the word *beh'éíhehi'* 'old man'. Addressing someone in this way is a sign of respect in everyday life. Given the nature of both the protagonists and the plot in this story, however, the term has an ironic tone here, somewhat like using "mister" when talking to a young person in English, as in "Listen, mister, you'd better clean up your room" (said to a ten-year-old). Similarly, Skunk several times uses 'us' and 'we' rather than 'me' and 'I', roughly like the "royal we" in English. It has polite and formal overtones in Arapaho but in this case comes across quite ironically.

Note, finally, that beyond the obvious moral lessons, an informant (likely the narrator) noted to Kroeber that the story is connected to traditional Arapaho medicinal practice. "Has reference to skunk bags and doctoring. Hurting of medicine, on eyes, etc. The squirting = spitting of medicine." Skunk hides were used as medicine bags by Arapaho medicine men, and the white stripe on the bag was interpreted as a road. Medicine was also commonly spit onto the patient. Moreover, another cure for aching eyes was to put a very old, smelly moccasin right up to the eyes, looking into the foot hole—this was said to make the eyes feel better. Thus there are broader connections between bad smells and curing of sight within Arapaho medicine, which this story seems either to echo or to be the basis of. Once this theme is understood, then the numerous references to sight in the story become all the more apparent and meaningful.

Xóuhu' he'ih-nosóusee boóón-e', teebe nohkúseic.
Little Skunk was still walking on the trail, just after morning had broken.

Nooku niixoo he'ih-nosóucoo.
Rabbit was still coming along the trail too.

He'ih-niisóho'-tou'uxóót{n}óneti-no'.
They both stopped right in front of each other.

"Koxuusee, hee3e'éisee-noo.
"Walk somewhere else, I'm coming through.

"Beeyoo hee3e'éisee-noo niíyoo3oo-',[1] béénii.
"I'm coming right down the middle of the path unobstructed, friend.

"Ceibís, nii3-é3en.
"Get out of the way, I'm telling you.

"Nii-nihi'néíhi-noo heesisee-nóóni," heeh-éhk xóuhu'.
"I insist on going wherever I want," said Little Skunk.

"Nohtóus heetih-ceibísee-noo?[2]
"Why do I have to get out of the way?

"Niixóó 3onookútii-noo bóoo.
"I'm following this trail too.

"Nonóónoko' ceibís.
"You might as well get out of the way instead.

"Konoo'eenéyei-n; hehnee=noohohóuhu-noo," heeh-éhk nóóku.
"You're an eternal slow poke; I'm in a hurry here!" said Rabbit.

"Hoowúuni: Hííko!
"I won't: No!

"Neenih-ceibis[ee-n]![3]
"You're the one to get out of the way!

"Nii-nihi'néíhi-noo hee3ooxúwu-nooni, béh'ee!
"I insist on going wherever I have determined to go, old man!

"Koxúús hee3e'éisee-noo.
"Walk somewhere else, I'm coming through.

"Hiineenowó'.
"Hurry up, I've got urgent business.

"Hei-tówuh-ei'ee, hootn-ooxonixóó-ni'," xouhu' nii-hok.
"You seem to be cutting us off, we must hit the road," Little Skunk said.

"Né-ihoowuuni.
"I won't do it.

"Ceibis béh'ee," nóóku nii-hok.
"Step aside, old man!" Rabbit says.

"Níixoo, wohéi heh-ni'óóxuwuh-ee.
"Well, let us set you straight here too.

"Yóh=hoowoh-wóxook.[4]
"You have the worst eyes imaginable.

"Nii-cii-noohóót-ow hee3e'éisee-noni.
"You can't see which direction you're going.

"Níi-cii-noohóot-ow.
"You can't see it.

"Nii3-é3en, niini'ítii-noo besíisei.
"I'm telling you, I can fix up bad eyes.

"Béh'ee, nohoní-kokóh'eenéet-ow?[5]
"Why don't you think about it, old man?

"Cih-nei'oohóot-oo nesíisei.
"Look here at my eyes.

"Heh='íí3eti-'i toh-'okecóúhuhú-'u.
"See how good they are, and nice and small.

"Tótoos hi3óóbe' nii-noohóó3ei-noo.
"I can even see things under the ground.

"Béh'ee, wohéi, koo-ne-et-cíi-ni'-niísitii heeyouhuu?
"Old man, well, what do you say, can't I do something for you?

"Noh henéi=neecó'oo."
"And then you'd be able to go on your way."

"Heetih-'e'ín-owoo toon-níisitoo-n.
"I need to know whatever it is that you do [to fix eyes," said Rabbit].

"Hootn-ooxonísee-noo.
"I must be on my way.

"Noh wo'éi3 wóótoo!
"Or else [if you're not going to help me], get out of the way!

"Koxúusee," nooku nii-hók.
"Walk somewhere else," says Rabbit.

"Hehé',[6] béh'ee.
"You forget, old man.

"Wóóce' hesíisei wosóó-no.
"You ought to remember that your eyes are bad.

"Hiinó3oon, neh-cíhnee."
"I insist, you'd better come over here."

Xouhú' he'ih-'iinee-too'uhce.
Little Skunk came to a stop and spun around right then and there.

3í'ooninee.
He had his tail up in the air.

"Bééyoo xóuuwuuhu' híhcebe'.
"Right straight in here real close.

"Cih-néí'oohoot-oo.
"Look in here.

"Ciibeh-néi3ecoo.
"Don't be afraid.

"Híhcebe' cih-tóó'us.
"Stop right close here.

"Cih-bébiis-nei'oohóót-oo.
"Look in here very carefully.

"Koo=woowuh híhcebe'?"
"Are you nice and close yet?"

"Hee," heeh-éhk nóóku.

"Yes," said Rabbit.

Xóuhu' he'ih-nonóokoonetii.[7]

Little Skunk let loose all of his spray on him.

"'o'xú!"[8]

"Ouch!"

Nóóku ceibihcehínoo'oo, toh-'otóuhuh-t.

Rabbit quickly jumped aside, because the little thing's eyes were burning.

Neesiineníhi-t.[9]

He rolled about.

Bee-be'e3i-níi-no'úusí'oo.

It had its eyes shut and its butt sticking up in the air.

"Nonó'otéíhi-noo nih-'ii3-é3en, béh'ee.

"I told you I'm powerful, old man.

"Ho-toustoo?

"What are you doing [rolling around like that]?

"Nii-níhi'néíhi-noo hee3ooxeihi-nóóni.

"I insist on going wherever I feel like making tracks.

"Niixoowó'-owoo,[10] nii-noo3-óú'u.

"I always overcome obstacles, and I leave my adversaries behind in my wake.

"Beetooh-é3en."

"I have blessed you with this medicine."

Notes

1. *Níiyoo3óó*- II.IMPERF, 'clean, clear'. The word often has moral overtones in Arapaho, as in 'live a clean life'. Furthermore, rabbits are associated with cleanliness and purity.

within Arapaho ceremonial tradition (the ceremony prior to the Sun Dance is the Rabbit Lodge). The usage thus has ironic undertones here, used by Skunk when talking to Rabbit.

2. *Nohtóu* is modern 'why'. *Nohtóús* is an older form.

3. Here *neníh-* is used with an imperative verb. Normally it is used with affirmative verbs, because the prefix itself has imperative force.

4. *Yóh=* 'exemplary' + *hoowóh-* 'barely [even]' + *wóxookú-* AI 'see badly'.

5. The form *nohoní-* is not recognized today. Kroeber glosses it 'for trial'. It would seem to be something more general like 'why don't you . . .' It also occurs in "Nih'oo3oo Cuts His Hair."

6. Alonzo Moss says that this is an older form that meant 'and next?' Kroeber glosses it as 'you forget'. Pragmatically, it seems to be more generally 'now wait a minute, you're heading off on the wrong track with what you're proposing next'.

7. The form is not used today but consists of *non-* 'away from X, lost to X' (cf. *noníikoh-* TA 'escape from', *noníikóóhu-* AI 'get lost running/driving') plus *ookóónitíí-* or *ookóónetíí-* AI.T final, 'act on s.t. using water or liquid'. Thus *nonookóónitíí-* AI.T 'let all his liquid substance escape from him onto s.t.'

8. This is the female word for 'ouch' (Rabbit is treated as female in this story, at least in terms of this word, or perhaps as unmanly).

9. This verb is unclear. Alonzo Moss points out that *neesiiniihíh-t* would be 'the little one is injured' (perhaps *nih-'esiiniihíh-t*, with past tense). William C'Hair notes that *-iní'iihi-* means 'pull, exert force', so *heesiininí'iihi-t* would be 'he is pulling/jerking around intensely', which seems the most likely reading, with /n/ being an error for /h/.

10. IMPERF form of *híixoowó'-* TI 'overcome' (cf. TA *híixoowó'on-* 'overcome, drive away, defeat').

The Bear Who Abused His Wife

Told by Cleaver Warden, Oklahoma, Summer 1928
Collected by Truman Michelson
NAA, MS 3087, 2 pp.

This fragment occupies two loose pages filed with a larger manuscript. Apparently the earlier and later pages were lost. It has no title, so this one was provided by the editors. The story is typical of Arapaho bear stories in that the bears are often portrayed as comical and buffoonish characters, always coming out the losers in their encounters with people or the trickster—see, for example, Dorsey and Kroeber [1903] 1997, narratives 96, 97, and 98. In this story the use of reduplication to describe the husband bear's reactions to finding his wife missing is a nice illustration of bear behavior: he 'screams and hollers' (*née-neeyéít-*) and 'scratches himself all over his face' (*kóo-kóú'u'éínetí-*). One thinks of Curly from the Three Stooges. Conversely, bears are also the most humanlike of all the animal figures in their portrayal, as this story also nicely illustrates. We would like to know how it ended!

Notíkoniihíí-ho' he'ih-noohob-eeno' wóx-uu tóh-tíci'ei-ni3.
Some warriors saw a bear abusing [his wife].

Héí'-iis-biih-oot hiníín, néhe' wóx tóh-'onow-oonoxúúheti-t,
hé'ih-nóko.
After he reduced his wife to tears, after the bear pleasured himself to his satisfaction, he went to sleep.

Hiníín he'ne'P . . . he'=kóxo'-kohei'i-ni3.
Then his wife . . . she slowly got up.

Héí'-e'inon-éít hé'ih-3ii'óóbe, kóxo'-hoseitísee-ni3.
Once she heard him snoring, she slowly backed out [of the den].

Héí'i-he'inon-eit tih-nosou-tíci'ei-t, ceese' wóx he'ih-'ííbinee-bisé'ein
neeyéíc-i'.

When he thought that the bear was still abusing his wife, another bear secretly poked his head out from the timber to see.

Néhe' [hii]níísi-t wóx[1] heï'i-ceniikoohu-t, he'ne'-won-nouxon-eit[2] ceexoo[n].
Once the wife of the first bear had run a long way, the other bear in the timber came and met her.

Beeyoo he'ih-xouu-ce3kóóhu-no' bóón-e'.
They ran off straight for the road/path.

Heï'i-cenííkoohu-3i', néhe' hiiniini-t wóx[3] he'ne'-owóto'oo-t.
Once they had run a long way, then the bear who was her husband woke up.

Xonóuu he'ih-noo-noti-noohob-ee hiniín.
Right away he looked around for his wife.

Tóh-cii-noohow-oot, kookiyon he'ih-koo-kou'u'éínet.
When he didn't see her, he just scratched his face all over.

Nee-neeyeit-o'.
He screamed and hollered.

Heï'-iis-bi'-nowúh-oot, beeyoo 3ooku3ei-t.
After he had tracked them, he followed right along after them.

Ne'=nii'-cé'e3eisi-'i.
Then they collided with each other.

[End of MS]

Notes

1. Literally 'this she-has-a-husband bear'.
2. The manuscript has *wotou[x]oneit* rather than *wonou[x]oneit,* but the gloss is 'was then met by her', which must be *woni-nóuxon-éít,* ALLAT-meet(TA)-4/3S.
3. Literally 'this he-has-a-wife bear'. This is an unusually precise way of identifying the different actors in the story and also exactly parallels the equally unusually precise expression in an earlier line (note 1 above). The storyteller's adjectival verbs serve to play up the importance of the marital relationship.

Anecdotal Stories of Wondrous Events

Big Belly's Adventure

Possibly told by Cleaver Warden: preceding narrative on
pp. 43–44 attributed to him
Collected by Alfred Kroeber, Oklahoma, 1899
NAA, MS 2560a, Notebook 6, pp. 44–45
Arapaho version published in Kroeber 1916: 125–26

This story occurs in Kroeber's field notes immediately after the story of "Nih'oo3oo and the Deer Women" and has a very similar theme. Both stories tell of men who let their sexual impulses get the best of them, making fools of themselves. The first story likely inspired the second one: the first is presented as a *heetéetoo* (myth), while this one is presented as a true-life example of the behavior pattern illustrated in the myth.

Although the word *bíh'ih* means 'mule deer', Kroeber glosses the word as 'antelope' through the entire story. This is a puzzling mistake on his part. The description of the animal 'jumping about' sounds much more like a deer than an antelope. More importantly, the deer was a traditional succubus figure in Arapaho myth. The female deer would try to seduce men; if they fell for her, they would become crazy. This story clearly fits in that tradition. The detail about the woman wearing antelope-derived buckskin is accurate, however, in the sense that the most attractive women are still called "buckskin beauties" in Arapaho English and buckskin is the traditional fancy dress of choice.

Kroeber added at the end as a note: "Acted thus because had to. Acted thus often, for some time. Cleaver [Warden] saw him act thus once." He also wrote "true" next to the title in the manuscript.

The Big Belly referred to in the title was possibly the same person who was a lower-level chief among the Arapahos in 1911 (Fowler 2002: 75). Most importantly, Fowler notes that he was a member of the Crazy Lodge Age-Grade Society. The members of this lodge were noted for taking a powerful root as medicine and then acting in crazy and perverse fashion (see Kroeber [1902–1907] 1983: 188–96). Thus the actions described here may be related to the Crazy Lodge.

Bih'ih he'ih-'iinoo'ei.
Deer went hunting.

Hitox-oohók wot=hih-tousi-ni'eihi-n hisei-n.
He came upon an extremely good-looking woman.

Behis-nisicehinoninouhu-yohkon.
She was dressed all in buckskin.

Xonóu he'ih-ceecii3énoo'oo.[1]
Immediately he could think of nothing else but obtaining her.

Tóh-noohówoot hísei-n, he'ih-'eenéitohowúun-e'.
When he saw the woman, she was gesturing for him to come toward her.

"Wohéi, hooti-bii'o'oo3-é3en," hee3-oohók bíh'ih.
"Well, I'll be your sweetheart," Deer said to her.

Noh "Niiheyoo heesitoo-nóni," hee3-éihok.
And "It's up to you to do as you want," she said to him.

He'ne'í-yihoo-t.
So then he went over to her.

Téébe hotni-iten-oohók, hiinoononox he'ih-wosetouuhú-n.
Just when he was going to embrace her, to his amazement she made the sound of an antelope.[2]

Ces[is]-cee-céno'oo.
She started jumping around.

Cee-cebite'éikoo.[3]
She was running back and forth across looking at him.

He'ih-bi'-nei'oohób-ee.
He just looked at her.

Bíh'ih, bíh'ih he'ih-teyéíh.
Deer, Deer was embarrassed/ashamed.

Howóh nih'ót-bii'é'ee-t!
And to think that he had been planning to be her sweetheart!

He'ne'-ce'eeckóóhu-t, toh-teyéíhi-t.
Then he went back home, because he was ashamed.

He'ih-'oote'éin bíh'ih toh-bih'ihínoo'oo-t.
It was sometime later that Deer turned into a deer.

Neeyéí3oon-e' he'ih-'iinikúhinee.
He was running about trying to escape in the middle of the camp
cluster.

Bíh'ih wootii bíh'ih, wootii bíh'ih nii3etouuh-éhk, wootii bih'ih
cee-céno'oo;
Deer, like a deer, he made sounds like a deer, he jumped around like a
deer;

wootii bih'ih he'=no'o'kuhnee-hék.
like a deer he ran out away from camp into the wilds, trying to escape.

He'=behi-yeihonee-téhk.
He was pursued by everyone.

Tih-'iis-iítenée-t, he'ih-nóo-noni3ooku'oo.
Once he had been caught, he was looking around in a very confused way.

Bíh'ih he'ih-te'etínoo'oo.
Deer opened his mouth.

He'ih-beh-'eenei'énoo.[4]
He was held close [to the camp] by everyone.

Hóónii hé'ih-ciin-íini bih'ihíin.
After a long time, he ceased being a deer.

Nee'ee3iisih'í-t bih'ih.

That is where his name Deer comes from.

Notes

1. Cf. *cíí3ecooh-* 'to preoccupy, bother, distract s.o.' and *cii3ecóót-* 'preoccupied with s.t., unable to think clearly'. The form here appears to be a variant, with an inchoative ending. It also seems to be a play on the word *céno'oo-* 'jump', which appears several times later in the text to describe Big Belly's ridiculous behavior.

2. Kroeber glosses 'antelope' here, but 'deer' is probably the correct gloss, given the rest of the story.

3. *Cebit-é'ei-kóóhu-* AI crossways-head-run-. The exact meaning seems to be running back and forth, with the head turned crossways to the path of the running, thus displaying in front of the man and looking at him. The manuscript has final *xoo* rather than *koo*. Kroeber glosses it as 'running looking back'.

4. TA *híí'en-* 'hold close by/to s.t.' > reduplicated TA *heenéi'en-* AI.MID *heenéi'enoo-* 'held near/close to s.t.'

The Woman and the Horse

Told by Caspar Edson, Oklahoma, August(?) 1899

Collected by Alfred Kroeber

NAA, MS 2560a, Notebook 13, pp. 6–14

English version published in Dorsey and Kroeber [1903] 1997:

121–22

W illiam C'Hair noted the following "good words": *hono'út* 'all, complete'; *ciinoocéíkuu3-* 'lower down quickly by rope' (due to its specificity); and *cebikoníítooni-* 'all the bands are traveling'. A number of Arapaho stories involve mysterious encounters between horses and people or people being or becoming horses. One of these told by Mary Kate Underwood (2010) involves a man who was raised by horses and then turns into a horse.

The teller specifies that the story is about the Southern Arapahos, which is a key indicator that this is considered a "true event" story and not a myth or legend.

Linguistically, this story is full of numerous markers of utter confusion and mystery. In the encounter between the woman and the horse we find *cee'ínooni3ecoo-* 'be in a confused state of mind'; *cee'ínon-* 'not know s.o.'; *he'iisííhi' nóhoó* 'some kind of stallion'; *híiyohóú' niisínihiit* 'there was nothing she could say/she was speechless'. When the riderless horse returns to camp, we see *híiyohóú' niisí3ecoot* 'he did not know what to think/his mind was blank'; *tótoos he'ih-cii-nowúh-e'* 'he did not even find any trail/tracks'.

Structurally, this narrative relies on line-initial *noh* 'and' to initiate new sequences in the story. We have segmented the story into sections based on the use of *noh* in this way. Once segmented, each strophe can be seen as a separate dramatic unit, containing a key event that advances the story in the eyes of the narrator.

Noowunenitee-no' nuhu' hoo3itoo.[1]

This is a story about the Southern Arapahos.

Teecixó' he'ih-cebikóniitoon noowuneniteeníít.[2]
Long ago the southern tribe was moving along in a group.

Ceeséy hiisí', noh céése' hiséi he'ih-'ii3íb-ee biiyo3oú'.
One day a certain woman realized that a colt was missing.

Toh-nousou-cebííhi-t, he'ne'i-ce'-notííh-oot hee3ikóniiní-t.[3]
While the group was still moving along, then she went back to look for
it where they had passed.

Noh toh-nosouséé-t, cenih-'ii3ííhi-t, he'ih-noohób-ee hinenitéé-n,
toh-cih-3ookutii-ni3 ceebíkoni-' bóoo.
And while she was still walking, where the group had traveled from,
she saw a person who was following the trail where they had passed.

He'ih-too'ús toh-noohów-oot núhu' hinenítee-n, toh-cee'inooní3ecoo-t,
tih-cii3o'-úu3óóhow-oot hinenítee-n heetee.[4]
She stopped walking because she saw this person, because she was
confused, since she had never seen this person before.

Noh he'ih-'ités-e'.
And he came to her.

He'ih-cee'inón-ee nuhu' honoh'é.
She did not know this young man.

'oh he'iisiihi' nóhoo.
And he was some kind of wild stallion.

Noh he'ne'-nottón-oot, "Toot=(h)éi-ihoo?" hee3-oohók.
And then she asked him, "Where are you going?" she said to him.

Noh "Nii-cih-noo3-é3en, toh-beetoh-niib-é3en."
And "I have come to fetch you, because I want to marry you," [he
said to her].

He'íh-'iiyohou niisí-nihii-t néhe' hísei.
This woman did not know how to respond.

Noh beexu-hoo3iíhi', he'né'-ii3-oot, "Heet-niib-ín," núhu' honóh'o.

And after a while, then she said to him, "You will marry me," [she said to] this young man.

Noh tih-'iis-íini ni'oob-éít, "Ciinooceikúus-in hotónih'{in}, cih-nii3óón-i," hee3-éihok.

And after she had agreed, "Drop your horse's reins, and come with me," the young man said to her.

He'né'-ciinikúu3-oot núhu' hiwóxuuhóóx-ebii hih-teexokúut-on.

Then she released the horse that she was riding.

Noh hiwóxuuhoox he'ih-seh-3ookukóó nih-cih-'iitíxoot-[o'].[5]

And the horse ran back there following the trail where he had come from.

He'né'i-nii3óón-oot núhu' honóh'o.

Then she accompanied this young man.

Noh nuhu' hiwóxuuhóóx-ebii hih-teexokúut-on hiséi toh-'etow-ooní3,

And when the horse that the woman had been riding caught up to them,

hiix, hih-teexokúut-on, he'ih-'iiyohou niisí3ecoo-ní3,

her husband, [with regard to] the horse she had been riding, he did not know what to think,

koúniihi' toh-no'ukoohu-ní3 hih-teexokúut-on.

when the horse she had been riding came running back all alone without her.

"Nuhu' hiwoxuuhóóx-ebii, nooxéihi' cenisib-éít, noh wo'éi3 nooxéihi' ce3ikoh-éít hiwóxuuhóóx, niis-no'eecikoohu-t," heeh-ehk, néhe' hinén, hísei híix.

"Maybe this horse threw her off, or maybe the horse got away from here, and it came home alone," he said, this man, the woman's husband.

Noh toh-'uusi-níiini-'i,[6] híix he'ne'-ce'-notíih-eit nih-'íitoh-noohob-éít.

And after they made camp, then he went back to look for her, where he had last seen her.

'oh he'ih-cii-bii'ííh-e'.

But he did not find her.

Tótoos he'ih-cii-nowúh-e' híix.

Her husband could not even find her tracks.

Noh he'i=nee'ei'í-biiwóóhu-t hi'íihi' hiníín, toh-cii-bii'ííh-oot.

And then he began to cry because of his wife, because he did not find her.

Noh toh-'úúsi-nóóke-', hono'út hinenteeníít he'ih-notííh-oo.

And the next morning the entire group looked for her.

Nih-cih-'íísiihí-3i' núhu' noowunenítee-no' he'ih-koutóótíi-no', toh-'uu-nótiih-oo3i' hinén-in hiníín-in.

They camped a long time where the southerners had moved from, because they were looking for the man's wife.

Noh hei'-kou3ííni notiihée-t néhe' hísei, he'né'-ce3ikóni-' heetoh-wóó3ee-t hii3einóón.

And after this woman had been looked for a long time, then they moved away to where there were a lot of buffalo.

He'ne'-i3óówu-noni3ó'oo-t néhe' hísei, hinén hiníín.

Then [they decided] this woman was truly gone, the man's wife.

Noh néhe' hísei hííx hé'ih-biiwóóhu-n hi'iihi' toh-'enih-éit.

And the woman's husband cried for her, because he had lost her.

[At this point Kroeber's manuscript says: "(cont. p.)." But no apparent continuation has been found. Kroeber printed the narrative in Dorsey and Kroeber (1903) 1997 complete as found above.]

Notes

1. Kroeber transcribes *hoowuneniteeno'*, but the expected form is *nóówuneníteeno'*.
2. The II verb *cebikoni-* means 'to move along as a band'. Impersonal verbs such as *cebikoníítooni-* normally are not formed from II verbs, only from AI verbs, but this II verb is unusual in that it refers to people (as a collective).

3. This sentence contains another unusual form of -*koni*- II 'move as a band'. One would expect *hee3íkoní*- for 'where they had moved as a band'. The form AI *hee3ikóniiní*- is not otherwise documented. William C'Hair suggested the pseudo-verbal prefix *hee3ikoniíni*- (formed from the II verb) as more appropriate.

4. The final verb is *híi3óóhow*- 'to have already seen s.o.'

5. *Cih-'iitísee*- AI 'come here from there' > *cih-'iitixóót*- TI 'come here from there on a path'.

6. The AI verb *níii*- means 'to make camp, to camp'. The form *níiini'i* appears to be an II form of this verb, with plural inflection: *níiini-'* 'a camp is made', *níiini-'i* 'camps are made'.

Anecdotal Stories

The Faithless Woman and the Kiowa

Told by Philip Rapid/Rabbit, Oklahoma, August 1899
Collected by Alfred Kroeber
NAA, MS 2560a, Notebook 10, pp. 1–5
English version published in Dorsey and
Kroeber [1903] 1997: 262

This narrative is untitled in Kroeber's manuscript. He supplied the title at time of publication. The story is notable for the narration of the central dramatic moment—the fight. A number of highly precise and relatively unusual words are used to describe the situation. The fight begins *xonóu*, 'immediately'. The verb *kouso'óóton-* means 'come at someone in a rage, a fury' and could be used to describe the behavior of hornets pouring (*kous-* 'pour') out of a nest to attack intruders. *Céece3ó'oh* means 'quick as a flash', 'before you know it.' *Híinci3-* 'grapple, wrestle' derives from the root *hiin-* meaning 'aimless, wandering, any direction', so the verb suggests the desperate grasping of hands seeking a solid hold. The reduplicated form *béebebííti'* 'each in his turn' serves to stress the changing fortunes of each participant as the fight shifts back and forth. *Kotóú'on-* means 'to come at s.o. and cover him or her' (*kotoy-* 'cover'). *Nó'uní'iihí-* indicates reaching a point or goal through great effort and struggle, such as dragging oneself to a place. The Kiowa has 'completely' (*nóxowu-*) forgotten about the knife in his desperation, and it has been '[violently] knocked away' from him (*hoséí[t]-* 'away' + *-[e]3eih-* 'by collision').

The violence of the fight is paralleled by the extraordinary unconcern of the woman. *Koowót=* indicates absolute lack (of help or attention in this case)—'not the tiniest little bit' does she pay him heed. She acts *konóhxuu*—despite any and all pleading and urging. This behavior earns her the formulaic expression *wo'úucéecíi3owu'*, meaning 'unbelievable callousness'. It should be noted that adultery per se could be punished more or less severely in Arapaho traditional society, with women potentially bearing the most severe penalty (cutting off the nose). In many cases, however, the matter was simply settled by payment of recompense. In addition, divorce was not especially difficult for either husbands or wives to obtain. Thus the violent condemnation of the woman here is more about her deceitfulness, which risks someone else's life, and her favoring of someone from another tribe over an Arapaho than about the issue of adultery per se.

Another interesting linguistic feature is the use of relationship terms to describe the actors: 'the one with the younger brother', 'the ones with a friend', 'the one with a wife', 'the one who had eloped'. Arapaho speakers can simply say *neehebéhe'* 'my younger brother' and so forth for all relatives. More complex are verbs derived from these nouns, such as *hineehebéh'i-* 'to have a younger brother'. These types of terms are relatively unusual in narratives and serve here to underline the different relationships at play in the story. This is a central moral element of the narrative, as the woman neglects family ties and duties for purely personal interest.

Note also the description of the Kiowa as *béebeenéíhit* 'he is good looking', using a more feminine type of word. The woman is described with exactly the same word. Thus she and the Kiowa are linked (negatively). The good-looking Arapaho man is described using a standard masculine verb for good looks, *ni'éíhi-*, which separates him from the Kiowa. Not surprisingly, the more manly Arapaho defeats the more effeminate Kiowa.

Finally, of course, the story contains one of the most graphic and shocking scenes in all Arapaho narratives: the woman left suspended in midair on a forest of arrows so thick that they keep her from falling to the ground, like a piece of cloth snagged on a thorn bush. This line includes a very creative use of the verb *hóóto'óu3i-* 'hang suspended'.

Hinóno'éi he'ih-bébeenéíhi-n hiníín.
An Arapaho had a wife who was very pretty.

'oh hunoohowóho' ci'=héh=he'ih-ni'éihi-n.[1]
And his younger brother certainly was very good looking too.

Nehe' honoóh'oe he'ih-'iinoo'éi.
The younger man went hunting.

Woowuh toh-ceníísee-t, he'ih-noníhi' hi-cóóxuuyo3oo.[2]
Now when he had walked quite a way, he [realized that] he had forgotten his bag.

He'né'-ce'i-no'kóóhuutii-t.
Then he ran to fetch it back.

He'ih-wotéés.
He went back into camp.

Toh-'uusííten-o' hi-cóóxuuyo3oo, he'ne'-cé3ei'oo-t.
After he had grabbed his bag, then he set off again.

He'né'-cee3i'ootowúún-oot[3] híisoh'ó.
Then he eloped with the wife of his older brother.

Nih-'iit-etéini-t, he'ih-cé'i-no'ús.
Where he had spent the night, he arrived back there.

Tóh-no'úsee-t, he'ih-nóuxon-ee niiciihéhiinen-in.
When he got there, he met a Kiowa man.

Wot=néhe' niiciihéhiinen nih-bébeeneih-éhk.[4]
This Kiowa man was very nice looking.

'oh nehe' hísei he'ih-bee3íh-ee, toh-ni'éenow-oot.
And this woman desired him strongly, because she liked him.

"Wohéi," heeh-éhk nehe' céé3i'ee-t, "Hootnii-hiicooh-ó'.
"Well," said the eloper, "I will give him a pipe to smoke.

"Beeto3ihi-no'óhk, heetni-í3kuu3-o'.
"When we finish smoking, I will seize him.

"Noh héét-cih-koo-koxukoh-óet."
"And then you will come here and keep stabbing him [until he's dead]."

He'ne'-biin-óot hi-wóoxe hiníín.
Then he gave his knife to his wife.

Xonóu he'ih-'iicóóh-ee.
Right away he gave the Kiowa man a pipe to smoke.

Hei'-béeto3ihi-3i', xonou hé'ih-kouso'ootón-ee.
Once they had finished smoking, he immediately attacked him with a fury.

Ceece3ó'oh he'ih-'iinici3etí-no'.
In a flash they were grappling with each other.

Bee-beebíiti' he'ih-kotou'óneti-no'.
Each in his turn kept getting on top of the other one.

He'ih-too-nóh'oo[5] néhe' hinóno'ei.
This Arapaho man was almost killed.

Koowot=hii3oohób-e' hiníín.[6]
But his wife did not pay the slightest heed to him.

"Wohéi, cih-koo-koxukoh-ún!" hee3-oohók hiníín,
"Well, come stab him!" he said to his wife.

Wo'úuceecii3owu'[7] he'ih-koo-koxkoh-u' híix!
But would you believe it, she stabbed her husband instead!

"Heetíh-neh'éihi-t," heeneesi3ecooton-oohók híix, "heetíh-niib-éinoo néhe' niiciihéhiinen."
"I prefer that he be killed," she was thinking about her husband, "so that this Kiowa man will marry me."

Konóhxuu[8] he'ih-cii-niitehéib-e'.
Despite his cries and pleading, she did not help him.

Hóónii wóotii he'ih-no'uní'iih[9] néhe' nih-'íit-ko'usé-ni' núhu'[10] wooxé:
After a good while the Arapaho man managed to struggle over to where this knife had fallen:

Wot=nih-{n}ósei3eihówuunée-téhk[11] néhe' niiciihéhiinen.
It had been knocked away from the Kiowa [in the struggle].

He'ih-'iibineeni-i3ikúutii néhe' hinóno'ei.
The Arapaho grabbed it without the Kiowa seeing him.

'oh hé'ih-noxowú-noníhi' nih-'iis-cesín-o' hi-wooxé nehe' niiciihéhiinen.
The Kiowa had completely forgotten that he had dropped his knife.

Tih-'iisí-i3ikúutii-t,[12] nehe' hinóno'éi xonóu he'i-césis-koo-koxukóh-uut núhu' niiciihéhiinén-in.
After he had seized it, the Arapaho immediately started stabbing the Kiowa.

Xonóu he'ih-néh'-ée.
He immediately killed him.

Tih-'iis-noh'-óot, he'né'-ce'iséé-3í'.
After he had killed him, then they walked back to camp.

Wot=nih-woo3ee-hék hinono'eitéén.
It was a big Arapaho village.

Toh-no'úsee-t néhe' nih-cée3i'ée-t hiisóh'o híyeih'-ín, xonóu hé'ne'-cesís-oo3itoon-oot núhu' heesi-too-neh'éihi-t,
When the one who had eloped got to his older brother's lodge, he immediately began to tell him the story of how he was almost killed,

núhu' hísei-n toh-niiteheiw-ooní3 niiciihéhiinen-in.
and of how this woman had helped the Kiowa man.

Toh-'uus-éi'tówuunée-t néhe' hiineehebéh'i-t,[13] he'ih-'esiníh-e' hiníín.
When the one with the younger brother had been told about this, he was angry with his wife.

"Wohéi neh-behíitoo'éi-'," hee3-oohók hiniiteh'éího-ho.
"Well, you'd all better arm yourselves," he said to his friends.

He'ih-cih-beh-no'oo'eiséé-no' núhu' hiiniiteh'eiheh'í-3i'.[14]
All who were friends with him came over and gathered at [his lodge].

Neehii3ei' he'ih-cih-'ookúuh-ee hiníín néhe' honóh'oe.
This man made his wife stand right in the middle of them.

Ceecíis he'=hiixoxo'onoo'oo nehe' hísei.
This woman suddenly found herself surrounded.

"Wohéi neh-beh-cébii-'," heeh-éhk néhe' hiiniiní-t.[15]

"Now you'd all better shoot," said the one who was her husband.

Xonou he'ne'-behí-ceb-iit nehe' hísei, honóot he'ih-'ootoo'ouu3[16] beic-é'.

Then immediately they all shot at this woman, until she hung suspended above the ground on the arrows.

Ne'=nih-'íís-noo-nó'o3ihee-téhk, tih-noo-nóxoo3itoo-t nehe' hísei.

That is how she was punished, since this woman acted so cruelly.

Notes

1. *Héhnee=* means 'certainly, surely'. It is unclear why the [n] is missing in the transcription. The form heh'ee= might be a variant of simple *héh=* (with the same meaning as *héhnee=*). Other forms in Kroeber's texts exhibit this extra syllable, as in modern *neníh-* 'let it be', transcribed by Kroeber (and in the Gospel of Luke) as *neníh'ee-*.

2. *Cóóxuuyo3óo.* William C'Hair says that this word, as far as he has heard it, is used mostly for 'afterbirth'. He occasionally heard it used for 'bag' when he was young. Perhaps it refers to a certain type of bag made from the internal organ of a buffalo, as was commonly done in the past.

3. *Céé3i'ee-* AI can mean 'date' or 'court' when used to describe young people. It can also mean 'go out with someone in a romantic way' (either inside or outside of marriage) for older people. Traditionally it referred to this kind of behavior outside the bounds of formal, gift-exchange marriages, either prior to the marriage (elopement) or after it (adultery). TA *céé3i'óótowuun-* means specifically to act like this with someone else's sweetheart or wife. We use the gloss 'elope' here, but 'steal his wife' or 'cuckold him' could also be used.

4. *Bébeenéíhi-* is normally used for women in modern Arapaho (glossed as 'buckskin beauty') though William C'Hair says that he has occasionally heard it used for a man. The normal male equivalent is *ni'éíhi-* or *hi3ówoonéíhi-* 'handsome'.

5. Modern AI middle voice verb ending /-ee/ is often replaced by /-oo/ in both Kroeber's texts and Michael Whitehawk's Gospel of Luke translation.

6. *Koowót=* 'not the least, none whatsoever, not a bit', etc. *Híi3óóhob-* means literally 'to have already seen s.o.' but more idiomatically in conjunction with the proclitic to 'pay attention to, notice, give heed to, help out'.

7. *Wo'úucéecíi3owu'* is used in response to a situation where someone exhibits extraordinary and unacceptable inattention and uncaring, as when a mother callously ignores a hungry child or an incapacitated elder is left unattended and suffering. Another version of the word is *wo'úucéecin3éí3ookowún*.

8. *Konóhxuu* 'despite all warnings to the contrary', 'despite all requests and pleading', 'despite everyone else's wishes' (the person goes ahead and does or does not do something). The word typically indicates a willful contrariness.

9. *Nó'uní'iihí-* AI 'struggle up to a point or place, reach a goal through great effort and strain'.

10. *Núhu'* 'this' is used here to introduce a new referent into the story that is going to be important in the subsequent discourse—a common feature in Arapaho discourse. This is

apparently not the knife that the man originally gave to his wife, unless the woman gave it to the Kiowa to use to stab her husband—something not stated in the text, but an interesting symbolic possibility.

11. *Hósei3eihówuunéé-* AI middle voice 'have s.t. knocked violently away'. The /n/ after *nih-* PAST TENSE is unexplained, unless it was intended as *neh-* deictic 'away from speaker/point of view'.

12. Kroeber gives *-itkuutii-*, but *-i3kuutii-* must have been intended.

13. *Hinééhebéh'i-* AI 'have a younger brother'.

14. *Hiniiteh'éiheh'i-* AI 'have a friend'.

15. *Hiníini-* AI 'have a wife'.

16. *Hóótoo'óuu3i-* 'hang suspended on something'. Often used to describe a kite or a ball stuck up in a tree or a person who has climbed up a cliff and now cannot get back down.

True Incident
(The Birth of Young Bull)

Told by Cleaver Warden?, Oklahoma, August(?) 1899
Collected by Alfred Kroeber
NAA, MS 2560a, Notebook 9, pp. 54–56

We have supplied the title in parentheses—Kroeber calls this text only "True Incident." The text is rich in the vocabulary of traditional life. It also tells the story of a somewhat amusing and even bizarre incident that was associated with the birth of the young man in question. Kroeber documented this narrative around 1900 and the incident in question happened roughly twenty-four years earlier, so the events must be from around 1875. This date seems a little questionable, as 1875 marked the very end of buffalo hunting on the southern plains. The 1903 Oklahoma census rolls for the Arapaho list a Young Bull who was born in 1859, which seems like a more reasonable date. See Fowler 2010: 152, 234, 236–37, 256, and 272, for references to Young Bull.

Upon hearing the lines in the narrative about the "choice" meats, William C'Hair recalled a very old hunting song that he heard when he was a young boy, sung by a man on his deathbed. The song went:

> Honóon-o3íiní3ee-t,
> It has very old/raggedy/frayed horns,
> ne-yenéíh'owóót
> the buffalo I am chasing.
> Nónii nookéí nónii nookéí.
> The back fat is my choice, the back fat is my choice.

The passage in the narrative below seems to recall a similar old hunting song. Parfleches are the bags normally used to store dried meat. But, as the story suggests, the Arapahos were almost overwhelmed with the amount of meat that they got and had nowhere to store it—and then were overwhelmed by the amount of maggots! Of course, in Oklahoma in 1899, the story would likely have been heard very ruefully by the often impoverished and hungry Arapahos. C'Hair remarked on hearing the story that he was always told that "we never took more than we needed" and that "going overboard always involves a consequence." So for him, at least, the story could be read as critical of Arapaho behavior at the time.

[Hee]toh-niisooneeto-' hooxeihii-niicíe tih-'óotee-' hiitéén.

At the forks of the North Canadian River, ['Wolf River'], a camp was set up.

Hii3éínoon noo'oeeníihi' tih'ini woo3ee-t.

There were many buffalo all around the area.

Heeyow-úúsi' nii'-o3ii'oohuutooni-'i,[1] nééyou heneenei3óú-'u no'ookéí-t.

Every day when people went out hunting, when evening came [each person] would come home with meat.

Bíi-biikoo woxuhóóx-ebii nih'ii-noo-no'etóuuhu-3i'.

As night fell the horses would all be arriving back in camp neighing and snorting.

Honóh'oehih'-o' hinenítee-no' conoo-cowookóé-ni3i, "wohóúwu!"[2] nih-'íí-3i'.

Boys and people, when they passed by with meat, would say, "Look at me!"

"Hítee nookéí,

"The heart is my choice,

"nónii nookéí,

"the back fat is my choice,

"noo-nóhk-koo-ko'éítouuhu" (nih-'íí-3i' honóh'oehíh'-o').

"come back with it all, yelling in a circle," [the boys would say].

'óh neeyou noh'ouutowoot heneen-eisiiní-'i.

And at that time there was inviting of people back and forth every day to eat.

Bíi-biikoo, heeyow-úúsi' hísei-no' hiicén-o nih'íí-béi3-oo3i'.[3]
When night fell, every day the women were scraping the meat off the hides.

Hoo3óó'o' nih'ii-kooneníii-3i'.
Others were tanning the hides.

Noh húúkoot nééyou se'ésoonoot.
And in addition at that time the meat was being sliced thin and flat.

Ho'úwoono3-o, ce'éiino3-o, hou-wó, hono'ut behííhi' nih'ii-tonóuhi-ni'.[4]
Parfleches, bags, blankets, everything available was being used to store the meat.

Tótoos séénook-uu, ceecenó'oo.[5]
Even rawhide ropes, they were just everywhere.

Nih'ii-bee-be'esoonouteyoonootiini-'.
People were hanging out red strips of meat to dry.

Betebíhoh'-o' kónowu-noo-noh'eenee-3i',[6] cee-cebei'í-3i'.
At the same time the old women were removing the marrow to make lard and making pemmican.

Tih-bii3oot,[7] núhu' nih-'ííhi-'.
"When there was plenty" is what this time/place was called.

Hihcebe' hix-óno tih-'oseikuuhu-'u, noh ciiyowoo-no, hi'íísoo-no' cee-cé3ei'oo-'.
Since the bones were thrown away nearby, along with food scraps, and maggots were showing up in every direction.

Kookuyón nih'íí-behinouhú-3i'[8] biito'owú-ú', 3o3óóxoyóowu-u'.[9]
They were just crawling all over the ground, even between the tipis.

"Hóeii, nexobeebéé-3i'.[10]
"Well, they are taking down their tipis.

"Hi'íísoo-no' wónoo3ee-3i'.

"There are too many worms.

"Noo-noxúhu-'! Wóów niih'éísee-no', híhcebe' hiit hí'iisoo-no'," hee3oooxúnee-t beh'eihehi'.

"Hurry up! Now we are splitting up and leaving, there are maggots near here," the old man who was the camp crier announced.

Ciitééx[11] hí'iisoo-no', né'=nih-'ii-'no'o'eso'on-óó3i'.

Because no one paid attention to the rules, the maggots drove them out of the camp.

Hí'iisóó-no' tih-no'o'eso'on-oo3i' ceitéé hoowúniihííhi', heneecééhe' ne'=nih-'íí'-cenísi-'.

When the maggots drove them out of camp over this direction downstream, that's when Young Bull was born.

Hi3íwoo,[12] niisoo' yéiniini' cécin-ii, nee'ee3éí'ookee-[t].

Let's see, twenty-four years, that's how old he is.

Notes

1. The verb here is AI.SELFB *ho3ii'óóhu-* (or *ho3ii'óúhu-*), from which an II impersonal form *ho3ii'oohúútooni-* is derived. This is an archaic term for hunting, which also occurs in this volume in the story "The Beheaded Ones."

2. This form is unrecognized today. We use Kroeber's gloss.

3. The word may be garbled in the manuscript. *Kóú'unbéxo'ei-* AI.O means 'remove the scraps of meat from a hide'.

4. This word is more normally *tonouníni-'.*

5. *Céecenó'oo* 'everywhere, common as can be, in abundance'. Cf. *wo'úucéecenó'oo* 'that's too much!' (for example, as a response when someone puts too much food on a plate).

6. *Nóonóh'oenee-* AI 'remove the marrow from large bones, to make grease or lard'. This was done with a small birch or red willow stick.

7. Alonzo Moss identified this term as correctly glossed, but it is archaic and apparently no longer a productive verb, as he could not provide further analysis.

8. *Behínouhú-3i'* AI 'they are visible everywhere'. The AI final here is *-inouhu-*, 'wear clothing, clothe', so more literally 'they are covering/clothing [the ground]'.

9. *3o3ooxoy-óowúú'* NI.LOC 'between, among the tipis', with *-oowúú'* NI.LOC 'lodge' being the final element. The word is apparently garbled in the manuscript, which gives *3ohoo3oxooy-oowuu'.*

10. *Nóh'-obeebee-* means 'to lift up a tipi and carry it away' The final element *obeebee-* is the same in this verb, but the initial *nex-* is not clear, unless it is *ne'-* as in *ne'-isee-t* '[the sun] goes down'.

11. *Ciitééx* means literally 'without orders'. Often it means that something is done spontaneously or voluntarily, without orders and planning, but here it means that an absence of orders and planning led to the situation with the maggots.

12. This is modern *3íwoo*. Kroeber actually transcribes *hisíwoo*.

Prayers and Ceremonial Speeches

Prayer: Blessing on This Food

Composed by Cleaver Warden, Oklahoma, August 1899

Collected by Alfred Kroeber

NAA, MS 2560a, Notebook 6, pp. 64–65

English version published in Kroeber [1902–1907] 1983: 314;

Arapaho version published in Kroeber 1916: 124–25

Normally Arapaho religious matters such as prayers are no longer published or documented outside the community, much like creation stories. However, the prayers and speeches here have already been published in English (and in one case in Arapaho). C'Hair and Moss, who are the co-chairs of the Northern Arapaho Language and Culture Commission and thus the individuals charged with reviewing research and publication decisions for the tribe, feel that their inclusion here is appropriate. The Arapaho versions can do full justice to the richness of this material as well as provide maximum accuracy. Note also that all of these items except the one by Spotted Bear's wife are not actual prayers that were used and then recorded but invented, sample prayers, meant to be representative of the genre. None of them are prayers from rituals such as the Sweat Ceremony or the Sun Dance Lodge.

The first selection here is a very eloquent prayer directed to the animals, thanking them for sharing their surplus population with humans so that they can eat. It concludes with an address to 'Man Above,' which is ambiguous. This term was used for the traditional Creator but could also be used for the Christian God (as in Michael Whitehawk's 1903 translation of the Gospel of Luke). Given the overall content of this prayer, here the Creator would seem to be the more likely addressee.

Note the parallel constructions in groups of threes and fours (illustrated here through the use of indentation). C'Hair notes that in traditional prayers people normally pray to the four types of animals: under the earth, on the earth, in the water, and in the air. Symbolically, this represents all of creation. Three of the four are mentioned here. Note also the way in which different nouns that are actually part of the same multiple-noun subject or multiple-noun object are placed symmetrically on each side of the verb in many lines (beginning line of section one and section four, ending lines of section three). Similarly, in the opening line of section two the modifier for 'animals' is placed after the verb, while the noun itself is placed before the verb. While the same syntax can be employed in everyday spoken Arapaho, it is much less common there: the balanced placement of components of the noun phrase on both sides of the verb is clearly an aspect of Arapaho high style and might vaguely remind some readers of the way in which classical Latin poetry often works. Note also that in sections two and three all the nouns and verbs are singular, but they could be translated as plurals: the intended reference is all animals below the earth, all the animals on the surface of the earth, and so forth.

1. Address to Extrahuman Intercessors

Hee heisonóón-in neniiton-éino', noh hebesiibéíh'-in.
Greetings, our Father, he who hears us, and our Grandfathers.

Hee3éí'i-noh'oeséíhiit, noh nohku-nihiit-owoo;
I say this in conjunction with all the heavenly lights;

    hiisi' nííhooyoo-',
    the yellow day,

    heséisen hii3eti-',
    the good wind,

    neeyeici' hii3eti-',
    the good timber,

    biito'owu' húu3eti-ni'.
    the good earth.

2. Address to Animals

Cese'éíhii heetih-ceh'e3tii-n hi3óówo'owú-u'!
The animal below the earth, I pray that you hear my words![1]

No'kúuto'owú-u' cese'éíhii,
The animal on the surface of the earth,

nec-i' cese'eihíí-ho',
and animals of the water,

cih-beh-ceh'e3tii-'!

listen, all of you, to my prayer!

3. Explanation to Animals

He-ciiyowoon-ínoo, heet-woní-biini-',

Your surplus is going to be eaten,

> heetih-'i3éíhi-[t],
> so that the people will prosper,[2]

> heetih-cih-kóutee-' hoowu3óów hiine'etíit,
> so that the breath of life will endure for a long time,

> heetih-'owoh'óu'oo-'[3] hinenteeníit:
> so that the tribe will be numerous:

>> tei'yoonéhe' heeneicxooyéih-t,
>> the child, whatever his age,

>> hiséíhihi' noh honóh'oehihi',
>> the little girl, and the little boy,

>> noh hinén heeneicxooyéih-t, hísei,
>> and man, whatever his age, and the woman,

>> beh'éihehi' heeneicxooyéihi-n, betebí.
>> you old man, whatever your age, and the old woman.

Heetnii-ni'oxon-éi'eenóu'u[4] bií3iwo, heenei'kóóhu-3i hiisíis.

[We pray that] these foods will keep us healthy as long as the sun follows its path in the sky.

4. Closing Request to Intercessors

Héé3-o', "Neixóó cih-ceh'é3tii, nebésiwoo," ne-nihii3óó.

I say to him, "My father, listen, and my grandfather," to what I am asking.

Kokoh'ú3ecoo,
[We ask for good] thoughts,

betée,
[good] heart,

bixoo3etíit,
love,

honowuune'etíit.
and a joyful life.

Heetnii-nii3iixoneeb-é3en.
I am now going to share this feast with you, [Man Above].

Notes

1. The verb has a 2S suffix, but the reference is really to all animals of the category. A looser translation more reflective of the implications of this phrase would be 'You animals below the earth'. The same goes for the next line as well.

2. Literally 'so that s/he [a person] will be good'. Again a singular person marking is used, but the implication is that the single person referenced is representative of the entire community, as in note 1 above.

3. *Howoh'-ou'oo-* II 'to be very large in size' (cf. *ciino'on-ei'oo-* 'to be fairly large in size').

4. TA *ni'óxon-* 'to make feel good'. Here, the 1P.EXCL direction-of-action theme *-éi'ee-* occurs, but it is then followed by the element *-noo* (> II.0PL *nóu'u*), which derives II verbs. Use of direct-of-action theme prior to an II derivational suffix is completely anomalous in Arapaho. What we read as an *i* may be a *c*, however, and if Kroeber left the tilde off the *c* then the phrase could be *ni'oxone3eenou'u. Ni'oxone3ei-* is an AI.O verb derived from *ni'oxon-*, meaning 'to make well, keep in good health', and the resultant II verb would be *ni'oxone3einoo-* 'it makes people be in good health'.

Speech of Man's Father at Marriage

Composed by Cleaver Warden, Oklahoma, August 1899

Collected by Alfred Kroeber

NAA, MS 2560a, Notebook 9, pp. 29–32

English version published in Kroeber [1902–1907] 1983: 315–16

This is a model speech, composed by Cleaver Warden, and not documentation of an actual speech. The same is true for all the prayers and speeches included in this volume other than the one to the model of the Sacred Pipe.

Marriage in traditional Arapaho society could be by elopement, but a public exchange of gifts between families was the preferred procedure. That is what is represented here (see Hilger 1952: 193–216).

Cowell has chosen to do a somewhat freer translation of this speech than in the other texts in this volume. The original style is notable in part for the many uses of 'where' (*héétoh-, niítoh-*) in place of 'when'. This is a not uncommon Arapaho stylistic device but is carried to a very high level of development here. These and related forms are underlined in the text. There is also a very strong emphasis on reciprocity. Two central roots that underline this point are *nohóuni-* 'marry into another family or group and become part of them' and *cee'i-* 'provide an [important, meaningful, permanent] gift, favor, service to, especially as a show of gratitude'. These forms are italicized in the text. Other central verbs emphasize more the shared nature of the new relationship, such as *woohonísee-* literally 'walk united' and of course *ni'ih-* 'treat well'.

Finally, the text is rich in forms expressing potential future events or obligations: it frequently uses the conjunct iterative (final *-i* and variants, indicating 'whenever') and conjunct subjunctive (final *-ehk, -ohk,* and variants, indicating 'when') verbal modes as well as the imperfective aspect with present and future imperatives, indicating general obligation. It also uses the proclitic *hi3=* 'later' for potential future events. In a related vein the text quite often uses the particle *hookóh* 'because', which is the strongest possible appeal to causality in Arapaho, in contrast to other forms (*tih-* 'since' and *toh-* 'because'). These other forms do not carry an implication of appeal to moral necessity as *hookóh* does. Thus *hookóh* is also used for future causality, whereas the other prefixes are only used for past events that causally precede some other main event (for example, 'because I fell down, I got hurt'). Therefore *hookóh* means more specifically 'because this is the way it must be'.

In summary, this is probably the richest text in this collection in terms of the treatment of futurity and potential (though see also the name-changing prayer) and in terms of the attempt to ground the response to future potentials in a framework of general moral duties and expectations.

1. Opening Address to the People

Hee né-neecee-no', neiteh'éího-ho', hísei-no'.
Greetings, my chiefs, my friends, and women.

Hoonónee benéesi-ni'í3ecoo-noo toh-u'-beh-cóó-nee, néih'e hoot-<u>niitoh</u>-'úniin[i-t],
I am so extremely happy that you have all come here for the sake of my son who is to be married today,

hóokoh heénoo nookónoonoo'oo-3i' hinén-no',
for we know that men always have great expectations,[1]

hiih'eh-ínoo <u>héetoh</u>-'úniini-ní3i, toh-nohk-etebinouhuuni-noo.
when their sons get married, [and I especially] since we are poor and pitiful.

Neniisoo yó'oh=heeyeih-'í3eti-n <u>héetoh</u>-woohonísee-t,
My son is making an even better marriage than I could have imagined,

hóokoh he'=<u>nee'éetoh</u>'óu3ecóó niihéyoo.
because I think that he has himself considered this decision very carefully.

'oh heesoo-' ciixootee-ní' <u>heetéíh</u>-t,
It will be a long way to where he will be living,

Tóóto'éé[2] hitesíi-no' beehiiniiní-3i' hinóno'ei.
but it is no matter because many Cheyennes have an Arapaho wife.[3]

2. Address to the Groom

Yo'oh=hú3et neih'e het-íniin.[4]

It is a wonderful choice that my son has made for his new wife and family.

3. Address to the Bride's Parents

Hohóu hee3-e3énee hiitoonehí-nee,

I say thank you to the parents of the daughter,

toh-ni'ih-ínee nohkuuhu' neih'é.

because you have treated both my son and me well.

Hi3óów-hínenteeníít <u>niitoh</u>-ni'eenéet-owoo <u>héetoh</u>-béhis-nih'oniitowootíini-'.

I lay my sympathies with truly good people, who all try their hardest to do their best.

Néih'e <u>heetoh</u>-bíí'iitoo-t hísei-n, *cenee'í3ecootobée-noo*.

I think that this is a great gift, the people with whom my son has found a wife for himself.

4. Extension of the Address to the Groom

Neí, tótoos hih-cii-ni'eteeb-eininéhk hetesih'e,

Son, even if your wife should say unpleasant things to you,

tótoos híh-to'ob-eininehk,

even if she should hit you,

noh wo'éi3 cii-ni'eteeb-eininehkóni',

or if others there say something unpleasant to you,

<u>héetoh</u>-*nohoúni*-n ciibéh-néi'oohoot-oo!

since you are married in with them, do not dwell on it!

Nih'oníitowoo neí!

Try your best, son!

Ciibeh-neetínoo'oo totéinee![5]
Don't be tired/discouraged no matter what!

Ciibeh-'eneesi3ecoo!
Don't think of yourself as a stranger there!

Hisiine'ítii!
Be gentle and kind!

Hi3í=*cee'ítii* heetoh-*nohoúni*-n!
Later you can provide benefits there where you are married in!

Hoonónee hií3eti-' héetoh-woohonísee-n.
The family you are joining is extremely good.

Hee3o3i'eeb-einoni neí, hesí3e,
Son, whatever your father-in-law asks you to do,

hehéihe, heyóo, het-ii-ni'óób-ei!
your mother-in-law, your brother-in-law, you must agree to it!

Ciibéh-'ii-no'o3i-nonouús[6] hétesih'e!
Do not travel about all over [without] your wife!

Kookuyon ciibeh-'iinís!
Don't just wander around for no reason!

Nei, nih'oníitowoo heetoh . . . , hóokoh heh=beetoh-*nohouhú*-n.
Son, try your hardest there where . . . , since you specifically wanted to marry in [to that family].

5. The Context of the Address/Invocation of Tradition

Héetee [he]t-iine'etiitóón-in nih-'í3eti' *nohouníit.*
In our old way of life it was good to marry in elsewhere.

Kookóós=nó-nosou-woonéíh, heneih-'iixonéíhi-noo bii3íbee;
I wish I were young again, I could be helpful in providing food;

'óh hookoh hiiyohóu-' he-ih-i'-iine'itíitoon-in.

but [that's not possible] because the things we lived on then are gone.

6. Extension of the Address to the Groom/Making a Living

Nihi'néé-ciinóuu hookóh nee'ees-iixoohoo3ih-eino' nih'óó3ou'u.

Plant lots of things to harvest, because that is what the white man has taught us.

Neí, hii-noo-notouukóóhu[7] hee3éíhi-noni.

Son, you must run to do whatever is demanded, wherever you are.

Hii-bebiis-benohwúun-in.

Water the livestock properly for [your relatives].

7. Extension of the Address to the Groom/How to Treat the Wife's Tribe

Hetesíh'e hiniihéí'i bixoox-ún, bíxoot-oo hinenteeníit.

Love your wife's family, love the Cheyenne people.

Cee'ihéiton-in hinenítee noo'úsee-3i heyeih'-é'.

Provide gifts to any person who arrives at your lodge.

Hií3eti' nei, heetoh-*nohoúni*-n.

It is good, son, where you are marrying in.

Hí3=heiteh'éi-no' heet[n]í-ites-éinoni.

Later new friends will come to you.

Hitesíi-no' hiites-éinoni "Wohéi!" het-íi3-oono'.

Whenever Cheyennes meet you, you must say to them, "Welcome!"

Ciibeh-'oto3iiton-in, hóokoh hítesii wonóóhonísee-n.

Don't be shy toward them, because now you are united with the Cheyennes.

8. Closing Address to the Groom

Ciibeh-'ii-nih'óuw-un hetesih'e.
Do not criticize your wife.

Kookóu'u het-ii-ni'íh-oo, het-owouunon-oo.
I implore you to treat her well and take pity on her.

Níí3eihi-3i' núhu'[8] neí, nii-ni'ihéihi-3i', noowóuunoneihi-3i'.
People who are good, my son, are treated well and pitied in their turn.

Ceecébi neí, ciibeh-neetinoo'oo!
Be dogged and persistent, son, do not become tired/discouraged!

Noh ní'i-noohoot-óó
Now, look well on

> heyeihe',
> your tent,
>
> het-iicooo,
> your pipe,
>
> he-bíi3iwo,[9]
> your food,
>
> heiteh'éi-no'.
> your friends.

Notes

1. Literally 'men treat [such occasions] with great seriousness', in the sense that they have much invested in the situation. The root *hookónoon-* is used to refer to 'serious', 'respect', and also to making ceremonial pledges.

2. *Tóóto'éé* 'nevertheless, despite this, it doesn't matter because . . .' Modern *tóóto'óé*.

3. Kroeber glosses this line in the manuscript 'Cheyennes all married into Arapaho tribe'. This does seem to be the broadly intended meaning, but the form used is *hiníini-* 'to have a wife', as opposed to *híisi-* 'to have a husband'. There is no gender-neutral word in Arapaho for 'to be married' other than the form *níiseekuu-* 'stand as two', which normally refers to the act of getting married rather than the state of being married.

4. This form is nonaffirmative, being still governed by *yó'oh=,* which requires nonaffirmative inflections.

5. *Totéinee* 'no matter what happens'.

6. *Nonóúúsee-* AI 'to travel, go on journeys'. This word is rare in modern Arapaho, but is the standard Gros Ventre word for travel (*nonóóúθaa-*).

7. The word *nouukóóhu-* means 'to roam or travel about', to go from lodge to lodge helping out.

8. The manuscript actually has what looks like *nohou,* so this may be a different, unrecognized word.

9. As in another speech, the manuscript actually has *he-bii3inoo* here.

Speech of Woman's Father
at Marriage

Composed by Cleaver Warden, Oklahoma, August 1899
Collected by Alfred Kroeber
NAA, MS 2560a, Notebook 9, pp. 27–28
English version published in Kroeber [1902–1907] 1983: 315

The words of the father's speech here are much briefer than those offered by the father of the groom. Note that the same formulaic opening is used here as in the other prayers and speeches—in particular, *núhu' nenéé'* and a dependent participle meaning 'this is what I am saying' or 'this is what I am thinking'. Similarly, the speech closes with a formal presentation of objects to the addressee, in formulaic groups. The same grammatical and lexical components present in the prayer for the groom occur here as well—future and potential forms, words emphasizing reciprocity, and *hóókoh* to indicate future causality and necessity arising out of moral obligation.

1. Words about the Daughter

Hee núhu' nenéé-' ne-ih-ni'eenee3oo heeneisoo-' toh-cih-'itóónehi-noo.
Greetings, this is the thing that I have been considering from all angles since my daughter was born.[1]

Héétee nih-'ooxuwu-noo notóóne hiis-éhk,
I planned ahead of time for my daughter, when she would be married,

Hi3í=heetih-'i3etí-ni' biito'ówu' hi-3í'okúu3oo; tih-'iisí3ecoo-noo.
So that later the land that she would occupy would be good; that is what I thought about.

Nee'ee'i-hí'-bebiisi-nótiitii-noo heet-í3eti-', nuhu' hí3=heet-3i'ookuu-' níiinon;
This is why I searched carefully for a good place, where the tipi would later stand;

440

notóóne heetih-'ónon-3eiísi-' ho'oowú-u'.

so that my daughter would live protected inside the house.

Hi3i=ne'=niiston-o', nih-'eihi-noo:

Later this is what I did for her, as I had said:

Toh-biisi(i)nówoo3-o' núhu' hi3=3ii'ookuu-'.

For this is the custom regarding where [one's home] will later stand.[2]

2. Words about the Son-in-Law

Hee hóókoh niiniisooní-3i' hinén-no' nii-cee'i-ni'i3ecóóton-oo3í' hi3e'exú-no.

Yes, [I do this] because men with children should make their sons-in-law happy with gifts for their lives.

Yó'oh=n-eeyeih-ciiwóxoeneb-e'[3] honóh'oe.

How good it is that this young man thinks favorably of me.

Yó'[oh]=heeyeih-cih-wóóhonis neyeih'-é'.

How good it is that he is uniting with my lodge.

3. Aside

Wóówuh nih-'iis-'eenéti3-o' notóóne,

Now I have talked to my daughter,

Hóokoh nenih'éi-3i'okú-no' hoo3óo'o' hiniito'éi-no notóóne, hih-'óówu-no'úsee-nino.

Because her other relatives live scattered about, they have not come to this ceremony.

4. Closing Gift/Marriage

Ne3é'ex, hiiyou héyeihe'.

My son-in-law, here is your lodge.

Hinee het-íicooo,

There is your pipe,

hiiyou hé-necib[4]

here is your water,

noh he-bii3íwo,[5] nohkúuhu' hetesíh'e.

and your food, together with your wife.

Neh-bii3ihi-bé.

Now let us eat.

Notes

1. Literally 'since I have had a daughter'.

2. Kroeber's gloss is used here, as the verb is not clear. *Biisiinowoo3-* means 'to learn to do s.t. from s.o. by watching and imitating'.

3. The *yó'oh=* requires nonaffirmative inflections. Here *ne-*(1S) + *hééyeih-* ('it is good that . . .') > *nééyeih-*.

4. The manuscript gives *he-neci3*.

5. The manuscript actually seems to have *he-bii3ino(o)*. While *he-bíí3ihiin-inoo* 'your (pl.) things to eat' would be grammatical, one would expect *he-bíí3iwo* 'your food' here.

Prayer of Spotted Bear's Wife
(to the Sacred Pipe)

Composed by Wife of Spotted Bear, translated by
Cleaver Warden, Oklahoma, August 15, 1899
Collected by Alfred Kroeber
NAA, MS 2560a, Notebook 9, pp. 16–19
English version published in Kroeber [1902–1907] 1983: 362–63

According to Kroeber, this was an actual prayer addressed to a model of the Sacred Pipe. Kroeber had models made of both the Sacred Pipe and the Sacred Wheel for collection purposes. The actual Sacred Pipe was owned/kept by Spotted Bear. Spotted Bear was also the "assistant director" of the Southern Arapaho Sun Dance in the early 1900s (Dorsey 1903: 24, 26) and thus one of the most important ceremonial men in the tribe.

His wife is the one praying (in the manuscript the prayer is entitled "Prayer of Spotted Bear's Wife"). The sale of the model to Kroeber is the specific occasion for the prayer.

Spotted Bear's wife clearly treats the model not just as an imitation but as another version of the original Sacred Pipe, with sacred powers. This is consistent with Arapaho beliefs to the present day. For example, children are not allowed to pretend to do a Sun Dance—the belief is that doing the motions and rites, no matter what the intention, is effectively a performance of the ceremony, with all the power and danger (if done wrongly) attendant upon that performance. The "Grandfather" of the prayer is the Pipe, and the "Father" is the Creator. Note that the prayer states that it is the will of the Creator that the Pipe go to Kroeber, not the personal decision of the one praying—a statement that could certainly be read from another perspective as an indication of hesitation and even doubt on the part of Spotted Bear and his wife about what they are doing or at least an attempt to avoid personal blame for the action. Note also that she includes the translator of the prayer (identified as Cleaver Warden in the manuscript) in the actual prayer, perhaps suggesting some doubt about his role in the process as well. C'Hair notes that today a reproduction of this sort for the purpose of sale or

443

public display where "there is no reverence" would be considered improper, and Moss agrees.

This prayer is full of key Arapaho moral terminology and images. Among the most important morphemes in this regard are *kout-/kou3-* indicating 'a long time'. Old age and long life are seen by the Arapahos as a sign of blessing from the Creator, and perseverance is a central virtue of Arapaho life. Also central is the notion of cleanliness (*hiiyoot-/hiiyoo3-*) in both a literal and a moral sense—people must both live cleanly and keep valued things clean. The one praying states that she and those she prays for are 'pitiful' (*hetebinouhuu-*) and therefore deserving of pity and mercy (*howouu-*). All of the words containing these roots have been marked with bold italics in the prayer. Other key terms include the contrast between remembering/thinking about (*kokóh'eeneb-*) people and the Creator and forgetting (*noníh'i-*).

Less immediately obvious but pervasive in the prayer is the morpheme *nohk-* meaning 'with' in the sense of accompaniment or aiding, along with the morpheme *niit-/nii3-* meaning 'with' in the sense of joint action. These morphemes are employed at several places in the poem, to link members of families, to link humans to the Creator, and to convey the idea of carrying blessings. They are in a sense the thread that weaves together the entire set of reciprocal relations that the prayer evokes (or the glue) and emphasize the fundamental principle that people do not pray for themselves in traditional Arapaho culture except to the extent that their own health and welfare can benefit others in the tribe. It is always the collective interest that is fundamentally at issue in prayers. The two morphemes are underlined where they occur in the prayer.

1. Opening Address to the Sacred Pipe

Hee, nenee-' net-***etebinouhuuniit*** hei-cii-noo3e3eet,
<u>nenii3</u>-***iiyoo3ih***-e3en.

Greetings, in my pitifulness, oh one whom I have never forsaken, I have kept you with me, pure and clean.

<u>Nenii3</u>-i'-eeneti3-e3en.

I have spoken with you regarding things.

Heeneisee-3i, he'=nihi'koohu-3i hiisiis, tih'ii-beetoh-ni'iine'etii-noo.

Wherever it goes, as long as the sun moves through the sky,[1] I have sought to live a good life.

Konoutootee-' hoowu3oow heetoh-tei'eekuu-' niiinon.
I [wish for] long breath of life where the tipi stands firm.

Koutonobetiit[2] ne'=nii3ee-<u>nohkuunisee</u>-noo tih'ii-niitowoon-in.
This is why I have roamed with you as you led me: since [I wished for]
a long and happy union.

Heetih-*'owouu3ecooh*-e3en, <u>nohkuuhu'</u> ne-tei'yooniiw-o',
I pray that I inspire you to merciful thoughts for me and my
children,

Hinen ne-<u>nii3</u>-iine'etiiw-ooo.
and for the man with whom I live.[3]

2. Parting with the Pipe

Hee hootni-i3eti-' hooton-onone-enitoo-n,[4] nebesiiwoo!
You will be in a good and safe place, my Grandfather!

Neixoo! Hii3eti-' heni'-ce3en-een.
Father! We part with you so that it will be good.

Heetih-cih-kokoh'eeneb-ei'een.
We pray that you keep us in your thoughts.

Heenei'i-nookei-'i *heetebinouhuuni-'*,
Each and every morning we will be pitiful [without you].

Hookoh he'=nee'ee3eeneb-eino' heisonoon-in.
[We do this] because our father has conveyed his wish to us.

3. Hope for Reunion

Nuhu' huuwoonihehe' cesisiihi',
From this time henceforth,

> *kou3iine'etiit*,
> [let there be] long life,

niiinon,
a tipi,

honowuune'etiit,
joyful living,

hii3eti-' betee,
a good heart,

honoot hei'-ooxuwutii-t heisonoon-in woohonixoot.
until the time that our Father has determined for our reunion.

Heetih-<u>nohku</u>-he'in-owoo, ne-tei'yooniiw-o', heenee3o'ouwu-noo,
I ask that my children and I, and all my relatives, will once again know

Hoxou'ei-bii3ihiit,
the pleasures of eating together,[5]

hoxou'ei-<u>niitokubetiit</u>,
the pleasures of sitting together,[6]

hitesetiit.
meeting up with each other.

4. Specific Requests to the Pipe

Heni'-hoo3itoohu-' hot-ooxuwuut noono'o3in, cii-niiheneihi-'.
We have told the rest of the tribe of your supremely powerful law,
which is from you, not us.[7]

Howouunon-ei'ee!
Have mercy on us!

Biito'owu' heenee3ixootonitii-'[8] heetih-'iiyoo3oo-',
Let the earth upon which we walk be pure and clean,

heetih-'ii-cee'eeto'o'obee-' hee3e'eixoo-ni'.
let the ground be smooth before us on our path.

Kookou'oo-'[9] heenei'-koh'uusi', hii3eti-' hiine'etiit heetih-'iteteihi-'.
Let things be easy during the days, so that we receive the good life.

Noo'oxooyoo-' heetih-ciixo'on-ei'eenoo'.[10]
Let pain and suffering be driven far from us.

5. Extended Request for the Benefit of the Interpreter

Nehe'eeno honoon-o3i'eeniini-t,[11]
This person who is working on behalf [of Kroeber],

heetoh-'i3eti-ni'[12] hiinixoot hiisi-i', nokohuut tece'-i'.
may his travels be good during the day and his sleep be good at night.[13]

Hi'-kokoh'eeneb-in nenii3o'on-ce'itesetiit.
I ask that you keep him in your thoughts so that he will enjoy a pleasant renewal of this acquaintance.[14]

6. Giving Thanks to the Deity

Hoot-<u>nohk</u>-ce3ei'oo-t heteneyooo nehe' nih'oo3oo.
Your body is departing with this white man.

Hohou! Yoh=n-ouu-heeyeis-bii'onou3ecoo![15]
Thank you! How wonderful that I happened to think of this idea![16]

Cii-nonihi'[17] heesi-<u>nii3in</u>-o', nebesiibehe' hit-ooxuwuut.
Let him not forget what he has, the commandment of my Grandfather.

Neisonoo yoh=n-ouu-cee'ih-e'
My Father, how wonderful that he provides me with

bii3iwo,
food,

bee3iyoo-no,
clothing,

hiwoxuuhoox heenee3oteheini-t.

horses of different colors.[18]

Hohou hee3-e3en!

Thanks I say to you!

7. Final Request to the Deity

Howouunon-i!

Have pity on me!

Ciibeh-nonih'ii3iton-ei'ee, toh-<u>nohk</u>-'etebinouhuuni-noo
ne-tei'yooniiw-o'.

Do not forget about us, because my children and I are poor.

Coon-ite3iine'itii-noo:[19] heni'-eeneti3-e3en.

I do not live in an acquisitive way: for this reason I am speaking to you
of these things.

Hohou! Hohou nebesiwoo noh neisonoo.

Thank you! Thank you, my Grandfather and my Father.

Hiisi-i' tece'-i' tei'-iine'etiit, nenee-' ne-nihii3oo-no.

Strong life day and night, these are the things I am asking for.[20]

Notes

1. This line could also be translated loosely as 'I have kept you company'. The sense is that the individual has attended to the Pipe, through both deeds (first line) and words (second line).

2. *Kóút-onób-etí-* = long-happy-RECIP.AI > AI Participle *kóútonóbetíit*.

3. I.e., her husband.

4. The manuscript has *hóóton-onon-iinitoo-n*.

5. Literally 'eating with a smile, smiling while eating'.

6. Literally 'sitting together while smiling, smiling and sitting together'.

7. Literally 'that we do not own'.

8. *Heenee3ísee-* AI 'wherever X walks' > *heenee3ixóóton-* TA 'wherever X walks up to [people]'. The addition of a further AI.T ending *-itii-* to the verb is anomalous, unless the RECIP ending *-eti-* was intended, in which case the verb would be *heenee3ixóóton-etí-'* 'wherever we (EXCL) walk up to each other'. This idea of meeting and reciprocity would actually fit quite well with the overall message of the prayer.

9. This is a less common word for 'easy', normally used in relation to life, existence, and so forth.

10. This verb includes the archaic inflection *-éi'eenoo',* 0S/1PL. In modern Arapaho an II passive verb would be used, terminating in *-éíhiinoo-'.* Despite the similarity of the two forms, Kroeber's manuscript text does not seem readable as the latter form.

11. This reduplicated form is glossed 'he who is a servant'. The reduplication indicates regular employment.

12. Although Kroeber gives *héétoh-* 'where' here, *heetíh-* 'we pray that, let it be that' seems much more likely.

13. Literally 'may traveling be good during the day and sleep at night'.

14. Literally 'meeting again in tranquillity'.

15. The reading here is uncertain. Our analysis is as follows: *yoh=nouu-heeyeisi-bii'on-ou3ecoo,* SUPERL/EXEMPLARY-1S.SUPERL (*no + houu*)-it is good that.PERF (*heeyei + iisi*)-fortuitously-think (AI). The proclitic *yoh=* requires nonaffirmative inflection of the following verb. Kroeber translates this as 'it is well. I think of you'.

16. I.e., to sell the Pipe. See the following sentences.

17. This form can be glossed with initial *cii-* NEG and AI 3S nonaffirmative *noníhi',* producing a hortative form 'let him not forget'. This is not a typical construction in modern Arapaho.

18. I.e., by selling the Pipe for a good price, these things are obtained. The willingness of the Creator to allow the selling of the Pipe allows for this newfound prosperity. The last line is literally 'a horse of whatever colors', but the sense is actually 'multiple horses, of different colors'.

19. *Coon-ite3-* = NEG-acquiring-. Cf. *hitét-* TI 'acquire s.t.', *hite3éi-* AI.O 'acquire things'.

20. Literally 'the things that I say'.

Prayer at a Young Man's Change of Name

Composed by Cleaver Warden
Collected by Alfred Kroeber
NAA, MS 2560a, Notebook 9, pp. 12–15
English version published in Kroeber [1902–1907] 1983: 313–14

In Arapaho culture individuals can change their name for a variety of reasons. Commonly, someone may be sickly and seek the name of a long-lived, healthy person or unsuccessful in life and seek a new start, to be provided by the name of a successful individual. Conspicuous achievement may also be the occasion for a new name. Either the individual himself/herself or parents or relatives can ask the current bearer of a name if the individual can have that name (in which case the bearer must take a new one) or else an elder can be asked to assign a new name to the individual. Names are considered to have power associated with them and to accumulate the power of conspicuous and successful bearers. This is then transferred to the new bearer of the name. Changes of names occur in circumstances ranging from a small private event to a major ceremony, typically as part of a larger social event, where the new name is announced to all present. The speech here is an example of this more formal and elaborate name-changing ceremony (see Hilger 1952: 58–67; Wiles 2011: 89–93, 170–73, for contemporary examples and photos).

Linguistically, this is perhaps the most carefully composed of all the speeches and prayers in this volume in terms of structure. It also has some of the most beautiful and complex polysynthetic expressions (see Cowell 2015 for further analysis of vocabulary and structure). C'Hair notes that the old men were "philosophers" when they prayed. The structure of ten sections is created by both specific themes of content and parallelisms of form. Note that this exact structure is unique to this prayer—name-changing prayers do not necessarily contain ten sections or the exact content of this prayer. They do, however, normally show divisions similar to the ones here. Both name-changing prayers and all prayers among the Arapahos tend to have a general structure that begins with an address to the higher powers, follows with prayers for the tribe as a whole, typically mentioning the different ages and genders, and then optionally concludes with a more specific request for one or more individuals.

In this prayer, section one opens with *nenee' nenihii3óó* = 'this is what I am saying'. Section two then addresses key Arapaho religious and mythological characters: the Seven Old Men, the Seven Old Women,[1] Found-in-the-Grass (see the story in this volume), and the myths (the various key heroes in all the myths). Section three opens with the closely parallel *ci'-céése' nenéé' nenihii3óo* = 'this is another thing that I am saying' and addresses the Seven Sweat Lodges (the seven age-grade societies of the tribe). It also establishes a strong duality between Rivers/Water and Land/Earth.

Section four opens with a series of parallel direct imperatives: *cih-tokoohob-eéi'ee! cih-'owóuunon-éi'ee! cih-'owóuunon-ín!* = 'look down upon/watch over us! Have mercy on us! Have mercy on him!' and is addressed to the Sun/Creator, evoking the daytime. Section five contains another direct imperative, *cih-ceh'é3itii-'!* = 'listen!' but evokes the night rather than the day, in the form of the animals of the night the moon, and a star (the Morning Star). Section six again contains direct imperatives, parallel to sections four and five: *cih-behisi-ceh'é3itii-'!* = 'you all listen!' The animals of all three realms (below ground, above ground, in the water) are the addressees. Section seven contains yet another set of direct imperatives: *cih-beh-ceh'é3itii-'!* = 'you all listen!', but now directed to those in the camp. In parallel with the various realms of the animal world, now the various realms of the tribal world are addressed, including all genders and ages.

Only in section eight is the actual name-changing explicitly mentioned and the new name of the young man given. Again the section opens with a direct imperative: *cih-tokoohób-e'!* = 'look down upon/watch over him!' Note that this command is a repetition of the one used in section four. There, however, it was for the Creator to watch over the tribe; now it is for the tribe to watch over the young man. The section continues with more specific directions to the tribe as a whole regarding the man, including five extremely parallel phrases that all use the iterative inflection ('whenever'). Section nine, with another direct imperative but also containing *wóówuh* 'now' (modern *woow*) does the actual work of giving the new name: *wóówuh híten-oo* = 'now take it!' the young man is told. In section ten the rest of the tribe is told, again with very close parallelism, *wóówuh neniitóbee-nee* = 'now you (PL) have heard it'. The section then moves back to the young man, again via parallelism, with *wóówúh hee'inónee-n* = 'now you (S) are known'.

The indentations below are intended to help illustrate the parallelisms of grammar and vocabulary that occur at different points in the prayer.

1. Opening Call for Attention

Nenéé-' ne-nihii3óó:
This is what I have to say:

henééceiniiciihéh-e' beescéneeco'on-e' tih-no'kóóhuutíí-noo wo'óteeet.
From the Cimarron ['buffalo bull'] River in Turkey Hills I brought back black paint in victory.[2]

Tei'yoonóh'-o' hootn-í'-iii'óó-3i'.
May the children prosper through it.[3]

2. Request to Intercessors

Niisootox beh'éihoho',
Seven old men,

niisootox betebíhoho',
seven old women,

Bii'oxuyóó,
Found-in-the-Grass,

noh heetéetoo-no,
and all the myths,

heetíh-'i3eti-ni' hinenteeníi[t] heeneicxóóyeihiinoo-'.
may they be for the good of the people of all ages.

3. Extended Request

Ci'=céése' nenéé-' né-nihii3oo;
There is something else I mention;

nii-cii-necííni-' tih-niisootoxéí-'i ciibéet-ino,
there were seven sweat lodges at Sand Creek,[4]

híisi' nonohku-nihiit-ówoo,
and I say this in conjunction with the day,

niicííhoh-o nonohkú-nihiit-ówoo,
I say this in conjunction with rivers,

noh biito'ówu',
and with the earth,

> heetíh-ciixo'onéihiinoo-' konoo'onó3oobe-'⁵ nó3oon
> may sickness stay far away rather than come here.

4. Specific Request to Intercessor-Sun

Nebésiiwoo! Hiisíis, niihoon-cebísee-n,
Grandfather! Sun, you who walk yellow,

cih-tokoohob-éi'ee!
look down upon us!

cih-'ówouunon-éi'ee!
have mercy on us!

cih-'ówouunon-ín,
have mercy on him,

> néhe' honóh'oe beeyoo yenii3é'eekuu-t,
> this young man standing facing in that direction [east],

> béébeet heetíh-nee'ee-nihi'ínee-cebixoot-o' híine'etíit.
> we ask simply that he be helped to walk firmly and steadily in his life.

5. Specific Request to Intercessor-Night

Hihcébe' nii3éi'-noh'eeséíhi-n biikóó,
You moon and all those shining up there above in the night,

cese'éíhii téce' néniihenéíhii niihíí3-een,
the animal who is the owner of night, we say to you,[6]

Nookóox noh neixóó! Cih-ceh'é3tii-'!
Morning Star and Father! Listen!

Heeyoocéí'oo-' hoowu3óów,
Long breath,

beneesoo-' hiine'etíit,
great life,

heni'-hihc-owooyeiti3-eenee.
we lift up our prayer to you for these things.

Nehe' honóh'oe nohkúuhu' hiniito'éi-no heenee3o'óuni-t,
This young man with all his relatives,

heetíh-nohkú-ni'-cebísee-t heet-í3eti-';
may he walk well and in a good place;

bii3íb ciiyóow,
with plentiful food,

bee3iyóó,
with [plentiful] possessions,

hiwoxuhóóx héet-cee-ce'íxooneihi-[t],
where his horse(s) will be of many colors,[7]

nii'éíhii heet-ní'etouuhu-t,
where the bird sings sweetly,

híisi' konoutóótee-',
where the day is long,

heet-í3eti-' heséisen.
where the wind is good.

6. Specific Address to Animals

Cese'éíhii no'kúúto'owú-u',
The animal on the surface of the earth,

hee3éí'-noh'oowuuniihí-n,
all of you who move on the ground,

cese'éíhii hi3oowo'owú-u',
the animal below the earth,

néc-i' heenitóot-ow,
you animal who occupies the water,

    cih-ceh'é3itii!
    listen to me!

    Cih-behisi-ceh'é3itii-'!
    You all listen to me!

        Nehe' 3ii'ookúu-t neníiitowuun-éinee hií3eti-ni' niisih'íit.
        The one who is standing here is asking you for a good name.

7. Address to People in the Camp

Téi'yoonóh'-o' heeneicxooyéíhi-n,
Children, of whatever age you are,

honóh'oe, híseihiitéí'yoo heeneicxooyéíhi-n,
young men and young women of whatever age you are,

betebí, beh'eihehi' heeneicxooyéíhi-n,
old women, old men of whatever age you are,

    cih-béh-ceh'é3itii-'!
    you all listen to me!

    noohób-e' nehe' honóh'oe!
    look at this young man!

ni'éenéb-e'!
think well of him!

hówouunón-e'!
take pity on him!

> benéetoh-beh'eihehííni-t.
> he desires to be an old man.

8. Address to the Lodges/Giving the Name

Beniiinén-no' neeneistóó-nee, nehe' honóh'e cih-tokoohób-e'!
Men of whatever age-grade society you are, look down upon this young man!

Hiisíis Téi'yoonehe' heet-ii3-óónee, hoo3i'ééw-oonei'i,
Call him Sun Child whenever you give him commands,

> heetí3-oonei'i,
> whenever you invite him to your place,

> hooxów-oonei'i,
> whenever you feed him,

> nenei'oohów-oonei'i,
> whenever you look at him,

> hiitéx-oonei'i.
> whenever you meet him.

9. Address to the Man with the New Name

Hiisiis Tei'yoonéhe' hooton-ní'ii3ée-n, hot-cee'ítii-n heito'éiteen.
Sun Child you will be called, so you will provide better for your kin.

Néé'eesíh'i-n: wóówuh híten-oo!
Thus you are named: now take this name!

Honoosootii-co'óteyoo' nenee3óotee-' híit,
Rainy Mountain remains behind here,

Hiisiis Tei'yoonéhe' neec-éh-nohku-cé3ei'oo he-niisih'íit.
Sun Child, set off on your way forward with your name.

10. Closing Address

Neixoo, Hihcébe' Nih'óó3oo sei'i3íixohu-[n]![8]
My Father Christ God above us,

Neixoo hóuu!
My Father Creator!

Cee'níibee-t nii'éíhii!
Thunderbird!

Wóówuh neniitóbee-nee.
Now you have heard his name.

Wohéi, wóówuh hee'inónee-n, béenii.
Wohei, now you are known to all, friend.

Notes

1. The Seven Old Men were also called the Water-Sprinkling Old Men and were the highest Arapaho age-grade society (see Kroeber [1902–1907] 1983: 207–209). The Seven Old Women were the members of the women's quillwork society (see Anderson 2013). See also Fowler 2010: 91–94 for the relationships and parallels between these two groups.

2. Names were often given by respected warriors. This line seems to be a reference to a war deed, which would add authority and power to the new name about to be conferred. The modern form for 'black paint' is *wo'(o)toeet*.

3. The reading of the final verb is ambiguous. It could be either *hootn-i'-iii'oo-3i'* = FUT-INSTR-grow(AI)-3P 'they will grow with the aid of it' or *hoot-ni'iii'oo-3i'* = FUT-grow well (AI)-3P, 'they will grow well'.

4. Seven is a sacred number for the Arapahos. There were also seven different age-grade societies, each of which was known as a 'lodge'. Note that the modern word for Sand Creek is *noobéí-niicíí* 'sand river'.

5. This word, glossed 'sickness', is not recognized by Alonzo Moss or William C'Hair and is a best-guess transcription based on Kroeber's manuscript.

6. I.e., all animals of the night; singular forms are often used in prayers as collective plurals (see the prayer "Blessing on This Food" in this volume).

7. I.e., he will have many different horses.

8. This word explicitly refers to the Crucifixion (literally 'attached flat to an object') and is thus a reference to the Christian God.

Song Texts

The following songs represent a number of different genres of Arapaho music, ranging from intensely religious songs that should be considered forms of prayer to humorous "love songs" that might be performed during free intervals at social dances when the dancers were taking a break. As far as we know, all song texts available from before 1950 have been included here, with the exception of songs recorded by Frances Densmore, which we have not had the opportunity to listen to. The songs here represent a relatively narrow range of documented Arapaho song genres. They should not be taken as representative even of the genres from which they come, because a great deal of variety could occur within a single genre such as Sun Dance Songs. The one exception is the Ghost Dance Songs, which represent an extremely rich selection as well as virtually the entire documentation of this genre. For further information on Arapaho music generally, see Densmore 1936; Nettl 1951; Mooney [1896] 1973; and Lah 1980. These texts cover the technical aspects of rhythm, melody, and structure that we do not discuss here.

With regard to the language of the texts, which is of course the focus here, the most important point to recognize is that Arapaho song texts often rely very little on what we might call "poetic" or "inventive" language for their effects. Compared to the language used in narratives, they normally lack unusual and highly descriptive words and do not often seek to evoke especially unusual or interesting scenes or create startling metaphoric juxtapositions (but see the second and third Hand-Game Songs below as well as a number of the Ghost Dance Songs). They rarely if ever stand as self-contained pieces of linguistic artistry as modernist poetry in the Euro-American tradition does. They are quite limited in length (though the words are repeated multiple times, often intermingled with long sections of non-meaningful "vocable" elements such as *hii-yoo-hou, hee-yoo-hou,* and so forth, which are not transcribed here but are included in Mooney's original transcriptions, though not in those of Kroeber or Gatschet). Instead they rely on a very different set of devices to achieve their power for the listener. In particular they tend to make use of certain key "loaded" words that evoke especially rich and complex associations and allusions. This allows the song to ground itself in the fuller world of Arapaho mythological, religious, or cosmological thought. The songs work most powerfully as brief evocations of a much richer complex of thoughts and emotions that are rarely if ever expressed directly in the songs themselves.

Moreover, the individual songs typically had specific interpretive traditions attached to them, provided by the maker of the song and then passed on orally. Without access to those individual details of meaning, it can be very hard to know exactly what a song is referring or alluding to. A very similar tradition was in place for Arapaho material culture items, as described by Alfred Kroeber ([1902–1907] 1983): while broadly similar decorative motifs were used on personal items, the exact meaning of the constellation of motifs on any given item could not be fully understood without actually talking to the maker of the item in detail—as Kroeber fortunately did. For these reasons, even modern fluent speakers of Arapaho likely can never have access to the full complexity of associations evoked by some of these songs. Many of the songs, however, do remain evocative or powerful for knowledgeable and fluent Arapaho listeners/readers who have access to the cultural complex they evoke. But these same songs can be very elusive for listeners/readers who lack this background, so we have tried to add modern commentary or report on field notes that accompanied the texts themselves. James Mooney's book on the Ghost Dance Songs [1896] 1973 does a good job of explaining that particular background in a fair amount of detail, however, so we simply retranscribe his texts into modern Arapaho orthography, with some purely linguistic commentary.

The word for 'song' in Arapaho is *niibóót*. When a particular type of song is referred to, however, the descriptive element comes first in the word then *–(ii)nóót* 'song' is added at the end.

Hand-Game Songs

The Hand Game (*koxóúhtiit* in Arapaho) is a social gambling game, widespread in both the nineteenth and twentieth centuries on the plains among many tribes and still widely played at present (see Wiles 2011: 216–19) but with roots in ceremonial contexts as well. It involves two teams: one team hides one or more game pieces in their hands, and the other team tries to guess the location of the pieces (which hand[s] they are hidden in). During each round of guessing, a singer with a hand drum sings Hand-Game Songs, with the hiders and guessers often moving their hands and bodies in rhythm. The name for such songs is *koxóúhtiinóót* 'hand-game song'. Note that even where the notes do not indicate repetition, the lyrics were likely all sung multiple times during a single performance of the song.

1

The first song here is from Albert Gatschet (MS 231, p. 274). He provides no information on who provided the song or assisted with documenting it.

> [Boo]h'óoobeee-noo,
> I am making thunder,
>
> [Ne]nééni-noo tih-'iséíni-noo.
> Since I am a woman.

Although Gatschet identifies this as a Hand-Game Song, he adds a note: "part of a spirit [Ghost Dance] song." The Hand Game was connected to the Ghost Dance for the Arapahos (see Mooney [1896] 1973: 1007–10; and Kroeber [1902–1907] 1983: 368–82). Elements of songs from the Ghost Dance were sometimes be used in Hand-Game Songs, as Gatschet's note suggests, and the Hand-Game Songs themselves often use imagery similar to that used in the Ghost Dances. The initial verb derives from the noun *boh'óoó* 'thunder'. It is not clear why the woman in particular would be associated with thunder in this song, but the song in general is almost certainly a reference to the Thunderbird. This could be direct or more likely indirect, in that some behavior of the woman is invoking thunder or the Thunderbird. The verb *boh'ooobee-* could mean 'acting so as to produce thunder' as well as 'making thunder'. There is a rich set of Arapaho beliefs surrounding thunder and lightning (which are the products of the Thunderbird) and how humans should behave during thunderstorms. For example, unless men and women (as well as girls and boys) sat on opposite sides of the tipi or house the Thunderbird would be jealous and strike. Women in particular also had to cover their hair with a cloth or clothing (an awareness of static electricity?). While we have no way of knowing if the song is specifically referring to one or more of these beliefs (is a woman courting during a thunderstorm?), the reader can see the richness of associations that only two lines can invoke.

2

The next song is also from Gatschet (MS 231, p. 298). It was provided by Alexander Yellowman:

> Neeneeceeni-noo,
> I act like a buffalo bull,
>
> kooxouhti-nóóni.
> whenever I am playing the Hand Game.
> [both lines repeated]

Gatschet's notes explain that the song compares the Hand-Game player using the guessing stick to a buffalo trying to hook or push an opponent with its horns. This is a good example of the way in which Arapaho songs achieved their effects for Arapaho listeners. The song itself simply refers very vaguely to connections with a buffalo, with no evocative specifics. But the full meaning of the song would have been passed on traditionally in the form of an interpretive tradition associated with the song (as expressed in Gatschet's note). The song, rather than linguistically re-creating that tradition, served to *evoke* the tradition through its performance. Thus this song, like most of the others in the Arapaho tradition, is in no way self-contained in terms of its meaning.

The song might also have had a comic meaning, as Hand Games are typically full of teasing, joking, and laughing. Exaggerated physical motions often surround the hiding of the playing pieces, the movement of the hands in rhythm to the songs and the hand drum, and the guessing motions.

3

The final Hand-Game Song is provided by Natalie Curtis ([1907] 1968: 201–202). Curtis explains that this song refers to the fact that the Indians turn their horses loose on the prairie to graze and then must go out looking for them to round them up. That situation is compared to the Hand Game, where the individual must look for game pieces hidden in the hands of the opposing team (201–202). The comparison of Hand-Game play to an aspect of everyday Arapaho experience on the prairies makes this song quite similar to the previous one in content. The song again offers the opportunity to incorporate the life situation being evoked into the movements of the Hand-Game players themselves. In their evocation of traditional life, the last two songs also function nostalgically in the context of reservation life.

Original:	*Retranscribed:*
natinachabena	Nootinooxobei-noo.
ni nananaechana	Nii-noononoo'eixoo-noo.
ni nananaechana	Nii-noononoo'eixoo-noo.
natinachabena	Nootinooxobei-noo.

Translation:

I am searching for horses.
I am circling my head all around [looking for them].
I am circling my head all around [looking for them].
I am searching for horses.

Frances Densmore documents (1936: song 44) what is apparently the same song, in English only:

I am out looking for my horse.
I am looking all around, I am looking all around.
Ha, He! (driving horse).

Lullabies

This lullaby is from Natalie Curtis ([1907] 1968: 201). Most Arapaho lullabies have the word *nókohukóóhu* 'go to sleep quickly, take a nap' in them. The use of *céi'teh'éí* is also very common: this is an affectionate vocative term used for younger siblings as well as babies, usually glossed as 'little round belly'. More information on lullabies can be found in Hilger 1952: 38–40. The text here closely matches modern lullabies. A lullaby is called *nókohuunóót* 'sleep song' in Arapaho. Curtis says that this song was sung by Maud Shawnee, Susie Sage, Jessie Sage, and Cappie Webster. Lullabies could be repeated as long as needed.

Original:	*Retranscribed:*
cheda-e	Cei'teh'ei,
nakahu-kahu	nokohuukoohu,
be-be	beebe

Translation:
Little round-bellied one,
go to sleep quickly/take a nap,
baby.

Age-Grade Society Songs

A rapaho religion traditionally consisted of a number of different organizations for men of different ages. Virtually all men belonged, advancing upward through the ranks of the societies as they matured. Details on these societies can be found in Mooney [1896] 1973; Kroeber [1902–1907] 1983; and Dorsey 1903. Each of the societies had its own set of ceremonial practices, dances, and songs. Many dozens of different songs were no doubt used in these ceremonies. The song here was provided by Natalie Curtis ([1907] 1968: 202) and is from the Tomahawk or Club Society (*hicé'eexóowu'*, hence *hicé'eexuunóót* 'tomahawk/club song'). The Tomahawk or Club Society was the third in order of the age-grade societies, after the Kit Fox Lodge and Star Lodge, and was thus for younger men.

Curtis reports that this song came to a member of the Tomahawk/Club Society in a vision and was sung by that individual. The song was a vision of two Arapaho warriors (White Horn and Whirlwind Passing By) who had been killed by the Pawnees (Curtis [1907] 1968: 202).

Original:	*Retranscribed:*
nananina nanakunithana	Neneeni-noo nonookuuni3ee-noo.
nananina neyachat-chawaat	Neneeni-noo neyooxet coowo'oo-t.
cha anitana	Cee'-enitoo-noo.

Translation:

I am White Horn.
I am Whirlwind Passing By.
I am present here again.

Love Songs

This is a loose category of songs that can be used for propositioning someone but also for turning down propositions, for teasing about love and desire, for warning against certain desires, and for other purposes. The songs are about love but not necessarily for the purpose of obtaining love or for seduction. They were not normally performed in private (though of course they could be) but rather were used publicly, often at social occasions such as dances and feasts. They are called *bii'ó'oonóót*, glossed in modern Arapaho as 'snagging song', also translatable as 'sweetheart song'. The word *bii'ó'oo* specifically means a sweetheart and not a spouse, and of course much of the teasing would revolve around sweethearts.

1

The first song here is from E. S. Curtis (1911: vol. 6, appendix). Note that Curtis was not a linguist: his transcriptions are the least accurate of any consulted for this volume.

Original:	*Retranscribed:*
hisse hiba bii3a	Hees he-ebeh-bii'e'ee3-ee.

Translation:
Your husband might be courting/snagging someone else.

The verb *bii'é'ee3-* is usually translated in Arapaho English as 'to snag' and refers to finding a sweetheart/lover. It can be used both for unmarried people and for married ones who are tired of a spouse and are looking for some variety. A classic context for the singing of this song would be when a brother-in-law or sister-in-law wanted to tease another sister-in-law in public.

2

The next two songs are both from Gatschet (MS 231, p. 24). He does not indicate who provided these two songs. The "D." referred to in the notes below is likely Dan Tucker, with whom Gatschet worked on several occasions and whose full name appears in his field notes. Since Tucker was reacting to the songs, he apparently did not provide them himself, although he may have been providing translations.

Noohow-únee hei3ébi.
Look, there is your brother-in-law.

Nénee'ee-hek cénoo-t.
There he is coming this way.

Woo'téénoubee-t.
He is wearing a black robe/blanket.

3

Néí3eboo, nééhebehe',
My brother-in-law! my younger sister,

Nééhebehe' bíxoox-un.
Love my younger sister.

[Ne]nééni-noo he-eti-tóúsih?
What are you going to do with me?

Bixóóx-unee.
Love [your wife] [instead].

Gatschet adds a note at the end of the second song: "D. [Dan Tucker] laughs at both songs."

Variant of 3

Later in his manuscript (MS 231, p. 253) Gatschet records the same songs, writing: "songs page 24 reproduced by O. Wilde." This is a reference to Oscar

Wilde, who evidently helped Gatschet retranscribe and retranslate the songs several years after his first visit to Oklahoma. The second song is slightly different the second time around:

Néí3ebi neehebehe', het-bixóó3-oo.
My brother-in-law! you must love my younger sister.

'oh nenééni-noo he-etí-tousih?
But what will you do with me?

Bixóóx-unee.
Love [your wife].

Both songs invoke the sexual tension in brother-in-law/sister-in-law relationships in Arapaho culture. While brothers and sisters traditionally were in a respect relationship that required minimal contact and no casual contact or joking, brothers-in-law and sisters-in-law were in the prototypical joking relationship, which not only allowed but expected joking and teasing. These were "institutional" relationships in that they involved cultural expectations. The teasing was often of an overtly sexual nature, and individuals in these relationships were encouraged to try to embarrass each other in public. Other members of the community looked on such teasing with approval, and it was an essential element of social events and the generation of communal good feelings. The particulars of the in-law relationship in part reflect the fact that it was not uncommon in the days of plural marriage for a brother to marry multiple sisters, especially if one of them lost her first husband. Thus a sister-in-law was in fact a potential sexual partner for a brother-in-law in the long run, if not necessarily at a given moment.

When Alonzo Moss heard songs 2 and 3, he recalled that his uncle used to tease about in-laws by asking someone *tééteehék* 'where is?' *hei3ébi-hóóhoe*? This last word combines *hei3ebi* 'your opposite-sex sibling-in-law' with *[h]ebihoohoe* 'toilet paper, thing for wiping the rear end', derived from *hébihoo* 'wipe your butt!' The joke is reinforced because the vocative form of *hei3ébi* is *nei3obóó,* with the final /oo/ echoing the scatological command. Although the songs above have no direct connection to this joke and the joke itself is specific to Moss's personal experience, his remark illustrates that the mere mention of the word *hei3ébi* for older Arapahos can evoke memories of hundreds of different occasions of in-law teasing and joking over the years, which inflect the hearing of this song for them.

One important but ambiguous detail in the first song is that the brother-in-law is wearing black. Cowell notes that the Arapahos use black as a symbol of victory, specifically after going to war. The man in the first song is wearing a black robe or blanket, which could be a way of saying that he would be quite the catch. In many tribes, however, Catholics were or are called "black robes." In Arapaho Catholics are called *heenínouhú3i'* 'they wear long robes', but Episcopals are known as *nonookúnouhú3i'* 'they wear white robes', suggesting a contrast with black robes. Moss and C'Hair would not speculate on this detail.

Songs such as these were often sung at breaks in larger social events, such as between rounds of dancing. Their exact use and meaning was flexible and dependent on the context, but they could be used for teasing an in-law playfully or for warnings to or about in-laws, intended more seriously but delivered through song to make the warning less personal and direct. The last song seems to have primarily this kind of playful warning/rebuke component.

War Songs

This song is from Natalie Curtis ([1907] 1968: 199). She calls it a Wolf Song or a Comanche Song and adds that advance scouts of war parties were called "wolves" because they prowled about camps at night. This song was thus sung by members of war parties (199).

According to William Powers (1990), 'wolf dance' was the general Arapaho name for the general Plains Indian 'war dance'. The Arapaho word for 'Comanche' is *cóó3o'* (archaically, *coox* in the singular), which also means 'enemy' more generally, so 'Comanche Song' could also be translated as 'Enemy Song'. The contemporary name for this type of song is *cóóxuunóót* 'Comanche/Enemy Song'. 'Wolf Song' would be *hooxéíhiinóót.*

This song was sung for Curtis by Chief Nookhoose'/Sage, an important figure in the Ghost Dance movement (Mooney [1896] 1973: 894). Curtis's translation actually provides much more of the contextual meaning than the more literal translation below. She translates:

> Look, O maid, behold me, I am going far away
> Upon the war-path roaming;
> And your words have caused the parting,
> Long shall be the time ere again you see me.

The original Arapaho given below is much more direct and less florid. Nevertheless, it does contain several words that increase its intensity. While *ceite'eini* simply means 'turn your head this way/look this way', *nonii* is a stronger word, used in Michael Whitehawk's translation of the Gospel of Luke for 'behold!' *Hii3e'* 'over there' is intensified by the use of *beebei'on* 'way off away over there'; and *hoonii* means 'eventually, finally, after a very long time'. Curtis's translation incorporates the context of the singing of the song and its social implications directly into the translation. We provide a literal translation.

Original:	*Retranscribed:*
nah'ni chita-ini	Nonii ceite'eini!
hitha babian niyihana	Hii3e' beebei'on nii-yihoo-noo.
hani hatinahawuni	Hoonii heet-noohow-un,
haka nihin	hookoh niihii-n.

Translation:

Behold, look here!
I am going way away over there.
After a long time you will see me,
because of [what] you have said.

Sun Dance Songs

The Sun Dance (*hoséihóowu'* 'offerings lodge'; *hoséihiinóót*, 'Sun Dance/ Offering Song') is the most complex of all Arapaho ceremonies, with a large variety of songs. Many of the songs are used for specific aspects of the ceremony, such as greeting the sunrise, closing, and so forth. In addition to the songs with very specific purposes, a number of other songs are sung more generally as the dancers are dancing, to provide encouragement. The song here—in two variants—is of the latter type. The verb *hówouu-non-* 'take pity on, have mercy on' is the central word of the song. It is the word most commonly used in prayers to express the same idea, so this song is really a quintessential prayer song. In his monograph on the Sun Dance, Dorsey (1903: 179) lists a number of Sun Dance Song texts, in English only. One of those is: "The sun will surely be merciful to us." This appears to be the same song as the one recorded below. Sun Dance Songs often have quite simple, single-sentence texts such as these, though there is also a great deal of variety.

1

This song is from E. S. Curtis (1911: vol. 6, appendix):

Original:	*Retranscribed:*
hisis hatawinoneinaa	Hiisiis heet[n]-owouunon-eino'.

Translation:
The Sun will take pity on us.

2

This song is from Natalie Curtis ([1907] 1968:

Original:	*Retranscribed:*
hedawunaneina	Heet[n]-owouunon-eino',
hishish nisana	hiisiis neisonoo

Translation:

He will take pity on us,
the Sun, my Father.

Ghost Dance Songs

S ongs from the Ghost Dance (*ko'éínohwóót* 'circle dance' in the north, *3ííkonohwóót* 'ghost dance' in the south) make up the vast majority of the songs included in this volume. Mooney [1896] 1973 provides a huge amount of information about the Ghost Dance in general and the Arapaho part in it (see also Fowler 1982 and Trenholm 1986, from which the information summarized below is taken). The Arapahos were in many ways central to the entire Ghost Dance movement. It movement began in Nevada, among the Paiutes and Shoshones. But the Northern Arapahos were crucial (especially due to their close contact with the Eastern Shoshones on the Wind River Reservation) in acting as intermediaries between the Great Basin to the west and the plains to the east, thus helping to spread the Ghost Dance much more widely on the northern plains.

The Northern Arapahos in turn spread the movement to the Southern Cheyennes and Arapahos, with the Southern Arapahos in particular being eager converts and practitioners. These two southern groups introduced the Ghost Dance widely in Oklahoma and among the tribes of the southern plains. Thus the Northern and Southern Arapahos are pivotal to any understanding of the Ghost Dance movement in the late nineteenth and early twentieth centuries.

Most of the Ghost Dance Songs presented below are from the work of Mooney. Because he provides a great deal of commentary along with the songs, we will not repeat that information. Before presenting Mooney's songs, however, we present songs from other sources, along with commentary, informed by a reading of Mooney.

The central aspect of the Ghost Dance was that the dancer fell into a trancelike state and ideally obtained visions of the spirit world or of a renewed earth, full of plenty and with white people gone (and vanished relatives reappearing). At the same time, the performance of the Ghost Dance was intended to bring about this new world as well or at least encourage the

476

Creator to provide it. Thus the songs were simultaneously a form of visioning and a form of prayer. The allusions in the songs are often to the general Ghost Dance doctrine, which was contained in summary form in letters dictated by the Paiute prophet Wovoka to Arapaho visitors. These letters are reprinted in Mooney [1896] 1973: 780–81, and some of the contents are reflected in the two Ghost-Dance–related texts at the conclusion of this section.

1

This song comes from Gatschet, MS 231, p. 252.

Níí-noo'eenih'óhu-noo bííto'owu-u' héénei'íse-'.
I fly around the land as far as it extends.

Hínee héé3i' nenííwoh'u-noo.
I carry along the end wing feather [as I fly].

The song refers to a person who presents himself as holding eagle wing feathers and using them to fly around like the eagle. This is typical of the visionary nature of many Ghost Dance Songs. Mooney records the same song (his song 17).

2

The following three songs come from Gatschet, MS 231, pp. 253–54, from Alexander Yellowman, March 19, 1893.

Hinee heisonóón-in,
There is our Father,

nii-béh-'ito'obéé-',
the ground is all damp,

Beetoooh-einóóni [twice],
whenever he makes me a dance,

hookoh heesi-biin-éínoo heisonóón-in [twice].
because that is what I have been given by our Father.

Although Gatschet offers no note on this song, the "Messiah Letter" from Wovoka that circulated among the Southern Arapahos specifically mentions that the Creator will send a great deal of rain, especially in the fall of 1891 (Mooney [1896] 1973: 781). The words of the preceding song may refer to that specific aspect of the Ghost Dance belief system. Alternately, there was a belief that a great fire would drive the whites back to the east and then would be extinguished by a twelve-day rain (Mooney [1896] 1973:786). 'Our Father' is a standard form used in Arapaho prayers for the Creator.

3

Neneeni-ni3 biis-hiixo'-owú'
He and I step into view upon the top [of the hill].

Neneeni-ni3 biis-hiixo'-owu'.
He and I step into view upon the top [of the hill].

Neniisóónehe', neniisóónehe',
My dear child, my dear child,

nee'ei'-nóóhootébeen-o'.
I see where he is at that spot.

nee'ei'-nóóhootébeen-o'.
I see how far he has gone.

This song is recorded by Mooney (his song 9), in a slightly different version—or else in a less well transcribed and translated version. He attributes it to Sitting Bull and explains it as a vision of the "messiah advancing at the head of all the spirit army" ([1896] 1973: 966). The 'dear child' may be a reference to a dead child, as the Ghost Dance was closely associated with the return of dead relations. The verb in the first line is an unusual and quite specific word: *bis-* 'appear, come into view'; *hiixó'-* TI 'step on/onto the top/summit of a hill, mountain' and the final inflection indicating 'we'. The idea of 'dear' is expressed by the diminutive *niisoon-éhe'* 'my little child'. The following TA verb *nóóhootébeen-* expresses most literally 'to see a specific place/thing/act associated with a person'. Thus the verb puts the focus on the specific place in relation to the person rather than on the person—as does the first line of the song.

Two other potential Arapaho ideas evoked by the song are the image of the four stages of life as four 'hills' or 'ridges' (see Anderson 2001), and the idea that the spirit world is a high hill to the west (Mooney [1896] 1973: 983).

4

Hinee heisonóón-in,
There is our Father,

cénih-biin-einóóni beexotíí-w,
whenever he gives the big wheel to me,

hííyou.
here it is.

Hííyou niih'kuutee-' bééxotíí.
Here is how the big wheel is rolled.

Gatschet notes that the word *bééxotíí* 'big wheel' can refer to a wagon as well as a wheel. The same word is also used to refer to a gambling wheel, which is rolled and then thrown at with a pair of sticks or shot at with an arrow (Mooney [1896] 1973: 994–95). Thus this song could involve a vision of a wagon loaded with provisions. Such visions of plenitude were common in Ghost Dance Songs. Another (recorded by Willard Rhodes in the 1950s) talks of so much meat piled around the campfire that a person cannot even walk through the area. Alternately, it could evoke gambling and games (as commonly occurs in the songs recorded by Mooney: [1896] 1973: 962, 964, 994–95, 1002, 1005–10) and more specifically good luck and winning at gambling, as a metaphor for the plenitude expected to arrive at the time of the renewal of the world. See the text "The White Crow," which begins with a depiction of the same gambling game and then leads to the discovery and unleashing of the buffalo in ancient times. Visions of the return of the buffalo were a central aspect of the Ghost Dance, so it is quite possible that this song is evoking the first mythical unleashing and flourishing of the buffalo through the allusion to the game wheel.

5

Gatschet (MS 231, p. 271) provides no information on who assisted him with the following song.

Nebesííbehe' nóóxou3-einoo [3 times].
My grandfather feathers arrows for me.

Nebesííbehe' tih'ii-yih'oowóó-no' [2 times].
My grandfather, since we go hunting for buffalo.

Once again, this song seems to invoke visions of the past plenitude of the buffalo. The verb *yih'óowóó-* AI is used specifically for group hunts conducted as chases, as opposed to the much more general verb *hiinóó'ei-* AI 'to hunt'. It refers prototypically to buffalo hunts by organized groups, pursuing whole herds.

To illustrate another possible meaning of the song (though purely speculative), one of the most famous of all Arapaho myths is the story of Tangled Hair and Found-in-the-Grass (see the versions in this volume). A key scene in that story involves a father making magical arrows for his two sons. The sons then use the arrows to shoot into the air and revive their dead mother, who has been placed in a sweat lodge. That myth is thus in part fundamentally about renewal and magical revitalization of the dead—much like the general goals of the Ghost Dance. Of course in this song it is a grandfather rather than a father making the arrows, and the reference is to hunting rather than to magical cures—we do not want to argue that the song refers specifically to the myth. But the evocation of the making of arrows in the context of the Ghost Dance movement and its focus on renewal almost inevitably resonates with other Arapaho mythological elements of a similar nature and enriches the power of the imagery in the song. Special arrows are also part of the story of "The White Crow," where the buffalo first come to flourish on the earth, and play a key part in Paul Moss's story of "The Forks" (Moss 2005), where an old man brings relief from famine to the tribe in part through the use of special powerful arrows.

As a final note, we could add that 'grandfather' can refer to a biological grandfather but also to a ceremonial grandfather (who aids a young man in the Sun Dance, for example). Again the making of arrows by the grandfather carries potential resonances of ceremonialism and ceremonial power.

6

Gatschet (NS 231, p. 274) classifies the following as a Ghost Dance or a war dance:

Nenééni-noo houu,
I am the Crow,

toh-no'ú-ce'eetíí-noo,
who arrives victorious [from the warpath],

neniiwoho'un-owoo niiwohéé-no.
I am carrying flags.

The word *hóuu* means both 'crow' and 'God/Creator' (and the crow is often interpreted in Ghost Dance Songs as a messenger to the Creator). In the second line the verb *ce'éétii-* means 'to be victorious in war' (cf. *ce'éétiinohwóót* 'victory dance'). The final line here likely refers to flags captured from enemy white cavalry units. The modern word *niiwohóe* can also refer to a 'signaling device', traditionally used by Indians even before the advent of cavalry flags.

7

The following song is also from Gatschet (MS 231, p. 275, March 21, 1893):

Hiiyou héé3-eino' heisonóón-in houu.
Here is what our Father the Crow says to us.

Yóó3on het-tou'usee-be nii3-éino' heisonóón-in.
Once you have done it five times you must stop, our Father says to us.

Gatschet notes: "They dance in a ring and while going through the whole ring they stop five times." In his notes is a circle with five dots evenly spaced on it and an arrow showing clockwise motion. Arapaho ceremonial acts are commonly done four times in a "pretend" fashion then "for real" on the fifth time. This song is recorded by Mooney (song 73). He reports that it was the closing song of the Ghost Dance.

8

Gatschet (MS 231, p. 276) records the following song:

Sénii'iheisee-nóó niihoonóówu-'.
I am going into the yellow river.

Nenéé-' be'énou-níícii niihoonóówu-'.
That is it, the turtle river with the yellow water.

This song was also recorded by Curtis. See the commentary on it below.

9

This song is from Gatschet's MS 231, p. 276:

Hoh'onookéi'i nonóónonóó'oo-noo [twice].
I am soaring around the rock(s).

Hííyohou-' níit-óówusee-noo [twice].
There is no place for me to walk down [to the ground].

This song likely evokes the vision of someone flying upward toward the spirit world (see Mooney [1896] 1973: 999). It also may evoke the idea of so much food and other resources that there is nowhere for the bird to land, a motif in other Ghost Dance Songs, as mentioned above.

10

The following songs were provided by Alexander Yellowman (MS 231, pp. 297–98):

Nónii neniisóónehe',
Look, my dear child,

heti-won-nóóhow-oo het-íícooo,
you must go and see your [sacred flat] pipe,

hee3-eínoo houu heisonóón-in.
our Father the Crow is saying to me.

The Crow is often directly linked to the Creator in the Ghost Dance or is the messenger of the Creator, as noted above. Gatschet also adds the following note, seemingly a quotation from a consultant: "In Wyoming and Montana they have the Sun(?) Dances, but the songs were made here." This seems to be a response to the directions in the song to go to see the Sacred Pipe, which is the most sacred religious possession of the Arapahos, held by the Northern Arapahos in Wyoming. The final comment in Gatschet's notes, which seems to come directly from his consultant, suggests a sense of rivalry between the Northern and Southern Arapahos, with the southerners here claiming priority in song creation, as opposed to the northerners having the Pipe.

11

Hóno'-u',
Up in the sky,

nii-xoxooyo'éti-' hóno'-u'. [repeated]
there are striped clouds in the sky.

Gatschet's notes say that the singer, who is identified as Alex[ander Yellowman], said the striped sky had no particular meaning to him (that is, the meaning was unknown or unclear to him). While that may be true, clouds are a common element of both songs and traditional narratives, with different cloud colors (yellow, white, black) often associated with thunderstorms and the Thunderbird, among other meanings. Moreover, the Messiah, according to the letter from Wovoka, was supposed to appear as a cloud (Mooney [1896] 1973: 780–82), so it is likely that this song represents a visionary looking at the clouds, waiting and searching for the appearance of the Messiah. Furthermore, the culture hero Young Bull (symbolically representing the buffalo) provided the paints worn in the Sun Dance by vomiting them across the sky in long streaks of color (Dorsey 1903: 158–59). Thus whether or not this song explicitly refers to these details, it is certainly rich in resonance with traditional Arapaho motifs.

12

The next song is from Natalie Curtis ([1907] 1968: 200). It is clearly the same song that Gatschet recorded in his MS 231 (p. 276). Curtis says that this song was sung by a group of Arapahos, and that Chief Sage (Nookhoose') explained the song—the same individual who provided the War Song above.

Curtis explains that the background of the song refers to the turtle diving under the water to bring up mud at the time of the creation of the earth. The turtle was thus an especially powerful being. More specifically, the yellow or turtle waters are the realm through which the spirit must pass in order to reach the spirit world. The song describes a ghost dancer/dreamer passing through the yellow turtle waters until he reaches the spirit world. More generally, this is the state that the ghost dancer singing this song hopes to attain.

Mooney adds more details: the earth was considered to be a disk, surrounded on all sides by water (apparently the primordial water of creation, upon which the land was created). The Arapahos believed that the spirit world was across this water and upward to the west (Mooney [1896] 1973: 983).

Curtis reports that this song was composed by Henéécee 3í'ok (Sitting Bull), who was a celebrated Arapaho leader of the Ghost Dance (see Fowler 1982: 122–23, 2010; Mooney [1896] 1973: 894–97). Fowler (1982: 123) reports that Sitting Bull sought to create a personal following for himself through his involvement with the Ghost Dance, outside of the traditional system of age-grade societies and ceremonial hierarchy. This has been a common tendency at many moments in Arapaho history among certain individuals and continues to occur at Wind River in the early twenty-first century. Thus, depending on when this particular song was composed (in Wyoming or in Oklahoma), it potentially represents not just a vision of spiritual inspiration and renewal. It may represent a more specific claim to visionary authority by one particular younger Arapaho man, in the context of competition for power and influence and, more broadly, in the context of the social debate over the relative status of traditional and newer forms of religious expression within the tribe. Fowler (1982: 123, 2010: 158–61, 184–85; Mooney [1896] 1973: 895–97) reports that Sitting Bull was eventually forced off the Wind River Reservation in 1891 and settled in Oklahoma, where he gained considerable influence.

Frances Densmore records several Ghost Dance song texts in English only in her book on Cheyenne and Arapaho music. One of those (song 35) is: "I am wading in yellow water. I guess it is a turtle pond." This is likely the same song as the one recorded by Curtis.

Original:	*Retranscribed:*
seniesana niha-nawu	Senii'iheisee-noo niihoonoowu-'.
nanai baeno nidjieh-hi niha-nawu	Nenee-' be'enou-niicie niihoonoowu-'.

Translation:

I am walking into the yellow water. [two times]
It is the turtle river, flowing yellow. [two times]

13

The next song is from Gatschet (MS 231, p. 255), provided by Oscar Wilde:

Nii-noo'oeexo'-owoo ciibeet [twice],
I step around the sweat lodge,

he'=heinootee beii, 3i'eyoon-e' [twice].

where the shell is lying on the earth mound.

This song was also recorded by Mooney (song 63). Wilde told Gatschet that "stones [are] piled up in heap to show that at a certain day or hour we passed that stone(?) building." He may be referring to a stone monument itself—when someone passed a monument alongside a trail, it was customary to add a stone. With regard to the shell, he specifically translates 'white shell' though *beii* simply means 'shell'. This is a reference to part of the sweat lodge ceremony.

14

Finally, we present two songs that seem to be the only ones that Kroeber recorded. They were both provided by Cleaver Warden, on July 24, 1899 (MS 2560a, Notebook 4, pp. 17, 27).

Tih-neneetoowu-' he'iiteihi3i,

When there was a flood everywhere, someone,

be'enoo nih-'o3i'eew-oohok nec-i',

he asked the turtle to go into the water,

toh-ceenotiitii-t biito'owu',

and to go down and search for land,

toh-cee'ih-eino'ohk.

which he has bestowed upon us gladly.

Kroeber's notes on the "meaning of song about turtle" offer a short version of the creation story (in English).

15

After recording several vocabulary items including *beeteenoo'* 'it is sacred'; *neenebe'eenoo'* 'it is dangerous, one must be careful, cautious not to use it'; *beexotii* 'gambling wheel game'; and *hoonowootinoti* (spelling?) 'the father of the buffalo', Warden offers a second song (p. 27):

'oh teebe tih-'iine'etiitooni-',
When people were first living on the earth,

neeni-hek be'enoo,
it was the Turtle,

ne-ih-cee'ih-eiit biito'owu',
who gladly bestowed on me the earth,

tih-'ei'towuun-einoo neisonoo.
as my Father has told me.

Kroeber's notes add "recent song, since Messiah agitation," referring to the rise of the Ghost Dance movement. This is song 26 recorded by Mooney, though with slightly different wording, revealing the fluidity of oral transmission.

Crow Dance Songs

The Crow Dance (*hóuunohwóót* 'Crow Dance', *hóuunohwóótnoot* 'Crow Dance Song') was an outgrowth of the Ghost Dance ceremony (Fowler 1982: 123–24; Mooney [1896] 1973: 901, 921–22). While the Ghost Dance passed out of practice early in the twentieth century at Wind River and in Oklahoma due to the failure of the promised miracles to occur, the Crow Dance continues to be performed as a healing ceremony around Christmastime each year. The link of the Crow to the Creator through the term *hóuu* has already been observed. Natalie Curtis ([1907] 1968: 201) notes this in relation to the following song as well as that black war paint was symbolic of success and that the crow is harmless and does not kill for its food.

Note that this same general ceremony (for which there are several specific songs) in modern times is also sometimes called the "Dog Dance" (a puppy is sacrificed and a ceremonial dog stew is served) and the "Kingfisher Dance" (one segment of the ceremony involves two specific men called "kingfishers," who symbolically dive into the kettle to bring out the dog meat). The actual earlier Arapaho name for the entire ceremony is *hookó'ooho'(o)yóót,* a word whose meaning is unknown.

Fowler (1982: 124) notes that, unlike the Ghost Dance, the Crow Dance was eventually better integrated with the traditional Arapaho religious practice and hierarchy. Thus, although it was embraced primarily by younger Arapahos rather than traditional ceremonial elders, it managed to survive through the years.

1

This song comes from Curtis ([1907] 1968: 201).

Original:	*Retranscribed:*
hesunani' ho-hu	Heisonoon-in houu,
bahinahnit-ti	beehiineenitii-[t].

hesunani' no   Heisonoon-in houu.
A e-yo he-ye ye-ye yo!   (vocables)

Translation:
Our Father the Crow,
he created everything.
Our Father the Crow.

2

The following Crow Dance songs are from Gatschet (both from MS 231, p. 252). He does not provide information about who assisted him with the songs.

Nii-nii-niitouub-eínoo houu,
The Crow calls repeatedly to me,

beetoooh-eínoo.
He is making me dance.

Nehínee hee3-eínoo.
Enough, he says to me.

Gatschet's note says: "After singing this (boys and women) they quit dancing. Somehow[?] crows while dancing." In other words, this was the final closing song of the Crow Dance. Note that Mooney ([1896] 1973) records this song as well (song 52). He says that it was the closing song of the Ghost Dance at one time (918, 996) but had been replaced in this function by his song 73 by the time of his publication (1011–12), which is Ghost Dance Song 7 above.

3

Nii-nii-niitouub-eínoo houu.
The Crow is calling to me.

Nonoo3-eínoo,
He comes to fetch me,

nenííton-o'.
I hear him.

Gatschet's note says: "This is another variant of song when dancers come to a stop." Note that Mooney ([1896] 1973) also records this song (song 38). He notes its resemblance to the preceding song and discusses the general importance of the Crow in the Ghost Dance in relation to this song (983) but does not connect it to the Crow Dance specifically. Mooney was present among the Southern Arapahos in 1891. Gatschet worked there in 1892 and 1893. Gatschet connects Mooney's Ghost Dance Song with the Crow Dance one or two years later. This might indicate a mistake by one of the two men or else an extremely rapid ceremonial evolution, as the Crow Dance borrowed songs from the Ghost Dance repertoire or, perhaps more precisely, elements of the Ghost Dance repertoire evolved rapidly into the semi-independent Crow Dance. Given what Mooney says about the shift in closing songs just within the time when he was present in Oklahoma, rapid evolution seems the more likely explanation.

Ghost Dance Songs from
James Mooney

The following texts are all taken from Mooney [1896] 1973, maintaining his numbering of the songs. We have provided retranscriptions and retranslations, emphasizing the actual textual content of the Arapaho as closely as possible. We have also added some linguistic notes for unusual lexical items or grammatical constructions but have not attempted to add additional poetic commentary. We do not repeat lines that he writes multiple times to show actual repetition in performance (virtually every line is sung twice) and do not include the vocables that he writes. In Mooney's transcriptions he often seems to have confused meaningless rhythmic elements added to words for actual parts of the words. This is especially the case with initial *'oh*, which functions somewhat like English *o* as in "O say can you see." But he also includes many final vocables as parts of words.

The following discussion is simply meant to provide linguistic clarification of Mooney's work, not to replace it. See Anderson 2005 for further analysis of some important thematic elements in these texts. In the context of this volume, note the pervasive presence of references to the creation story in these songs, usually indicated by references to the Sacred Pipe, the earth, gifts of the Pipe or of the earth, the use of 'our Father' or 'my Father', and the act of taking pity (as the Creator did for humans at the time of the creation of the earth). The songs attempt to invoke a second creation and a renewal of the world via these references.

In terms of specific linguistic elements, the related AI verbs *niitóuuhu, -etóuuhu-* 'to holler' and the II *-etóuuse-* 'to resound' (along with several variants) are extremely common in the songs. This is the sound of the Thunderbird and of thunder as well as of humans hollering and other birds and animals calling and gives the songs a powerful aural component.

The obligatorily possessed word *ne-níísoo* 'my child' is used pervasively. This is an older word in comparison to modern *téi'yoonéhe'* 'child' (which is not obligatorily possessed). The word contains the ending *-soo* 'young of', which resonates with the same ending used in various songs to refer to 'young Thunderbirds', 'young crow', 'young bird/eagle', and 'young relative', thus contributing to the general emphasis on youth and transformation. In comparison, images of old age are relatively few in the songs.

The instrumental prefix *hi'-* is used much more than in normal speech (or even other song genres) and clearly emphasizes the importance of sacred help and aid (songs 15, 33, 35, 43, 44, 49, 68). Note, however, that this prefix is equally common in the prayers and ceremonial speeches in this volume.

The verb for 'he says' or 'he says to me' and variants is always the more formal, present-tense form *hee3-*, never the more informal, past-tense form *-ii3-* (see the general introduction for more on these forms).

The iterative mode ('whenever') is used here much more commonly than in other songs or the narratives (17, 31, 38, 52, 59, 71)—but again see its use in prayers and speeches, including the speech of a man's father at his wedding and the name-changing prayer. Here it gives many of the songs a general sense of anticipation, as if people were always eagerly awaiting the next call or gift from the Creator (as indeed the Ghost Dancers were).

The image of circling flight is also pervasive, expressed by two roots, *noo'(ó)ée-* 'around a central point' and *nonóó'oo-* 'around in circles, soaring, gliding'. These songs stand out for these complex derivational morphology used in the verbs of flight as well as others. Rather than just saying 'fly' (or 'stand'), secondary verb stems are derived, meaning 'to fly in relation to s.o.' or 'to stand in relation to s.t.' (AI *nonóó'oo-* > TA *nonoo'óóton-*, AI *3i'óókuu-* > TI *3i'ookúút-*, etc.). This gives the verbs, and the songs generally, a more specific and dynamic feeling than would otherwise be the case, tying different participants together not only thematically but grammatically through the inflections.

Finally, these Ghost Dance Songs contain perhaps the greatest overall density of unusual verbs (both lexically and in terms of secondary grammatical constructions and derivations) and unusual images (expressed either as individual words or in combinations of verbs with prefixes) of any texts in this volume. This underlines that the Ghost Dance was clearly a break with past Arapaho ceremonial traditions in many ways, even as it borrowed much practice and imagery from them. This was certainly perceived by the Arapahos themselves at the time (Fowler 2010: 158–65), and the linguistics of the songs reinforces this point. This of course makes the texts very difficult to transcribe and translate well: several questions remain in what follows.

1

Neniisoo-no',
My children,

hinee ceese' het-iicooon-inoo,
that other one of your pipes,

noh'oe'eini-'! Ne'-nii3etouuhu-noo,
lift up your heads and look at it! That is how I holler,

biito'owu' toh-noh'ooben-owoo.
when I move/raise the earth.

This is the opening song of the Ghost Dance and originated in the north (Mooney [1896] 1973: 958).

2

Se'iicooo hei'towuun-einoo,
The Flat Pipe tells me,

heisonoon-in,
our Father,

hootni-i3oowu-ce'-woohoneni-no',
we will truly all be reunited,

heisonoon-in.
our Father.

3

This song was composed by Nowoo3/Left Hand of the Southern Arapahos (Mooney [1896] 1973: 961).

Teebe tih-'owouunon-ou'u neniisoo-no',
When I first took pity on them, my children,

nih'oo3ou'u,
the white people,

nih-biin-ou'u koo'ohwoot-ino.
I gave them canned goods/fruits.

4

Beenii!
Friend [male]!

Heetih-cebiihineesee-no' ciiciitoon-e'.
I ask that we go to where they are gambling at ciiciitoo (meaning unknown).

5

Neisonoo,
My Father,

heecis-hiinixoh-einoo,
while he was taking me all over,

(hi?)heesi-nookowuuhuuni-t.
he transformed into a moose.

Mooney says the word *nookowuu* means 'moose'. It is otherwise unrecognized and completely undocumented for Arapahos. It seems to contain the imperfective/habitual form of *hookow-* 'bent/crooked' (as in *honookowúúbeet* 'elephant,' literally 'it has a bent nose') along with the agent suffix *–uuhuu*, thus 'bent one'. The verb derived from this word would be *nookowuuh-úúni-* 'to be a moose or moose-like/a bent one(?)'. The song is attributed to Woxu'eisei/Ugly Face Woman (Mooney [1896] 1973: 962).

6

Wonooyou-'u,
They are new,

hookon-o.
the buffalo hide [bed covers].

Hookono (NI.PL) is likely a variant of *héecéno* 'buffalo hides'. It is documented in Kroeber, NAA, MS 2560a.

7

Hiseihihi',
Girl/friend,

houunee-to'ow-unee koh'owooo.
hit the ball as hard as possible.

Hooton-eeteehinee-noo.
I am going to win the game.

The modern form for 'ball' is *kokoh'owóoó*.

8

Neniisoo-no',
My children,

nenii-niibeineesei-'i wookuu-no,
the plumes worn on the head are singing in the wind,

neniisoo-no'.
my children.

9

[Ne]nee-ni3 biis-iixo'-o',
That one stepped into view on top of the hill,

neniisoo-no',
my children,

ne'i-noohootebeen-o'
then I saw what it was that he was doing.

Mooney provides the gloss 'I saw the multitude plainly' for the last line. The verb *nóóhootébeen-* refers to seeing/knowing about some specific action by the referenced object of the verb. When used in conversation, the specific action normally is clear and identifiable from preceding context—indeed it must be for the verb to be used. Here that is not the case, but the action seems to be 'leading a multitude of followers', as supplied by Mooney's consultant. This song was composed by Sitting Bull (Mooney [1896] 1973: 965).

10

Neniisoo-no',
My children,

honoon-owouunon-ou'u ne-ei'towuun-ooono'.
I take pity on those I have told/taught.

Teco'on-nih'oniitowoo-3i',
They always try their hardest,

nii3-einoo heisonoon-in.
thus our Father says to me.

11

Neixoo, woow neniibeit-owoo,
My Father, I am singing it now,

hini' koo-koyetouuse-',
that [song] whose sound escapes far into the distance,

hini' nii-niitouuse-' niibeit-owoo.
I am singing the one that sounds out.

Koy-etóuuse- means 'the sound escapes' (i.e., resounds far and wide). Cf. AI *koy-íh'ohu-* 'fly away, escape by flying'. This is an unusual verb. Mooney writes the inflection on the verb *niibeit-* as *-ia,* which does not fit well with the necessary *-owoo.* One would also expect *neniibóót-owoo* today, rather than *neniibeit-owoo.*

12

Hooyoh=noh'oeseiyoo.
How wonderfully bright it is,

biikoo toh-cowooxu-noo.
at night as I carry along [game] on my horse.

Hooyoh= is a variant of *hiiyoh=*'an exemplary instance of' or 'what a wonderful example of'. Frances Densmore (1936) records (in English only) what appears to be either the same song or a close variant, though she calls it a hunting song:

It is dark, but the moon is shining.
I am carrying home my game.

13

Hohooti-niiboot,
The cottonwood song,

neniibeit-owoo.
I am singing it.

One would expect *neniibóót-owoo* here.

14

Nii'ehiisoo-no',
Young birds/eagles,

boh'ooonii'ehiisoo-no'.
young Thunderbirds.

15

Heisonoon-in neyooxet,
Our Father the whirlwind,

heni'-nihi'koohu-noo.
by means of him I am running fast.

Heisonoon-in heni'-noohow-o'.
By means of it I have seen our Father.

Heni'- is the initial changed form of the instrumental prefix *hi'-*.

16

Heisonoon-in neyooxet,
Our Father the whirlwind,

woow ceniinookuuni-t houu-no'.
now he has put on crow [feathers] as plumes.

17

Nii-noo'eenih'ohu-noo biito'owu-u',
I fly around the earth,

heeneisei-'i.
as far as it extends.

Hine'e3 neniiwouh'u-noo.
I am carrying the wing [feathers] [of the eagle].

Hi-3e'en is 'his wing [feather]'. The first word of the last line is apparently an error by Mooney in transcription.

18

Hoh'onohowuunen beniin-einoo hinow-un.
The Hoh'onohowu' man has given me red paint.

Koonen-einoo.
He has wiped me clean [of the previous paint].

The last verb is not recognized today. The ending is clearly TA 3S/1S. Alonzo Moss suggests that the verb is likely related to *kóo-kónoh-* TA 'dust s.o. off', as the root *kon-* 'shake' appears in both forms (with initial change in the form in the song).

19

Teebe toh-no'usee-t heisonoon-in,
When our Father first arrived,

nih-'owoten-o',
I woke him up [with prayers],

toh-notineenow-o' neito'eisoo.
because I sought for him in my mind, my young relative.

This song is by Be'eekuuni'/Paul Boynton (Mooney [1896] 1973: 971).

20

Nih-'eni3o-he'inon-einoo neisonoo.
My father did not recognize (?) me.

Hei'-ce'-noohob-einoo,
When he saw me again,

houusoo hee3-einoo.
Crow Child, he said to me.

The preverb in the first line is unclear to modern speakers, though the verb *he'inon* means 'to know'. It could possibly be based on *heni3ei-* 'to lose things', thus 'he lost knowledge of me'? The song is by Sitting Bull (Mooney [1896] 1973: 972).

21

Neniisoo-no',
My children,

hootowouh-oono',
we have made them sad/depressed,

nih'oo3ou'u hoohookeeni-3i'.
The white people are crazy [now].

Hotowóú-3ecoo- means 'grieving, mourning', so the root of the verb in the second line specifically refers to a sense of loss or depression.

22

Neniisoo-no',
My children,

noohoot-oo biito'owu'!
look at the earth!

Heet-noh'oowo'owuhu-'.
The earth will be shaken.

Hee3-einoo neisonoo.
Thus my Father says to me.

The verb in the third line is *nóh'oow-o'owú-h-u-=* move/shake-earth-CAUS-PASS.IMPERF, 'it will be caused to move/shaken'.

23

Heisonoon-in,
Our Father,

heecixoohow-o',
as/while I look at him,

(hi?)heesi-nii'eihiini-t.
he is turning into a bird.

24

Hoh'onookei'i,
On the rock(s),

teneesookuut-owoo.
I am standing on top of them.

Heisonoon-in heni'-noohow-o'.
By means of them I have seen our Father.

25

Neniisoo-no',
My children,

woow no-oton-etei'oo,
now I suppose I shall make a buzzing noise,

neniisoo-no'.
My children.

The verb in the second line has nonaffirmative inflection, giving the phrase the sense 'So I guess that' or 'I suppose that' in everyday Arapaho. The buzzing noise is a reference to a toy noise-maker, either the hummer or the bull-roarer. The bull-roarer was also used to start the singing in the Ghost Dance (Kroeber [1902–1907] 1983: 396–97). It was said that playing with this toy could bring rain and thunder (Hilger 1952: 93–94) and thus the Thunderbird.

26

Teebe tih-'iine'etiitooni-'ehk,
When people first started to live,

nih-'iite(i)h-ehk be'enoo ne-ih-cee'ih-eiit,
it was the Turtle who bestowed this on me,

biito'owu',
the earth,

tih-'ei'towuun-einoo neisonoo.
as my Father told me he would.

The verb in the second line is *hiitéíhi-* AI 'indefinite person/it is who?' It normally occurs with a dubitative prefix, as in *he'=íite(i)hí-3i* 'I wonder who it is/it is someone'. The exact meaning is something like 'they say that it was Turtle' or 'Turtle is said to be the one'.

27

Neniisoo-no'
My children,

neneeni-noo toh'uu-noo'eeneenih'ohu-noo.
I am the one who is always flying around [you].

Neneeni-noo toh-'eteinih'ohu-noo.
I am the one who flies with a rumbling noise.

28

Neixoo neh-cih-'owouunon-i!
Father! You must take pity on me!

Woow biixonokooyei-noo.
I am crying from thirst.

Hiiyohou-' ne-bii3hiit.
All of my food is gone.

29

Nii-nihoonih'ohu-noo.
I fly yellow.

Yeiniisetii-nookuunih'ohu-noo,
I fly wearing the rose bush [flower] in my hair,

hihcebe'.
up above.

Yéiníis NI 'rose bush,' > *yéiníisetii* NI.PL 'rose bush foliage' (cf. *co'óx-etii* NI.PL 'thick grass, vegetation') + *nookuun-ih'ohu-* AI 'fly with a plume in one's hair/on one's head'. As the reader may have guessed, this is not a commonly occurring verb in Arapaho.

30

Niihoonotoyeicee-t,
The one with the yellow hide,

nonookoxonee-t,
the one with the white skin,

woow hookoo3en-o'.
now I have changed him for another.

Woow ne-ihoow-owouunon-oo.
Now I have no pity for him.

31

Be'3eino'o,
The cedar/juniper tree,

Heetnii-3i'ookuut-oono'.
we will stand around it.

Beeteeen-ooni'i,
Whenever we dance for it,

heetnii-3i'ookuut-oono'.
we will stand around it.

The first verb here is TA *3i'ookúút-*, but one would expect *3i'ookúúton-*, inflected as *3ii'ookúúton-óóno'. 3ii'ookúúton-ó'* would be 'I am standing at its location', but the translation clearly gives 'we'. The verb *beeteeen-* is likewise problematic: for 1P/3.ITER inflection, one would expect *-oonóú'u*, not *-ooní'i*.

32

Neniisoo-no',
My children,

woow nonoo-nonoo'ookuutii-[noo] wookuu.
now I am waving the plume in circles.

Hiiyou neenih'ibeihi-[t].
Here is a spotted [eagle] one.

Heetih-'inookuun[i-n], hee3-einoo neisonoo.
So that you have a plume, says my Father.

The verb in the second line is *nóo-nonóó'ookúutii-* AI.T 'move s.t. in circles'. Note the resemblance to the cognate AI verb *nóo-nonóó'oo-* used to describe the soaring motion of eagles, the crow, the Thunderbird, and so forth in several other songs. The lack of person inflections on all the verbs is unexplained.

33

Niixonookee,
Lone Bull,

hooton-ni'ii-notonihei-noo.
I will make medicine using him.

The more common noun for buffalo bull *is henéécee,* but several archaic words contain the noun final *-onóókee* as here, as in *bo'onóókee* 'red bull'. Lone Bull is a reference to the symbolic buffalo of the Sun Dance.

34

Ne'=ii3i-biiwoohu-noo,
That is where I start crying from,

3i'eyoon-e'.
at the fasting monument/sweat lodge earth pile.

A *3i'éyoo* (NA) can be a rock marker, used to mark a race course or set up at a fasting spot, but it is also the pile of earth created when the fire pit is scooped out inside a sweat lodge and the earth pile is left outside the lodge.

35

3i'eyoo hei'-noohow-o',
Once I have seen the fasting monument,

ne'=hi'-biiwoohu-noo.
that is why I am crying.

36

Houu hookeeeniistii-t booo.
The Crow is making a road across the river.

Heniistii-t.
He has finished it.

Hiniisoo-no,
His children,

ne'-oo'eixoh-oot.
then he gathered/assembled them [on the other side].

Hokéee- AI 'wade across/cross a river' is combined with *niistii-* AI.T 'make'. This is not a usual Arapaho verb and means literally 'make a wading place'.

37

Biito'owu', houu,
The earth, the Crow,

nonohku-no'uxotii-[t] houu.
[the Crow] has brought it with him.

38

Nenii-niitouub-einoo houu.
The Crow is calling to me.

Nonoo3-einooni houu,
Whenever the Crow is coming to fetch me,

nii-niiton-o'.
I hear him.

39

Nonoo-nonoo'ooton-einoo houu,
The Crow is soaring all around me,

toh-cih-noo3-einoo houu.
because the Crow has come to fetch me.

40

Neniisoo-no',
My children,

hiiyou hee3eben-owoo,
here it is, I am passing it there to you,

biito'owu'.
the earth.

41

Honoh'oehi', koo'ohuno',
Little boy, the coyotes' [gun],

seniiy-ookun-owoo.
I have really untied it now.

Neeyou heneinootee-' hi-3ooxe.
There is the scabbard lying there.

Mooney gives the form *koo'ohuno'* for 'coyote men' (i.e., the men posted to guard the camp). *Koo'óh* is 'coyote', but the full root is *koo'ohw-* and the plural is *koo'óhwuu*, so the form that he gives is puzzling, though it appears to have NA.PL *-no'* finally. This song was composed by Nookhoose'/Sage (Mooney [1896] 1973: 985).

42

Heisonoo nonoohoo3ih-[einoo],
Your Father has showed me,

niitoh-'oowukoni-'.
where the band is moving down here.

43

Neniisootoxu-3i' ciineciiciibeh'ei-ho',
The seven water-sprinkling old men,

nii-noohow-oono'.
we see them.

Nii-behiinookuuni-3i',
They are all wearing plumes,

bonoh'ooo-no'.
Thunderbirds.

Ne'=hi'-biiwoohu-noo.
That is why I am crying.

One would expect *boh'óoó-no'* for NA.PL. The initial changed form *bonoh'óoó-* would be expected with a verb, not a noun.

44

Neniisootoxu-3i' ciineciiciibeh'ei-ho',
The seven water-sprinkling old men,

beeh-i'-biiwoohu-noo.
I am crying for all of them.

Beexotii heni'-biiwoohu-noo.
I am crying for/because of the gambling wheel.

In this song as in the preceding one, the instrumental prefix *heni'-/hi'-* is used, as it is commonly in these songs in general.

45

Noo-nonoo'ooton-einoo houu,
The Crow soars all around me,

toh-cih-biin-einoo hi3e'-eno.
because he is giving me his wing [feathers].

46

No-tonouyoo cebiini,
This that I am using as pemmican,

noh=ci'=cebooo-ni'.
we are making it too.

AI.O *ceb-éee-* 'make pemmican' > *cebóóó-ni'* with 1P.

47

Hee'in-owoo heeneitoox-unoon-i',
I know, the pitfall,

niinen, nenee-' heeneitoox-unoon-i'.
Tallow, that is what [is used as bait] in the pitfall/eagle trap.

The exact spelling and analysis of the word 'pitfall' is unclear. *Heeneit-* is the reduplicated form of *hiit-* 'here', while *-oox-* means 'hole' (cf. AI.T *nooxcítii-* 'dig a hole by hand'), but the rest of the term is obscure.

48

Beehiin-eeneinootee-' niitobee-noo.
I hear everything in all directions.

Neneeni-noo houu.
I am the Crow.

49

Beexotii heni'-cebiihinee-noo.
I am gambling with the gambling wheel.

Woo'teenooni-' ni'-eeteehinee-noo.
I win the game thanks to the black mark.

50

Nii-hesooku'oo-noo,
I watch closely,

toh-cebiihetiitooni-' beexotiib-e'.
when people gamble with the gambling wheel.

Niih'otiibikuu3oo-[t] beexotii,
The gambling wheel is set rolling,

tih-cebiihetiitooni-'.
when they gamble with it.

Níh'otíibikuu3- TA 'set s.t. rolling' > *níh'otíibikúu3oo-* AI.MID 'is set in motion/rolling'. Cf. *níh'kúutii-* AI.T 'set off/fire a gun'. The locative marker on 'gambling wheel' in the second line is an example of the archaic usage of this marker in instrumental constructions.

51

Niicie hii3eti-'.
A good river.

Coonohootiini-t.
There is not a single tree.

Koun boh'oooníbi-no 3ii'ookuu-'u.
Only hawthorns stand/grow there.

Hawthorns (*Crataegus* spp.) are literally 'thunder berries'. The verb in the second line combines *cii-* NEG with *hóon-ohootíini-* AI.REDUP 'be trees in an area'.

52

Nih-nii-niitouub-einoo houu.
The Crow has called out to me.

Beetoooh-einooni houu,
Whenever the Crow gives me a dance,

nehinee hee3-einoo.
that is enough/you can stop now, he says to me.

53

Niihooyoo-' hooton-ii-tonoun-owoo,
I will use the yellow [paint],

hee3-einoo heisonoon-in.
thus our Father says to me.

Toh-cee'ih-einoo heisonoon-in.
Because our Father has graciously bestowed it upon me.

Cee'ih- TA 'to give s.t. out of gratitude, to show favor towards s.o.'

54

Neniisoo-no',
My children,

nii-noo'eenih'ohuut-owoo biito'owu-u',
I am flying all around the earth,

tih-nii'eihiini-noo neniisoo-no'.
since I am a bird, my children.

Hee3-einoo heisonoon-in.
Thus our Father has said to me.

55

Nii-too-too'usee-nee.
You will all stop walking there.

He-et-niitouubi-be houu,
When you are called to by the Crow,

het-noohow-oobe houu.
you must see/look at the Crow then.

Niitóuubi- AI.PASS.IMPERF 'hollered at'. The nonaffirmative inflections indicate a more specific meaning 'should you be hollered at'. This song is by the Southern Arapaho chief Little Raven (Mooney [1896] 1973: 998).

56

Neniisoo-no',
My children,

woow he3ebi-ce'-ceniinobeen-ookuu-',
I have given you plumes to wear again.

Woo'uh'ei-nooko3-ii.
Magpie tail feathers.

Hee3-einoo neinoo.
Thus my mother has said to me.

The long polysynthetic form is unclear. *Hé3ebi-* means 'there/over there', used here in the sense 'I have given something to you over there'. *Ce'-* is 'again'. The final element is *-ookuu-* 'plumes that are worn'. The entire thing is likely an imperative addressed to multiple listeners (thus the final glottal stop). The middle element *ceniinobeen-* is the unclear part. As an independent verb, it would be 'to lay s.t. specific down for s.o.', which would make sense given the gloss by Mooney, but such a verb should not have the preceding or following elements.

57

Neixoo, heetebinouhuuni-noo.
Father, I am pitiful.

Hooton-owouunon-einoo heisonoon-in.
Our Father is going to take pity on me.

Hooton-iinih'ohuuh-einoo heisonoon-in.
Our Father is going to make me fly about.

58

Neniisootoxu-3i' houu-no',
Seven crows,

hi-bii3hiin-ínoo gasitu.
they are 'flying about' their food/carrion.

The form *gasitu,* glossed as 'flying about', is completely unclear. Mooney ([1896] 1973: 1016) actually glosses it 'carrion' in his glossary, but the first word in the second sentence ('their food') must be the form that means 'carrion'. The final element may be *-ih'ohu-t* 'fly-3S'.

59

Hunee heisonoon-in,
Our Father there,

niitoh-betooo-ni' beetoooh-einooni,
where we are dancing is wherever he has asked me to dance,

hookoh heesoo' biin-eino' heisonoon-in.
because this is the way our Father has given it to us.

60

Koh'owooo
The ball,

nihi'neekuuš-inee!
throw it quick!

Hooton-eeteehinee-noo.
I am going to win.

61

Houu niihi'koohu-[t].
The Crow is running fast.

Hooton-niiton-einoo.
He is going to hear me.

62

Neisonoo,
My Father,

yoo3oyoonoo-' toh-no'uxoh-einoo,
there are five places/parts he took me to,

toh-biin-einoo hit-iicooo-n,
when he gave me his [Sacred Flat] Pipe,

biito'owu-u' toh-3i'ookuut-owoo.
when I stood on the earth.

63

Nii-noo'eexo'-owoo ciibeet.
I step around the sweat lodge,

Heinootee-' beii, 3i'eyoon-e'.
where the shell is lying, on the dirt mound.

64

Hisei,
Woman/friend,

heetnii-beikuu3-oono',
we will play the awl game,

heetih-to'usetoo-no'.
let's play the dart/dice game.

A *to'úsetoo* (NI) is a wooden, dartlike stick slid along the ground, usually on snow, as part of a game testing accuracy and distance of sliding as well as a die—it literally means 'thing thrown down'.

65

Neniisoo-no',
My children,

not-ouu{woni}soo,
my spinning top,

heneeteehinee-t.
it is winning the game [for me].

The modern word for a toy top is *hóuusoo*, possessive *notóuusoo*.

66

Hei'-nookonohwoo-ni',
When we dance all night/until the morning,

ne'-owouunon-eini' biikoušiiš heisonoon-in.
then our Father the Moon takes pity on us.

Nii3-einoo heisonoon-in.
Thus says our Father.

The 3/1P inflection *-eini'* is nonstandard. It may be that *-eino'* was
intended.

67

Neniisoo-no',
My children,

neneeni-noo tih-'inookuuni-noo nookoox,
I am the one who wears the Morning Star as a plume,

tih-noohoo3ih-ou'u neniisoo-no'.
for I show it to my children.

Hee3-einoo heisonoon-in.
Thus our Father says to me.

68

Neinoo tih-biin-einoo net-ihtowoo,
Since my mother gave me my game stick,

niinih'ohuukoohu-noo,
I flit all around,

toh-u'-noohoo3ih-einoo neniisoo-no'.
because it makes me [able to] see my children.

The exact spelling of the word 'game stick' is unknown, as the term is not recognized today. The initial element is 1S.POSS 'my'. The -*u'*- prefix in the third Arapaho line is the instrumental, with vowel harmony shifting *i* to *u*.

69

Heneen-eehiikuu3-o' koxouhee.
I am throwing the hand-game button.

The verb here is unclear. *Heneen*- is reduplication, and the ending -*kuu3*- indicates throwing or other rapid motion.

70

Neixoo!
Father!

Xouuwusee-noo,
I walk straight to it,

koxouhee.
the hand-game button.

71

Hinow hu'uuhu',
By means of red paint,

hooton-ni'ii-bei'i-noo.
I am going to paint myself red with it.

Kooxouhti-nooni,
Whenever I play the hand game,

hinee'ee-hek koxouhee.
there is the button.

The form *hínee'eehék* was becoming obsolete even when these songs were recorded. Modern Arapaho has only the simple demonstrative *hínee*, but the longer, pseudo-verbal forms equivalent to the Arapaho are documented for Gros Ventre and the language of the Béesóowúunénino'.

72

Neixoo nookoox!
My Father, Morning Star!

Hii-noohob-ei'ee!
You must look at us!

Nih-nookonohwoo-ni'.
We have danced all night long/until morning.

Howouunon-ei'ee!
Take pity on us.

This is the penultimate song of the Ghost Dance ceremony (Mooney [1896] 1973: 1011).

73

Hee3-eino' heisonoon-in,
Our Father says to us,

yoo3on het-too'usee-be.
five [times] and you must stop.

Nii3-eino' heisonoon-in.
This is what our Father tells us.

This is the closing song of the Ghost Dance (Mooney [1896] 1973: 1012). Other than the closing song, there were apparently no fixed sequences of songs.

3ííkoniibetooot/The Ghost Dance

Told by Paul Boynton, April 1893
Collected by Albert Gatschet
NAA, MS 231, pp. 310–11

This text was provided by Paul Boynton. Note that the Southern Arapaho word for Ghost Dance, at least at this time, was literally 'ghost dance' (*3iikoníbetóoot*) whereas the modern Northern Arapaho word is 'circle dance' (*kó'einohwóót)*. Boynton's claim that Sitting Bull brought the dance to Oklahoma is verified by other historical sources as well. The term 'earth above' is a reference to the idea that a new earth would slide down over the old earth, bringing with it renewal and driving out the white people. The exact term, *hihcébe' bííto'ówu'*, resonates with the general term *hihcébe'* 'above, heaven' and *hihcébe' nih'óó3oo* 'above white man, the Creator' (both of these terms are used in the translation of the Gospel of Luke done in the early 1900s).

The Ghost Dance was notable for the lack of musical instruments, and the Crow was the central symbolic mediator figure between humans and the Creator in the Ghost Dance theology. The exact term used for the crow is *betee3óúnii'éíhii,* with the first element derived from *betéé3oo* 'shadow, spirit, soul', thus 'spirit bird'.

The last line of the text is interesting in that it suggests a more close conflation of Christianity with the Ghost Dance (on the part of this consultant, at least) than is normally the case. Whites were called *nih'óó3oo* (also meaning 'spider' and 'trickster') by the Arapahos as early as anyone can recall and at least since the early nineteenth century. At the same time Hihcébe' Nih'óó3oo was a traditional term for the Creator, evidently predating white contact. The speaker suggests that Jesus was called Hihcébe' Nih'óó3oo 'above/heavenly white man' because he was white, thus providing a reconceptualized folk etymology of the connection between the Christian Messiah and the traditional Arapaho Creator figure. He also seems to be saying that the Hihcébe' Nih'óó3oo that the Ghost Dancers pray to is associated with Jesus Christ, at least in his mind. It should be borne in mind, however, that this claim may have been made to appease the white ethnographer/linguist, either due to fear of repression of the ceremony or out of a desire on the part of the Carlisle-educated informant (see the following paragraph) to appear more favorably "civilized" from a Euro-American perspective.

Paul Boynton was a younger Arapaho man who had attended Carlisle School in Pennsylvania and spoke English (he worked as an interpreter at the agency). The fact that the dances occurred at his camp shows that not only strongly traditionalist Arapahos but also those who had experienced closer contact with the Euro-American world took part in the Ghost Dance movement.

Henéécee 3i'ok, hinóno'ei hihíí3íihi' bo'óóceiteen, nóh nih-no'úxotii-t betooot híít.
Sitting Bull, an Arapaho from the Northern Arapahos, he brought the dance here.

Nih-nó'oteihi-t Zack Wilson, pénehti' hihíí3iihi'.
Zack Wilson was powerful, from Peyote.

Heneecee 3i'ok nih-neyéí3eih-oot hihii3iihi' nenítee-no,
Sitting Bull taught people from here,

hiit hihcebe' bííto'owu' hóót-no'úseenoo-' nóhohoonííhi'.
[that] Earth Above will arrive here soon.

Betooot tonounu-'.
A dance is held.

Hii3oowot-ou'u hoot-no'úseenoo-' wónooyoo-' biito'owu'.
They believe that a new earth will arrive here.

Nii-bi'-niiboo-ni' betooot.
We just sing at the dance.

Hii-hóówu-niitou3oo.
There are no whistles [or other musical instruments].

Ceese' hóuunohwoot, hóókoh houu betéé3ounii'éíhii.
One [of the dances] is the Crow Dance, because the crow is the spirit bird.

Nii-beteee-3i' yóó3on-íiiš, heh-yéínei-'i bííkoo.

They dance five days and four nights.

Heh-yeinei-'i betoooh-ou'u bííkoo, nii-nookonohwóó-ni'.

On the last night of the dance, we dance [the Crow Dance] all night.

Be'eekuuni' hi-yéíh'-e', béénihehe' nenebííhi' hihciniihiihi', nee'eetiíni betooo-ni'.

At Paul Boynton's camp, a little bit north and upstream [from here], that is where we dance.

Hihcebe' Nih'óó3oo neniiših'ee-t,

We name [the one we pray to] White Man Above,

hóókoh Hihcebe' Nih'óó3oo, toh-nookeihi-t.

the reason we say White Man Above is because [Jesus Christ] was white.

Account of the Ghost Dance

Told by Henry North, Oklahoma, probably early 1890s
Collected by Albert Gatschet
NAA, MS 231, pp. 220–21

This untitled text is especially interesting due to the evidence that it provides for the "discourse" of the Ghost Dance. Not only the images evoked but specific linguistic content in the text can be linked to the Ghost Dance Songs recorded by James Mooney. Clearly the language of the songs and the language used to talk discursively about the Ghost Dance were intimately related and mutually reinforcing. For example, vocabulary here that evokes the songs includes *heisonóónin nii3éínoo* 'our Father tells me'; *wonóóhoyóó'* 'reunion, all will be together' and the root *woohon-* 'together, united'; *hí3oowu-* 'truly, certainly'; and the pervasive references to relatives, both living and dead.

Niiyou ní'íi-t Heneecee 3i'ók:
Here is what Sitting Bull says:

hootni-i3oowu-wóóhoyoo-', nii3-éínoo heisonóón-in.
it is for certain that a gathering will occur, our Father tells me.

Níí3ei'-nih'oníítowoo-3i' hoot-nóhohoon-noohow-oo3i' hinííto'éín-inoo.
All those who are striving hard will soon see their relatives.

Hínee héito'éín-in cénii-nih'oníítowóó-3i' tohúú-no'otib-éinee.
Our relatives who have passed away are striving hard because they have much to say to you.

Woohoyóó-(o)hk, hoton-éénee3eti-' hííne'etiit, nii3-éínoo heisonóón-in.
When all are gathered, life will be different, our Father tells me.

Wóóhoyóó-(o)hk, heetní-í3etí-' hees-iine'etíí-nee.
Once we are gathered, it will be good how we live.

520

Híí3einoon noh hee3ei'-cée-ce'eseihi-t heetné-énitoo-t cese'éíhii
he-etn-ii-bii3híítoon-in,

The buffalo and all kinds of animals will be there, which we will feed on,

nii3-éínoo heisonóón-in.

our Father tells me so.

Heisonóón-in heetni-i3oowu-hówóuunon-eino'.

Our Father is sure to take pity on us.

Heet-nóhohoon-woohonen-éíno'.

He will hurry and gather all of us together.

Neniiton-éíno' tohuu-biibi3ehii3iton-óóno'.

He hears us when we pray to him.

Noh huunoxuusóó-no' tohuu-no'otiw-óó3i' hiinoon-ínoo noh
hiteséíb-inoo.

And the orphans have much to say to their mothers and their brothers
and sisters.

Hinee heisonóón-in néé'eetoo-t, cenéíto'oo-t bííto'owu-u'.

That Father of ours who is far off, he is coming to the earth.

Noh hóót-cih-'itex-o' nuhu' bííto'owu'.

And he will come over/cover this earth.

Ne'=néé-yehk he-et-niit-tees-iine'etíítoon-in, cénih-'ooúte-' hínee
bííto'owu'.

And that is the kind of place on which we will live, high above that
[old] earth.

Noh hííyou hoot-níísoo-' cih-no'xoo-'ohk hínee bííto'owu'.

And this is how it will be when that [new] earth arrives.

Hinee heito'éín-in noh núhu' hiniito'éín-inoo, hóót-ne'-nii3ixow-oo3i'
hinííto'éín-inoo.

Our relatives and their relatives, then they will come together with their
relatives.

Appendix A
Other Early Arapaho Texts

Unpublished Early Arapaho-Language Texts
(manuscript only, not included in this anthology or otherwise
published, excluding missionary materials and translations)

"A Bear Eating Chokecherries," collected by Alfred Kroeber, NAA, MS 2560a, Notebook 1, p. 95. [account of bear looking for and eating berries]

"The Bent Gun," collected by Alfred Kroeber, Ms 2560a, Notebook 1, p. 45. [tall tale or "believe it or not" story]

"The Boy and the Bear," told by John Goggles, collected by Zdeněk Salzmann, American Heritage Center, University of Wyoming, Salzmann Papers, Box 15 (June 21, 1949), pp. 10–11. [story/anecdote of a boy escaping from a bear]

"Comanche and Kiowa Story," collected by Zdeněk Salzmann, American Heritage Center, University of Wyoming, Salzmann Papers, Box 15 (date?), p. 65. [initial few sentences of a story about a woman falling in love with her brother–in–law—resembles the story of the faithless woman and the Kiowa in this volume]

"The Conjurer," collected by Albert Gatschet, NAA, MS 231, pp. 67–68. [account of traditional medicinal healing, from patient's perspective/experience]

"Conversation," collected by Zdeněk Salzmann, American Heritage Center, University of Wyoming, Salzmann Papers, Box 15 (July 18, 1949), p. 8. [brief invented conversation]

"The Coyote and the Tick," told by Robert Goggles, collected by Zdeněk Salzmann, American Heritage Center, University of Wyoming, Salzmann Papers, Box 15 (July 7, 1949), p. 4. [race between the coyote and the tick, won by the tick through trickery]

"Dress of the Women," collected by Albert Gatschet. NAA, MS 231, pp. 69–70. [ethnographic account]

"Festivities in Lander WY," told by Robert Goggles, collected by Zdeněk Salzmann, American Heritage Center, University of Wyoming, Salzmann Papers, Box 15 (July 4, 1949), p. 12. [brief recounting of Fourth of July events in Lander, Wyoming, involving Indians]

"Fetching Rations," collected by Alfred Kroeber, NAA, MS 2560a, Notebook 3, p. 30. [anecdote of going to town to fetch rations]

"The Fourth of July in Oklahoma," told by Bruce (Goes-Back), collected by Truman Michelson, NAA, MS 2703 (January 22, 1912), 2 pages. [description of Arapaho celebration of Fourth of July, with races, rodeos, parade, dances, and so forth]

"Hunting Buffalo," told by Dan Tucker, retold by Henry North. Collected by Albert Gatschet, NAA, MS 231, pp. 65–66, 294–95 (1882). [ethnographic account]

"The Last Tomahawk Lodge," told by John Goggles, collected by Zdeněk Salzmann, American Indian Heritage Center, University of Wyoming, Salzmann Papers, Box 15 (date?), 17 pages. [account of the last time the Tomahawk Lodge was held in Wyoming, in the 1920s]

"The Life of Medicine Grass," told by Medicine Grass, collected by Jesse Rowlodge for Truman Michelson, NAA, MS 2267 (November 1929), 50 pages. [ethnographically oriented autobiography]

"The Life of Mrs. White Bear," told by Mrs. White Bear, collected by Jesse Rowlodge for Truman Michelson, NAA, MS 2182 (1929), 22 pages. [ethnographically oriented autobiography]

"Making a Bow and Arrows," collected by Alfred Kroeber, NAA, MS 2560a, Notebook 28, p. 11. [ethnographic account]

"A Man and His Wife Went Hunting," told by Cleaver Warden, collected by Truman Michelson, NAA, MS 3087 (summer 1928), 2 pages. [comic anecdote of man teasing his wife by carrying his gun over his shoulder, pointed back at his wife to scare her, and her getting angry and scolding him]

"A Man Goes Hunting," collected by Zdeněk Salzmann, American Heritage Center, University of Wyoming, Salzmann Papers, Box 15 (date?), pp. 13–16. [incomplete narrative, may be the initial part of Tangled Hair/Found-in-the-Grass]

"Oscar Wilde," told by Oscar Wilde, collected by Albert Gatschet, NAA, MS 231, pp. 143–146. [brief autobiography]

"Paul Boynton," told by Alexander Yellowman, collected by Albert Gatschet, NAA, MS 231, pp. 312–14. [brief biography]

"Prayer for Sweat Lodge Ceremony," told by John Goggles?, collected by Zdeněk Salzmann, American Heritage Center, University of Wyoming, Salzmann Papers, Box 15 (date?), p. 75. [brief prayer]

"Raiding the Utes," collected by Alfred Kroeber, NAA, MS 2560a, Notebook 21, p. 4. [account of an attack on a party of Utes]

"The Singing Porcupine," told by Robert Goggles, collected by Zdeněk Salzmann, American Heritage Center, University of Wyoming, Salzmann Papers, Box 15 (July 21, 1949), p. 7. [anecdote about a man hearing a lullaby while out walking and discovering a porcupine singing]

"Sleeping Boy," told by John Goggles, collected by Zdeněk Salzmann, American Heritage Center, University of Wyoming, Salzmann Papers, Box 15 (date?), 13 pages. [a version of "The Beheaded Ones" included in this volume]

"The Southern Arapaho Sun Dance," told by Jesse Rowlodge, collected by Truman Michelson, NAA, MS 1791 (1929), 1 page. [account stating that the Sun Dance is no longer done because the old men who knew the ways have passed on]

"The Toad," told by Robert Goggles, collected by Zdeněk Salzmann, American Heritage Center, University of Wyoming, Salzmann Papers, Box 15 (July 20, 1949), p. 9.

[comic anecdote/story about man mowing a field, disturbing a toad, and the toad making a mocking gesture at him]

"Wichitas," collected by Alfred Kroeber, NAA, MS 2560a, Notebook 2, p. 57. [anecdote of seeing a group of Wichitas in town, looking for a friend who is in jail]

"Yellow Hair's Illness," told by Alexander Yellowman, collected by Albert Gatschet, MAA, MS 231, pp. 305–306. [account of recovery from an illness]

Untitled, teller unknown, collected by Zdeněk Salzmann, American Heritage Center, University of Wyoming, Salzmann Papers, Box 15 (no date), 5 pages. [unfinished story of an intertribal gathering for a race, won by an Arapaho man with medicine power, who then has a vision that allows him to see a strange visitor to the gathering]

This list constitutes all known Arapaho-language texts from before the advent of Salzmann's recorded texts from the early 1950s (Salzmann 1956a, 1956b). All of these texts have been retranscribed (when necessary), translated (when necessary), interlinearized, and included in a digital database created by Andrew Cowell. A printout copy of the database has been deposited at the American Heritage Center, University of Wyoming.

Published Arapaho Narratives, Prayers, and Songs
(English, or bilingual where noted)

Published versions of Arapaho narratives, prayers, and songs can be found in: Anderson 2005 (bilingual; texts included in this volume), The Arapaho Language Project website (bilingual), the Arapaho Project website (bilingual), C'Hair 2005, Cowell 2001 (bilingual), Cowell 2005, Cowell and Moss 2011 (bilingual; texts included in this volume), E. Curtis 1911 (bilingual; texts included in this volume), N. Curtis [1907] 1968 (bilingual; texts included in this volume), Densmore 1936, Dorsey 1903, Dorsey and Kroeber [1903] 1997 (many included in this volume), Haas 2011, Hopper n.d., A. Kroeber [1902–1907] 1983 (texts included in this volume), A. Kroeber 1916 (bilingual; texts included in this volume), Mooney [1896] 1973 (bilingual; texts included in this volume), P. Moss 1993 (bilingual; texts included in P. Moss 2005), P. Moss 1995 (bilingual; texts included in P. Moss 2005), P. Moss 2005 (bilingual), R. Moss 2006 (bilingual), Salzmann 1950, Salzmann 1956a (bilingual), Salzmann 1956b (bilingual), Salzmann 1957, Salzmann 1980 (bilingual; revised versions of Salzmann 1956a, 1956b), Salzmann and Salzmann 1950, Salzmann and Salzmann 1952, Underwood 2010 (bilingual), Voth 1912, and Wake 1904.

Appendix B

Grammar

In this appendix we provide a list of the most common prefixed and suffixed grammatical elements found in this collection as well as the most common particles (invariable words) and nouns. This will of course not be sufficient to analyze the entire collection, especially as many verbs in Arapaho have one or more lexical prefixes attached to them as well as grammatical elements. Common lexical prefixes are *ce'(i)-* 'again, back'; *ni'(i)-* 'able to'; *ciin(i)-* 'quit doing'; *bee3(i)-* 'finish doing'; *cesis(i)-* 'start doing'; *no'o3(i)-* 'lots, many'; *teco'on(i)-* 'often, always'; *bis(i)-* 'all'; *beh-* 'all'; *nosou(n)-* 'still'; and *hee3nee(n)-* 'very, really'. Serious students of the language will need to consult the grammar (Cowell and Moss 2008) and the currently available dictionary (Cowell et al. 2012). However, the following lists account for the large majority of grammatical prefixes and suffixes as well as particles in terms of total number of occurrences. We include pitch accents for the particles but not for prefixes or suffixes, because the pitch accent on the prefixes is variable in most cases, depending on what follows, while the suffixes in many cases do not have their own pitch accent but force pitch accent patterns onto the preceding nouns or verbs. Pitch accent is controlled from the right end of the word in Arapaho.

After the tables and lists, we provide two Arapaho narratives with interlinear analysis, to give readers a better sense of how the Arapaho language and these narratives in particular are structured.

Grammatical Abbreviations

ADV	adverbial derivational suffix, forms adverbial particles
AFF	affirmative order inflections
AI	verb, animate subject, intransitive
AI.O	verb, animate subject, pseudotransitive with indefinite object
AI.T	verb, animate subject, pseudotransitive with definite object
ALLAT	allative, 'go to' do s.t.

AN	animate
CAUS	causative
CONTR	contrary to fact
DEPPART	dependent participle ('the one who . . .' used in relative clauses)
DETACH	derivational suffix, forms independent adverbials
DIM	diminutive
DUBIT	dubitative
EMPH	emphatic
EXCL	exclusive
f.	female speaker (form used only by females)
FUT	future tense
HABIT	habitual aspect
IC	initial change
II	verb, inanimate subject, intransitive
IMPER	imperative
IMPERF	imperfective aspect
IMPERS	impersonal verb
INAN	inanimate
INCHOAT	inchoative (developing, changing)
INCL	inclusive
INSTR	instrumental
INTERR	interrogative
ITER	iterative mode
LOC	locative
m.	male speaker (form used only by males)
MID	middle voice
NA	noun, animate
NARR	narrative marker
NEG	negative, negation
NI	noun, inanimate
NONAFF	nonaffirmative order inflections
NPAST	narrative past tense
OBLIG	obligation
OBV	obviative
P	plural
PART	particle
PASS	passive voice
PAST	past tense
PERF	perfective aspect
POSS	possessive marker
PROX	proximate
RECIP	reciprocal

REDUP	reduplication
REFL	reflexive
RESULT	resultative
S	singular
SELFB	self-benefactive
s.o.	someone (used in definitions)
s.t.	something (used in definitions)
SUB	subordinate
SUBJ	subjunctive mode
SUGG	suggestive (imperative)
SUPERL	superlative
TA	verb, transitive, animate object
TI	verb, transitive, inanimate object
0	inanimate
1	first person
2	second person
3	third person
4	fourth person/obviative

Common Prefixes, Suffixes, Particles, and Nouns

Grammatical Prefixes
(* = NONAFF inflection required)

beet(oh)	want to . . .
beex(u)-*	should
beh-	all
behis(i)-	all
bis(i)-	all
-eeneis(i)-	REDUP of -iis-
-eeneit(oh)-	REDUP of -iit(oh)-
-eh-	from here
-et(n)(i)-	FUT
cih-	to here
cii-	NEG
ciibeh-	don't, prohibitive
ci'=	too, also
-ebeh-*	might
eeneis(i)-	REDUP of iis(i)-
he(t)-	2, 2POSS
heecis(i)-	while
heeneet(oh)-	REDUP of heet(oh)-

hees(i)-	what/how . . .
heet(n)(i)-	FUT
heet(oh)-	where . . .
heetih-	so that, in order that (SUB) . . .
heetnii-	FUT.IMPERF
hee3nee-	very, really
heh-	precedes number verbs
heh-*	let's . . .
hei'(i)-	when.PERF (SUB) . . .
het(i)-*	FUT.IMPER
het(n)(i)-	FUT.OBLIG (SUB)
he3eb(i)-	over there, to over there
he'(i)=(*)	DUBIT
he'ih-*	NPAST
he'ih'ii-*	NPAST.IMPERF
he'ih'iis(i)-*	NPAST.PERF
he'ne'(i)-	then, next
he'ne'=	this/that is . . .
hi(t)-	3, 3POSS
hih-*	PAST
hi3i=	later, perhaps, if (future)
hi'(i)-	INSTR
ho(t)-	2, 2POSS
hoot(n)(i)-	FUT
hoow(u)-*	NEG
hoowooh-*	no longer
hot(i)-*	FUT.IMPER
hot(n)(i)-	FUT.OBLIG (SUB)
how3o'(u)-*	never
-(e)(i)hoow(u)-*	NEG
-ih-	PAST
-ii-	IMPERF
-iis(i)-	PERF
-iis(i)-	what/how . . .
-iit(oh)-	where . . .
-ii'(i)-	when . . .
-i'(i)-	INSTR
koo=	INTERR, yes/no question
koox=	again, yet again
ne(t)-	my; I
nee'ees(i)-	thus, that is what/how . . .
nee'eet(oh)-	that is where . . .

nee'ei'(i)-	that is when . . .	
neh-	from here	
neh-	you had better . . . (IMPER)	
ne'(i)-	then, next	
ne'=	this/that is . . .	
nih-	PAST	
nih'et(n)-	supposed to	
nih'ii-	PAST.IMPERF	
nih'iis(i)-	PAST.PERF	
nih'ot(n)-	same as nih'et(n)-	
nii-	IMPERF, HABIT	
niis(i)-	what/how.HABIT	
niit(oh)-	whereHABIT	
nii'(i)-	whenHABIT	
-oow(u)-*	NEG	
-ot(n)(i)-	FUT	
tih-	when.IMPERF (SUB)	
tih'et(n)-	supposed to (SUB)	
tih'ii-	when.IMPERF.HABIT (SUB)	
toh-	when/after/because (SUB)	
toh'et(n)-	supposed to (SUB)	
toh'ot(n)-	same as toh'et(n)-	
toh(')uu-	when/after/because.IMPERF (SUB)	
toon=	indefinite	
toot=*	where.INTERR	
tous(i)-*	what/how?	
won(i)-	ALLAT	
wot=	I guess, supposedly	

Most Common Inflections:
Intransitive Verbs, Affirmative

	S	P
0	-'	-'i, -'u
0.OBV	-ni'	-ni'i
1	-noo	-no' (INCL), -ni' (EXCL)
2	-n	-nee
3	-t, -'	-3i', -'i
4	-ni3	-ni3i

Intransitive Verbs, Nonaffirmative

0	-	-no
0OBV	-n	-nino

1	ne-	he- -(i)n (INCL), ne- -be (EXCL)
2	he-	he- -be
3	-	-no'
4	-n	-nino

Imperative Verbs
(Objects)

0	-oo	-oo
1	-i, -u	-ei'ee
3, 4	-in(ee), -un(ee)	-in(ee), -un(ee)

Iterative Mode
(Third Person Only)

| 3 | -3i | -noo3i |

Subjunctive Mode
(Third Person Only)

| 3 | -hek, -ehk | -(h)ehkoni' |
| | -hok, -ohk | -(h)ohkoni' |

Transitive Verbs, Inanimate Object, Affirmative (TI.AFF)

1	-owoo	-owuni' (EXCL), -owuno' (INCL)
2	-ow	-owunee
3	-o'	-ou'u
4	-owuni3	-owuni3i

Transitive Verbs, Inanimate Object, Nonaffirmative (TI.NONAFF)

1	ne-	he- -ow (INCL), ne- -eebe (EXCL)
2	he-	he- -eebe
3	-	-owuu
4	-owun	-owunino

Transitive Verbs, Animate Object (TA)
1S acting on 2: -e3e- inflections
1P acting on 2, 3: -ee- plus inflections
1S acted on by 2, 3P: -i- plus inflections
1P acted on by 2, 3: -ei'ee- plus inflections
1S, 2, 3 acting on 3, 4: -oo- plus inflections
1S, 2, 3 acted on by 3, 4: -ei- plus inflections

The inflections are the same as for intransitive verbs, both affirmative and non-affirmative, with a few irregularities. For the first four "themes" (-e3e-, etc.) the inflections refer to the final element (2, etc.). For the final two themes, the in-flections refer to the first element (1S, 2, 3, etc.). The most common forms are:

	AFF	NONAFF
3S-4	-oot	-ee
3P-4	-oo3i'	-eeno'
4-3S	-eit	-e'
4-3P	-ei3i'	-ei'i

Nouns

INAN.P.	-(o)no, -ho, -ii, -uu
AN.P.	-(i)no', -ho', -ii, -uu
AN.OBV.	-(i)n, -o, -ii, -uu
AN.OBV.P.	-(i)no, ho, -ii, -uu
LOC	-(n/b)e', -i'
POSS	use NONAFF prefixes
P. Possessor	-inoo, (EXCL, 2, 3) -in (INCL, 4)

Most Common Particles

be	friend! (m.)
béébeet	only, just
beeníí	friend! (m.)
bééxoo3ííhi'	a little later
beh'éé	old man!
bííkoo	at night
bííti'	one after the other, in turn
céésey	one time, once
céése'	one, another, other
hee	yes (m.)
heeyóu	what (is it)?
héíhii	soon
híh'oo	okay! agreed!
hííko	no
hííkoot	what's more, moreover
híínoononóx	to one's astonishment
hiit	here
hííwo'	indicates surprise, wonder
híiyóu	here it is
hínee	that
híni'	that (aforementioned)
hi'ííhi'	with, by means of
hohóú	thank you
hónoot	until
hóonii	after a long while
howóh	who would have thought!

huut	here
húú3e'	over there
kook(uy)ón	just, any, no reason
kou3ííhi'	a long time afterward
nebésiiwóó	grandfather!
neehéé	friend! (f.)
néeyóu	there it is
néhe'	this (AN.PROX.S)
neisíe	grandchild!
neiwóó	grandmother!
neixóó	father!
niixóó	too, also
níiyóu	here it is
noh	and
nooxéíhi'	maybe, perhaps
no'óó	mother!
núhu'	this (AN.PROX.PL; OBV; INAN)
téébe	just now
tótoos	even
wohéí	okay, now then (m.)
wootii	like, seems
wóów(uh)	now, already
(noh) wo'éí3	or
xonóu	right away
yéin	four (times)
'íne(hous)	okay, now then (f.)
'oh	but; and
'oo	yes (f.)

"Nih'oo3oo and the Burrs" by John Goggles

Nih'oo3oo he'ih'oowuniihisee niihiihi' niiciihehe'.

Nih'oo3oo	he'ih-'oowuniihisee	niih-iihi'	niiciiheh-e'
Nih'oo3oo	NPAST-go down river(AI)	along-ADV	river-LOC

Nih'oo3oo was walking downstream along a river.

He'ihnoohobee hiseihih'o hooxono'o.

He'ih-noohob-ee	hiseihih'-o	hooxono'o
NPAST-see(TA)-3S/4	woman.DIM-OBV.P	across the river

He saw some girls on the other side of the river.

He'ih'okeee he'iitooni3i, noh hee3eihok,

He'ih-'okeee	he'=iitoo-ni3i		noh	hee3-eihok
PAST-wade across(AI)	DUBIT=where(AI)-4P		and	say (TA)-4/3S. SUBJ

He crossed over to where they were, and they said to him,

"Nih'oo3oo heh'i3ooxuhee," hee3eihok.

Nih'oo3oo	heh-'i3ooxuh-ee		hee3-eihok
Nih'oo3oo	2.IMPER.SUGG-delouse (TA)-1P.EXCL		say(TA)-4/3S.SUBJ

"Nih'oo3oo, let us delouse you," they said to him.

"Hih'oo," hee3oohok.

Hih'oo	hee3-oohok
all right	say(TA)-3S/4.SUBJ

"All right," he said to them.

Noh he'ne'icesisii3ooxuheit.

Noh	he'ne'i-cesisi-i3ooxuh-eit
and	then-begin-delouse(TA)-4/3S

And then they began to delouse him.

Noh beenihehe' hoo3iihi' he'ihnokohunoo'oo.

Noh	beenihehe'	hoo3-iihi'	he'ih-nokohunoo'oo
and	a little	later-ADV	NPAST-fall asleep(AI)

And a little while later he fell asleep.

Kou3iihi' he'ih'owoto'oo.

Kou3-iihi'	he'ih-'owoto'oo
long time-ADV	NPAST-wake up(AI)

After a long time, he woke up.

Noh he'ihbii'inee woniseineehiisii hinii3ee'eene'.

Noh	he'ih-bii'in-ee	woniseineehiis-ii	hi-nii3ee'een-e'
and	NPAST-find(TA)-3S/4	burr-OBV.P	3-hair-LOC

And he found burrs in his hair.

He'ihbeh'eibinino.

He'ih-beh'eibi-nino
NPAST-all stuck/attached(II)-0.OBV.P

They were stuck all over his hair.

He'ihciinoohobee hiseihih'o.

He'ih-cii-noohob-ee	hiseihih'-o
NPAST-NEG-see(TA)-3S/4	woman.DIM-OBV.P

He didn't see the girls.

'oh heehehk, "Heet3iiyouhetinoo."

'oh	heeh-ehk	heet-3iiyouheti-noo.
and	say(AI)-3S.SUBJ	FUT-cut own hair(AI.REFL)-1S

And he said, "I will cut my hair."

He'ne'ihiteno'wooxe.

He'ne'i-hiten-o'	wooxe
then-get(TI)-3S	knife

Then he got a knife.

He'ne'3iiyouheti-t.

He'ne'i-3iiyouheti-t
then-cut own hair(AI.REFL)-3S

Then he cut his hair off short.

Hei'iisi3iiyouhut, he'ne'iheecikoohut.

Hei'iisi-3iiyouhu-t	he'ne'i-heecikoohu-t
when.PERF-cut own hair(AI.SELFB)-3S	then-go home(AI)-3S

Once he had cut his hair off, then he went home.

Noh he'ne'ice'no'eecikoohut, noh hiniin hee3eihok, "Heihtousitoo?"

Noh	he'ne'i-ce'-no'eecikoohu-t	noh	hiniin	hee3-eihok	he-ih-tousitoo
and	then-again-arrive home(AI)-3S	and	3.wife	say (TA)-4/3S. SUBJ	2-PAST-what do(AI)?

And then he arrived back home, and his wife said to him, "What have you done?"

Noh heehehk Nih'oo3oo, "Nihniitobeenoo nih-'iiyohoote-ninehk," hee3oohok.

Noh	heeh-ehk	Nih'oo3oo	nih-niitobee-noo	nih-'iiyohoote-ninehk	hee3-oohok
and	say(AI)-3S.SUBJ	Nih'oo3oo	PAST-hear(AI)-1S	PAST-dead(AI)-2S.SUBJ	say(TA)-3S/4.SUBJ

And Nih'oo3oo said, "I heard that you were dead," he said to her.

"Nee'ee3iiyouhunoo."

Nee'ee-3iiyouhu-noo
that why-cut hair for myself(AI.SELFB)-1S

"That's why I cut my hair."

Noh nih'oo3ou'u, ne'=nii'i3iiyouhehkoni' nih'oo3ou'u.

Noh	nih'oo3ou'u,	ne'=nii'i-3iiyouh-ehkoni'	nih'oo3ou'u.
and	white person.PL	that=when-cut	white person.PL
		hair(AI.SELFB)-3PL.SUBJ	

And the white men, that's why the white men cut their hair.

Nee'ei'ise'.

Nee'ei'ise-'.

thus end/extend(II)-0S

That's how the story ends.

"Pemmican Floating Downstream" by Cleaver Warden

Ceb toh'oowuniihou'oo'.

ceb	toh-'oowuniihou'oo-'
pemmican	when-float downstream(II)-0S

Pemmican floating downstream.

Nih'oo3oo hoowuniihiseehek.

nih'oo3oo	hoowuniihisee-hek
trickster	walk down along (stream)(AI)-3S.SUBJ

Nih'oo3oo was walking downstream.

Ceb he'ihcowou'oo.

ceb	he'ih-cowou'oo
pemmican	NPAST-float past/along(II)

Some pemmican floated by.

He'iisooyeikoo.

he'=iis-ooyeikoohu

DUBIT=PERF-run around in front of to catch(AI)

He managed to run around ahead of it and caught up to it.

"Heitohuu3ei'ko'obee?"

hei-tohuu3ei'i-ko'ob-ee

2S.IMPERF-what amount?-bite off(TA)-1P

"How much of you can we bite off?" [he asked the pemmican].

"Beenihehe' nii'ko'obeen."

beenihehe'	nii'-ko'ob-een
a little	IC.able-bite off(TA)-1P/2S

"You can bite off a little bit."

Kooxhe'ihce'no'o'us.
Koox=he'ih-ce'i-no'o'usee
yet again=NPAST-back-walk out of water(AI)
[After doing this, Nih'oo3oo] got back out of the water again.

He'ih'ooyeikoo.
he'ih-'ooyeikoohu
NPAST-run around in front of, to catch(AI)
He ran around ahead of it again.

"Heitohuu3ei'ko'obee?" niito'ohk ceb.

hei-tohuu3ei'i-ko'ob-ee	niit-o'ohk	ceb
2S.IMPERF-how much?-bite off(TA)-1P	IMPERF.say to(TI)-3S.SUBJ	pemmican

"How much of you can we bite off?" he said to the pemmican.

"Beenihehe'."
beenihehe'
a little
"A little bit."

He'iisooyeiko'oot konohxuu.

he'=iis-ooyei-ko'oot	konohxuu
DUBIT=PERF-most-bite off(TI)	despite/nevertheless

Despite [what the pemmican said], he managed to bite off most of it.

Kooxci'he'ih'ooyeikoo, beebei'on.

Koox=ci'=he'ih-'ooyeikoohu	beebei'on
yet again=too=NPAST-run around in front of to catch(AI)	far away

Then yet again he ran around ahead of it, way on downstream.

"Heitohuu3ei'ko'obee?" Nih'oo3oo niihok.

hei-tohuu3ei'i-ko'ob-ee	nih'oo3oo	nii-hok
2S.IMPERF-what amount?-bite off(TA)-1P	trickster	IMPERF.say(AI)-3S.SUBJ

"How much of you can I bite off?" Nih'oo3oo said.

"Beenihehe'," nih'ii3eetehk.

beenihehe'	nih-'ii3ee-tehk
a little	PAST-said to(AI.MID)-3S.SUBJ

"A little bit," he was told.

He'ihbeesko'oot konohxuu.

he'ih-beesi-ko'oot	konohxuu
NPAST-big-bite off(TI)	despite/nevertheless

Despite what he was told, he bit off a big piece.

He'ne'ouucenooyeikoohut.

he'ne'i-houuni-cenooyeikoohu-t
then-SUPERL-run down around in front of to catch(AI)-3S

Then he ran way on down around ahead of it as fast as he could.

"Heitohuu3ei'ko'obee?" niihok.

hei-tohuu3ei'-ko'ob-ee	nii-hok
2S.IMPERF-what amount?-bite off(TA)-1P	IMPERF.say(AI)-3S.SUBJ

"How much of you can we bite off?" he said.

Beeyoo he'ihko'oot.

beeyoo	he'ih-ko'oot
just right	NPAST-bite off(TI)

He bit some off right in the middle.

Hiiwoonihehe' he'ne'beneebe3, beesko'ooto'.

hiiwoonihehe'	he'ne'i-beneebe3	beesi-ko'oot-o'
now	then-one last/final time	big-bite off(TI)-3S

Now he took a big bite and got the whole thing.

"Howoh heenee3ehtoneihi3i Nih'oo3oo!"

Howoh	heenee3-ehtoneihi-3i	nih'oo3oo
Who would have thought	what/how.REDUP	trickster
	clever/tricky(AI)-3S.ITER	

"Who would have imagined how clever/tricky Nih'oo3oo is!" [he said about himself].

He'ihce3ikotii hookoo3iihi'.

he'ih-ce3ikotii	hookoo3-iihi'
NPAST-wander off(AI)	to home-ADV

He set off for home.

Biikoo, tohnokohut, hitouw he'ihbiibii3i3ee.

biikoo	toh-nokohu-t	hit-ou-w	he'ih-bii-bii3i3-ee
at night	when-sleep(AI)-3S	3S-robe-OBV	NARRPAST-REDUP-crap/ excrete on(TA)-3S/4

That night, when he was sleeping, he crapped on his buffalo robe.

He'ihnohkce3ikotii.
he'ih-nohku-ce3ikotii
NARRPAST-with-wander off(AI.T)
He set off with it.

"Nehe' hou, heetiitouwu beh'ee," heeto'ohk hihnoohoo3oo.

nehe'	hou	he-eti-itouwu	beh'ee	heet-o'ohk	hih-noohoo3oo
this	robe	2S-FUT-have	old man!	say to(TI)-	3S.PAST-
		robe(AI)		3S.SUBJ	see(TI.DEPPART)

"This robe, it can be your robe now, old man," he said to whatever thing he saw.

Neenowo', teebe tohceniiseet,

neenowo'	teebe	toh-ceniisee-t
hurry, it's urgent!	just now	when/after-walk a long way(AI)-3S

Rushing along, once he had gone a good distance,

he'ihce'e'ein, nih'iitohbeit hitouw.

he'ih-ce'e'eini	nih-'iitoh-bei-t	hit-ou-w
NARRPAST-turn	PAST-where-giveaway(AI.O)-3S	3S-robe-OBV
head/gaze back(AI)		

he looked back, where he had given away his robe.

Wotkeisiiyooteihin.
Wot=koo=hiis-iiyooteihi-n
DUBIT=INTERR=PERF-clean(AI)-4S
He was amazed to see that it was all clean!

"Ceisin ce'iihi' yono'oh'itouwun," heehehk Nih'oo3oo.

ceis-in	ce'i-iihi'	yono'oh-'itouwu-n	heehi-ehk	nih'oo3oo
bring here(TA)-	back-ADV	IC.thinks so, but is not-	said(AI)-	trickster
3.IMPER		have robe(AI)-2S	3S.SUBJ	

"Give it back to me, what in the heck are you doing with a robe?" said Nih'oo3oo.

He'ihnohkce3ikotii.
he'ih-nohku-ce3ikotii
NPAST-with-wander off(AI)
He set off with it.

Kooxhe'ihce'beeniin.
Koox=he'ih-ce'i-beeniini
yet again=NPAST-again-excrement on s.t.(AI)
Then once again it was covered with crap [after he slept on it].

"Beh'ee, nuhu' heetiitouw," niihok, tihyihkuutiit heeyouhuu.

beh'ee	nuhu'	he-eti-itouwu	nii-hok	tih-yihkuutii-t	heeyouhuu
old man!	this	2S-FUT-have robe(AI)	IMPERF. say (AI)-3S. SUBJ	when.PAST. IMPERF-throw over there(AI.T)-3S	thing

"Old man, this can be your robe," he said, when he tossed it away toward something or other.

Heet3i'ookuuni' wotnehe'nih'iistoohok.

Heet-3i'ookuu-ni'	wot=nehe'=nih-'iistoo-hok
where-stand(II)-0S.OBV	DUBIT=that=PAST-what/how do(AI)-3S.SUBJ

Wherever something was standing, that's what he would do.

Cee'beeniinini3i, howoh'uuhu' . . .

cee'i-beeniini-ni3i	howoh'-uuhu'
IC.again-excrement on s.t.(AI)-4S.ITER	many-ADV

Whenever it got covered with lots of crap again . . . [he would do the same thing].

Koox hitouw, he'ihce'eso'oo3ihee hitouw.

koox=hit-ou-w	he'ih-ce'i-so'oo3ih-ee	hit-ou-w
yet again=3S-robe-OBV	NPAST-again-make dirty, soil(TA)-3S/4	3S-robe-OBV

Then once again his robe, he soiled his robe again.

Noosouseet, he'ihcih'itesee {no}hoh'onookeen.

noosousee-t	he'ih-cih-'ites-ee	hoh'onookee-n
IC.still walking(AI)-3S	NPAST-to here-come upon(TA)-3S/4	rock-OBV

He is still walking [with his robe dirty again], and he came upon a rock here.

"Beh'ee, nuhu' heetiitouw," hee3oohok.

beh'ee	nuhu'	he-eti-itouwu	hee3-oohok
old man!	This	2S-FUT-have robe(AI)	said to(TA)-3S/4.SUBJ

"Old man, this can be your robe now," he said to it.

Tohceniiseet, he'ihce'e'ein.

toh-ceniisee t   he'ih-ce'e'eini
when/after-walk a long way(AI)-3S   NPAST-turn head/gaze back(AI)
When he had walked a good way, he looked back.

Koowotnehe' hou he'ih'iisiiyooteih.

Koo=wot=nehe'   hou   he'=ih-'iis-iiyooteihi
INTERR=DUBIT=this   robe   DUBIT=PAST-PERF-clean(AI)
To his surprise, this robe was all clean!

Ce'ikotiihok.

ce'ikotii-hok
go/hurry back(AI)-3S.SUBJ
He hurried back.

"Yono'oh'itouwun," hee3oohok.

yono'oh-'itouwu-n   hee3-oohok
IC.thinks is, is not-have robe/blanket(AI)-2S   said to(TA)-3S/4.SUBJ
"What is someone like you doing with a robe?" he said to the rock.

Ce'itenowuunoohok, he'inee'eesce3ei'oot.

ce'itenowuun-oohok   he'i=nee'eesi-ce3ei'oo - t
take s.t. back from s.o.(TA)-3S/4.SUBJ   DUBIT=thus-set off(AI)-3S
When he took it back from the rock, he set off again.

Tohceniiseet, heeyouti' he'ih'etei'oo.

toh-ceniisee-t   heeyouti'   he'ih-'etei'oo
when/after-walk a long   something   NPAST-rumbling rolling
   way(AI)-3S   sound(AI)
When he had gone a good way, there was a rumbling sound from something.

Nih'oo3oo he'ihce'e'ein.

nih'oo3oo   he'ih-ce'e'eini
trickster   NPAST-turn head/gaze back(AI)
Nih'oo3ooo looked back.

Noonononox, hoh'onookee beeyoo heetoot he'ihceitetei'oo.

noononox   hoh'onookee   beeyoo   heetoo-t   he'ih-ceitetei'oo
to one's   rock   exactly where   NPAST-rumbling
   surprise   located(AI)-3S   rolling sound
                                                       to here(AI)
To his astonishment, the rock was rumbling right toward where he was.

Cihnoonoh'uhcehisine'.
cih-noo-noh'uhcehisine-'
to here-REDUP-bounce(TA)-3S
It was tumbling and bouncing along toward him.

Xonou he'ihce3ikoo.
xonou   he'ih-ce3ikoohu
immediately   NPAST-set off (running)(AI)
Right away he took off running.

Hoh'onookee he'ihcih3ookukoo'ouuto'oo.
hoh'onookee   he'ih-cih-3ooku-koo'ouuto'oo
rock   NPAST-to here-following- go/roll along making dust(AI)
The rock was following behind him, kicking up clouds of dust.

"Hihtonot, hehkuhneenoo,
Hih-tonoti   hehkuhnee-noo
if-be hole(II)   where fleeing/chased(AI.MID)-1S
"If only there was a hole in the direction where I am running.

"He[i]hno'o3oo hehkuhneenoo," niihok.
Heih-no'o3oo-'   hehkuhnee-noo   nii-hok
POTENT-powerful(II)   where fleeing/chased-   IMPERF.say(AI)-
                                (AI.MID)-1S   3S.SUBJ
"[I wish there was] a strong/powerful place [for protection] where I'm fleeing,"
he was saying.

He'ne'ii'P, he'ne'houunihi'koo, tohto3iheit,
he'ne'=hii'P   he'ne'i-houun-nihi'koohu   toh-to3ih-eit
that=when-pause/break   then-SUPERL-run (AI)   because-
                                                      follow(TA)-4/3S
Then he was running as fast as he could, because it was following him.

"'uuh beh'ei."
'uuh beh'ei
ugh old man
"Uhh, old man," [he said].

Hei'neetikoohut, kotoukoo.
hei'i-neetikoohu-t   [he'ih]-kotoukoohu
when.PERF- tired from running-3.S   NPAST-run under cover(AI)
When he was tired from running, then he ran under the cover [of a stream bank].

"Hi3iheetcebkoohut," heehehk.

hi3i=heet-cebikoohu –t   heehi-ehk

maybe=FUT-run past(AI)-3S   said(AI)-3S.SUBJ

"It would be good if it would go past," he said.

He'ihkoxo'teesteeteco'oo hikoobe'.

he'ih-koxo'-tees-tee-teco'oo   hi-koob-e'

NPAST-slowly-on/over-REDUP-roll along(AI)   3S-back-LOC

The rock slowly rolled on top of his back.

"Beh'ee, toh'oobenin," nii3oohok hihnoohowooono cese'ehiiho.

beh'ee	toh'-ooben-in	nii3-oohok	hih-noohowooo-no	cese'eihii-ho
old man!	[I ask] that-take down off(TA)-2S/1S	IMPERF.say to(TA)-3S/4. SUBJ	3S.PAST-see(TA. DEPPART)-OBV.PL	animal-OBV.PL

"Old man, take it off me," he said to the animals he saw.

Koowothe'ihceh'e3ihe'.

Koo=wot=he'ih-ceh'e3ih -e'

INTERR=DUBIT=NPAST-listen to(TA)-4/3S

To his disappointment, they did not listen to him.

Cisihi' he'ihcihnoononoo'oo.

cisihi'   he'ih-cih-noononoo'oo

nighthawk.DIM   NPAST-to here-soaring/circling(AI)

A little nighthawk came soaring around this way.

"Neehee, cih'oobenin nehe' hoh'onookeen," niihok.

neehee!	cih'-ooben-in	nehe'	hoh'onookee-n	nii-hok
friend!	EMPH-take down off(TA)-3.IMPER	this	rock-OBV	IMPERF.say(AI)-3S.SUBJ

"Friend, take this rock off me," he said.

Kou3iihi' cisihi' cenih'ohukoo beenihehe'.

kou3-iihi'	cisihi'	[he'ih]-cenih'ohukoohu	beenihehe'
long (time)-ADV	nighthawk.DIM	NPAST-fly down quickly(AI)	a little

Eventually the nighthawk dove down a little bit.

He'ihko'oxouhuu.
he'ih-ko'oxouh-uu
NPAST-chip off by blow/tool(TA)-3S/4
He blasted off some of the rock [by farting/with his anus].

Heeyowceenih'ohukoohu3i, ceneeti3i,

Heeyow=ceenih'ohukoohu-3i	ceneeti-3i
every time=IC.fly down quickly(AI)-3S.ITER	IC.fart(AI)-3S.ITER

Every time he dove down, when he farted,

noonoxoo he'ihko'unoo'oo nehe' hoh'onookee.

noonoxoo	he'ih-ko'unoo'oo	nehe'	hoh'onookee
one at a time	NPAST-pieces being removed(AI)	this	rock

Gradually, bit by bit, this rock was getting chipped away.

Beneebe3 he'ne'hihcinoononoo'oot beebei'on.

beneebe3	he'ne'i-hihci-noononoo'oo-t	beebei'on
One last/final time	then-upward-soaring/circling(AI)-3S	far away

One final time, he soared way up high far away.

Nii3ei'iinit cenih'ohukoo hetebiihi'.

nii3ei'iinit	[he'ih]-cenih'ohukoohu	heteb-iihi'
with all one's might	NPAST-fly down quickly(AI)	overtake(TA)-ADV

He dove down at the rock on a collision course, with all his might.

Ceeti3ee, behis3o'ohoe.

[he'ih]-ceeti3-ee	[he'ih]-behis-3o'oh-oe
NPAST-fart on/at(TA)-3S/4	NPAST-all-shatter with tool(TA)-3S/4

He farted at it and shattered it all to bits.

Nih'oo3oo he'kohei'ihok.

nih'oo3oo	he'i=kohei'i-hok
trickster	DUBIT=stand up(AI)-3S.SUBJ

Nih'oo3oo jumped up.

"Neehee, neheic, hotniini'ibe3en," hee3oohok cisiho'.

neehee	neheic	hot-nii-ni'ib-e3en	hee3-oohok	cisiho'
friend!	come here!	So that-REDUP-praise/speak well of(TA)-1S/2S	said to(TA)-3S/4.SUBJ	nighthawk. DIM.OBV

"Friend, come here, I am going to share some good words with you," he said to the nighthawk.

"Neiteh'ei, yohouhiixoneih hetowouuyoo{n}.

neiteh'ei	yohou=hiixoneihi	het-owouuyoo
1S.friend	examplary=useful,	2S-take pity,
	helpful(AI)	mercy(TI.DEPPART)

"My friend, how helpful you have been, in taking pity on me.

"Hi3tee'etineen," hee3oohok.

hi3i=tee'etinee-n	hee3-oohok
if/maybe=open one's mouth(AI)-2S	said to(AI)-3S/4.SUBJ

"Will you open your mouth?" he said to him.

He'ihkoxo'etineen.

he'ih-koxo'etinee-n

NPAST-have mouth stretched apart(AI.MID)-4S

The nighthawk got his mouth stretched apart.

"Yono'oh'uuxoneih, wottowuuhuu," hee3oohok.

yono'oh-'uuxoneihi	wotitowuuhuu	hee3-oohok
IC.thinks is but is not-useful,	dirty scoundrel	said to(TA)-3S/4.SUBJ
helpful(AI)		

"You thought you were so useful/helpful, you dirty scoundrel," he said to him.

"Beebeet heet[n]iinee'eenii[ni] beesetineenee.

Beebeet	heetn-ii-nee'een-iini	beesetinee-nee
just/only	FUT-IMPERF-thus-DETACH	have a big mouth(AI)-2P

"You will just have a big mouth like this from now on."

References

Anderson, Jeffrey D. 2001. *The Four Hills of Life.* Lincoln: University of Nebraska Press.

———, trans. 2005. "Ghost Dance Songs." In Swann 2005, 448–71.

———. 2013. *Arapaho Women's Quillwork: Motion, Life, and Creativity.* Norman: University of Oklahoma Press.

The Arapaho Language Project. "Bilingual Curricular Materials." http://www.colorado.edu/csilw/alp/Curricular%20Materials.html.

The Arapaho Project. "Stories." http://www.colorado.edu/csilw/arapahoproject/language/storytelling.htm.

Basso, Keith H. 1990. *Western Apache Language and Culture: Essays in Linguistic Anthropology.* Tucson: University of Arizona Press.

Bauman, Richard. 1986. *Story, Performance, and Event: Contextual Studies of Oral Narrative.* Cambridge: Cambridge University Press.

Berthrong, Donald J. 1976. *The Cheyenne and Arapaho Ordeal: Reservation and Agency Life in the Indian Territory, 1875–1907.* Norman: University of Oklahoma Press.

———. 1994. "Jesse Rowlodge: Southern Arapaho as Political Intermediary." In *Between Indian and White Worlds: The Cultural Broker,* ed. Margaret Connell Szasz, 223–39. Norman: University of Oklahoma Press.

Bringhurst, Robert. 1999. *A Story As Sharp as a Knife: The Classical Haida Mythtellers and Their World.* Lincoln: University of Nebraska Press.

Brittain, Julie, and Marguerite MacKenzie. 2005. "Two Wolverine Stories. Told by John Peastitute." In Swann 2005, 121–58.

Buszard-Welcher, Laura. 2005. "Three Tales. Told by Alice Spear and Jim Spear." In Swann 2005, 201–14.

"Carlisle Indian Industrial School." http://home.epix.net/~landis/.

"Census of the Arapahoe Indians of Shoshone Agency, Wyoming." Taken by H. G. Nickerson, U.S. Indian Agency, July 1900. Bureau of Indian Affairs: Shoshone Agency, Wyoming.

C'Hair, William. 2005. *Crazy Man and the Plums.* Ft. Washakie, Wyo.: Painted Pony Press.

Costa, David. 2005. "Culture-Hero and Trickster Stories. Told by George Finley, Elizabeth Vallier, and an Unknown Shawnee Speaker." In Swann 2005, 292–319.

Cowell, Andrew. 2001. *Telling Stories: Arapaho Narrative Traditions.* A collaborative project of the Northern Arapaho Tribe and Dr. Andrew Cowell, University of Colorado. 46-minute video plus booklet. Laramie: Wyoming Council for the Humanities.

———. 2002. "The Poetics of Arapaho Storytelling: From Salvage to Performance." *Oral Tradition* 17 (1): 19–52.

———, ed. and trans. 2005. "Three Stories. Told by Richard Moss." In Swann 2005, 472–94.

———. 2015. "Editing Arapaho Text: A Comparative Perspective." In *New Voices for Old Words: Editing Algonquian Texts,* ed. David Costa. Lincoln: University of Nebraska Press.

Cowell, Andrew, and Alonzo Moss, Sr. 2003. "Arapaho Place Names in Colorado: Form and Function, Language and Culture." *Anthropological Linguistics* 54 (4): 349–89.

———. 2008. *The Arapaho Language.* Boulder: University Press of Colorado.

———, eds. and trans. 2011. "Arapaho Songs." *Bombay Gin* 37: 125–32.

Cowell, Andrew, with Alonzo Moss, Sr., William C'Hair, and Wayne C'Hair. 2012. *Dictionary of the Arapaho Language.* 4th ed. Ethete, Wyo.: Northern Arapaho Tribe.

Curtis, Edward S. 1911. *The North American Indian; Being a Series of Volumes Picturing and Describing the Indians of the United States and Alaska.* Vol. 6: 137–50, 159–73. Cambridge, Mass.: self-published. Available on-line at: http://curtis.library.northwestern.edu/curtis/toc.cgi.

Curtis, Natalie. [1907] 1968. *The Indians' Book.* New York: Dover.

Densmore, Frances, 1936. *Cheyenne and Arapaho Music.* Southwest Museum Papers, No. 10. Los Angeles: Southwest Museum.

DePasquale, Paul W. 2005. "Omushkego Legends from Hudson Bay. Told by Louis Bird (Pennishish)." In Swann 2005, 247–91.

Doris Duke Collection of American Indian Oral History. Western History Collections, University of Oklahoma, Norman. Available online at http://digital.libraries.ou.edu/whc/duke/.

Dorsey, George A. 1903. *The Arapaho Sun Dance: The Ceremony of the Offerings Lodge.* Field Columbian Museum, Publication 75, Anthropological Series, Vol. 4. Chicago: Field Columbian Museum.

———. [1904] 1995. *The Mythology of the Wichita.* Norman: University of Oklahoma Press.

———. [1906] 1997. *The Pawnee Mythology.* Lincoln: University of Nebraska Press.

Dorsey, George A., and Alfred L. Kroeber. [1903] 1997. *Traditions of the Arapaho.* Lincoln: University of Nebraska Press.

Fowler, Loretta. 1982. *Arapahoe Politics, 1851–1978: Symbols in Crises of Authority.* Lincoln: University of Nebraska Press.

———. 2002. *Tribal Sovereignty and the Historical Imagination: Cheyenne-Arapaho Politics.* Lincoln: University of Nebraska Press.

————. 2010. *Wives and Husbands: Gender and Age in Southern Arapaho History.* Norman: University of Oklahoma Press.

Gatschet, Albert. 1882–93. Field Notes. National Anthropological Archives, MS 231.

Grinnell, George Bird. 1926. *By Cheyenne Campfires.* Lincoln: University of Nebraska Press.

Haas, Merle. 2011. *Fox and the Woodtick.* Ft. Washakie, Wyo.: Painted Pony Press.

Hilger, Sister Inez. 1952. *Arapaho Child Life and Its Cultural Background.* Bureau of American Ethnology Bulletin 148. Washington, D.C.: Smithsonian Institution.

Hopper, Ralph. n.d. *Stories from Yellow Calf.* Collected by Frances Merle Goggles [Haas]. Laramie: Wyoming Council for the Humanities.

Hymes, Dell. 1981. *"In Vain I Tried to Tell You": Essays in Native American Ethnopoetics.* Philadelphia: University of Pennsylvania Press.

————. 2003. *"Now I Only Know So Much": Essays in Ethnopoetics.* Lincoln: University of Nebraska Press.

Kâ-Nîpitêhtêw, Jim. 1998. *Ana kâ-pimwêwêhahk okakêskihkêmowina/The Counselling Speeches of Jim Kâ-Nîpitêhtêw.* Edited, translated, and with a glossary by Freda Ahenskew and H. C. Wolfart. Winnipeg: University of Manitoba Press.

Kroeber, Alfred. 1899–1901. Field Notes. National Anthropological Archives, MS 2560a (Arapaho), 2560b (Gros Ventre).

————. [1902–1907] 1983. *The Arapaho.* Lincoln: University of Nebraska Press.

————. 1907. "Gros Ventre Myths and Tales." *Anthropological Papers of the American Museum of Natural History* 1 (3): 55–139.

————. 1916. "Arapaho Dialects." *University of California Publications in American Archaeology and Ethnology* 12 (3): 71–138.

Kroeber, Karl, ed. 1997. *Traditional Literatures of the American Indian: Texts and Interpretations.* 2nd ed. Lincoln: University of Nebraska Press.

Lah, Ronald. 1980. "Ethnoaesthetics of Northern Arapaho Indian Music." Ph.D. dissertation (Anthropology), Northwestern University.

Leman, Wayne. 2005. "The Rolling Head. Told by Laura Rockroads." In Swann 2005, 501–509.

LeSourd, Phillip S. 2005. "Traditions of Koluskap, the Culture Hero. Told by Peter Lewis Paul." In Swann 2005, 99–111.

Lévi-Strauss, Claude. 1978. *The Origin of Table Manners.* Vol. 3 of *Introduction to the Science of Mythology.* Translated by John and Doreen Weightmann. New York: Harper and Row.

Lord, Albert Bates. 1965. *The Singer of Tales.* Cambridge, Mass.: Harvard University Press.

Lowie, Robert H. 1915. "Myths and Traditions of the Crow Indians." *Anthropological Papers of the American Museum of Natural History* 11, 8: 3–308.

Medicine Grass. 1929. *The Life of Medicine Grass (Woxu'uubee), Arapaho.* Recorded by Jesse Rowlodge, National Anthropological Archives MS 2267. Retranscribed and retranslated by Andrew Cowell and Alonzo Moss, Sr., 2005. Boulder: Center for the Study of Indigenous Languages of the West.

Michelson, Truman. 1910–29. Field Notes. National Anthropological Archives, MSS 1791, 2707, 2708, 2988, 2994.

———. 1933. "Narrative of an Arapaho Woman." *American Anthropologist* 35: 595–610.

Milligan, Marianne. 2005. "The Origin of the Spirit Rock. Told by Charles Dutchman (Naehcīwetok)." In Swann 2005, 411–28.

Mooney, James. [1896] 1973. *The Ghost Dance Religion and Wounded Knee.* New York: Dover.

Moss, Paul. 1993. *The Stories of Paul Moss.* Transcribed and translated by Alonzo Moss, Sr., with Sara Wiles. Laramie: Wyoming Council for the Humanities.

———. 1995. *More Stories of Paul Moss.* Transcribed and translated by Alonzo Moss, Sr., with Sara Wiles. Laramie: Wyoming Council for the Humanities.

———. 2005. *Hinóno'éínoo3ítoono/Arapaho Historical Traditions.* Edited by Andrew Cowell and Alonzo Moss, Sr. Winnipeg: University of Manitoba Press.

Moss, Richard. 2006. *Modern Arapaho Narratives/Hinono'einoo3itoono.* Edited by Andrew Cowell and Alonzo Moss, Sr. Laramie: Wyoming Council for the Humanities.

Nettl, Bruno. 1951. "Musical Culture of the Arapaho." M.A. thesis (Anthropology), Indiana University.

Parks, Douglas R. 1991. *Traditional Narratives of the Arikara Indians.* 4 vols. Lincoln: University of Nebraska Press.

Parry, Milman. 1971. *The Making of Homeric Verse: The Collected Papers of Milman Parry.* Edited by Adam Parry. Oxford: Clarendon Press.

Powers, William. 1990. *War Dance: Plains Indian Musical Performance.* Tucson: University of Arizona Press.

Preston, Richard J. 2005. "Louse and Wide Lake. Told by George Head." In Swann 2005, 215–29.

Preston, Susan M. 2005. "A Pair of Hero Stories. Told by John Blackned." In Swann 2005, 230–46.

Radin, Paul. 1972. *The Trickster: A Study in American Indian Mythology.* New York: Schocken Books.

Rice, Julian. 2004. "Double-Face Tricks a Girl." In Swann 2004, 397–407.

Salzmann, Zdeněk. 1950. "An Arapaho Version of the Star Husband Tale." *Hoosier Folklore* 9: 50–58.

———. 1956a. "Arapaho II: Texts." *International Journal of American Linguistics* 22: 151–58.

———. 1956b. "Arapaho III: Additional Texts." *International Journal of American Linguistics* 22: 266–72.

———. 1957. "Arapaho Tales III." *Midwest Folklore* 7: 27–37.

———. 1980. *Arapaho Stories—Hinóno'éí hoo3ítóono.* Anchorage, Alaska: National Bilingual Materials Development Center.

———. 1983. *Dictionary of Contemporary Arapaho Usage.* Wind River Reservation, Wyo.: Northern Arapaho Tribe.

Salzmann, Zdeněk, and Joy Salzmann. 1950. "Arapaho Tales I." *Hoosier Folklore* 9: 80–96.

———. 1952. "Arapaho Tales II." *Midwest Folklore* 2: 21–42.

Sherzer, Joel, and Anthony C. Woodbury, eds. 1987. *Native American Discourse: Poetics and Rhetoric.* New York: Cambridge University Press.

Swann, Brian, ed. 1992. *On the Translation of Native American Literatures.* Washington, D.C.: Smithsonian Institution Press.

———, ed. 2004. *Voices from Four Directions: Contemporary Translations of the Native Literatures of North America.* Lincoln: University of Nebraska Press.

———, ed. 2005. *Algonquian Spirit: Contemporary Translations of the Algonquian Literatures of North America.* Lincoln: University of Nebraska Press.

Swann, Brian, and Arnold Krupat, eds. 1987. *Recovering the Word: Essays on Native American Literature.* Berkeley: University of California Press.

Taylor, Allan. 1996. "'Mexican' in Arapahoan Languages." In *Nikotwâsik iskwâhtêm, pâskihtêpayih! Studies in Honour of H. C. Wolfart,* ed. John D. Nichols and Arden C. Ogg, 383–86. Memoir 13, Algonquian and Iroquoian Linguistics. Winnipeg, Manitoba: University of Manitoba.

Tedlock, Dennis. 1983. *The Spoken Word and the Work of Interpretation.* Philadelphia: University of Pennsylvania Press.

Thompson, Stith. 1953. "The Star Husband Tale." *Studia Septentrionalia* 4: 93–163.

Toll, Oliver W. 1962. *Arapaho Names and Trails: A Report of a 1914 Pack Trip.* Reprinted 2003: Estes Park, CO: Rocky Mountain Nature Association.

Trenholm, Virginia Cole. 1986. *The Arapahoes, Our People.* Norman: University of Oklahoma Press.

Underwood, Mary Kate. 2010. *Arapaho Stories, History, and Culture.* Book and 2 CDs. Narratives collected by Andrew Cowell, Hartwell Francis, and Lisa Conathan. Edited and translated by Andrew Cowell. Boulder: Center for the Study of Indigenous Languages of the West.

U.S. Indian Census Schedules, 1903 Census of the Arapahoe Tribe in the Oklahoma Territory. http://genealogytrails.com/oka/arapahoe1903census.html.

Valentine, Rand. 2004. "The Birth of Nenabozho." In Swann 2004, 486–514.

Voth, H. R. 1912. "Arapaho Tales." *Journal of American Folklore* 25: 43–50.

Wake, C. Staniland. 1904. "Nihancan, the White Man." *American Antiquarian Oriental Journal* 26: 225–31.

Walker, Willard. 2004. "Thunder and the Ukten" (told by Willie Jumper). In Swann 2004, 357–67.

Whitehawk, Michael, trans. 1903. *Hethadenee Waunauyaunee Vadan Luke Vanenāna/ The Gospel according to Saint Luke.* New York: American Bible Society.

Wiles, Sara. 2011. *Arapaho Journeys: Photographs and Stories from the Wind River Reservation.* Norman: University of Oklahoma Press.

Wissler, Clark, and D. C. Duvall, comps. and trans. 1995. *Mythology of the Blackfoot Indians.* Lincoln: University of Nebraska Press.

Index

CPSIA information can be obtained
at www.ICGtesting.com
Printed in the USA
LVOW11s0428100318
569207LV00004B/46/P